B. Sharon Byrd

Einführung in die anglo-amerikanische Rechtssprache

Introduction to Anglo-American Law & Language

2nd edition

Einführung in die anglo-amerikanische Rechtssprache

2. Auflage

von

B. Sharon Byrd

Verlag C.H. Beck oHG, München
Manz'sche Verlags- und Universitätsbuchhandlung, Wien
Stämpfli Verlag AG, Bern
2001

Über die Autorin

Die Autorin, derzeit Leiterin des "Law & Language" Programms an der Universität Jena und Honorarprofessorin für anglo-amerikanisches Recht an der Universität Erlangen, verfügt aufgrund ihrer akademischen Ausbildung (J.D. University of California, Los Angeles; LL.M., J.S.D. Columbia University, New York) über langjährige Erfahrungen mit dem amerikanischen Recht. Als Stipendiatin der Alexander von Humboldt Stiftung studierte sie darüberhinaus zwei Jahre deutsches Recht. Die Autorin hat mehrere Jahre als Dozentin für anglo-amerikanisches Recht in Augsburg Erfahrungen gesammelt, bevor sie nach Jena ging, um dort das "Law & Language" Programm aufzubauen.

Die Deutsche Bibliothek – CIP-Einheitsaufnahme

Byrd, B. Sharon:
Introduction to Anglo-American law & language = Einführung in die anglo-amerikanische Rechtssprache / von B. Sharon Byrd. – 2nd. ed. – München : Beck; Wien : Manz; Bern : Stämpfli, 2001
(Rechtssprache des Auslands)
ISBN 3-406-47290-7 (Beck)
ISBN 3-214-02946-0 (Manz)
ISBN 3-7272-9066-8 (Stämpfli)

C.H. Beck ISBN 3-406-47290-7
Manz ISBN 3-214-02946-0
Stämpfli ISBN 3-7272-9066-8

© 2001 Verlag C.H. Beck oHG München
Wilhelmstr. 9, 80801 München
Druck und Bindung: Nomos Verlagsgesellschaft
In den Lissen 12, 76547 Sinzheim
Satz: Herbert Kloos, München
Umschlag: Christiane Rauert, München
Gedruckt auf säurefreiem, alterungsbeständigem Papier
(hergestellt aus chlorfrei gebleichtem Zellstoff)

Meinen Studenten,
die mir so viel beigebracht haben

Vorwort zur 2. Auflage

In der Neu-Auflage habe ich versucht, einige Lücken zu schließen, die mir bei der Verwendung dieses Buches in meinen Vorlesungen aufgefallen sind. Eine dieser Lücken bestand hinsichtlich des Zivilprozeßrechts. Da common-law-Systeme Systeme der Verfahrensgerechtigkeit sind, ist das Prozeßrecht ein Gebiet von zentraler Bedeutung. Deshalb habe ich in Unit I Kapitel 3 das Verfahren Schritt für Schritt beschrieben. Die erste Auflage enthält auch nichts zur juristischen Ausbildung und zum Berufsbild des Juristen. Die Informationen, die ich jetzt einfüge, sind für die Leser von Interesse, die einen Studienaufenthalt als LL.M. Kandidaten oder ein Praktikum als Referendar in den USA oder in England planen. Schließlich habe ich im allgemeinen versucht, mehr speziell zum englischen Rechtssystem zu sagen.

Für die großzügige Unterstützung durch das British Council, das mir einen Forschungsaufenthalt in England ermöglicht hat, möchte ich mein Dank aussprechen. Darüber hinaus möchte ich Monsieur François Feij für sein Interesse an diesem Buch und seine hilfreichen Vorschläge danken. Nicht zuletzt danke ich der Rechtswissenschaftlichen Fakultät der Friedrich-Schiller-Universität Jena für ihre Unterstützung des Law & Language Programms und ihr Bemühen, der juristischen Ausbildung ein internationales Flair zu geben.

Ich möchte meine Leser einladen, mich Online zu besuchen bei www.recht.uni-jena.de/llp/index.html. Ihre Kommentare zu diesem Buch sind mir sehr willkommen.

Jena, den 30. April 2001   B. Sharon Byrd

Vorwort zur 1. Auflage

Die Grenzen meiner Sprache bedeuten die Grenzen meiner Welt.

Ludwig Wittgenstein, *Tractatus logico-philosophicus*, 5.6

Recht ist Sprache, und wenn Sie das nicht glauben, sollten Sie einen Blick in das BGB werfen und dabei versuchen, den Text ganz mühelos zu verstehen. Wenn Sie Jurist sind, ist es Ihnen wahrscheinlich bewußt, daß Sie bei Ihren nicht-juristischen Kollegen und Freunden schlecht ankommen, wenn Sie über ein Delikt mit überschiessender Innentendenz sprechen oder einfach über "p.V.V.", "c.i.c." oder "a.l.i.c." reden. Falls Sie die Rechtswissenschaft noch studieren, haben Sie vielleicht die Zeit schon vergessen, als diese Begriffe für Sie völlig neu und unverständlich waren.

Dieses Buch versucht, Ihnen eine andere Rechtssprache beizubringen, die des Common Law - eines Rechtssystems, das unter anderem in England und in den Vereinigten Staaten gilt. Dieses Rechtssystem und deshalb die Art und Weise, wie Juristen dort über Rechtsprobleme denken und miteinander diskutieren, ist von den anderen europäischen Rechtssystemen und der mit ihnen verbundenen Weise zu denken grundverschieden. Aus diesem Grunde führt dieses Buch in die Rechtssprache *und* das Rechtssystem ein, weil das eine ohne das andere wie ein Wort ohne Sinn ist.

Introduction to Anglo-American Law and Language ist aus vielen Jahren Lehrerfahrung an verschiedenen deutschen Universitäten – jetzt an der Friedrich Schiller-Universität Jena – gewachsen. Meine Dankbarkeit muß in erster Linie meinen Studenten ausgesprochen werden, die mir Klarheit darüber verschafft haben, wie sie am besten lernen, und die auch durch ihr eigenes Engagement mir die Aufgabe, ihnen etwas beizubringen, zur großen Freude machten. Darüber hinaus gebührt mein Dank insbesondere Gunther Biewald (Los Angeles), Angelika Drescher (München), Professor Mark F. Grady (Los Angeles), Jochen Hoffmann (Erlangen), Professor Dr. Jan C. Joerden (Frankfurt/Oder), Arthur B. Laby (Washington), Matthias Lehmann (Jena), Dr. Rembert Niebel (Jena), Christoph Reichert (Augsburg), Dr. Martin Schnell (Augsburg), Irina von Schilling (Erlangen), Jan Schuhr (Erlangen), Hannes Unberath (Erlangen), Sebastian Walter (Erlangen), Anne Witt (Jena) und Andreas Zuber (Edinburgh) dafür, daß sie das Manuskript in den verschiedenen Phasen seiner Entwicklung gelesen und mir wertvolle Vorschläge dazu gegeben haben. Für eine langjährige freundschaftliche Unterstützung möchte ich ganz besonders Professor Dr. Wilfried Bottke (Augsburg) und Professor Dr. Karl M. Meessen (Jena) danken.

Jena, April 1997   B. Sharon Byrd

Einführung und methodische Hinweise

I. Lernziele

Introduction to Anglo-American Law & Language ist gedacht als Einführung in die anglo-amerikanische Rechtssprache, in das Rechtssystem des Common Law und in einige ausgewählte Rechtsgebiete. Sie sollten von diesem Buch erwarten,

- daß Sie mit seiner Hilfe ca. 500 juristische Fachbegriffe im Kontext lernen können, was es Ihnen ermöglicht, sich mit Juristen und Juristinnen in einem englischsprachigen Land über Rechtsprobleme zu unterhalten; Sie schaffen sich damit eine Grundlage, auf der aufbauend Sie Ihren Fachwortschatz später selbständig erweitern können;
- daß Sie sich mit seiner Hilfe eine Arbeitsmethode aneignen können, die Sie befähigt, eigenständig englischsprachige juristische Texte aufzufinden, zu lesen und genau zu verstehen;
- daß Sie mit seiner Hilfe ein Verständnis für die fundamentalen Unterschiede zwischen einem common law-System und einem civil law-System gewinnen können;
- daß Sie mit seiner Hilfe einen Einblick in die Grundlagen ausgewählter Rechtsgebiete bekommen können, was Sie befähigt, sich in diesen Rechtsgebieten selbständig weiter auszubilden, die Lösungen juristischer Probleme selbständig zu erforschen und die dafür notwendige Rechtsterminologie zu verstehen.

II. Adressaten und Benutzer

Introduction to Anglo-American Law & Language ist gedacht als

- eine Unterstützung für den Fachsprachen-Unterricht im Rahmen eines Studiengangs an einer Universität oder einer anderen Institution für den Unterricht von Rechtssprachen (Dolmetscher- und Übersetzerinstitute);
- eine Einführung für Anwälte, die sich wegen ihrer beruflichen Tätigkeit selbständig einen Einblick in das anglo-amerikanische Recht und seine Rechtssprache verschaffen möchten;
- eine Vorbereitung für Studenten, die es vorhaben, ein Aufbaustudium (LL.M.) oder ein Praktikum in einem Land mit einem common law-System zu absolvie-

ren, d.h. in Australien, England, Irland, Kanada, Neuseeland oder in den Vereinigten Staaten, auch in Indien oder in Schottland, die beide vom common law-System beeinflußt sind;

• eine Grundlage für Rechtsreferendare, die vorhaben, eine Auslandswahlstation in einem Land mit einem common law-System zu verbringen.

Englischkenntnisse, wie sie in 7 bis 9 Jahren an einem Gymnasium, und juristiche Grundkenntnisse, wie sie in 2 Semestern an einer Universität erworben werden können, werden für die Lernenden vorausgesetzt. Für das Unterrichten mit Hilfe dieses Buches sind Rechtskenntnisse zwar nützlich, aber nicht unbedingt erforderlich. *Introduction to Anglo-American Law & Language* versucht, die Rechtsprobleme, die in den verschiedenen Orginaltexten ans Licht kommen, auch im Detail sprachlich und fachlich zu untersuchen, damit sie für jeden Leser klar sind. Das Buch liefert ein Lehr- und Lernprogramm, das die Studierenden auch auffordert, zwischen ihrem eigenen Rechtssystem und dem common law-System Vergleiche zu ziehen. Diese Orientierung erleichtert dem Nicht-Juristen das Unterrichten insofern, als er sich in aktiven Diskussionen während des Unterrichts die Lösungen der Rechtsprobleme, die in dem Buch angesprochen werden, von den Studierenden nach dem einheimischen Recht erläutern lassen kann. Darüber hinaus werden die Studierenden dadurch veranlasst, über ihr eigenes Rechtssystem in der englischen Fachsprache zu reden.

III. Struktur und Aufbau des Lehr- und Lernprogramms

Introduction to Anglo-American Law & Language besteht aus drei Einheiten, die jeweils in mehrere Kapitel unterteilt sind. Wenn das Buch als Unterstützung für den Unterricht im Rahmen eines Recht- und Sprachenprogramms oder einer fachspezifischen Fremdsprachenausbildung an einer Hochschule benutzt wird, kann es bei einer Unterrichtsdauer von 2 SWS innerhalb von 3 bis 4 Semestern durchgearbeitet werden, und zwar nach dem folgenden Zeitplan:

    Unit I. Fundamental Characteristics of the Common Law (2 Semester)

    Unit II. The Courts and their Jurisdiction und

    Unit III. Constitutional Law (1 bis 2 Semester)

Unit I: Fundamental Characteristics of the Common Law steht dabei im Vordergrund, und das common law-System als Ganzes wird betont. Das common law unterscheidet sich zu sehr von den Rechtssystemen der Länder des europäischen Kontinents, um in einer kürzeren Zeit angemessen behandelt zu werden. Es ist auch nicht so, daß die Grundzüge des Systems in Unit I lediglich abstrakt angesprochen würden. Statt dessen führt Unit I in das Lesen von englischen und U.S.-amerikanischen Gerichtsentscheidungen – die wichtigste Quelle der common law-Rechtsprinzipien – ein und versucht, den Studierenden nahezubringen, wie sie diese Rechtsprinzipien in den Entscheidungen erkennen können. Die Studierenden sollten dabei auch lernen, Fälle miteinander zu vergleichen und voneinander zu unterscheiden, damit sie Analogien zu weiteren Fällen bilden können und dadurch lernen, in der Weise englischsprachiger Juristen zu argumentieren. Die Texte in Unit I sind überwiegend Gerichtsentscheidungen, die sich mit dem Strafrecht befassen. Am Anfang eines solchen Programms kommen die Studierenden erfahrungsgemäß mit der strafrechtlichen Terminologie besser zurecht als mit der Terminologie anderer Rechtsgebiete. Darüber hinaus kommt auf diese Weise auch das Strafrecht zur Sprache.

Unit II: The Courts and their Jurisdiction fährt mit einer genauen Beschreibung des Gerichtssystems und der etwas komplizierten konkurrierenden Zuständigkeit der einzelstaatlichen Gerichte und der U. S.-Bundesgerichte fort. Es enthält in erster Linie Gesetzestexte aus dem *United States Code*, umfasst aber auch Gerichtsentscheidungen und Sekundärliteratur zu diesen Themen. Das U.S.-Gerichtssystem habe ich ausgewählt, weil es einige fachsprachliche Bücher zum englischen, aber, soweit ich weiß, keine in Deutschland erhältlichen Bücher zum U.S.-amerikanischen Gerichtssystem gibt.

Unit III: Constitutional Law führt Sie in ausgewählte Rechtsgebiete ein. Dieser Abschnitt versucht, die Fähigkeiten, die die Studierenden durch die Arbeit mit den beiden ersten Abschnitten entwickeln konnten, noch weiter zu fördern. In ihm kommen sowohl authentische Gerichtsentscheidungen als auch Gesetzestexte, Kommentare zu Gesetzen und Sekundärliteratur zur Sprache.

Natürlich ist es nicht möglich, in einer *Introduction to Anglo-American Law & Language* eine umfassende Darstellung des Rechtssystems zu geben. Doch habe ich versucht, dadurch eine solide Grundlage zu schaffen, daß die Darstellung etwas mehr in die Tiefe der juristischen Problematik eindringt und dafür weniger in die Breite geht.

IV. Arbeiten mit *Introduction to Anglo-American Law & Language*

Aus welchem Grunde auch immer Sie Interesse an diesem Buch gefunden haben, sollten Sie – um den höchsten Erfolg zu erzielen – folgendes beachten:
• Dieses Buch baut Ihre Sprachkompetenz und Ihr Verständnis für die common law-Lösung von Rechtsfragen kontinuierlich auf und sollte deswegen langsam von vorne nach hinten durchgearbeitet werden; dabei sollte die Rechtsterminologie im ersten Kapitel verstanden und gelernt sein, bevor Sie mit dem zweiten Kapitel anfangen, usw.

- Bevor Sie mit den verschiedenen Rechtstexten konfrontiert werden, führt das Buch Sie erst einmal in jedes der einzelnen Rechtsgebiete ein. Dabei wird die für das Verstehen der Texte notwendige Terminologie durch **Fettdruck** hervorgehoben und erläutert. Die Terminologie wird auch in Listen aufgeführt, die Sie in den einzelnen Kapiteln finden. Dort finden Sie auch Definitionen und, soweit das sinnvoll ist, Übersetzungen oder Übertragungen ins Deutsche. Darüber hinaus versucht das Buch, Ihren allgemeinen Wortschatz dadurch zu erweitern, daß es auch solche englische Wörter in Wortschatzlisten aufführt und definiert, die nach meiner Erfahrung Studenten oft nicht geläufig sind.

- Wenn Sie die Einführung verstanden und die Terminologie gelernt haben, sollten Sie die originalen Rechtstexte durchlesen und dabei versuchen, ihren Sinn auch ohne die mitgelieferten Analysen der Rechtsprobleme so gut wie möglich zu verstehen. Überlegen Sie sich, was Ihnen noch nicht klar ist und wie Sie vorgehen würden, um die Unklarheiten selbständig zu beseitigen.

- Nach jedem Text finden Sie eine ausführliche Analyse der Rechtsprobleme und der benutzten Rechtsterminologie. Achten Sie darauf, wie sich Probleme lösen lassen, die beim Verständnis eines Textes immer noch bestehen bleiben. Sie werden sehen, daß das Buch oft ein Rechtswörterbuch "Englisch-Englisch" und/oder eine Enzyklopädie wie das *Corpus Juris Secundum* sowie Kommentare und andere Sekundärliteratur als Hilfsmittel heranzieht. Diese Methode sollte Ihnen klar werden, damit Sie lernen, solche Verständnisprobleme selbständig zu lösen. Ich habe bewußt die Hilfsmittel, die ich bei der Analyse benutze, danach ausgesucht, daß Sie sie auch in einer relativ schlecht ausgestatteten juristischen Bibliothek noch finden können.

- Wenn Sie einen Text als Ganzen verstanden und sich mit der Terminologie vertraut gemacht haben, sollten Sie ihn nochmals durchlesen und sich dieses Mal darauf konzentrieren, die genaue Bedeutung jedes einzelnen Satzes zu verstehen.

- Im Anschluß an die Texte finden Sie Übungen, die Sie anregen sollen, das Gelernte noch einmal zu überdenken und sich dabei selbst zu prüfen, ob Sie die im Text angesprochenen Probleme wirklich verstanden haben. Diese Übungen sind auch für die aktive Diskussion im Rahmen eines Lehrprogramms besonders geeignet.

- Bei der Bearbeitung der Texte sollten Sie sich den sprachlichen Rahmen merken, in dem die Terminologie benutzt wird. Um Sie dabei zu unterstützen, liefert das Buch zusätzliche Terminologie-Übungen ("Language Exercises"), die Sie am Ende jeder Lehr-Einheit ("Unit") finden.

- Jeweils am Ende der Kapitel mache ich Vorschläge, was Sie lesen können, um sich weiter in das jeweilige Rechtsgebiet einzuarbeiten. Die Gerichtsentscheidungen, die ich anführe, sind dafür geeignet, daß Sie sie gewissermaßen als Hausaufgabe lesen und bearbeiten und dann Ihren Freunden vortragen. Auf diese Weise wird Ihre Fähigkeit gefördert, juristische Texte selbständig zu verstehen, zu erläutern und darüber zu diskutieren. Darüber hinaus ist die Methode fraglos dafür geeignet, in das Rechtsgebiet, um das es jeweils geht, immer weiter einzudringen.

- Am Endes des Buches finden Sie im Anhang II Hinweise darauf, wie man englische und U.S.-amerikanische Gerichtsentscheidungen auffindet und zitiert. Das soll Ihnen bei einer selbständigen Erforschung der Rechtsquellen helfen. Darüber hinaus finden Sie ein vollständiges Glossar, das die juristische Terminologie mit Definitionen und deutschen Übersetzungen und Übertragungen enthält. Das Glossar gibt auch Hinweise darauf, wo die Ausdrücke in dem Buch zu finden sind und kann deshalb auch als Sachregister benutzt werden.

Eine Bemerkung zum Thema "Politically Correct Speech": In diesem Buch verwende ich in den Beispielen, bei denen es um Kläger, Rechtsanwälte, Richter usw. geht, die Ausdrücke "he" und "she" gleichermaßen. Das ist in Großbritannien und in den U.S.A. heute üblich. Sie sollten deswegen nicht denken – was viele Leser schon gedacht haben -, daß es sich um einen Druckfehler handelt, wenn "The judge.... she" vorkommt.

Eine Bemerkung zum Unterschied zwischen britischem und amerikanischem Englisch: Sie werden in diesem Buch authentische Texte sowohl aus England als auch aus den U.S.A. finden. Dabei werden Sie sicher merken, daß in der Rechtssprache die Unterschiede nicht so groß sind, wie sie auf der Konversationsebene Ihnen vielleicht erscheinen mögen. Sogar die Rechtsterminologie im engeren Sinne ist meistens dieselbe oder doch so ähnlich, daß die Unterschiede als nicht sehr problematisch bewältigt werden können. Nichtsdestoweniger habe ich mich in den Fällen einer Differenz in der Terminologie darum bemüht, sowohl die englischen als auch die U.S.-amerikanischen Ausdrücke und Begriffe zu liefern. Auch versuche ich, auf die manchmal unterschiedliche Schreibweise in England und in den Vereinigten Staaten hinzuweisen.

Table of Contents

Unit I
Fundamental Characteristics of the Common Law

Most legal systems of the world may be classified into two major groups, referred to as **civil law** and **common law** systems. Continental European nations have civil law systems, whereas England has a common law system. Common law systems are also found to a greater or lesser extent in Australia, Canada, India, Ireland, New Zealand, Scotland and the United States. The distinguishing characteristics of these two systems lie in the **source of law** and the **procedure** used in the courts.

Unit I comprises four chapters. The first deals with the source of law in civil law and common law systems. The second, on the jury, and the third, on the adversary system, consider the procedure used in trial courts. The final chapter deals with the retroactive application of judicial decisions, a problem particularly relevant for a common law system. Although Unit I focuses in the *differences* between the two systems, indeed many people would argue quite correctly that the two systems are merging in a number of respects. Still, it is important first to grasp the fundamental distinctions because they explain to a great extent the different approaches lawyers from these legal systems take when tackling legal problems.

Chapter 1
The Source of Law

A. Civil Law Systems

In a civil law system, the primary source of law is a **code**, such as the *Code civil* in France or the *Bürgerliches Gesetzbuch* (BGB) in Germany, which in English would be called the **Civil Code**. These codes developed historically from the *Codex Iustinianus* of the sixth century, which until the end of the eighteenth century was the law "common" to all of continental Europe (*ius commune*). Over time, the various individual European nations developed their own national codes and the "common" nature of the applicable law was to some extent lost. Still, the influence of Roman law is strong in the civil codes of continental Europe today, which is why they are to some extent similar.

It is important to realize that a code is not merely a collection of **statutes**, or written laws, which have been **enacted**, or adopted by a **legislature**. Instead, it is a highly sophisticated, organized treatment of an entire body of law. A code contains a **general part**, which deals with issues common to the entire body of legal problems the code is designed to govern. It also has one or more **specific parts** containing **provisions** relating to particular legal questions. The *BGB*, for example, consists of five books, the first of which is the general part for the following four on the **law of obligations** (**contract law** and **tort law**), **property law, family law** and **inheritance law** (or the law of **estates and trusts**). Furthermore, the second book on the law of obligations is also divided into a general part and a specific part, the specific part covering both the law of voluntarily assumed obligations (contracts) and the law of obligations imposed by law (torts). The intellectual achievement embodied in the codes of continental Europe can hardly be exaggerated. Berthold Brecht formulated the respect owed them by placing the *BGB* on a level with the Bible when, in characterizing Mackie Messer's despicable nature, he wrote: "Er hält sich nicht an die Bibel. Er lacht übers BGB."

Codes are generally published with a **commentary** written by a scholar or a group of scholars in the particular legal field. It is to these commentaries that a lawyer will first look when trying to find the status of the law relating to a case she is handling. The opinion of these scholars on the status of the law is based on their own and other scholars' theories and on decisions of the higher courts. Although court decisions are important, scholarly opinion certainly receives a great deal of respect as providing a theoretical basis for solving legal issues. Often the courts will adopt these theories themselves as the bases for their opinions.

B. Common Law Systems

In a common law system, the primary source of law is **judicial opinion,** or the opinion of judges as developed over the centuries. In twelfth century England, King Henry II (1154-1189) increased his own power and reduced the power of the local courts by opening the King's Court (*Curia Regis*) to the entire realm. Before that time, royal justice was available only to the elite. The common man's legal problems were solved locally, with the Norman barons exercising their authority within their own manors. When disputes arose between their subjects, it was the law of the manor that applied to the dispute. Henry II established a central court manned with his appointees who were to act as judges to hear complaints from the whole realm. Court was held at Westminster Hall, but royal justices also **rode circuit,** traveling around all of England to hear cases and bring the King's justice to the people locally. The law that developed from the decisions reached in the King's Court thus became superior to the law of the manors. In this way, the King's authority increased as did legal security regardless of the time or place of the decision. The law that developed in the King's Court thus became "common" to all of England, or the **common law** of England.

Today people use the term "common law" to denote the system of law that developed in England and was imported into countries the English strongly influenced. The common law has its main source in the opinions of judges. These opinions contain legal principles which can be applied to solve future cases. English common law was exported to the United States in 1607 when the first colonists settled in Virginia. Consider the following entries in *Corpus Juris Secundum*, a leading legal encyclopedia in the United States:

> I. § 1.b. The term "common law of England" refers to the general system of law derived from England as opposed to the Roman or civil law. Although it has been used to represent the entire body of law, including statute law, administered in the common-law tribunals, it generally designates only the unwritten law.

5 I. § 2. The common law is one of the forms of law, and is a controlling system of rules
and principles, flexible and susceptible of adaption to new conditions, although
fundamentally immutable, which is developed and stated in, although not established by, judicial decisions.

The common law is one of the forms of law, and is the embodiment of principles and
10 rules inspired by natural reason, an innate sense of justice, and the dictates of
convenience, and voluntarily adopted by men for their government in social relations. The authority of its rules does not depend on positive legislative enactment,...but on general reception and usage, and the tendency of the rules to accomplish the ends of justice. However, except where altered by statute, it is just as much
15 a part of the local jurisprudence as are enactments of the legislature, and where a
principle of such law has entered into our form of government, it is controlling, until
by legislation express in its terms it is modified or negatived by the substitution of a
new declaration on the subject.

20 II. § 3 The greater part of the common law in the United States is derived from the
common or unwritten law of England.

The English common law in its enlarged sense...became by the principle of coloniza-
tion the fundamental jurisprudence of the American colonies, as far as it was adapted
to their several conditions. When the colonies renounced their allegiance to the
25 British government and passed into states, that law, with that limitation, became the
fundamental jurisprudence of the states. The common law is the system from which
our judicial ideas and legal definitions are derived; and the greater part of the
common law in the United States is derived from the common or unwritten law of
England. This portion of the English law, in so far as it remains applicable to their
30 conditions and has not been changed by Constitution or statute, is in force in most of
the states...either by reason of its having been expressly adopted by constitutional or
statutory provision, or because of its having been recognized by the courts as in
force.

Corpus Juris Secundum, New York: West Publishing Co.: St. Paul, Minnesota, vol.
15A, "Common Law" (1964, updated by 1994 Pocket Parts). Cross references and
footnotes have been omitted from the original.

Terminology

source of law	origin of legal principles actually applied by judges to solve cases (**Rechtsquelle**)
civil law system	a system of law, such as the legal systems of continental European nations, with a strong Roman law tradition and the main source of law in written codes

Civil Code	translation of the German **Bürgerliches Gesetzbuch** or the French **Code civil**
code	organized and theoretically consistent treatment of an entire body of law (**Gesetzbuch**); **to codify**: to formulate a body of law in sections (§§) of a code (**kodifizieren**)
general part	the introductory book or part of a code in a civil law system containing basic sections or **provisions** that apply to the rest of the code provisions (**Allgemeiner Teil**)
specific part(s)	one or more books or parts of a code dealing with a particular area of the law (**Besonderer Teil**)
commentary	expert's analysis of the law including references to cases and legal theories (**Kommentar**)
common law system	a system of law such as found in England and in countries influenced by England with the main source of law in the opinions of judges
judiciary	branch of government responsible for hearing and deciding legal disputes (**rechtsprechende Gewalt**); a **judge** or **justice** (for higher courts) is the person who determines the rights of the parties to a law suit (**Richter**); **to judge**: to act as a judge in a case, to determine the rights of the parties to a law suit; **judicial**: of or relating to a judge, as in **judicial opinion** (**Urteil**)
to ride circuit	to travel as a judge from one area to another and back again to hear cases
procedure	manner of conducting a case from start to finish in a court of law (**Verfahren**); as a body of law it contains rules on how to initiate a law suit and conduct it to its close (**Prozeßrecht**)
legislature	one of three branches of government common to democratic republics; the branch of government responsible for making law (**Legislative**); **legislator**: person who is a member of the legislature (**Abgeordneter**); **legislative**: of or relating to the legislature, as in **legislative enactment**
to enact	to formally adopt a law and put it into force (**verabschieden**)
statute	a single written law that has been adopted by the legislature; sometimes used to designate a single section or paragraph of a code (**Gesetz**); **statutory**: of or relating to written enacted law
provision	what the law **provides** (**vorsieht**), laws and parts of laws (**gesetzliche Bestimmungen**)
law of obligations	English translation of the German: **Schuldrecht**
contract	agreement between two private parties or between a private party and the state (**Vertrag**); term *is not* used for international agreements, which are called **treaties, conventions, agreements** (**Verträge**)

contract law	the law of obligations as between two or more persons who have voluntarily entered into an agreement involving rights and obligations for each of those persons (**Vertragsrecht**); **contract** is *not* used for international agreement (**treaty**)
estates and trusts	another name for the law of inheritance (**Erbrecht**)
inheritance law	the law governing property disposition on death, also called **estates and trusts** (**Erbrecht**)
family law	the law of marriage, divorce, responsibilities to children (**Familienrecht**)
property law	the law of ownership, possession and other rights relating to movable and immovable objects (**Sachenrecht**)
tort law	the area of the law dealing with rights against a person who has committed a tort (**Deliktsrecht**), also referred to simply as "**torts**"; **tort**: an injury inflicted intentionally or accidentally upon s.o. for which that person can sue for compensation, pain and suffering, etc. ([zivilrechtliches] **Delikt**); **to sue in tort**: to sue s.o. for a tort

Vocabulary

allegiance	loyalty
disposition	transfer of property, giving away of s.th.
express	actually stated and not merely implied
immutable	unchangeable
implied	not directly stated, suggested so that one can drawn as a conclusion
innate	inborn, of the essence of s.th.
scholar	highly educated specialist engaged in research and often teaching; "scholar" is the correct translation of "Wissenschaftler"; "scientist" is the correct translation of "Naturwissenschaftler"; accordingly, a "Rechtswissenschaftler" is a legal scholar and not a scientist

1. The Doctrine of Stare Decisis

Once a principle of law was developed and applied in a case to resolve a dispute, lawyers in similar cases came to rely on what the court had said in the past and used the past decisions as arguments for the way a new case should be decided. In common law systems today, judges indeed are bound by their previous decisions and by the decisions reached by higher courts. A case decided in the past establishes a principle of law which is referred to as **binding precedent**. The binding nature of the precedent was expressed in the Latin: *stare decisis et non quieta movere*, meaning "to stand by decisions and not to disturb settled questions." Accordingly, when we speak of the **doctrine of stare decisis** we are referring to the binding nature of previous judicial decisions on a particular point of law.

The **House of Lords,** as the highest court in England, makes final determinations of what the law of today's England is. Its decisions are final and binding for all lower courts throughout England. They were also absolutely binding on the House of Lords itself. In 1898, in *London Tramways v. London City Council* [1898] A.C. 375, the House of Lords **held** that it was bound by its own decisions and could not depart from them in future similar cases. Of course, this degree of rigidity restricts the natural development of the law and its conformity to changing standards and customs within society. Increasingly aware of this problem, the House of Lords officially retracted its decision in *London Tramways* in a published announcement in 1966. The **Lord Chancellor (L.C.),** who is the head of the British **judiciary** and the speaker of the House of Lords, delivered this announcement. He delivered it "on behalf of himself and the **Lords of Appeal in Ordinary,"** also called "**Law Lords,**" who are the judges of the House of Lords.

Practice Statement (Judicial Precedent)
[1966] 3 All E.R. 77

Before judgments were given in the House of Lords on July 26, 1966, Lord Gardiner, L.C., made the following statement on behalf of himself and the Lords of Appeal in Ordinary:

5   Their lordships regard the use of precedent as an indispensable foundation upon which to decide what is the law and its application to individual cases. It provides at least some degree of certainty upon which individuals can rely in the conduct of their affairs, as well as a basis for orderly development of legal rules.

Their lordships nevertheless recognise that too rigid adherence to precedent may lead to injustice in a particular case and also unduly restrict the proper development of the 10   law. They propose therefore to modify their present practice and, while treating former decisions of this House as normally binding, to depart from a previous decision when it appears right to do so.

In this connection they will bear in mind the danger of disturbing retrospectively the basis on which contracts, settlements of property and fiscal arrangements have been 15   entered into and also the especial need for certainty as to the criminal law.

This announcement is not intended to affect the use of precedent elsewhere than in this House.

Analysis

The announcement was published in the **All England Law Reports** (**All E.R.**) in the third volume of the 1966 Law Reports on page 77 (See Appendix II for an explanation of citations).

The announcement states that, when departing from former precedent, the House of Lords will "bear in mind the danger of disturbing retrospectively the basis on which contracts, settlements of property and fiscal arrangements have been entered into and also the especial need for certainty as to the criminal law." This statement appears somewhat problematic. It could be interpreted to mean that principles of law announced in cases on which people have relied should not be **overruled,** or declared invalid and thus not applied. Since the assumption is that people do rely on the law and that decisions of the House of Lords embody principles of law, then it would remain impossible for the House of Lords to overrule itself even after this announcement. On the other hand, the announcement was published, which puts people on notice that decisions might be overruled and that therefore they cannot rely on them totally. Yet since one cannot predict when the House of Lords might overrule itself, one could argue that in principle their decisions cannot be relied upon at all.

In fact, the House of Lords has overruled itself even in criminal cases where the more recent decision had the effect of making conduct criminal that was not criminal under the former precedent. An interesting example is the case *Regina v. Shivpuri*. The problem in *Shivpuri* began with the House of Lord's earlier precedent in *Regina v. Smith (Roger)* [1975] A.C. 476. In *Smith* the **prosecutor** had **charged** the **defendant** with the **attempt** to handle or deal in stolen goods. Although the **defendant** believed the goods to be stolen, in fact they were not. This type of attempt is generally classified as a so-called **impossible attempt,** because regardless of what the defendant did, it was impossible to actually **consummate** the crime. The House of Lords held that the defendant could not be **convicted** because his act was entirely innocent. After this decision, the legislature adopted the **Criminal Attempts Act** 1981. Section 1 of this Act provides as follows:

> (1) If, with intent to commit an offence to which this section applies, a person does an act which is more than merely preparatory to the commission of the offence, he is guilty of attempting to commit the offence. (2) A person may be guilty of attempting to commit an offence to which this section applies even though the facts are such that the commission of the offence is impossible ...

The legislature thus abolished any **defense** (U.K. **defence**) of impossibility to a **charge of attempt.** Accordingly, a defendant charged with the attempt **to commit a crime** could not argue to his benefit that what he was doing could never result in the actual commission of the crime and thus he should be **acquitted** of the attempt. In addition, the **Law Commission** published a report in 1980 using exactly the example of the attempt to handle stolen goods when the goods were, unbeknownst to the defendant, not stolen. The Law Commission indicated that in this case the defendant would be guilty in theory under the proposed Criminal Attempts Act, although prosecution would probably not occur.

Following the adoption of this act, the House of Lords was confronted with the case *Anderton v. Ryan* [1985] A.C. 560; [1985] 2 W.L.R. 968; [1985] 2 All E.R. 355. Here the **defendant**, Ms. Ryan, had purchased video equipment believing it to be stolen. In fact the equipment was not stolen. Consequently, Ms. Ryan was **prosecuted** for "dishonestly attempting to handle a video cassette recorder knowing or believing it to be stolen, contrary to the **Criminal Attempts Act 1981**." The **trial court**, which is the lowest level court and the first one to hear a case, dismissed the **charges** against Ms. Ryan, but the **Divisional Court of the Queen's Bench Division**, the first **court of appeal** in this case, **reversed** the trial court's decision. On appeal to the House of Lords, however, the trial court's decision was **upheld** and Ms. Ryan was **acquitted,** or found not guilty. In deciding this case, the House of Lords relied on *Regina v. Smith* and overlooked the Law Commission's Report.

A great deal of scholarly literature developed around this decision, much of it extremely critical of the House of Lords' failure to apply the Criminal Attempts Act 1981. Two years later *Regina v. Shivpuri* came to the House of Lords. In *Shivpuri*, the defendant was charged with "attempting to be knowingly concerned in dealing with and harbouring a controlled drug, namely, heroin, in violation of the Criminal Attempts Act 1981." In fact, the substance he was carrying was not a restricted drug, but merely harmless vegetable material. The trial court convicted Shivpuri; the **Court of Appeal (Criminal Division)** and the House of Lords upheld the conviction. On appeal to the House of Lords, Shivpuri had argued that according to the holding in *Anderton v. Ryan*, he should have been acquitted. Just as in that case, where the defendant incorrectly thought goods were stolen, Shivpuri incorrectly thought the substance was heroin. Consequently, he argued, his act was also completely innocent. The House of Lords disagreed. The following excerpt is from Lord Bridge of Harwich's **speech** representing the opinion of the majority of the House of Lords in *Regina v. Shivpuri*:

Regina v. Shivpuri

[1987] A.C. 1

I am thus led to the conclusion that there is no valid ground on which *Anderton v.*
5   *Ryan* can be distinguished. I have made clear my own conviction, which as a party to
the decision (and craving the indulgence of my noble and learned friends who agreed
in it) I am the readier to express, that the decision was wrong. What then is to be
done? If the case is indistinguishable, the application of the strict doctrine of precedent would require that the present appeal be allowed. Is it permissible to depart
10   from precedent under the *Practice Statement (Judicial Precedent)* [1966] 1 W.L.R.
1234 notwithstanding the especial need for certainty in the criminal law? The following considerations lead me to answer that question affirmatively. First, I am
undeterred by the consideration that the decision in *Anderton v. Ryan* was so recent.
The *Practice Statement* is an effective abandonment of our pretention to infallibility.
15   If a serious error embodied in a decision of this House has distorted the law, the
sooner it is corrected the better. Secondly, I cannot see how, in the very nature of the
case, anyone could have acted in reliance on the law as propounded in *Anderton v.*
Ryan in the belief that he was acting innocently and now find that, after all, he is to
be held to have committed a criminal offence. Thirdly, to hold the House bound to
20   follow *Anderton v. Ryan* because it cannot be distinguished and to allow the appeal
in this case would, it seems to me, be tantamount to a declaration that the Act of
1981 left the law of criminal attempts unchanged following the decision in *Reg. v.*
Smith [1975] A.C. 476. Finally, if, contrary to my present view, there is a valid
ground on which it would be proper to distinguish cases similar to that considered in
25   *Anderton v. Ryan*, my present opinion on that point would not foreclose the option
of making such a distinction in some future case.

Analysis

The House of Lords states here that its decision in *Anderton v. Ryan* was incorrect and confronts the problem of what to do to correct that decision (lines 7-8).
It acknowledges that the **strict doctrine of precedent** would bind it to its previous
decision. In such case, the House of Lords would have to **allow the appeal**,
meaning that it would have to apply the holding in *Anderton v. Ryan* and acquit
Shivpuri (lines 8-9). On the other hand, it points out that the *Practice Statement*
may be applicable, which would permit the House of Lords to overrule its previous precedent and uphold Shivpuri's conviction. The *Practice Statement*, however, requires the House of Lords to take special note of the need for certainty in
the criminal law when overruling its precedents (lines 9-11). Still, the House of
Lords overruled *Anderton v. Ryan* and applied its new insights in the *Shivpuri*
case.

Questions on the Text

1. Some argue that the power to overrule should be exercised only prospectively, or with regard to the future. Disagreement exists on how to treat the party to the law suit who convinced the House of Lords to overrule its previous precedent. Should that party receive the benefit of the new rule as the prosecution did in *Shivpuri*? Or should the new rule first be announced and then applied only in future cases?

2. Would it make more sense in criminal cases than in civil cases to limit application of the new rule to the future? Is the argument stronger when the new rule makes conduct criminally punishable that would not have been punishable under the prior precedent? The problem raised by retroactive application of new judicial precedents is of particular importance in a common law system, because precedents are the primary source of law. We shall return to the problem later in Chapter 4.

3. State in your own words the four arguments the House of Lords makes in defense of its decision in *Shivpuri*. Discuss each of them and indicate your agreement or disagreement, including the reasons for your opinion.

Terminology

Act	an enactment, a law that is in force (**Gesetz**)
doctrine of stare decisis	principle that courts are bound by their former decisions when deciding later similar cases
precedent	principle of law announced by a court when reaching a decision that binds that court and all lower courts when reaching decisions in the future in similar cases, thus **binding precedent**
to hold	(held, held) to make a determination which resolves a legal dispute (**für Recht erkennen**)
judgment	judge's decision in a case (**Urteil**); (U.K.) judgement
to overrule	to declare a previous decision of either a lower court or of the court itself invalid (when the court overrules its own precedent) (**außer Kraft setzen**); this term is used in relation to a past precedent announced in a *different case* from the case in which it is overruled (e.g. *Shivpuri* overruled *Anderton v. Ryan*); the term is also used to mean: to deny the request or objections of a lawyer during a trial (**einen Antrag oder Einspruch ablehnen**); opposite of: **to sustain**

to reverse	to declare the decision of a lower court invalid; this term is used in relation to a lower court's decision in the *same case* as the one in which the decision is reversed (e.g. the court of appeal in *Anderton v. Ryan* reversed the trial court's decision in *Anderton v. Ryan* (**aufheben**)
to uphold	to maintain the validity of, for example, a decision reached by a lower court (**aufrechterhalten**)
to appeal	to turn to a higher court with the argument that a legal error occurred during the trial (**in die Revision gehen**); on appeal: during the appeal (**in der Revision**); appellant: the person bringing the appeal (**Revisionskläger** [Zivilrecht]; **Revisionsführer** [Strafrecht]); appellee: the person against whom the appeal has been brought (**Revisionsbeklagter** [Zivilrecht]; **Revisionsgegner** [Strafrecht]); appellate: of or relating to an appeal, as the **appellate** court, meaning the **court of appeal(s)** (**Revisions-**)
court of appeal(s)	court on a level higher than the trial court, which considers issues of law and not of fact (**Revisionsgericht**)
to allow an appeal	(U.K.) to decide in favor of the person bringing an appeal (**der Revision stattgeben**)
House of Lords	highest appellate court in England; term more commonly used to designate the upper house of the British Parliament
Law Lords	judges of the House of Lords (**Lords of Appeal in Ordinary**)
Lord Chancellor (L.C.)	head of the British judiciary and speaker of the House of Lords
Lords of Appeal in Ordinary	judges of the House of Lords (also "**Law Lords**")
speech	the opinion of a judge of the House of Lords in a case
Law Commission	committee of judges, lawyers and professors appointed to review the law, make proposals for reform and prepare draft codifications in an attempt to simplify the law and make it more consistent
trial	the first proceeding in which a legal dispute is resolved (**Hauptverhandlung**); trial court: the lowest court to consider a legal dispute, a court which considers both **issues of fact** and **issues of law** (**Tatsacheninstanz**)
to try a case	to act as a judge in a trial court in resolving a legal dispute (ca. **über einen Fall gerichtlich verhandeln**)
charges	formal legal claims made against s.o. (criminal law: **Anklagepunkte**; civil law: **Ansprüche**)
to prosecute	to formally charge s.o. with a crime (**anklagen**)
prosecutor	public official responsible for developing and bringing criminal cases to court (**Staatsanwalt**)

to commit a crime	to act in a way, or to bring about a result, that is criminally prohibited (**eine Straftat begehen**); **commission** as contrasted with **omission** means acting, as opposed to not acting, and thereby fulfilling the definition of a criminal offense; an omission is a failure to act to avoid the occurrence of criminally prohibited harm when one has the duty to so act (**Handlung – Unterlassung**)
to consummate a crime	to act in a way that fulfills all of the elements of the definition of a criminal offense (**eine Straftat vollenden**)
offense	(U.K. **offence**) crime (**Straftat**)
defendant	in a private law dispute, the person against whom a law suit has been brought (**Beklagter**); in a criminal case, the person who has been formally charged with a crime (**Angeklagter**)
defense	(U.K. **defence**) anything a defendant to criminal or civil law charges can argue to his benefit (**Verteidigungsvorbringen**)
to acquit	to find not guilty of a criminal charge (**freisprechen**); **acquittal**: a not-guilty judgment (**Freispruch**)
to convict	to find the defendant in a criminal trial guilty of the offense charged (**für schuldig erklären**)
intent	a state of mind required by the law for holding a person responsible for the commission of a crime; indicates that the actor was aware of what he was doing and did it purposely (**Vorsatz**)
attempt	trying to do s.th. that is criminally prohibited but being unsuccessful in actually bringing about the prohibited harm (**Versuch**)
impossible attempt	the attempt to do s.th. that is criminally prohibited in a situation in which the criminally prohibited harm cannot possibly occur (**untauglicher Versuch**)

Vocabulary

to abandon	to depart from s.th. with no intent to return to it
adherence	sticking to s.th.; following s.th.
benefit	advantage
to crave	to desire strongly
to deter	to keep s.o. from doing s.th.; **undeterred**: not stopped from doing s.th.
to distort	to twist out of shape so that appearance is different from what it should be
fiscal	relating to financial matters; relating to taxation

to foreclose	to prevent, to hinder
to harbour	(U.S. **to harbor**) to hide s.th., to keep s.th. secretly
indispensable	cannot be done without, necessary to have
infallibility	quality of never making a mistake
notwithstanding	regardless of
pretention	a claim, the truth of which is doubtful
to propound	to put forward, to set forth
prospectively	with regard to the future
retrospectively	with regard to the past
to be tantamount to	to be almost the same as, to have the same effect as
unduly	improperly

2. Ratio decidendi and obiter dicta

Since the main source of law in a common law system lies in judicial decisions, which are binding precedents, a common law lawyer or judge must be able to find those precedents within the somewhat lengthy case decisions published. Here, the case decisions referred to are decisions reached by the various courts of appeal and by the highest court of the land, the British **House of Lords,** for example, or the **United States Supreme Court.**

Not every word of a judicial decision is part of a precedent for future cases. Often judges discuss a wide range of issues in their opinions, such as **legislative intent,** historical and cultural developments, analogous and hypothetical cases, distinguishable cases, economic efficiency and the philosophy behind the law.

Judicial decisions also contain a statement of 1) the **facts of the case,** 2) the **legal history of the case,** 3) the **issue or issues raised on appeal** and 4) the **holding.** The statement of the **facts of the case** include only those facts that are relevant for the appellate court's decision. The **legal history of the case** is the disposition of the case by the first court to consider it, the **trial court,** and by any lower appellate courts that also considered the case. The **issue raised on appeal** is always a legal issue that one of the parties to the law suit claims was incorrectly resolved by any one of the lower courts. The **holding** is the resolution of this legal issue by the court whose decision one is reading. When you read a case, you should always be prepared to give a brief statement of these four elements of the decision.

The precedent in a case is the principle of law necessary to reach the holding in the case. This legal principle is referred to as the **ratio decidendi** of the case. Any general discussion included in the opinion which is not necessary for resolving the issue raised on appeal is referred to as **obiter dicta** or simply **dicta**.

Although the distinction between the **ratio decidendi** and **dicta** may seem fairly straightforward, being able to make it is crucial to the practice of law in a common law country. For a judge it is crucial because the judge needs to know what precedents bind him in arriving at a decision in a new case. For a lawyer it is crucial because the lawyer may only argue a case on the basis of binding precedents and not dicta. Indeed the entire legal process revolves around discovering the ratio decidendi of a case and thus defining the precedent, or law applicable. In a civil law system, one could say that the sections of the various codes represent what in a common law system are the rationes decidendi of one or many cases. Whereas a judge or lawyer in a civil law system has the problem of applying the general principles of law in the codes to the various and complex problems that arise in individual cases, the common law judge or lawyer has the problem of sorting out the general principle of law from the specific case.

Two U.S. torts cases, *Ploof v. Putnam* and *Vincent v. Lake Erie Transportation Co.*, provide good examples of rationes decidendi which correspond exactly to provisions in the German *Civil Code*. In *Ploof*, the **plaintiff**, who is the person suing the **defendant**, was sailing with his family on Lake Champlain when a severe storm suddenly developed. In an effort to save his sailboat from capsizing, the plaintiff moored it at the defendant's dock. The defendant, however, unmoored the boat, which the storm then drove upon the shore. The boat and its contents were destroyed and the plaintiff and his family injured. In a law suit the plaintiff filed against the defendant for compensation for the loss of the boat and the injuries to himself and his family, the defendant argued that the plaintiff had no right to use his dock. In upholding the lower court judgment for the plaintiff, the court held in pertinent part as follows:

Ploof v. Putnam
8 Vt. 471, 71 A. 188 (1908)

There are many cases in the books which hold that necessity, and an inability to
5   control movements inaugurated in the proper exercise of a strict right, will justify entries upon land and interferences with personal property that would otherwise have been trespasses … .

This doctrine of necessity applies with special force to the preservation of human life. One assaulted and in peril of his life may run through the close of another to escape
10   from his assailant…One may sacrifice the personal property of another to save his

life or the lives of his fellows. In Mouses's Case...the defendant was sued for taking and carrying away the plaintiff's casket and its contents. It appeared that the ferryman of Gravesend took 47 passengers into his barge to pass to London, among whom were the plaintiff and defendant; and the barge being upon the water a great
15 tempest happened, and a strong wind, so that the barge and all the passengers were in danger of being lost if certain ponderous things were not cast out, and the defendant thereupon cast out the plaintiff's casket. It was resolved that in case of necessity, to save the lives of the passengers, it was lawful for the defendant, being a passenger, to cast the plaintiff's casket out of the barge; ...

20 It is clear that an entry upon the land of another may be justified by necessity, and that the declaration before us discloses a necessity for mooring the sloop. But the defendant questions the sufficiency of the counts because they do not negative the existence of natural objects to which the plaintiff could have moored with equal safety. The allegations are, in substance, that the stress of a sudden and violent
25 tempest compelled the plaintiff to moor to defendant's dock to save his sloop and the people in it. The averment of necessity is complete, for it covers not only the necessity of mooring, but the necessity of mooring to the dock; ...

Analysis

In *Ploof v. Putnam,* the plaintiff sued to force the defendant to pay for the damage to the plaintiff's sailboat and for the injuries to himself and to his family. The defendant, however, argued that the plaintiff had no right to moor the boat at the defendant's dock and thus that the plaintiff had committed the tort of **trespass** (see subsection 3 on common law forms of action for a more detailed explanation of "**trespass**"). If that were true, the defendant would have had a right to defend his dock against the plaintiff's use of it and would therefore not be responsible for the damage caused. The court, on the other hand, discusses whether the plaintiff might have had a **justification** for using the defendant's dock.

In the first paragraph of the case excerpt, the court considers what it calls "the **exercise of a strict right**," namely the **right of necessity**, as a **justification** for the plaintiff's otherwise unlawful use of the defendant's dock. If the plaintiff was justified in using the defendant's dock, then the defendant would not have had the right to untie the plaintiff's boat. Untying the boat therefore would have been an unlawful act, or a **tort** for which the plaintiff could sue the defendant.

The court goes on to consider similar cases where the right of necessity had been affirmed in the past. As you should be aware, this type of consideration is appropriate in a common law system, because the law to be applied in a case is the law as established through judicial precedent in previous similar cases. One of these cases concerned an individual who was attacked, or **assaulted** by an attacker, or **assailant,** and who ran through someone else's property (**close**) to escape. The court notes that it was permissible for the individual to do so (line 9). The court also considers the famous *Mouse's Case*, in which a ferryman had overloaded his ferryboat and consequently it was in danger of sinking. Here too, the court notes that it was permissible for a passenger to throw someone else's property overboard in order to keep the ferry from sinking and save the lives of the passengers (lines 11-19).

In the last paragraph of the opinion, the court affirms that the plaintiff's **declaration** is sufficient. A **declaration** is another word for a **complaint**, the formal document a plaintiff must file with a court in order to initiate a law suit. The defendant had argued that the plaintiff's individual legal claims, or **counts**, were insufficient under the law because the plaintiff did not state that there was no way to save his boat other than by tying it to the defendant's dock. What issue does this raise in light of your knowledge of German law? Another way of stating the problem in English would be that the damage to the defendant's dock was "otherwise unavoidable."

The court dismisses this argument by stating that the plaintiff's claims, which are referred to as **allegations** and **averments**, were sufficient to support the **counts** in the **declaration**. That is another way of saying that the plaintiff's factual claims in his complaint were sufficient under applicable law to permit the plaintiff to win the law suit.

The **issue raised on appeal** here is whether a situation of necessity provides an individual with a right to use someone's property to save himself from injury and from the loss of his own property. The holding in the case is that it does. What is the ratio decidendi of this case? It is important to define it narrowly enough so that it will not apply in cases where a person should not be justified in using someone else's property, but also broadly enough so it establishes a precedent that courts can apply in future cases. Consider the following possibilities and determine which one is the best and which ones are too narrow or too broad:

1) When, in a storm on a body of water, an individual violates someone else's property rights to save himself from personal injury he is justified;

2) When, in a situation of danger, an individual violates someone else's rights he is justified;

3) When, in a situation of danger, an individual violates someone else's property rights he is justified;

4) When, in a situation of danger, an individual violates someone else's property rights to save himself from physical injury he is justified;

5) When, in a situation of danger, an individual violates someone else's

property rights to save himself from physical injury and injury to his
property he is justified if he could not have avoided the danger in any other
less harmful way;

6) When, in a situation of danger, an individual violates someone else's
property rights to save himself or his property from injury he is justified if
the injury he is preventing would be greater than the injury he is causing;

7) When, in a situation of danger, an individual violates someone else's
property rights to save himself or his property from injury he is justified if
the injury he is preventing would be greater than the injury he is causing
and he could not have avoided the danger in any other less harmful way.

To further refine the rule of law announced in *Ploof*, compare it to the decision
in *Vincent*:

Vincent v. Lake Erie Transportation Co.
109 Minn. 456, 124 N.W. 221 (1910)

O'Brien, J. The steamship Reynolds, owned by the defendant, was for the purpose of
5   discharging her cargo on November 27, 1905, moored to plaintiff's dock in Duluth.
While the unloading of the boat was taking place a storm from the northeast developed, which at about 10 o'clock p.m., when the unloading was completed, had so
grown in violence that the wind was then moving at 50 miles per hour and continued
to increase during the night. There is some evidence that one, and perhaps two, boats
10 were able to enter the harbor that night, but it is plain that navigation was practically
suspended from the hour mentioned until the morning of the 29th, when the storm
abated, and during that time no master would have been justified in attempting to
navigate his vessel, if he could avoid doing so. After the discharge of the cargo the
Reynolds signaled for a tug to tow her from the dock, but none could be obtained
15 because of the severity of the storm. If the lines holding the ship to the dock had been
cast off, she would doubtless have drifted away; but, instead, the lines were kept fast,
and as soon as one parted or chafed it was replaced, sometimes with a larger one. The
vessel lay upon the outside of the dock, her bow to the east, the wind and waves
striking her starboard quarter with such force that she was constantly being lifted
20 and thrown against the dock, resulting in its damage as found by the jury, to the
amount of $500.

We are satisfied that the character of the storm was such that it would have been
highly imprudent for the master of the Reynolds to have attempted to leave the dock
or to have permitted his vessel to drift away from it...Nothing more was demanded
25 of them than ordinary prudence and care, and the record in this case fully sustains the
contention of the appellant that, in holding the vessel fast to the dock, those in charge
of her exercised good judgment and prudent seamanship...

The appellant contends...that, because its conduct during the storm was rendered

30   necessary by prudence and good seamanship under conditions over which it had no
     control, it cannot be held liable for any injury resulting to the property of others, and
     claims that the jury should have been so instructed. An analysis of the charge given
     by the trial court is not necessary, as in our opinion the only question for the jury was
     the amount of damages which the plaintiffs were entitled to recover, and no com-
35   plaint is made upon that score.

     The situation was one in which the ordinary rules regulating property rights were
     suspended by forces beyond human control, and if, without the direct intervention
     of some act by the one sought to be held liable, the property of another was injured,
     such injury must be attributed to the act of God, and not to the wrongful act of the
40   person sought to be charged. If during the storm the Reynolds had entered the
     harbor, and while there had become disabled and been thrown against the plaintiffs'
     dock, the plaintiffs could not have recovered. Again, if while attempting to hold fast
     to the dock the lines had parted, without any negligence, and the vessel carried
     against some other boat or dock in the harbor, there would be no liability upon her
45   owner. But here those in charge of the vessel deliberately and by their direct efforts
     held her in such a position that the damage to the dock resulted, and, having thus
     preserved the ship at the expense of the dock, it seems to us that her owners are
     responsible to the dock owners to the extent of the injury inflicted...

     This is not a case where life or property was menaced by any object or thing belong-
50   ing to the plaintiff, the destruction of which became necessary to prevent the threat-
     ened disaster. Nor is it a case where, because of the act of God, or unavoidable
     accident, the infliction of the injury was beyond the control of the defendant, but is
     one where the defendant prudently and advisedly availed itself of the plaintiff's
     property for the purpose of preserving its own more valuable property, and the
55   plaintiffs are entitled to compensation for the injury done.

Questions on the Text

[1] A person dissatisfied with the decision of a lower court may **appeal** to a
     higher court. The person who appeals is called the **appellant** and the other
     party is referred to as the **appellee**. Who was the original **plaintiff** in this
     case, the ship owner or the dock owner? Who lost the case at the trial court
     level? Who is the **appellant** in the decision you have just read? What are the
     facts of this case? What is the **legal history of the case** (what was the result
     of the trial)? What is the **issue on appeal**? What is the **holding** of the court
     whose decision is reported above?

[2] Since this is a torts case, the issue of the defendant's **negligence** is of import-
     ance. Negligence is the failure to exercise the care a **reasonable person** in the
     defendant's position would have exercised. If the defendant's negligence
     causes the plaintiff's injury, the defendant will be required to compensate for

the damage he has caused. The court, however, states here that the **appellant** ship owner was not negligent: "the **record** in this case fully **sustains** the **contention** of the **appellant** that, in holding the vessel fast to the dock, those in charge of her exercised good judgment and prudent seamanship..." The **record** in a case contains all of the documents relevant to a law suit including the **transcript**, which is a written documentation of every word that was said during the trial. **Contentions** are claims and "**to sustain**" is used primarily in a legal context and means "to uphold" or "to support." Accordingly, the court here is saying that the **evidence** presented during the trial supports the ship owner's claims that he was not negligent. What other basis could there be for holding someone responsible for a tort other than negligence?

[3] The **appellant** then argued that since he was not negligent in tying to the appellee's dock, he should not be **held liable**, which means he should not be found responsible and thus not have to pay for the damage. He also argued that this was a purely legal question, because he claimed that the **jury should have been instructed** that he was not liable if not negligent. As is more fully described in Chapter 2, the jury is responsible for determining what the facts of a case are and applying the law as the judge instructs it to those facts. If the judge instructs or **charges** the jury that the defendant is not liable if not negligent, then the jury has to determine only whether the defendant exercised the care a reasonable person in the situation would have exercised and if so then reach a decision in favor of the defendant. In this case, the trial court did not instruct the jury in this way, and the higher court, whose decision you have just read, does not find that to be an error. In other words, the court here thinks that the appellant was liable for the damage caused to the appellee even though the appellant was not negligent. Furthermore, it states that the only question for the jury was the amount of money the appellant should pay, or the "amount of **damages** which the plaintiffs were entitled to **recover**" ("**damage**" means the injury caused and "**damages**" is the compensation the defendant has to pay for causing the damage). Why does this case not raise a question of negligence?

[4] In the fourth paragraph of the decision as reported here (lines 36-48) the court discusses damage attributable to the **act of God**, which is the way the common law characterizes a situation where damage is caused by some natural catastrophe, such as a storm or flood, and not by human conduct. In the fifth paragraph (lines 49-55) the court states that this was not a case where damage was caused by an act of God. Furthermore the court considers the somewhat different case where the object destroyed belongs to the plaintiff and is the cause of the danger to the defendant (lines 49-51). What parts of this decision contain **dicta**? What is the **ratio decidendi** of the case? When formulating it, include the ratio decidendi from the *Ploof* decision.

5 Students in U.S. law schools usually read these two cases together. They generally have a great deal of difficulty understanding them, because they focus on who won the case. In *Ploof*, the person who tried to moor his ship at another person's dock won the case (the dock owner had to pay for the damage to the ship) and the court even said that the ship owner had the right to do so. In *Vincent*, the person who moored his ship at another person's dock lost the case (the ship owner had to pay for the damage to the dock) even though he had a right according to the *Ploof* holding to do so and was not negligent. For a German law student, these cases should be fairly simple to understand because they say nothing other than what § 904 of the German *Civil Code* provides. The ratio decidendi of *Ploof* is almost identical to the first sentence of § 904 and the ratio decidendi of *Vincent* is identical to the second sentence of § 904. Reconsider the first sentence of the last paragraph of the *Vincent* decision (lines 49-51). Does it refer to a situation also covered by another section of the German *Civil Code*? Does the *Vincent* decision say anything about that situation which could be considered to be binding precedent?

Terminology

facts of a case	truths that directly relate to the issue raised in a law suit (**Sachverhalt**)
legal history (of a case)	the disposition lower courts, such as the trial court and any intermediate appellate court, reached in a case (ca. **die Entscheidung(en) der Vorinstanz(en)**)
issue raised on appeal	the legal problem confronting an appellate court when deciding a case (**Rechtsfragen in einem Revisionsverfahren**)
holding	the decision of a court that resolves the actual dispute before it (**Urteilstenor**); the part of the opinion that becomes a binding precedent, or principle of law, for the future; contrasted to **dicta** or **obiter dicta**, which are the additional comments, hypotheses, speculations, analogies, arguments of a court in the court's opinion and which are not binding precedents
ratio decidendi	(pl. **rationes decidendi**) the principle of law necessary to arrive at the holding in a case
dictum	(pl. **dicta**) any comment or discussion in a judicial opinion that is not necessary for resolving the dispute in the case; often includes hypotheticals used for the sake of argumentation, analogies, legislative history; sometimes referred to as **obiter dictum**

	or **obiter dicta,** especially if the discussion goes far astray from the basis of the decision
legislative intent	the purpose or reason the legislature had for adopting a law (**Wille des Gesetzgebers**)
plaintiff	in a private law dispute, the person who sues, who initiates the law suit (**Kläger**); also called the **complainant,** because it is the plaintiff who files a complaint to initiate a law suit
complaint	formal document setting forth the plaintiff's claims against the defendant to a private law suit (**Klage, Klageschrift**); the law suit is initiated by the plaintiff's filing the complaint with the appropriate court
declaration	another name less commonly used for **complaint** (**Klageschrift**)
allegation	claim; used primarily in a legal context (**Behauptung**); **to allege** (**behaupten**)
averment	claim; used primarily in legal context to refer to a claim contained in the plaintiff's complaint or the defendant's answer to the complaint (**Behauptung**); **to aver** (**behaupten**)
contention	claim (**Behauptung**); **to contend**: to claim (**behaupten**)
count	a separate and distinct legal claim; one crime charged in the indictment (**Anklagepunkt**) or one civil law claim made in a complaint (**Anspruch**)
liability	responsibility in the legal sense that the person responsible has to pay for damage he has caused (**Haftung**); conclusion of a private law dispute determining that the defendant has to pay for the plaintiff's injuries; also used in a criminal context but only if specifically referenced, as **criminal liability; to hold s.o. liable**: to determine as a court that s.o. is responsible and must pay for the damage caused (**jemanden haftbar machen**)
recovery	judge's award to a successful plaintiff to be paid by the defendant in order to make up for the injury the defendant caused the plaintiff; also **redress, relief, remedy** (ca. **Klagebegehren**)
damages	money that the defendant has to pay the plaintiff for causing the plaintiff's injuries (**Schadensersatz**); to be distinguished from **damage,** which is the common word for harm; **to recover damages**: to be awarded damages by a court to be paid by the defendant to a private law dispute for injury caused
charge given by the trial court	the trial court judge's instructions to the jury on the law (see Chapter 2) (**Belehrung der Geschworenen**)
jury instructions	explanation by the prosecutor to the grand jury or by the judge to the petit jury on what the applicable law is (ca. **Belehrung der Geschworenen**); the judge **instructs the jury on the law** (see Chapter 2)

United States Supreme Court	highest court in the U.S. federal court system
act of God	natural cause of some event; used to refer to natural catastrophes, as opposed to human actions, which cause damage (**höhere Gewalt**)
justification	a good reason recognized by law for committing what otherwise would be a civil or criminal wrong; a justification negates the wrongfulness normally associated with conduct defined as a crime or tort and gives the actor a right to commit it (**Rechtfertigungsgrund**); examples include **self-defense** (**Notwehr**) and **necessity as a justification** (**rechtfertigender Notstand**)
necessity	a justification or excuse based on a situation of emergency that can only be avoided by harming s.o. else's legally protected interest to protect one's own interest; distinguished between **necessity as a justification** (**rechtfertigender Notstand**) and **necessity as an excuse** (**entschuldigender Notstand**)
record	all of the documents relevant to a law suit assembled by the court (**Gerichtsakten, Protokoll**)
transcript	written record of everything said during a court proceeding, such as the grand jury hearings (also called **minutes**) or the trial (usually called the **trial transcript**) (**Wortprotokoll**)
evidence	proof offered at trial (**Beweismaterial**)
to sustain	to uphold, to grant or support the validity of a formal request made by a lawyer during a trial; the opposite of **to overrule**; (**einem Antrag oder Einspruch stattgeben**)
to assault	to attack or threaten s.o. (ca. **angreifen**); an assault is a criminal offense and a tort
assailant	s.o. who assaults another person (**ca. Angreifer**)
negligence	failure to take reasonable care in a situation to avoid damage to s.o. else; failure to recognize risk of causing harm in a situation in which a reasonable person would have recognized the risk; (**Fahrlässigkeit**)
reasonable person standard	standard used in all areas of the common law as a test for whether conduct was that of a normal, average person in the situation under consideration (vgl.: **die im Verkehr erforderliche Sorgfalt**)
personal property	movable property (**Fahrnis, bewegliche Sachen**); also referred to as **chattels, movables, personalty**; contrasted to **real property**, which is land and things attached to it (**Liegenschaften**)
trespass	a tort at common law involving direct injury to s.o. committed either intentionally or negligently for which the injured party could sue for compensation

Vocabulary

to abate	to stop, to nullify, to diminish in strength
to avail oneself of	to make use of, to turn to for assistance
barge	a flat-bottomed boat, usually used for transporting goods
bow	front of a boat; **stern**: back of a boat
to capsize	to tip over
casket	box; today generally used only to mean a box in which s.o. is placed for burial
to chafe	to rub and become thin or weak
close	area enclosed by walls, a narrow passage leading to a courtyard
to compel	to force
crucial	central, of primary importance
disposition	treatment of a matter, problem, case, etc. that resolves the issue and finishes the case
dock	a structure, often of wood, which extends from the land into the water to which one can tie a boat
imprudent	unwise, unadvisable
to inaugurate	to initiate, to begin
to inflict	to impose pain, damage or injury on s.o.; to deliver (a blow)
intervention	s.th. that occurs between two other events, s.th. that happens in between two other things
menace	s.th. annoying or bothersome
to moor	to tie a boat to s.th. on shore to keep it from drifting out onto the water
peril	danger; **in peril of his life**: in danger of losing his life
pertinent	relevant; **in pertinent part**: the part which is relevant to the discussion here
ponderous	heavy; **to ponder**: to think deeply and at length about s.th., to weigh s.th. in one's mind
prudent	wise, advisable
to render	to make, to cause to be
sloop	type of sailboat
starboard	right side of a boat; **port**: left side of a boat
tempest	strong storm
tug, tugboat	a strong boat used for pulling (towing) or pushing larger less easily turned boats, usually in harbors
vessel	general term for a boat or any hollow container

3. Common Law Forms of Action

As you recall from the last section, the plaintiff in *Ploof v. Putnam* sued the defendant in **trespass**. The word "trespass" is used in everyday English to mean that an individual has entered someone else's property without permission. In legal English, it refers to one of the so-called "**forms of action**" in the common law. To more fully understand this term, it is necessary to return briefly to the history of the common law.

A person seeking justice from the King's Court had to purchase a **writ** from the King's Chancellor. A "**writ**" is simply a formal *writ*ten order. Originally the various writs were addressed to the individual whom the plaintiff claimed had caused him injury, or to the sheriff or the lord of the manor where the injury had occurred or where the defendant resided. If addressed to the defendant, they usually required him to appear in the King's Court to answer or defend himself against the plaintiff's claims. If addressed to the sheriff, they required him to hear a case to determine the facts and then do justice as required by the King's law.

Over time the King's Chancellor developed different writs for different types of cases. The case specification, called "**form of action**" or "**cause of action,**" included factual, procedural and remedial elements. The factual elements described the type of injury for which a plaintiff could sue a defendant. The procedural elements specified the formal steps the plaintiff had to take to go forward with the law suit, such as what type of evidence he was permitted or required to present, who had to be joined as defendants, whether a trial by jury was available, and so forth. The remedial elements provided what **remedy** or **relief** the King's judges granted for the plaintiff's type of injury. A **remedy** or **relief** is what the court could then order the defendant to do in order to compensate the plaintiff for his injuries. In order to sue a defendant, therefore, the plaintiff first had to purchase from the King's Chancellor the **writ** that was appropriate for the particular **cause** or **form of action** and then follow the procedural rules associated with it in an effort to attain the remedy it provided.

Each of the common law **forms of action** had names and included most prominently over the course of history: **account, assumpsit, covenant, debt, detinue, ejectment, replevin, trespass, trespass on the case,** and **trover.** The various forms of action were abolished in England and the United States in the nineteenth century and today one simply refers to them as "**civil actions.**" Still they remain relevant because they each dictate the elements of the legal claim a plaintiff has to prove in order to be successful against the defendant. Although the plaintiff today simply files what is called a "civil action," rather an "action in trespass," for example, he may base his claim on a common law theory of **liability,** or responsibility, as embodied in any one of the original forms of action. If he does so, he must prove the elements of the form of action which is the basis of his claim.

The Most Well Known Forms of Action

At least superficial knowledge of the most well known forms of action is necessary for any real understanding of the common law. Read the following definitions:

account	form of action to force the defendant to give an explanation, or **account**, of how he has used the plaintiff's money which has been entrusted to his management or care.
assumpsit	form of action for **damages** to compensate for the defendant's failure to perform as promised under a simple contract, whereby the promise may be implied by law (**general assumpsit**) or expressly made by the defendant (**special assumpsit**)
covenant	form of action for **damages** to compensate for the defendant's failure to perform as promised under a contract which is written and has been **signed, sealed and delivered** to the plaintiff
debt	form of action to recover a specific sum of money the defendant owes the plaintiff
detinue	form of action to recover specific personal property, or for the value of the property, which the defendant unlawfully **detains**, or refuses to give back to the plaintiff, who is the owner of the property, and for **damages** to compensate the plaintiff for the loss of the use of that property
ejectment	form of action to recover possession of real property from the defendant who is in unlawful possession of it and for **damages** for loss of use of that land
replevin	form of action to recover personal property from defendant who unlawfully detains it, whereby the plaintiff may secure possession of that property on the posting of a **bond** or **security** at any time before judgment
trespass	form of action to recover **damages** to compensate for injury caused by the defendant's unlawful interference with the plaintiff's person, property or rights
trespass on the case	form of action to recover **damages** to compensate for injury resulting from the defendant's wrongful act which was not an act of direct or immediate force (**trespass**) but instead which caused the harm indirectly or as a secondary consequence; generally referred to simply as "**case**"

| trover | form of action to recover **damages** to compensate for the value of personal property which the defendant has wrongfully **converted** to his own use, such as by finding the plaintiff's property and keeping it for himself |

Comparison to the German Civil Code

At first glance, these definitions appear confusing even for Anglo-American law students, but they are not as complex as they might seem, at least on a level that is relevant for modern legal studies. First, they may be grouped into **actions ex contractu** and **actions ex delicto**. **Actions ex contractu** are law suits based on a contract the parties closed. Accordingly, the relationship between the plaintiff and defendant was voluntarily assumed by the two parties. **Actions ex delicto** are law suits based on some loss the plaintiff suffered as a result of the defendant's wrongful act in situations independent of whether the plaintiff is in a contractual relationship with the defendant. Here it is usually not the case that the plaintiff and defendant voluntarily entered into a mutual relationship before the cause of action arose. Instead these actions usually are based on a claim that the defendant acted intentionally or negligently to cause the plaintiff harm. **Actions ex contractu** include **account, assumpsit, covenant** and **debt**. **Actions ex delicto** include **case, ejectment, replevin, trespass** and **trover**. The action of **detinue** is considered to be a hybrid with mixed contractual and delictual elements.

Second, one may find at least rough parallels to these causes of action in the German *Civil Code*. Lawyers in the civil law tradition are accustomed to referring to causes or forms of action by a section number in their respective codes. In the common law tradition, names, such as those in the above definitions were used, but that should not be a source of confusion when trying to understand the nature of the legal basis for the plaintiff's complaint. To improve understanding, one can compare the above-listed **forms of actions** to German *Civil Code* provisions:

1. The action of **account** was appropriate against someone who had agreed to keep or manage the plaintiff's money and give him a periodic account of that money, but who had failed to do so. (see *BGB* §§ 666, 675).

2. The action of **assumpsit** was appropriate against someone who had breached a simple, informal contractual agreement. Here the comparison to German law is somewhat more complicated, because normally in a common law system the plaintiff sues the defendant for **damages**, which is the amount of money that will compensate for the loss the plaintiff suffered from the breach. In Germany, on the other hand, the typical **remedy** for

breach of contract is **specific performance,** namely forcing the defendant to do what he promised. Still, under some circumstances the German defendant to a contract action does have to pay damages (BGB §§ 325, 326).

3. The action of **covenant** is the same as **assumpsit,** but was appropriate when the contract had been formalized through **notarization** or by placing a wax **seal** on it. German law does not distinguish between the actions of **assumpsit** and **covenant** and this distinction in the common law is the result of historical development rather than any significant difference in the law suit itself.

4. The action of **debt** was appropriate to recover money loaned to the defendant (see *BGB* § 607).

5. The actions of **detinue** and **ejectment** were appropriate to recover possession of personal (**detinue**) or real (**ejectment**) property that the defendant was unlawfully detaining. Again the common law distinction between these two causes of action is a matter of historical development, rather than of any significant difference between the two. German law treats them together in §§ 985, 987 et seq. of the *BGB*.

6. Furthermore, the action of **replevin** functioned the same as the action of **detinue,** but the plaintiff could recover possession of the personal property immediately on filing his law suit with the appropriate court and posting a bond of security. Sections 916 et seq. of the German *Code of Civil Procedure* provide for this additional twist to the actions under *BGB* §§ 985, 987 et seq.

7. The actions of **trespass on the case,** or simply **case,** and **trespass** are non-contractual actions to recover **damages** to compensate for injury the defendant caused the plaintiff through the defendant's wrongful act. The historical difference between **trespass** and **case** was that **trespass would lie,** meaning a plaintiff could sue a defendant successfully **in trespass,** for the direct consequences of the defendant's interference with the plaintiff's person, property or rights, whereas **case would lie** for the indirect consequences of the defendant's wrongful act. A typical example used to explain the difference is the falling-tree example. If the defendant's tree fell on the plaintiff travelling by on a public road, the plaintiff could sue **in trespass.** If the tree fell on the public road and the defendant failed to remove it, the plaintiff could sue **in case** if he later fell over it and injured himself. This distinction is irrelevant for German law and both causes of action are relatively comparable to the cause of action provided by *BGB* § 823.

8. Finally the action of **trover** was appropriate when the defendant had unlawfully **converted** property to his own use after gaining possession of it. Comparable to the treatment German law gives this type of case (*BGB* § 992), **trover** was considered to be a **tort** or **action ex delicto.**

Again, the forms of action have disappeared today, but often you will find cases of the twentieth century with references to them. In addition, the common law as it developed over the centuries is applicable law today unless it has been expressly replaced by statute. Consequently, today's plaintiff may base a law suit on any one of the above theories of recovery, in which case the nature of the claim is important even though the name given it is in some sense obsolete. At very minimum, a student of the common law must recognize from these names 1) that a common law cause of action is meant and 2) whether that action is based on **tort** (**actions ex delicto**) or **contract** (**actions ex contractu**).

Terminology

actions ex contractu	law suit based on breach of an obligation voluntarily assumed in a contract (**Ansprüche aus Vertrag als Klagegrund**)
actions ex delicto	law suit based on breach of obligation imposed by law and independent of any contractual relationship (**Ansprüche aus Delikt als Klagegrund**)
bond	instrument of security for a debt (**Sicherungsleistung**)
civil actions	law suits based on theories of private law (**privatrechtliche Ansprüche als Klagegrund**)
conversion	"An unauthorized assumption and exercise of the right of ownership over goods or personal chattels belonging to another, to the alteration of their condition or the exclusion of the owner's rights. Any unauthorized act which deprives an owner of his property permanently or for an indefinite time..." *Black's Law Dictionary* (ca. **Unterschlagung**)
form of action	case specification at common law including factual, procedural and remedial elements and contained in a writ issued by the King's Chancellor, which a plaintiff had to purchase in order to file a private law suit; includes the actions of **account, assumpsit, covenant, debt, detinue, ejectment, replevin, trespass, trespass on the case** and **trover**, which today are merely referred to as "**civil actions**"; for a definition of each of these forms or **causes of action,** see above
cause of action	set of facts that permit a person to file a law suit against s.o. else (**Klagegrund**)
notarization	method of formalizing a document by having a **notary** witness the signing of the document and place her stamp on it (**Beurkundung durch einen Notar, notarielle Beurkundung**)
remedy	what plaintiff to a law suit is suing to obtain from defendant to compensate plaintiff for injury defendant is claimed to have caused him; what a court can order a defendant to do to com-

	pensate for causing injury to a plaintiff (**Klagebegehren**); also called "**relief**," "**recovery**," "**redress**," examples being money damages or specific performance
specific performance	remedy for breach of contract whereby the defendant is forced to do exactly what he promised to do under the contract (**Vertragserfüllung**)
writ	*writ*ten order issued by a court or some other official responsible for judicial matters (**gerichtliche Anweisung**)

4. Equity

As the common law developed in the **writ** system, it became more and more specific, complicated and rigid. As a result, justice was being sacrificed to formality. The King's Chancellor, who was usually a bishop and responsible for issuing the common law writs, began considering **petitions** individual subjects addressed to the King asking for **relief** from the injustice that would ensue from the common law. If the Chancellor was convinced, he would order the person responsible for the injustice to do or refrain from doing some act that could cause this injustice. As a consequence, a separate body of legal principles developed, which are referred to as principles of "**equity**." They developed parallel to the principles of the common law in the King's Court through the decisions of the King's Chancellor in certain exceptional cases.

Read the following text on this development:

> ... The Chancery was originally the royal secretariat, the place where all kinds of royal documents were prepared and authenticated by the Great Seal. Its head was the Chancellor, whose office came to be one of the great offices of state. In medieval times, most Chancellors were bishops and graduates in civil or canon law. Some
> 5   holders of the office were in effect the King's chief minister.

> The plaintiff was obliged to obtain a writ in a form appropriate to the claim. At first, if there was no precedent the Chancery would be prepared to draft a new one, but by the end of the thirteenth century this could no longer be done. Once the writ was obtained it governed the detailed form the action would take: if the wrong one had
> 10   been chosen, the plaintiff was required to recommence proceedings.

> Among the duties of the Chancellor were those of determining questions relating to Crown property, hearing common law actions concerning his clerks, servants and officials, and entertaining "petitions of right" (*i.e.* claims against the Crown). In addition, the Chancellor came to deal exclusively with petitions addressed to the
> 15   King or the Council in respect of grievances which for some reason were not redressed or redressible by proceedings in the common law courts. This might be because of corruption or undue influence affecting proceedings (*e.g.* the bribery of

jurors), or because in a particular case strict common law requirements for proof appeared to lead to injustice, or because the matter did not fall within the scope of
20   writs recognised by the common law. The Chancellor would give relief in particular cases by an order directed to the parties, his intervention being based on the dictates of their consciences judged in accordance with his own view of what was just. Proceedings before the Chancellor were simpler, and were in other respects advantageous when compared with the procedures of the common law courts. Moreover, the
25   Chancellor developed several remedies which were not available in other courts, most notably specific performance and the injunction – an order requiring the person to whom it is addressed to perform or to refrain from performing a stated act. When performing these judicial functions, the Chancellor came to be regarded as constituting a court: the Court of Chancery.

30   The standard illustration of how the Chancellor operated was provided by the person who borrowed money, acknowledged the debt by entering into a bond under seal, subsequently paid the debt, but failed to have the bond cancelled. For a common law court, the sealed bond provided incontrovertible proof of the existence of the debt: the court would enforce a second payment if proceedings were instituted by the
35   creditor. However, the Chancellor could restrain such unconscionable action on the part of the creditor by an injunction directed to him, and order that the bond be cancelled.

At first it was not thought that there were separate systems of "law" and "equity." The Chancellor was frequently advised by the common law judges, and there were
40   suggestions that the common law courts could take account of matters of conscience. However, tensions developed. The arguments on each side indeed reflected what is an inevitable dilemma in any system of law, the problem of reconciling the competing demands of justice and certainty. The more general a rule, the less likely it is to do justice in the particular cases to which it applies; moreover, an attempt to construct
45   in advance the qualifications to the rule necessary to do justice in all cases would lead to a system of rules of enormous complexity, even if all the problems could be foreseen. Hence, the need for some means whereby particular cases could be dealt with justly. Ad hoc decision-making can however be unjust if like cases are treated differently and, in any event, tends to be unpredictable. The Chancellors reacted to
50   criticisms from common lawyers and to the need to introduce regularity into the processing of an increasing caseload by developing principles of "equity" or justice from their ad hoc interventions ...

The principles of equity were progressively refined and developed, most notably during the course of the seventeenth and eighteenth centuries... By the nineteenth
55   century the organisation of the Court of Chancery was totally incapable of dealing with the business, and a series of reforms increased the number of judges sharing the work of the court with the Lord Chancellor. It was also obvious that the presence of two systems with separate courts was highly inconvenient for litigants....

S.H. Bailey & M.J. Gunn, *Smith and Bailey on the Modern English Legal System*, 2 ed., Sweet & Maxwell: London (1991) pp. 5-7 (footnotes omitted)

Analysis

In the first paragraph of the text (lines 1-5), the author notes that "most Chancellors were...graduates in **civil** or **canon law**. **Canon** or **canonical** law is church law. In this context, **civil law** refers to the law prevalent on the Continent, or the law that evolved from Roman law and later became the basis for modern **civil law systems,** such as the German and French systems. Since **civil law** preceded English **common law**, legal experts in England were originally trained in it for lack of any real body of common law principles that could be the basis for legal education. The term "**civil law,**" however, is also used in another sense to mean **private,** as opposed to **public** law. One can tell only from the context in which the term is used whether the reference is to a civil law system or to private as opposed to public law.

The second paragraph of the text (lines 6-10) discusses what you have already learned from the section on the **common law forms of action,** namely that the plaintiff had to decide what type of law suit to pursue against the defendant, purchase the appropriate **writ** from the King's Chancellor and follow the procedural rules relating to it. As the text points out, if the plaintiff was mistaken, he had to start all over again with the law suit, namely he had to **recommence proceedings**.

In the third paragraph of the text (lines 13-20), the author discusses three reasons for the development of **equity** jurisprudence. All three relate to the inadequacies of the common law system as it had developed up to the thirteenth century to **redress grievances,** or to compensate for some problem a defendant had caused a plaintiff. **Equity** developed as the Chancellor tried to take care of these problems in a way that corresponded to his own sense of justice. In lines 24-27, the author points out that the Chancellor developed his own **remedies** to deal with these problems. One of them was **specific performance.** Recall from the section on **forms of action** that the **common law action of assumpsit** for **breach of contract** only permitted the plaintiff to claim **money damages** as a **remedy.** As you know from your own studies of contract law, the primary **remedy for breach of contract** in a **civil law system** is **specific performance**, which involves the court requiring the defendant to do exactly what he promised to do under the contract. This alternative was not available in the King's Court and in some cases the result was clearly unjust, for example when the subject matter of the contract was unique and thus could not be obtained elsewhere even with the amount of money the plaintiff had received as **money damages.** To avoid such injustice the Chancellor simply exercised his own power and ordered the defendant to **perform specifically** under the contract. Another **equitable remedy** the Chancellor developed was the **injunction,** an order addressed to an individual telling her to perform or stop performing some act.

Another example of injustice that resulted from rigid application of the common law system involves the action on a debt whereby a **bond** or security had been given **under seal** to secure repayment on the debt. Even when the defendant had already repaid the debt to the plaintiff, if the sealed bond had not been cancelled, it served as **incontrovertible proof** that the debt was still unpaid. Thus no amount of evidence the defendant offered would be sufficient to disprove the existence of the debt; the law simply assumed it still existed.

Paragraph 5 (lines 38-52) discusses how **law** and **equity** developed as separate systems. On the one hand, the judges of law in the King's Court were deciding cases on the basis of developing and developed common law principles. On the other, the Chancellor was undermining that system by ordering the parties to the law suit to do something different from the requirements of the judgments attained in the courts of law. Although the reasons the author gives seem plausible to any student of law, this development is bound to confuse the student in a civil law system. A rather simple parallel, however, may serve to make this development more understandable. Imagine that German judges, who are deciding cases under the provisions of the *BGB*, do not have § 242. Some cases, however, cannot be decided justly without it. To avoid injustice in these few cases, some higher state official starts issuing orders much like those judges would issue if they could rely on § 242. In addition, imagine that the judges start criticizing this state official with the argument that his decisions are too uncertain, that individuals cannot predict the result of a law suit because of the official's case-by-case intervention. The official understands the need for certainty in the law and begins to develop his own body of principles. It is this body of principles that would be comparable to what is known as "**equity**" jurisprudence in the English legal system.

In the final paragraph of the text (lines 53-58) the author skips to a much later period in history. As he notes, the courts of law and courts of equity were still separate in the nineteenth century, but this separation caused **litigants,** or the parties to a law suit, inconvenience. Consequently, these courts were merged and today one judge will apply both principles of law and principles of equity in reaching a decision in a particular case. Accordingly, the distinction between the two has to some extent been lost. Still, it is important for the English or U.S. American lawyer. One rather simple example of this importance relates to the right to a trial by jury in a private law dispute as guaranteed by the Seventh Amendment to the U.S. Constitution. This Amendment provides: "In Suits at common law, where the value in controversy shall exceed twenty dollars, the right of trial by jury shall be preserved,..." "Suits **at common law**" are law suits based on principles of the common law and not on principles of equity. As a result, the U.S. Constitution does not give a person a right to a jury trial, for example, if that person is suing for **specific performance** of a contract (an **equitable remedy**) rather than for **money damages** (a **common law remedy**).

Final Questions on Chapter 1

1. State the differences between the source of law in a common law and civil law system.
2. What is the doctrine of *stare decisis*?
3. What five elements of a case decision are of particular importance?
4. What is the difference between the holding and dicta?
5. What is the ratio decidendi of a case?
6. How does one refer to the parties to a law suit: a) on the trial court level; b) on the appellate court level?
7. Which of the following forms of action are contractual and which are delictual: a) assumpsit; b) trespass; c) case; d) replevin; e) ejectment
8. What is a remedy? List some remedies you are now familiar with. What are some different words for the word "remedy."
9. Explain what a "writ" is. What aspects of the writ system led to the development of a system of equity?

Terminology

equity	body of principles that developed to compensate for the rigidity of the common law; permitted the King's Chancellor to do justice in cases that could not be resolved justly under common law principles alone (**Billigkeit; Billigkeitsrecht; Recht nach Prinzipien von Treu und Glauben**)
Court of Chancery	original court of equity
canon law	church law (**kanonisches Recht**)
petition	formal request (**Antrag**)
grievance	complaint, suffering, distress (**Beschwer**); **to redress a grievance**: to compensate for injury caused
injunction	equitable remedy ordering a defendant not to do s.th. (ca. **gerichtliche Verfügung**); there are various types of injunctions depending on the length of time they are to last, such as the **preliminary** or **temporary injunction**, which remains in force until a final judgment on the matter can be reached (**einstweilige Verfügung**), or the **perpetual injunction**, which stays in force permanently (**Leistungsurteil auf Unterlassung**); see Unit III, Chapter 2
litigant	party to a law suit (**Partei**)

Vocabulary

to ensue	to follow, to result
incontrovertible	cannot be refuted
inevitable	cannot be avoided, necessary, sure to happen
to recommence	to start again
to refrain from doing	to hold back, to forbear from doing
to reside	to live somewhere, to be an inhabitant of some place
to restrain	to hold s.o. back, to keep s.o. from doing s.th.
unconscionable	contrary to conscience, in violation of good morals

Suggested Reading

I. Legal Dictionaries

English-English

U.S. American: *Black's Law Dictionary* (7th ed.), West Publishing Co.: Saint Paul, Minnesota (1999)

Merriam Webster's Dictionary of Law, Merriam-Webster, Incorporated: Springfield, Massachusetts (1996)

D. Mellinkoff, *Mellinkoff's Dictionary of American Legal Usage*, West Publishing Co.: St. Paul, Minn. (1992)

Bryan A. Garner, *A Dictionary of Modern Legal Usage* (2 ed.) Oxford University Press: New York/Oxford (1995)

Steven H. Gifis, *Barron's Law Dictionary*, Barron's Educational Series, Inc.: New York/London/Toronto/Sydney (1991)

U.K.: D. Walker, *Oxford Companion to Law*, Clarendon Press: Oxford (1980)

J. James, *Stroud's Judicial Dictionary*, Sweet & Maxwell: London (1986)

English-Deutsch-English

Romain/Byrd/Thielecke, *Wörterbuch der Rechts- und Wirtschaftssprache / Dictionary of Legal and Commercial Terms* (4. Auflage), Beck Verlag: München, vol. 2 German-English (2001)

Romain/Bader/Byrd, *Dictionary of Legal and Commercial Terms / Wörterbuch der Rechts- und Wirtschaftssprache* (5th ed.) Beck Verlag: München, vol. 1 English-German (2000)

C. Dietl, E. Lorenz, *Wörterbuch für Recht, Wirtschaft und Politik / Dictionary of Legal, Commercial and Political Terms*, Beck Verlag: München, vol. 1 English-German (2000), vol. 2 German-English (1992)

W. Schäfer, *Wirtschaftswörterbuch*, Verlag Vahlen: München, vol. 1 Englisch-Deutsch (1998), vol. 2 Deutsch-Englisch (2000)

G. Köbler, *Rechtsenglisch*, Verlag Vahlen: München (2000)

P. Flory, B. Froschauer, *Grundwortschatz der Rechtssprache / Basic Vocabulary of Legal Terminology*, Luchterhand Verlag: Neuwied (1995)

II. Legal Encyclopedia

Corpus Juris Secundum, West Publishing Co.: St. Paul, Minn. (annual supplementation)

III. Writing Aids

G. Block, *Effective Legal Writing* (4th ed.), Foundation Press: Westbury, N.Y. (1992)

B. Garner, *The Elements of Legal Style*, Oxford University Press: New York/Oxford (1991)

D. Mellinkoff, *Legal Writing: Sense & Nonsense*, West Publishing Co.: St. Paul, Minn. (1982)

R. Neumann, Jr., *Legal Reasoning and Legal Writing* (2d. ed.), Little Brown and Co.: Boston/New York/Toronto/London (1994)

H. Shapo, M. Walter, E. Fajans, *Writing and Analysis in the Law* (2d. ed.), Foundation Press: Westbury, N.Y. (1991)

J. Williams, *Style*, University of Chicago Press: Chicago/London (1990)

IV. The Common Law System

U.S. American:
E.A. Farnsworth, *An Introduction to the Legal System of the United States* (3 ed.) Oceana: New York (1996)

Bodenheimer, Oakley, Love, *Introduction to the Anglo-American Legal System*, West Publishing Co.: St. Paul, Minn. (1988)

Fundamentals of American Law, Alan B. Morrison, ed., New York University School of Law, Oxford University Press: New York (1996)

U.K.:
S.H. Bailey, M.J. Gunn, *Smith and Bailey on The Modern English Legal System* (3rd ed.), Sweet & Maxwell: London (1996)

G. Slapper D. Kelly, *English Legal System*, Cavendish Publishing Ltd.: London (1995)

German:
D. Blumenwitz, *Einführung in das anglo-amerikanische Recht*, 5th ed., C.H. Beck Verlag: München (1994)

P. Hay, *Einführung in das amerikanische Recht* (4th ed.) Wiss. Buchgesellschaft: Darmstadt (1995)

Chapter 2
The Jury

A central feature of the common law is its use of juries. The right to **trial by jury** is anchored in the English Magna Carta, a charter of rights signed by King John in 1215, and in the Bill of Rights, which comprises the first ten amendments to the United States Constitution. Some civil law systems use lay persons in the legal process as well. Germany, for example, incorporates **lay assessors** in criminal trials, but these lay persons consult with a professional judge in the process of reaching their decision. A unique feature of the common law jury system is that jurors decide cases in the absence of any person professionally trained in the law. Granting this authority to a group of people who are supposed to represent a cross-section of the general population and who have had no legal training has often been the topic of heated debate. Proponents of the jury system focus on its democratic elements; opponents concentrate on the **miscarriages of justice** that can result from legally untrained minds. Much of the opinion held regarding the jury, however, is the product of ignorance on how this body actually functions.

A. Types of Juries: Grand and Petit

Most people are familiar only with the **petit jury**, which is the jury used at trial. In a criminal case, it is the petit jury which decides whether the **defendant** is guilty or not guilty. In fact, the common law traditionally used two types of juries, the **grand jury** and the petit jury. Use of the grand jury was abolished in England in 1933, but in the United States the right to a grand jury proceeding is firmly entrenched in the Bill of Rights, a document which has never been changed in its over 200 years of existence.

1. The Grand Jury

The grand jury convenes only in criminal matters of a serious nature and is responsible for deciding whether an individual should be formally accused of having committed a crime. This formal accusation is called the "**indictment**." The indictment is a document which is written by the **prosecutor**. It contains a list of criminal offenses the prosecutor claims **the accused** has committed. Only if the grand jury agrees, will the individual actually be charged with these crimes, or **indicted**. Consider the text of the Fifth Amendment to the U.S. Constitution, which guarantees the right to a grand jury proceeding:

> Amendment V: No person shall be held to answer for a capital, or otherwise infamous crime, unless on ... indictment of a Grand Jury, ...

The idea behind the grand jury system is to assure that individuals are not **brought to trial** for serious crimes by prosecutors who are overly zealous. Facing criminal prosecution in a courtroom open to the public and the media can cause an individual serious emotional and psychological pain and create a risk of damage to his reputation. Since the prosecutor conducts the criminal investigation in conjunction with the police, he may be too strongly influenced by the side of the story he is trying to establish, namely the individual's guilt. In order to avoid this one-sidedness, a group of lay persons meets to review the prosecutor's **evidence** before the prosecutor can go to trial and in this way acts as a buffer between the individual citizen and the state. In some sense, this division of authority between the prosecutor and the grand jury reflects concern with the problems generally associated with an **inquisitorial** mode of trial, where one person is both prosecutor and judge. The division of authority between these two roles was deemed necessary to avoid having the person convinced of the defendant's guilt (in the role of the prosecutor) also judging at the trial whether the defendant was guilty or innocent. Similarly, the grand jury is intended to split the prosecutor's role of establishing **the evidentiary case** against the accused and deciding whether the quantity and quality of this evidence is sufficient for bringing the accused to trial.

Classically the grand jury is composed of twenty-three members, twelve of whom (a simple majority) have to agree with the prosecutor in order to indict the accused. The members of the grand jury are selected randomly from the general population. Usually the **jury commissioner**, who is the public official responsible for calling **prospective jurors** into court, will select names from the list of registered voters, the list of licensed drivers or simply from the telephone book. The selection must be random so that a true cross-section of the community will participate in the process. Discrimination in juror selection on the basis of race, color, religion, gender, national origin, economic status or age is illegal and disqualifies the prospective jurors so selected. On the other hand, there are certain requirements that the prospective jurors need meet in order to be permitted to serve on either the grand or petit jury. They must be citizens of the United States, at least eighteen years of age, able to read, write and speak English, and not be charged with, or serving time in or out of prison for a crime.

Since the grand jury is part of a secret criminal investigation, it meets in sessions closed to the public and, most importantly, to the press. If the grand jury hearings were open to the media, one major purpose behind this body would be frustrated, namely protecting the accused from inappropriate harassment from the state prosecutor and the accompanying damage to reputation occasioned by a public criminal trial. Although a judge will be responsible for supervising the sessions, usually the grand jury convenes only with the prosecutor. The **defendant** is not present during the hearings and is not **represented by a lawyer**. Every word spoken during the hearings is recorded in a written **transcript**, which is also referred to as the **minutes**. The transcript is forwarded daily to the judge supervising the hearings so that the judge can control whether the prosecutor is observing the legal requirements applicable to grand jury hearings. If the judge notices any violation, she must pass this information on to the defendant's **legal representative**. On the basis of this information, the defendant can challenge the legitimacy of the hearings and hence of any indictment the grand jury may hand down.

The proceedings in the grand jury room are somewhat similar to the proceedings at a normal trial, but limited to the presentation of evidence by the prosecutor and thus to only one side of the case. The prosecutor may call in **witnesses**, who have some knowledge of the facts of the case, to **testify**, or tell the grand jury what they know. At the end of the hearings the prosecutor will **instruct the jury on the law** applicable to the case. The jurors, of course, have to know what the relevant criminal law is in order to determine whether the prosecutor has enough evidence to convict the defendant of the crimes charged. The prosecutor will formulate the law in terms that lay persons can understand. It is here that the greatest difficulties occur, because if in an effort to simplify the legal explanation, the prosecutor incorrectly states the law, any decision the grand jury reaches on the basis of this explanation is invalid and can be challenged by the accused. If the prosecutor is unsuccessful with the first grand jury he convened for the indictment hearing, he may gather more, or more reliable, evidence and initiate grand jury hearings again with a new jury at a later date.

2. The Petit Jury in the United States

a. *The Right to Trial by Jury*

The petit jury is the **trial jury**, which in a criminal case decides on the defendant's guilt and in a civil case decides in favor of one of the parties to the law suit. The Bill of Rights guarantees the right to **trial by jury** for both criminal and civil trials:

> Amendment VI: In all criminal prosecutions, the accused shall enjoy the right to a speedy and public trial, by an impartial jury of the State and district wherein the crime shall have been committed, ...

> Amendment VII: In Suits at common law, where the value in controversy shall exceed twenty dollars, the right of trial by jury shall be preserved ...

The Sixth Amendment guarantees the right to trial by jury for all criminal prosecutions, although the United States Supreme Court has interpreted this guarantee as applying only to prosecutions for crimes of a more serious nature. The Seventh Amendment guarantees the right to trial by jury for private law disputes based on the principles of the common law, if the **value** or **amount in controversy**, which is the amount of money for which the **plaintiff** is suing the **defendant**, exceeds twenty dollars – perhaps at one time a significant hurdle to overcome, but rather insignificant today. Although these amendments guarantee the *right* to trial by jury, they do not require that a jury actually be used for every trial. If, for example, the defendant to a criminal prosecution or *both* parties to a private law dispute **waive their right** to a trial by jury, then the trial generally will be conducted by a judge alone. In the criminal law context, however, some states in the United States do not permit the defendant to waive his right to trial by jury when the defendant has been charged with a more serious crime, and indeed under the original common law rule, juries could not be waived for such trials. In practice today, juries are commonly used for criminal trials and for private law disputes when the plaintiff is suing the defendant **in tort**, which is a type of law suit based on some injury the defendant has intentionally or negligently caused the plaintiff, such as through an automobile accident.

The classic petit jury was composed of twelve members, who were required to decide unanimously in order **to reach** their **verdict**. The verdict in a criminal case is the decision of the jury as to whether the defendant is "guilty" or "not guilty." In a private law case, it is the decision in favor of the plaintiff or the defendant. Whatever the jury's decision, it traditionally had to represent the agreement of all twelve members. Similar to the members of the grand jury, the members of the petit jury are selected **randomly from the community** and the jury commissioner may not use any irrelevant or discriminatory criteria in making this selection.

The petit jury is responsible for determining the facts of a case and applying the law, as the judge explains it, to those facts in order to reach a verdict. To determine what the facts of a case are, the jury considers the evidence presented by both parties to the dispute, either in the form of **physical exhibits**, the **testimony** of lay witnesses as to what they believe to be true or the testimony of **expert witnesses,** such as medical doctors, as to their opinions on matters within their particular range of expertise. Because lay persons may overly react to certain types of evidence, there are complex **rules of evidence** in a common law system governing what exactly they are permitted to hear or see. Although civil law systems also have rules on what evidence a judge may consider, they are far fewer in number and lack the complexity of common law rules. To determine what the law is, the jury needs the judge's instruction at the end of the trial. The judge will explain the law in terms that lay persons can understand. **Jury instruction** is one of the most difficult aspects of the judge's responsibility in the courtroom. The law is often complex and lawyers easily disagree on what it actually provides. The judge must simplify this complex material and present it in a way that does not distort its meaning. Obviously, if the judge's instructions are incorrect, the jury may come to a false conclusion and the losing party at the trial can use this mistake as an argument **on appeal** to justify holding a new trial.

b. Jury Size

Although the traditional jury consists of twelve members, the U.S. Supreme Court has approved the use of juries with fewer than twelve members. In 1970, the Court held that a jury of six, as provided for by Florida state law, was sufficient to meet the Constitutional guarantee of the Sixth Amendment:

Williams v. Florida
399 U.S. 78, 90 S.Ct. 1893, 26 L.Ed.2d 446 (1970)

Mr. Justice WHITE delivered the opinion of the Court.

5   Prior to his trial for robbery in the State of Florida, the petitioner filed a ... pretrial
     motion to impanel a 12-man jury instead of the six-man jury provided by Florida law
     in all but capital cases. That motion ... was denied. Petitioner was convicted as
     charged and was sentenced to life imprisonment. The District Court of Appeal
     affirmed, rejecting petitioner's claims that his ... Sixth Amendment rights had been
10   violated. We granted certiorari ...

Analysis

Williams v. Florida is a U.S. Supreme Court case, which you can see from the case **citations**, telling you where to find the case (see Appendix II for an explanation of case citations). The United States Supreme Court is composed of nine justices, a simple majority of whom is sufficient for reaching a decision. Here Justice Byron White wrote the opinion for the majority of the Court, which means that Justice White was himself in the majority and was designated by the Chief Justice, at that time Warren Burger, to write the official decision. To **deliver the opinion of the Court** means to announce the holding of the majority of the court and to give reasons for the holding.

The short paragraph here contains both the **legal history of the case** and the **legal issue raised on appeal** to the U.S. Supreme Court. The **petitioner** is Williams. He is called the petitioner because he had to petition, or formally request, the Supreme Court to hear his case. This petition is called a **petition for a writ of certiorari**. The writ of certiorari is an order that the Supreme Court can issue if it decides to hear a case. Generally, the losing party at trial has a right to appeal once. From the decision of a court of appeal, however, the dissatisfied party does not have a right to appeal. The second appeal **lies within the discretion of** the higher court. Accordingly, a person dissatisfied with the decision of the court of appeal has to petition for a writ of certiorari, requesting that the supreme court hear the case. If the supreme court decides to hear the case it will **grant the writ of certiorari**, or as stated in the *Williams* opinion "**grant certiorari**," ordering the lower court to certify the record in the case and send it up to the supreme court for appellate review.

In this case, the petitioner, Williams, was tried for the crime of robbery in a Florida trial court. According to applicable Florida law, the jury in criminal cases had to consist of only six persons. Before the trial began, Williams formally requested the trial court to impanel the traditional number of twelve jurors. This formal request is called a "**motion**," and since it was **filed** before the trial began it is called a "**pretrial motion**." The trial court then **denied this motion** and impaneled the six-person jury for the trial. This jury found Williams guilty of the crime which the prosecutor had accused him of committing, or he was **convicted as charged** in the indictment. The trial court judge then imposed a punishment of life imprisonment, or **sentenced** Williams to **life imprisonment**. Williams then appealed to the Florida District Court of Appeal, the first level appellate court in the State of Florida. This court agreed with the trial court's decision and therefore **affirmed** it, or upheld the result reached at trial. Normally the next step would have been for Williams to petition for a writ of certiorari to the Florida Supreme Court, but according to Florida rules of appellate review, which are not of direct concern here, that step could not be taken in Williams' case. Since Williams based his appeal on the Sixth Amendment to the U.S. Constitution, the United States Supreme Court was the next available court of appeal. The issue raised before the U.S. Supreme Court was whether a jury of only six persons violated Williams' right to a trial by jury as guaranteed by the Sixth Amendment to the U.S. Constitution.

Continue reading the case:

The purpose of the jury trial ... is to prevent oppression by the Government. "Providing an accused with the right to be tried by a jury of his peers gave him an inestimable safeguard against the corrupt or overzealous prosecutor and against the compliant, biased, or eccentric judge." Duncan v. Louisiana, *supra*, 391 U.S., at 156,
15   88 S.Ct., at 1451. Given this purpose, the essential feature of a jury obviously lies in the interposition between the accused and his accuser of the commonsense judgment of a group of laymen, and in the community participation and shared responsibility that results from that group's determination of guilt or innocence. Their performance of this role is not a function of the particular number of the body that makes
20   up the jury. To be sure, the number should probably be large enough to promote group deliberation, free from outside attempts at intimidation, and to provide a fair possibility for obtaining a representative cross-section of the community. But we find little reason to think that these goals are in any meaningful sense less likely to be achieved when the jury numbers six, than when it numbers 12 – particularly if the
25   requirement of unanimity is retained. And, certainly the reliability of the jury as a factfinder hardly seems likely to be a function of its size.

It might be suggested that the 12-man jury gives a defendant a greater advantage since he has more "chances" of finding a juror who will insist on acquittal and thus prevent conviction. But the advantage might just as easily belong to the State, which
30   also needs only one juror out of twelve insisting on guilt to prevent acquittal. What few experiments have occurred – usually in the civil area – indicate that there is no discernible difference between the results reached by the two different-sized juries. In short, neither currently available evidence nor theory suggests that the 12-man jury is necessarily more advantageous to the defendant than a jury composed of fewer
35   members.

Similarly, while in theory the number of viewpoints represented on a randomly selected jury ought to increase as the size of the jury increases, in practice the difference between the 12-man and the six-man jury in terms of the cross-section of the community represented seems likely to be negligible. Even the 12-man jury
40   cannot insure representation of every distinct voice in the community ... As long as arbitrary exclusions of a particular class from the jury rolls are forbidden, ... the concern that the cross-section will be significantly diminished if the jury is decreased in size from 12 to six seems an unrealistic one.

We conclude, in short, as we began: the fact that the jury at common law was
45   composed of precisely 12 is a historical accident, unnecessary to effect the purposes

of the jury system and wholly without significance "except to mystics." Duncan v. Louisiana, *supra*, ... To read the Sixth Amendment as forever codifying a feature so incidental to the real purpose of the Amendment is to ascribe a blind formalism to the Framers which would require considerably more evidence than we have been able to
50   discover in the history and language of the Constitution or in the reasoning of our past decisions. We do not mean to intimate that legislatures can never have good reasons for concluding that the 12-man jury is preferable to the smaller jury, or that such conclusions – reflected in the provisions of most States and in our federal system – are in any sense unwise. Legislatures may well have their own views about the
55   relative value of the larger and smaller juries, and may conclude that, wholly apart from the jury's primary function, it is desirable to spread the collective responsibility for the determination of guilt among the larger group. In capital cases, for example, it appears that no State provides for less than 12 jurors – a fact that suggests implicit recognition of the value of the larger body as a means of legitimating society's
60   decision to impose the death penalty. Our holding does no more than leave these considerations to Congress and the States, unrestrained by an interpretation of the Sixth Amendment that would forever dictate the precise number that can constitute a jury. Consistent with this holding, we conclude that petitioner's Sixth Amendment rights, as applied to the States through the Fourteenth Amendment, were not vio-
65   lated by Florida's decision to provide a six-man rather than a 12-man jury. The judgment of the Florida District Court of Appeal is

Affirmed.

Analysis

The U.S. Supreme Court in the *Williams* opinion held that the Sixth Amendment guarantee of a trial by jury in a criminal case does not mean that a criminal defendant has a right to a jury of twelve persons and that a jury of six is sufficient under the U.S. Constitution. The import of this decision is that the legislatures of the individual states and the U.S. Congress can decide on whatever number of jurors they want to use as long as it is at least six. Whether a jury of less than six is sufficient under the Sixth Amendment has not been decided by *Williams*.

At the end of the opinion, the Court states that Williams' rights under the Sixth Amendment **as applied to the States through the Fourteenth Amendment** were not violated. To understand this statement, it is necessary to consider the Fourteenth Amendment:

Section 1. All persons born or naturalized in the United States, and subject to the jurisdiction thereof, are citizens of the United States and of the State wherein they reside. No State shall make or enforce any law which shall abridge the privileges or immunities of citizens of the United States; nor shall any State deprive any person of life, liberty, or property, without due process of law; nor deny to any person within its jurisdiction the equal protection of the laws.

The Fourteenth Amendment was adopted in 1868, which was three years after the end of the Civil War. The central purpose of the Amendment was to protect freed slaves from unjust state action. The Fourteenth Amendment does this by declaring freed slaves citizens of the United States since they were born in the U.S. and are **subject to the jurisdiction** of the U.S. Government. In this context "jurisdiction" means the power of the United States to govern its citizens through passing legislation, interpreting, applying and enforcing it. By virtue of being a U.S. citizen, every individual has certain rights that may not be interfered with, which is the same as saying that the citizen has **privileges and immunities**. The Fourteenth Amendment further prohibits depriving any U.S. citizen of life, liberty or property without **due process of law**. Simply stated, this expression means that if a state in the U.S. takes away a person's liberty, for example by putting that person in prison, then the person must have had a fair trial. The Fourteenth Amendment also prohibits any state from denying a person equal rights under the law.

In the context of the *Williams* case, the Fourteenth Amendment plays a fundamental role because of the **due process clause**. Over the years following the adoption of the Fourteenth Amendment, the U.S. Supreme Court was confronted with cases in which it had to decide whether state action violated the **due process guarantee**. To resolve this question, it turned to the Bill of Rights, which was originally intended to protect individuals from oppression by the federal government. In its opinions, the U.S. Supreme Court has gradually extended most of the protections contained in the Bill of Rights to also prohibit oppression by the individual state governments. This extension was justified on the basis of the Fourteenth Amendment's guarantee of due process. Accordingly, in the *Williams* case, the question really is 1) does the Sixth Amendment guarantee the right to a trial by a twelve-person jury in *federal criminal trials* and if so 2) does the Sixth Amendment's guarantee of a right to trial by a twelve-person jury in federal court also guarantee that right for criminal trials held in state courts. The *Williams* decision answers the first question negatively and therefore does not have to answer the second.

Questions on the Text

1. Describe the function of the grand jury, distinguishing it from the petit jury. Use the following terms in your description: **to indict, the indictment, prosecutor, random selection, jury commissioner, defendant, accused, to bring someone to trial, the evidentiary case, the trial jury, the right to a trial by jury, verdict.** Does your own legal system have a means of protecting individuals from harassment by an overly zealous prosecutor? Describe your own system in English and in a way that a lawyer from a common law system with her background in the grand jury system can understand. Discuss the pros and cons of the use of grand juries. Consider such issues as costs, the prosecutor's influence, the time factor, the jury's lay nature.

2. In your own words give a statement of a) the facts of *Williams*, b) the legal history of the case, c) the issue(s) raised on appeal and d) the holding of the case.

3. What are the various arguments the Court discusses in *Williams* when trying to determine whether a 6-person jury is sufficient under the Sixth Amendment to the U.S. Constitution? State each of them individually. Do you agree with the Court that a reduction of 12 to 6 jurors is irrelevant in light of the various arguments discussed?

4. Consider that the United States is a society of widely diverse racial and ethnic groups. What will happen to the representation of these groups on juries as the size of the jury decreases? Suppose a criminal trial is to be held in a community with a 10% Hispanic population. The defendant is a member of this group. How large does a jury have to be to give him a fair chance that at least one member of the Hispanic community will be on the jury? What are his chances with a 6-person jury? With a 12-person jury?

5. What is the ratio decidendi of *Williams*? Consider the following and determine which is the best statement of it, which are too broad and which too narrow:
   a. A 12-person jury is not required by the Sixth Amendment to the U.S. Constitution.
   b. A 6-person jury satisfies the requirements of the Sixth Amendment.
   c. A jury of 6-12 is enough under the Sixth Amendment.
   d. A jury of at least 6 persons is enough under the Sixth Amendment.
   e. A jury of at least 6 persons is required under the Sixth Amendment.

After *Williams* was decided, a significant number of studies were conducted on the effect a reduction in group size can have on the group's decision-making process. Eight years after *Williams*, the U.S. Supreme Court heard a case involving a Georgia statute that provided for a five-person petit jury. Read the following case. You should now be familiar with all the terminology you need to understand it. Be prepared to answer the following questions: a) What are the **facts of the case**? b) What is the **legal history of the case**? c) What is the **issue on appeal** to the U.S. Supreme Court? d) What was the U.S. Supreme Court's **holding**? e) What is the **ratio decidendi** of the case? Be prepared to explain from the text how you know the answers to those questions and where you found those answers in the text.

Ballew v. Georgia
435 U.S. 223, 98 S.Ct. 1029, 55 L.Ed.2d 234 (1978)

5   Mr. Justice BLACKMUN announced the judgment of the Court and delivered an opinion in which Mr. Justice STEVENS joined.

This case presents the issue whether a state criminal trial to a jury of only five persons deprives the accused of the right to trial by jury guaranteed ... him by the Sixth and Fourteenth Amendments. Our resolution of the issue requires an application of
10 principles enunciated in *Williams v. Florida*, 399 U.S. 78, 90 S.Ct. 1893, 26 L.Ed.2d 446 (1970), where use of a six-person jury in a state criminal trial was upheld against similar constitutional attack ... .

On September 14, 1974, petitioner was charged in a two-count misdemeanor accusation with

15   "distributing obscene materials in violation of Georgia Code Section 26-
        2101 in that the said accused did, knowing the obscene nature thereof,
        exhibit a motion picture film entitled 'Behind the Green Door' that contained
        obscene and indecent scenes ..."

Petitioner was brought to trial in the Criminal Court of Fulton County. After a jury
20 of 5 persons had been selected and sworn, petitioner moved that the court impanel a jury of 12 persons ... .

The motion for a 12-person jury was overruled, and the trial went on to its conclusion before the 5-person jury that had been impaneled. At the conclusion of the trial, the jury deliberated for 38 minutes and returned a verdict of guilty on both counts of
25 the accusation ... The court imposed a sentence of one year and a $1,000 fine on each count, the periods of incarceration to run concurrently and to be suspended upon payment of the fines ... After a subsequent hearing, the court denied an amended motion for a new trial. Petitioner took an appeal to the Court of Appeals for the State of Georgia. There he argued: ... Fifth, the use of the five-member jury deprived him
30 of his Sixth and Fourteenth Amendment right to a trial by jury ...

The Court of Appeals rejected petitioner's contentions. 138 Ga.App. 530, 227 S.E.2d 65 (1976) ... In its consideration of the 5-person jury issue, the court noted that *Williams v. Florida* had not established a constitutional minimum number of jurors. Absent a holding by this Court that a five-person jury was constitutionally

35 inadequate, the Court of Appeals considered itself bound by *Sanders v. State*, 234
    Ga. 586, 216 S.E.2d 838 (1975), cert. denied, 424 U.S. 931, 96 S.Ct. 1145, 47
    L.Ed.2d 340 (1976), where the constitutionality of the five-person jury had been
    upheld ...

    The Supreme Court of Georgia denied certiorari ...

40 In his petition for certiorari here, petitioner raised three issues: the unconstitution-
    ality of the five-person jury; ... We granted certiorari ... Because we now hold that
    the five-member jury does not satisfy the jury trial guarantee of the Sixth Amend-
    ment, as applied to the States through the Fourteenth, we do not reach the other
    issues.

    Williams v. Florida and *Colgrove v. Battin*, 413 U.S. 149, 93 S.Ct. 2448, 37 L.Ed.2d
45 522 (1973)(where the Court held that a jury of six members did not violate the
    Seventh Amendment right to a jury trial in a civil case), generated a quantity of
    scholarly work on jury size. These writings do not draw or identify a bright line
    below which the number of jurors would not be able to function as required by the
    standards enunciated in *Williams*. On the other hand, they raise significant questions
50 about the wisdom and constitutionality of a reduction below six. We examine these
    concerns:

    First, recent empirical data suggest that progressively smaller juries are less likely to
    foster effective group deliberation. At some point, this decline leads to inaccurate
    fact-finding and incorrect application of the common sense of the community to the
55 facts. Generally, a positive correlation exists between group size and the quality of
    both group performance and group productivity. A variety of explanations have
    been offered for this conclusion. Several are particularly applicable in the jury set-
    ting. The smaller the group, the less likely are members to make critical contributions
    necessary for the solution of a given problem. Because most juries are not permitted
60 to take notes ... memory is important for accurate jury deliberations. As juries
    decrease in size, then they are less likely to have members who remember each of the
    important pieces of evidence or argument. Furthermore, the smaller the group, the
    less likely it is to overcome the biases of its members to obtain an accurate result.
    When individual and group decisionmaking were compared, it was seen that groups
65 performed better because prejudices of individuals were frequently counterbalanced,
    and objectivity resulted ...

    Second, the data now raise doubts about the accuracy of the results achieved by
    smaller and smaller panels. Statistical studies suggest that the risk of convicting an
    innocent person (Type I error) rises as the size of the jury diminishes. Because the risk
70 of not convicting a guilty person (Type II error) increases with the size of the panel,
    an optimal jury size can be selected as a function of the interaction between the two
    risks. Nagel and Neff [Deductive Modeling to Determine an Optimum Jury Size and
    Fraction Required to Convict, 1975 Wash.U.L.Q. 933] concluded that the optimal
    size, for the purpose of minimizing errors, should vary with the importance attached
75 to the two types of mistakes. After weighing Type I error as 10 times more significant
    than Type II, perhaps not an unreasonable assumption, they concluded that the
    optimal jury size was between six and eight. As the size diminished to five and below,

the weighted sum of errors increased because of the enlarging risk of the conviction of innocent defendants ... .

80   While we adhere to, and reaffirm our holding in *Williams v. Florida*, these studies, most of which have been made since *Williams* was decided in 1970, lead us to conclude that the purpose and functioning of the jury in a criminal trial is seriously impaired, and to a constitutional degree, by a reduction in size to below six members. We readily admit that we do not pretend to discern a clear line between six members

85   and five. But the assembled data raise substantial doubt about the reliability and appropriate representation of panels smaller than six. Because of the fundamental importance of the jury trial to the American system of criminal justice, any further reduction that promotes inaccurate and possibly biased decisionmaking, that causes untoward differences in verdicts and that prevents juries from truly representing

90   their communities, attains constitutional significance ...

Petitioner, therefore, has established that his trial on criminal charges before a five-member jury deprived him of the right to trial by jury guaranteed by the Sixth and Fourteenth Amendments.

The judgment of the Court of Appeals is reversed, and the case is remanded for

95   further proceedings not inconsistent with this opinion ... .

Analysis

The *Ballew* case involves a criminal prosecution for a **misdemeanor**. Criminal offenses are categorized as **petty offenses, misdemeanors and felonies**. A **felony** is a serious crime often defined as any offense threatened with a possible prison term of more than one year. A **misdemeanor** is a less serious criminal offense but one for which the judge may impose a prison term. A **petty offense** is punished only with a fine. Here the criminal accusation contained **two counts**. A **count** is a separate and distinct criminal offense charged in the indictment. In the section of the U.S. Supreme Court's opinion that was omitted from the above text, the Court indicates that the defendant had shown the film twice and each time police officers had viewed it. Accordingly, the prosecutor charged Ballew with having committed the offense twice, each commission being contained in a separate count of the indictment.

Here the U.S. Supreme Court **reversed** the decision of the Georgia Court of Appeals and **remanded** the case **for further proceedings not inconsistent with** the U.S. Supreme Court's own opinion. The Georgia Court of Appeals had upheld the decision of the trial court to use a five-person jury. When the U.S. Supreme Court **reversed** this decision, it declared that the trial court had erred in using a five-person jury. The U.S. Supreme Court then **remanded the case**, or handed the case back to the Georgia Court of Appeals, ordering it to apply the holding of the U.S. Supreme Court to the case, or to conduct **proceedings not inconsistent with** the Supreme Court's opinion. As a result, the Georgia Court of Appeals will have to declare the decision of the trial court erroneous and order a new trial, this time with at least a six-person jury.

Jury **selection, impaneling, swearing in, and deliberation** will be explained in subsection c.

Questions on the Text

1. It is fairly safe to say that almost every person from Great Britain or the United States knows the adage "It's better to let ten guilty people go free than to convict one innocent man." One of the most interesting aspects of the *Ballew* decision is the Court's application of this principle in determining whether a jury of five is constitutionally sufficient. Find this discussion in the case and consider whether you agree with this weighting (Friedrich der Große is claimed to have insisted on a ratio of 20 to 1).

2. In lines 35-37 of the Court's opinion there is the following citation: *Sanders v. State*, 234 Ga. 586, 216 S.E.2d 838 (1975), cert. denied, 424 U.S. 931, 96 S.Ct. 1145, 47 L.Ed.2d 340 (1976). Which court denied certiorari in the *Sanders* case? If you cannot answer that question, review the citations in Appendix II and look them up in your library. Why did the Georgia Court of Appeals feel bound by the *Sanders* holding? Which court upheld the constitutionality of the five-person jury? What court's decisions are binding precedents for the Georgia Court of Appeals?

3. In *Johnson v. Louisiana*, 406 U.S. 356 (1972), the U.S. Supreme Court approved verdicts **rendered,** or given, by a majority of 9 to 3 and in *Apodaca v. Oregon*, 406 U.S. 404 (1972), it approved verdicts rendered by a majority of 10 to 2. What advantages and disadvantages does the requirement that verdicts be unanimous have? Read these cases and report on them. Remember to include the facts of the case, the legal history of the case, the issue(s) raised on appeal, the holding and the ratio decidendi.

Terminology

Bill of Rights	first ten amendments to the U.S. Constitution, relate primarily to individual rights
grand jury	body of traditionally 23 persons from the community which is responsible for determining whether an individual should be charged with a serious crime
to indict	to charge an individual with a serious crime (**anklagen**); pronounced with a silent "c" as "in-dite"
indictment	formal document containing criminal charges against a defendant (**Anklageschrift**); pronounced "in-dite-ment"
to bring s.o. to trial	to file charges against s.o. in a court of law; usually used in the criminal law context (**anklagen**); also **to charge s.o. with an offense**
the accused	person who has been charged with a criminal offense (**Beschuldigter, Angeschuldigter**)
petit jury	jury used to determine the facts and apply the law as the judge instructs in order to reach the outcome of a trial (**die Geschworenen**); traditionally a body of 12 persons chosen randomly from a cross-section of the community; also called the **trial jury**, as opposed to the **grand jury**; note that "jury" is singular in U.S. and plural in British English! (U.S. "the jury is"; U.K. "the jury are")
to be tried by a jury	to have a petit jury as the factfinding body at a trial; also called **trial by jury** (ca. **Geschworenenprozeß**)
a jury of one's peers	expression used to emphasize the lay, or non-professional, nature of a jury composed of individuals who are like the parties to a law suit; a group of fair-minded individuals who are representative of the community in general
layperson	person who is not an expert (**Laie**)
random selection	choice made in a manner intended to ensure that every member of the group from which one is selecting has an equal probability of being chosen (**Auswahl nach dem Zufallsprinzip**)
cross-section of the community	group of people who represent all demographic aspects, such as income, educational and professional or vocational levels, race, gender, political opinion, religious persuasion, ethnic background, etc. of a particular area where they live (**Bevölkerungsdurchschnitt**)
jury commissioner	public official responsible for selecting prospective jurors for both the grand and petit juries; (U.K.) **summoning officer** (ca. **Beamter, der für die Auswahl der Geschworenen zuständig ist**)

prospective juror	a person the jury commissioner has selected to come to court for potential jury duty (**möglicher Geschworener**); it is from this group that the actual jurors on a grand or petit jury will be selected
lay assessor	term used as translation of layperson who participates in the trials of most civil law systems (**Schöffe**)
legal representative	a person who acts for s.o. else in legal matters, usually a lawyer (**juristischer Vertreter**); **to be represented by a lawyer** means to have a person trained in the law act for you in legal matters
witness	a person who has personal knowledge of facts relevant to a law suit called into court to tell the court those facts (**Zeuge**)
expert witness	a person who has expertise on an issue raised in a law suit, such as a medical doctor, who can provide this knowledge to the court (**Gutachter**)
to testify	to tell what one knows relating to a law suit in a court of law (**aussagen**)
physical exhibits	objects, such as the murder weapon, that can be considered in a court of law as evidence (**Gegenstand des Augenscheins**)
rules of evidence	formal legal rules specifying what can and cannot be used as proof at a trial (**Beweiserhebungs- und Beweisverwertungsregeln**)
the evidentiary case	the sum total of proof for or against s.o. who is a party to a law suit
factfinder	the person or body responsible for determining the facts of a case from the evidence presented at trial; it is the jury if a jury is used, otherwise the judge acts as the factfinder (**Richter oder Geschworenenbank, die für die Feststellung des Sachverhalts zuständig ist**)
to instruct the jury on the law	to explain, as a judge, the applicable law to the jury at the end of a trial in terms that lay persons can understand and apply to the facts as they determine them (**die Geschworenen belehren**); **jury instructions**: the explanations of the law the judge gives at the end of the trial
verdict	result of trial as jury determined; in a criminal case the verdict will be "guilty" or "not guilty;" in a private law dispute either "for the plaintiff in the amount of ... " or "for the defendant;" (ca. **Spruch der Geschworenen**); also referred to as a **general verdict** in contrast to a **special verdict**, which is merely a list of facts the jury believes are true to which the judge will apply the law in reaching the final judgement in a case; a **special verdict** is required when, for example, the judge feels the law is too complicated for the jury to apply correctly (ca. **Tatsacheninterlokut**)
to reach a verdict	to come to a resolution of a trial as a jury (ca. **zu einem Urteilsspruch [der Geschworenenbank] kommen**)

to render a verdict	to give, announce a verdict as a jury (ca. **das Urteil [der Geschworenenbank] verkünden**)
unanimous verdict	a verdict in which all members of the jury agree (**einstimmiges Geschworenenurteil**); usually a requirement for jury trials in the U.S.
to deliver an opinion	to announce, as an appellate judge, the holding one has reached for a law suit on appeal and to give reasons for that holding (**ein Urteil verkünden**)
opinion of the court	refers to the holding of the majority of the judges on a court
citation	indication of where to find a case, indication of the volume, page and year of a decision (**Fundstelle**)
supra	commonly used in legal texts to mean "see above"; contrasted to "**infra**" meaning "see below"
motion	formal request addressed to a judge in a law suit (**Antrag**); one **files** or **makes** a motion (**einen Antrag stellen**)
pretrial motion	motion made before the trial begins (ca. **Antrag, der während eines Vorverfahrens gestellt wird**)
motion for a new trial	motion claiming that some significant error affected the outcome of the trial such that a new trial should be held (**Antrag auf Wiederaufnahme des Verfahrens, das aufgrund schwerer Rechtsfehler als ungültig behauptet wird**)
to affirm	to uphold, as an appellate court, the decision reached by a lower court (**die Entscheidung aufrechterhalten**)
to overrule	to reject or disagree, as a court, with a motion or objection a party to a law suit has made; e.g. to overrule the plaintiff's motion to impanel a 12-man jury (**den Antrag ablehnen**); to overrule the plaintiff's objection (**den Einspruch ablehnen**)
to deny	to reject or disagree, as a court, with a motion a party has made (**ablehnen**); or with a remedy a party seeks
to reverse	to change, as an appellate court, the decision of a lower court in the same case (**aufheben**)
to remand	to send back, as an appellate court, a case to a lower court for some specified treatment of the case (**zurückverweisen**), such as **to remand for further proceedings not inconsistent with this opinion,** meaning the lower court has to deal with the case as directed in the decision of the higher appellate court
to petition	to formally request that a court do s.th. (**einen Antrag stellen**)
writ of certiorari	formal order issued by a supreme court and addressed to a lower court ordering the lower court to certify the record in a case and send it to the higher court for further judicial review (ca. **Zulassung der Revision**); if the supreme court agrees to hear a case it

	will: **grant the writ, grant certiorari, grant cert.**; if it decides not to hear the case it will: **deny the writ, deny certiorari, deny cert.**
petitioner	name given to the person who files for a **writ of certiorari** (**Revisionskläger** [Zivilrecht]; **Revisionsführer** [Strafrecht])
discretion	power or right to exercise judgment in making a decision independent of any exact rules on how to proceed (**Ermessen**); **discretion** is **abused** if the person exercising it acts unfairly or arbitrarily (**Ermessensmißbrauch**)
to sentence	to impose, as a judge, some form of punishment on a person found guilty of a crime (ca. **das Strafmaß festsetzen**); the **sentence** is the formal order of punishment, not to be confused with the **judgment**, which is the judge's formal conclusion in a law suit in favor of, or against, one of the parties to that suit; in a criminal case with a jury, if the jury **renders a verdict** of guilty, the judge will **enter judgment on the verdict**, meaning that the judge will give the jury's verdict the force of law, and then the judge will determine the punishment and **sentence** the defendant to, for example, five years in prison
incarceration	imprisonment (**Haft**)
to run concurrently	to begin to expire on the same day (**gleichzeitig ablaufen**); used with prison sentences to mean that if a person has been sentenced to more than one prison term, the terms start to run together, such that the first day in prison counts as serving one day of two or more prison terms simultaneously (**gleichzeitig zu verbüßende Gefängnisstrafen**)
to run consecutively	to expire one after the other (**nacheinander ablaufen**); used with prison sentences to mean that if a person has been sentenced to more than one prison term, the first term runs first and after that term has been served, the second term starts to run (**nacheinander zu verbüßende Gefängnisstrafen**)
to suspend a sentence	to cancel the defendant's obligation to actually serve time in prison; not to be confused with **probation** (**Bewährung**), which requires the defendant to fulfill certain conditions, such as attending regular meetings with a **probation officer** (**Bewährungshelfer**), keeping a certain job, curfew, etc.; also not to be confused with **parole** (**bedingte Entlassung**), which is the release of a prisoner, under the imposition of requirements, before his prison sentence has been fully served
robbery	*Model Penal Code*, Section 222.1 Robbery. (**Raub, räuberische Erpressung**)
	(1) <u>Robbery Defined.</u> A person is guilty of robbery if, in the course of committing a theft, he:
	(a) inflicts serious bodily injury upon another; or

(b) threatens another with or purposely puts him in fear of immediate serious injury; or …

An act shall be deemed "in the course of committing a theft" if it occurs in an attempt to commit theft or in flight after the attempt or commission.

amount in controversy	the amount for which the plaintiff sues the defendant (**Streitwert**); also called **value in controversy**
to waive a right	to give up a right, to not insist on exercising a right (**auf ein Recht verzichten**)
The Framers	the writers of the U.S. Constitution; also called the **Founding Fathers**
federal system	the legal system of the United States as opposed to the legal systems of the individual states (**System des Bundesrechts**)
naturalized	made a citizen of a nation, having received citizenship rights on application rather than on birth (**eingebürgert**)
jurisdiction	the authority of a court to hear and decide a case (**Zuständigkeit**); **the court has jurisdiction** (**das Gericht ist zuständig**); the area over which a legal system is applicable, e.g. "the jurisdiction of California" means the State of California as a distinct legal system where California laws apply and are applied by California courts
due process of law	expression used in the U.S. Constitution to mean fairness in legal procedures (**Rechtsstaatlichkeit**); the due process guarantee is contained in the Fifth and Fourteenth Amendments and as a part of the Fourteenth Amendment is referred to as "the **due process clause**"
equal protection of the laws	expression used in the Fourteenth Amendment to the U.S. Constitution to mean that every U.S. citizen has equal rights; to distinguish this guarantee from other guarantees it is referred to as being contained in "the **equal protection clause**" (**Gleichheitsgrundsatz**)
count	a separate and distinct legal claim; one crime charged in the indictment (**Anklagepunkt**) or one civil law claim made in a complaint (**Anspruch**)
felony	a serious crime for which the prison term threatened normally exceeds one year (ca. **Verbrechen**)
misdemeanor	a less serious crime, for which a prison term of not more than one year is threatened (ca. **Vergehen**)
petty offense	a minor criminal violation, usually punished with a fine (ca. **Ordnungswidrigkeit**)
capital crime	a crime the commission of which is threatened with the death penalty (**Kapitalverbrechen**)

capital case	a criminal trial involving a crime which can be punished by death

Vocabulary

to abridge	to shorten, to make smaller
to adhere to	to stick to
arbitrary	irrational, not based on reason, capricious
to ascribe	to impute, to attribute
bias	prejudice
buffer	a cushion against s.th., a protective shield
compliant	submissive, likely to give in
to comprise	to consist of, to contain (the whole comprises the parts); compare: **to compose**: to constitute, to form the substance of (the parts compose the whole).
to constitute	to amount to, to form, to make up
to convene	to come together, to meet
to be deemed	to be considered, to be viewed as
to deprive	to prevent s.o. from having s.th. to which the person has a right or claim
entrenched	firmly established, solidly rooted
to enunciate	to announce, to articulate
to foster	to nurture, to care for
gender	sex
harassment	constant annoyance, causing s.o. to have anxieties
to impair	to damage, to lessen in value
impartial	fair, not prejudiced
implicit	part of the nature of s.th. although not directly stated, implied
import	consequence, meaning
infamous	disgraceful, detestable; **infamous crime:** crime of a serious nature
to intimate	to hint at without saying directly, to imply, to suggest
to intimidate	to make fearful or timid, to bully, to make afraid by using threats
negligible	insignificant, very small
to promote	to advance, further, support
untoward	unfortunate, improper

by virtue of	as a result of
zealous	impassioned, eager, enthusiastic

c. Jury Selection: Randomness, Impartiality, Tactical Choices

As noted above, the initial selection of prospective jurors must be random and not based on any personal characteristics other than those required for jury service, such as being at least eighteen years of age, being able to read, write and speak English, and being a citizen of the United States. The jury commissioner is responsible for selecting the **array**, which is the group of individuals who are qualified to serve on a jury, who are not exempt from jury duty and who have not been excused from service. Individuals are exempt from service if they are serving their country in another way, such as police officers, fire fighters, soldiers and politicians. Other individuals will be excused because service would be an unfair burden on them in light of their other responsibilities, such as taking care of young children. Once the jury commissioner has eliminated the unqualified, exempt and excused, he will send a **summons** to the individuals who are required to appear in court for service. A summons is an order to appear under threat of penalty for failure to do so. A person who fails to appear can be charged with **contempt of court** and fined a certain amount of money. The individuals who have been **summoned** make up what is called the **array** or **venire**, and each of them is referred to as a **venireperson**.

Once the individual has appeared in court for jury service, he will be assigned to a courtroom for a trial. Here the selection process for the twelve venirepersons who will actually serve on the jury in the particular case continues. Although all of the venirepersons are generally qualified to serve on some jury, they may not be qualified to serve on the jury in the specific case before the court. The process of selecting the twelve, referred to as the **voir dire**, is conducted in court in the presence of the judge presiding over the case and the two lawyers representing the two parties to the law suit. The judge is responsible for ensuring that the twelve people chosen are legally suitable for service in the case, meaning primarily that they can be fair and impartial. The lawyers, of course, will be interested in selecting a jury whom they think they can convince of their client's view of the case. The interest of the judge in a fair and impartial jury is somewhat different from the interests of each of the lawyers. This aspect of jury selection – the tension between the demands of impartiality and the conflicting interests of the two parties – makes jury selection one of the most difficult aspects of a trial.

The process usually begins with the judge questioning members of the venire as a group. To determine whether they can be impartial in the particular case, the judge will explain to them the nature of the trial and inform them of the identities of the two parties and of the lawyers representing them. One initial question will be whether any venireperson knows one of the parties or lawyers either from a personal or business context. If the case has been widely publicized in the media, which usually happens only in criminal cases, another question will be whether any of the prospective jurors is already convinced that the defendant is guilty. Again, if a crime is involved, the judge will probably want to determine whether any prospective juror was the victim of the same or a similar type of crime, because this experience could result in the juror favoring the victim of the crime charged. If the judge is of the opinion that any particular individual could not be fair as a juror in the case, the judge must excuse the juror from service.

After the judge has completed questioning the prospective jurors, usually each of the lawyers will be able to examine them individually. Rules on how intensely and concerning what matters the lawyers may question prospective jurors vary from state to state. The more leeway a lawyer has in conducting the voir dire examination, the more he will be able to delve into the prospective juror's personality and determine whether this particular person will be advantageous to keep on the jury. In states where the lawyer has considerable latitude in his examination and in cases where a large amount of money is involved, it may be worthwhile to undergo significant expense in selecting the jury. Sometimes lawyers will hire psychiatrists or sociologists to sit in court and observe prospective jurors as they answer questions on voir dire. This expert on human attitudes may assist in determining whether a person has a stronger or weaker personality, has a sense of self-esteem or suffers from an inferiority complex, is easy to convince or is more discriminating in adopting a certain position. All of these factors relate to how the individual will react when actually serving on the jury. Other lawyers, even in important cases, do not pay so much attention to jury selection and are essentially willing to accept any random group of individuals as jurors.

The lawyers can affect the composition of the jury through **exercising challenges,** which the judge will either accept or reject. There are three major types of challenges the lawyer may exercise: the **challenge to the array,** the **challenge for cause,** and the **peremptory challenge.** A challenge to the array, which is also called a **motion to quash the venire, a motion to quash the panel** or a **motion to quash the array,** is based on the argument that the method for selecting prospective jurors from the general population was not in accordance with legal requirements, usually meaning that the process was not truly aimed at random selection. Jury commissioners of the past have intentionally excluded, for example, African Americans or women from jury duty. Even though the jury commissioner may not be acting intentionally to discriminate against a certain group of people, still his selection method might in effect be discriminatory. If the judge accepts the challenge to the array, then a new group of prospective jurors must be summoned to court for the voir dire.

A **challenge for cause** is based on the argument that one particular juror is biased regarding the issues to be raised at trial. Although the judge will have excused some jurors for this reason based on her own questioning, the lawyer may discover a new difficulty based on his examination. Of course, lawyers will disagree on whether the juror should be excused. Bias against one party to the law suit may simultaneously be bias in favor of the other. Whereas one party may want the juror excluded, the other might be quite happy to keep that person. Ultimately, the judge will have to decide whether to accept or reject the challenge.

A **peremptory challenge** is not based on any argument, but is merely a privilege each lawyer has to exclude a certain number of individuals from the jury. Each party has the same number of peremptory challenges, which the judge will determine before the voir dire begins and which the party may exercise without giving any reason. The purpose of the peremptory challenge is to permit the lawyers to have some real input into who will actually serve on the jury to judge their particular case. It permits them to have prospective jurors excused when they cannot give any reason why that person should not serve, other than perhaps just the "feeling" they have about the person. Here the idea is that both of the parties to the law suit should feel fairly comfortable with the final group of twelve who will decide their fate in court. After all, the jury is there to protect the individual, so the individual should have a feeling of confidence in the final jury selected. Many people disagree on whether peremptory challenges should be granted at all. They argue that as long as the judge considers a juror to be impartial, there is no reason to exclude him or her. Permitting the parties to eliminate prospective jurors on any basis other than impartiality arguably permits them to re-introduce bias into the final selection process. Be that as it may, peremptory challenges are still permitted in the United States, although a lawyer's freedom in exercising them is currently being restricted by the courts.

The jury selection process can usually be accomplished within a few hours at most. It continues for as long as challenges can be exercised. When both of the lawyers have exhausted their peremptory challenges and no juror can be challenged for cause, then the twelve remaining in the **jury box** will try the case. Usually several **alternates** will also be selected. These are individuals who will sit and hear the evidence presented throughout the trial, but who usually take part in jury deliberation only if one of the twelve becomes ill or is excused for some other reason before the verdict has been reached. The use of alternates helps to guarantee that the final verdict will be reached by twelve persons (or, as we have seen in some states, six). In some highly publicized cases, jury selection can take several months. It is often difficult to get a group of twelve persons who know very little about a spectacular criminal case if it has been discussed constantly in the newspapers and on television. If an individual has already formed a firm opinion about the case from information in the media, he is considered unfit to serve on the jury. Furthermore, the longer the trial is expected to last, the more difficult it will be to get a juror who will not suffer considerable hardship through serving. In many states, mandatory service is limited to several weeks. If the judge expects a trial to last significantly longer, she will depend on the individual's voluntary commitment to serve. Furthermore, the more publicized the case, the more peremptory challenges the judge will allow. Although normally the lawyers might have only three each, for some trials the number will exceed twenty. As a result, jury selection can take up a significant amount of time.

Once the selection process has been completed, the jury will be **impaneled,** which is the formal recording of the names of the jurors by the court. Once the jury is impaneled, the members select from among themselves a **foreperson**, who is the spokesperson for the entire twelve and who will thus announce the verdict to the court at the end of the trial. The jury members are required to **take an oath** or **make an affirmation** that they will render a verdict based on the evidence presented to them. After the trial has been completed, the judge will instruct the jury on the law and send it into **deliberation**. While deliberating on their verdict, the members of the jury are usually **sequestered**, which means that they are separated from the public and kept only in their own company. If deliberation continues over the course of several days or even weeks, the jury members will usually be accommodated in a hotel and guarded. They are not permitted to discuss the case with anyone except themselves. They are also not permitted to be in the company of either of the parties or the judge alone. If the jury needs clarification of the instructions or has any request to make of the court, the judge must first contact the lawyers for both parties and wait until they have both appeared before she may call in the jury. If the case has been highly publicized and the judge fears that the jury might be unfairly influenced by the media, the judge may sequester the jury from the beginning of the trial. If the trial lasts for several months, sequestration can be a real hardship for the jurors. When the jury has reached a verdict, the court will reconvene and the verdict will be announced by the foreperson. If the jury cannot agree on a verdict after long deliberation, the jury is called a **hung jury**. At the point at which a verdict appears hopeless, the judge will have to declare a **mistrial**. In such case, the trial will have to be repeated.

A recent line of U.S. Supreme Court cases addresses the use of peremptory challenges to exclude jurors solely on the basis of their race or gender. The landmark decision for what has become a significant change of approach to peremptory challenges is the following:

Batson v. Kentucky

476 U.S. 79, 106 S.Ct. 1712, 90 L.Ed.2d 69 (1986)

Justice POWELL delivered the opinion of the Court.

5   Petitioner, a black man, was indicted in Kentucky on charges of second-degree burglary and receipt of stolen goods. On the first day of trial in Jefferson Circuit Court, the judge conducted *voir dire* examination of the venire, excused certain jurors for cause, and permitted the parties to exercise peremptory challenges. The prosecutor used his peremptory challenges to strike all four black persons on the
10 venire, and a jury composed only of white persons was selected. Defense counsel moved to discharge the jury before it was sworn on the ground that the prosecutor's removal of the black veniremen violated petitioner's rights under the Sixth and Fourteenth Amendments to a jury drawn from a cross section of the community, and under the Fourteenth Amendment to equal protection of the laws ... the trial judge
15 observed that the parties were entitled to use their peremptory challenges to "strike anybody they want to." The judge then denied petitioner's motion, reasoning that the cross-section requirement applies only to selection of the venire and not to selection of the petit jury itself.

20 The jury convicted petitioner on both counts. On appeal to the Supreme Court of Kentucky, petitioner pressed, among other claims, the argument concerning the prosecutor's use of peremptory challenges ...

The Supreme Court of Kentucky affirmed ... We granted certiorari ... and now reverse.

Questions on the Text

1️⃣ If you have understood the previous cases and analyses, you should be able to analyze this part of the *Batson* decision on your own. Try to answer the following questions:
a. What are the facts and the legal history of the case?
b. What is the legal issue on appeal to the U.S. Supreme Court?

2️⃣ Explain the difference between the **venire** and the **impaneled jury**. This distinction is important for understanding the rest of the *Batson* opinion.

3️⃣ How do you think this case SHOULD be decided by the U.S. Supreme Court? Which of the two constitutional claims do you think the Supreme Court based its opinion on, the cross-section requirement or the equal protection of the laws guarantee?

Continue reading the case:

25   More than a century ago, the Court decided that the State denies a black defendant
equal protection of the laws when it puts him on trial before a jury from which
members of his race have been purposefully excluded. *Strauder v. West Virginia*, 100
U.S. 303, 25 L.Ed. 664 (1880). That decision laid the foundation for the Court's
unceasing efforts to eradicate racial discrimination in the procedures used to select
30   the venire from which individual jurors are drawn … .

Purposeful racial discrimination in selection of the venire violates a defendant's right
to equal protection because it denies him the protection that a trial by jury is intended
to secure. "The very idea of a jury is a body … composed of the peers or equals of the
person whose rights it is selected or summoned to determine; that is, of his neighbors,
35   fellows, associates, persons having the same legal status in society as that which he
holds." *Strauder, supra*, 100 U.S., at 308 …

Accordingly, the component of the jury selection process at issue here, the State's
privilege to strike individual jurors through peremptory challenges, is subject to the
commands of the Equal Protection Clause. Although a prosecutor ordinarily is
40   entitled to exercise permitted peremptory challenges "for any reason at all, as long as
that reason is related to his view concerning the outcome" of the case to be tried, …
the Equal Protection Clause forbids the prosecutor to challenge potential jurors
solely on account of their race or on the assumption that black jurors as a group will
be unable impartially to consider the State's case against a black defendant.

45   … a defendant may establish a prima facie case of purposeful discrimination in
selection of the petit jury solely on evidence concerning the prosecutor's exercise of
peremptory challenges at the defendant's trial. To establish such a case, the defendant
first must show that he is a member of a cognizable racial group, … and that the
prosecutor has exercised peremptory challenges to remove from the venire members
50   of the defendant's race. Second, the defendant is entitled to rely on the fact, as to
which there can be no dispute, that peremptory challenges constitute a jury selection
practice that permits "those to discriminate who are of a mind to discriminate." …
Finally, the defendant must show that these facts and any other relevant circumstances raise an inference that the prosecutor used that practice to exclude the
55   veniremen from the petit jury on account of their race. This combination of factors
in the empaneling of the petit jury, as in the selection of the venire, raises the
necessary inference of purposeful discrimination …

Once the defendant makes a prima facie showing, the burden shifts to the State to
come forward with a neutral explanation for challenging black jurors. Though this
60   requirement imposes a limitation in some cases on the full peremptory character of
the historic challenge, we emphasize that the prosecutor's explanation need not rise
to the level justifying exercise of a challenge for cause … But the prosecutor may not
rebut the defendant's prima facie case of discrimination by stating merely that he
challenged jurors of the defendant's race on the assumption – or his intuitive judg-
65   ment – that they would be partial to the defendant because of their shared race …
Nor may the prosecutor rebut the defendant's case merely by denying that he had a
discriminatory motive … The prosecutor therefore must articulate a neutral expla-

nation related to the particular case to be tried. The trial court then will have the duty
to determine if the defendant has established purposeful discrimination … .

70   In this case, petitioner made a timely objection to the prosecutor's removal of all
black persons on the venire. Because the trial court flatly rejected the objection
without requiring the prosecutor to give an explanation for his action, we remand
this case for further proceedings. If the trial court decides that the facts establish,
prima facie, purposeful discrimination and the prosecutor does not come forward
75   with a neutral explanation for his action, our precedents require that petitioner's
conviction be reversed …

Analysis

In line 45, the Court refers to a **prima facie case.** Generally, a **prima facie case** is
established when the plaintiff has presented enough evidence to justify giving the
issue raised to the jury for consideration. Usually the plaintiff has to offer evidence
of all of the elements required for her to win the law suit, assuming the defendant
says nothing. After the plaintiff has made a **prima facie case,** the defendant must
rebut the plaintiff's evidence or lose the suit, which is what is meant by the expression "the **burden shifts**" to the other party. The burden here is the **burden of
proof,** or the obligation to prove or disprove facts relevant to the legal claim. In the
context of *Batson*, it is the defendant who has to establish a **prima facie case** of purposeful discrimination. Here the **prima facie case** is the defendant's evidence that
the prosecutor has exercised his peremptory challenges on the basis of the juror's
race. Once the defendant has made a **prima facie showing** of racial discrimination,
the **burden shifts** to the prosecutor to prove that he had some non-racial basis for
the challenge. The claim that the prosecutor has based his peremptory challenge on
racial bias and essentially challenging his challenge, or asking the judge to not dismiss the prospective juror, is referred to today as a **Batson challenge.** As you will
see after reading the following *Questions on the Text*, the Batson challenge has
been expanded over the years to include most types of prejudice exhibited by either
party in exercising peremptory challenges.

Questions on the Text

1 What does the defendant have to do according to *Batson* to establish a
prima facie case of the prosecutor's racial discrimination in exercising his
peremptory challenges?

2 What is the holding of the *Batson* case? Remember that you may not interpret a decision too broadly. You need the minimum principle necessary to decide this case. That always depends on the facts of the case under consideration, because in reaching a decision the Supreme Court is actually resolving a dispute, namely the dispute in the case before it. Since the holding has the status of binding law, the Court usually will be very careful to limit its holding as much as possible so as not to establish any precedent it may later regret. Do you think the *Batson* rule applies to the exercise of peremptory challenges by the defendant's lawyer (**defense counsel**)? Do you think it applies to exercising peremptory challenges in order to discriminate against persons on the basis of gender? age? religion? national origin? Do you think that it applies in cases involving private law (as opposed to criminal law) disputes?

3 In *Edmonson v. Leesville Concrete Co., Inc.*, 111 S.Ct. 2077 (1991), the U.S. Supreme Court held that a private party to a law suit in a civil case could not exercise peremptory challenges to exclude prospective jurors on the basis of race. In *Georgia v. McCollum*, 112 S.Ct. 2348 (1992), the Court held that a criminal defendant may not exercise peremptory challenges on the basis of race. In *J.E.B. v. Alabama ex rel. T.B.*, 114 S.Ct. 1419 (1994), the Supreme Court held that peremptory challenges may not be exercised on the basis of gender. In all these cases the Court based its decision on the Equal Protection Clause of the Fourteenth Amendment and not on the Sixth or Seventh Amendment guarantees of trial by jury. This constitutional basis permitted the Court to focus on discrimination against the prospective juror rather than on the party's right to a trial by a jury of his peers. If the Court had used the Sixth or Seventh Amendment guarantees, what do you think the result would have been if a party who was *not* of the race being excluded made the objection to the discrimination? In *Powers v. Ohio*, 111 S.Ct. 1364 (1991), the U.S. Supreme Court was confronted with a criminal case where the defendant was white. He objected when the prosecutor exercised his peremptory challenges to exclude black jurors. The trial court overruled his objection and the jury convicted him. On appeal, the U.S. Supreme Court stated that the Sixth Amendment right to a trial by jury in a criminal case did not prohibit the discriminatory exercise of peremptory challenges. Instead, it was the Equal Protection Clause of the Fourteenth Amendment that prohibited this practice. Does it make any sense to permit lawyers to exercise peremptory challenges at all? See the following Section *3. The Petit Jury in England* to discover how the British legal system deals with this issue.

3. The Petit Jury in England

The petit jury plays a less significant role in the administration of justice in England than it does in the United States. In a civil law case, there is no absolute right to trial by jury, but rather a qualified right for a narrow range of law suits, including primarily tort claims such as those based on **false imprisonment, malicious prosecution, libel, slander** and **fraud**. The trial court judge has the authority to exclude the jury even in these cases if the law suit appears too complicated for laypersons to deal with effectively and efficiently. The court also has the discretion to order trial by jury in other cases, but in practice it is difficult to persuade a judge to agree to a jury trial.

The petit jury, however, is used for criminal trials where the accused has been charged with a more serious crime. The pre-selection process is carried out by a **summoning officer**, who is responsible for random selection from the electoral register. Selection criteria are aimed at attaining a representative sample of the general population and at excluding discrimination in jury selection. The group of people summoned for jury service is referred to as the **panel**, which is the body from which the final jury of twelve will be selected. If a lawyer suspects that the summoning officer acted improperly or discriminatorily in selecting the panel, he may make a **challenge to the array**.

The lawyers' ability to influence the composition of the trial jury is much more limited in England than in the United States. Before the trial begins both lawyers have the jury list available to inspect. The only information this list contains, however, is the names, addresses and dates of attendance for the members of the panel. A practice referred to as **jury vetting**, which is a formal investigation into the jurors' background, may be carried out by the Attorney-General, with the information attained passed on to the prosecutor and to defense counsel. Jury vetting is primarily limited to an investigation of the jurors' criminal conviction record, and in cases involving national security or terrorism, to inquiry regarding a few other matters. Furthermore, the lawyers are not permitted to conduct any *voir dire* examination of the prospective jurors, so information that could lead a lawyer to challenge a juror is hardly available.

At the beginning of the criminal trial, the clerk of the court has a stack of cards with the names of the panel members. The cards are shuffled and the clerk draws cards from the top of the deck, reading out the name of the juror drawn. That juror then proceeds to the jury box to be sworn in as a juror in the case. If the prosecution or defense intends to challenge a juror, the juror must be challenged before she is sworn in. Defence counsel only has the right to **challenge for cause**, **peremptory challenges** having been abolished in England in 1988. The prosecutor may challenge for cause or require a **juror to stand by for the Crown**. The **right**

to stand by is very similar to the peremptory challenge, because the prosecutor may assert this right without giving any reason for doing so. Essentially, the **right to stand by** is only limited by the number of **jurors in waiting,** or those on the panel who have not yet been called for swearing in. When the prosecutor requires a juror to stand by, the juror's card will be placed at the bottom of the stack and the selection process will continue with the next juror. Only when there are no more jurors available, will the prosecutor have to accept the jurors he has required to stand by or exercise a challenge for cause in order to have them excused. Since there are usually many more jurors in the panel than the twelve needed, the prosecutor's right is basically unlimited. It has, however, been limited by the *Attorney General's Guidelines on Exercise by the Crown of its Right of Stand-by* (1989) 88 Cr App R 123. These guidelines restrict the right to cases involving national security or terrorism on the express authorization of the Attorney-General and to cases where a juror is obviously unfit to serve, and the defense lawyers agree with the prosecution on this question.

Twelve jurors are sworn in, but only nine are needed for a valid verdict. The number of jurors may drop during the trial if the judge finds it necessary to **discharge** a juror. Jurors may be discharged because of illness or other reasons relating to the juror's own needs, or for inappropriate conduct during the trial. At the end of the trial the judge will instruct the members of the jury on various points of law and provide them with a summary of the evidence in the **summing up.** The points of law relate to the jury's responsibility to decide on matters of fact, the judge's responsibility for matters of law, the standard and burden of proof and the elements of the definition of the offense that must be proved for the defendant to be convicted. In addition the judge will give his summary of the evidence presented during trial. This power granted the English judge goes far beyond what the U.S. judge may do in the way of instructing the jury. The English judge may comment on the value of the evidence, the credibility of the witnesses and even on his opinion as to what the verdict may be.

After the summing up, the jury retires to deliberate. It is instructed to reach a unanimous verdict. If it returns to the courtroom at least two hours and ten minutes after it began deliberating, a non-unanimous verdict is acceptable, subject to the judge's determination that the jury has had enough time to deliberate in light of the complexity of the case. In such case, if the jury consists of at least eleven members, ten have to agree on the verdict. If the number of jurors is ten, then nine is sufficient to reach a verdict. If the number has dropped to nine, then the verdict has to be unanimous.

B. Why Integrate the Public?

One traditional reason for trial by jury is to protect the accused in a criminal trial from state oppression. There are enough examples in the history of England and the United States where the jury simply refused to convict a criminal defendant of the crime charged, even though the evidence was absolutely clear on the person's guilt. The jury as factfinder has the sole authority to determine what evidence to believe. Generally, the jury will be instructed at the end of the trial to apply the law as the judge explains it to the case. In fact, however, in a criminal case the jury can ignore the law completely and acquit the defendant. This practice, which is referred to as **jury nullification,** has also been the topic of heated debate. It is possible because a verdict of "not guilty" cannot be overthrown by any judge at any time, and the defendant can never be tried again for the same offense under the **double jeopardy** prohibition of the Fifth Amendment to the U.S. Constitution (unless the trial results in a hung jury, in which case a mistrial is declared and a valid trial is not considered to have taken place). Accordingly, if the jury finds the law unjust, or unjust under the circumstances of the particular case, and decides to acquit the defendant even though it is clear from the evidence that she is guilty, that determination is final. Accordingly, if the state attempts to use the criminal law as a means of suppression and the jury recognizes this motive and refuses to convict the defendant as charged, the defendant is a free person and the state can do nothing about it. Consider the interesting description of the trial of William Penn and William Mead, which Jeffrey Abramson gives in his book *We, the Jury*:

> On September 1, 1670, the Quakers William Penn and William Mead entered Old Bailey Courtroom in London to stand trial on charges of unlawful assembly and breach of the peace. The charges grew out of events on August 14 of that year, when Penn addressed a group of Quaker worshipers standing outside the Friends' Meeting
> 5   House on Gracechurch Street. Persecution of the Quakers was at its height, with soldiers standing guard over locked meetinghouses. The recently renewed Conventicles Act forbade worship other than that performed according to Anglican form. Penn therefore knew he was courting arrest when he began speaking. In fact, even before he uttered his first word, a warrant had been drawn up charging him with
> 10 "preaching seditiously and causing a great tumult of people on the royal street to be there gathered together riotously and routously." Armed with this warrant, two London constables arrived at Gracechurch Street, arrested Penn and fellow Quaker William Mead, and dispatched the pair to Newgate prison.

Trial began on September 1, on an indictment that did not charge the defendants
15   under the Conventicles Act but instead with the common-law crimes of unlawful
assembly and disturbance of the peace ... .

The defense for Penn and Mead was more legal than factual. Penn freely "confessed"
to preaching and praying to a crowd on the street. Far from wishing to deny evidence
of his preaching, Penn trumpeted his "indispensable duty" to worship God. But he
20   denied that any law of England made it a crime for people to assemble with a design
to worship God. Thus, when the court asked him whether he pleaded guilty to the
indictment, Penn saucily shot back that the question was not "whether I am guilty of
this Indictment but whether this Indictment be legal." ...

... The court grew increasingly irritated by Penn's attempt to invite the jury to go
25   "behind" the indictment and assess for itself what the common law meant by unlawful assembly and disturbance of the peace ...

[Penn] stated the essence of the legal question he was trying to put before the jury:

> Because to worship God, can never be a crime, no meeting or assembly
> designing to worship God can be unlawful ... That is properly an unlawful
30   > assembly, according to the definition of the law, when several persons are met
> together, with design to use violence and to do mischief, but that dissenters
> meet with no such intention, is manifest to the whole world, therefore their
> assemblies are not unlawful.

35   In other words, a conviction for the common-law crime of unlawful assembly required the jury to determine, among other things, that the defendants met with an
intent to do violence or harm to persons and property. Penn sought to put this
question of unlawful intent squarely before the jury; by contrast, the court's view was
that the act itself of preaching in the street and drawing a large and tumultuous
40   crowd was enough to establish guilt ... .

... After "some considerable time," the jury returned to the court with a verdict:

> CLERK: Is William Penn Guilty of the matter whereof he stands indicted in
> manner and form, or Not Guilty?
> FOREMAN: Guilty of speaking in Gracechurch-street.
45   > COURT: Is that all?
> FOREMAN: That is all I have in commission.
> REC: You had as good say nothing.
> MAYOR: Was it not an unlawful assembly? You mean he was speaking to a
> tumult of people there?
50   > FOREMAN: My Lord, This is all I had in commission.

The exchange makes clear the jury's initial attempt to give a partial verdict, pronouncing Penn "guilty" of preaching on Gracechurch Street, but leaving unresolved
the issue of whether this made Penn guilty of unlawful assembly. However, the court
required a definitive verdict and sent the jury back to reach one. A little more than
55   half an hour later, the jury returned with a written verdict repeating that Penn was
"Guilty of speaking or preaching to an assembly, met together in Gracechurch-
street ... Furious at the repeated nonverdict as to Penn, the court ordered the jury
locked up without "eat, drink, fire, and tobacco" until it reached a proper verdict ...

The next morning, the same scenario was repeated – the jury informing the court that
60 it had no other verdict to render than the one already given. Again the jury was
discharged, and again they came down to say Penn was guilty of speaking on
Gracechurch Street. The bench's insults to the jury grew in passion; threats were
made to starve the jurors and cart them about the city. When the jurors balked at
retiring yet another time to reconsider their verdict, the sheriff forcibly escorted them
65 back to their deliberations.

Finally, the next morning the jury avoided its attempt to walk a tightrope and
rendered a verdict of not guilty for both Penn and Mead. The court accepted the
verdicts but then promptly fined the jurors for rendering a decision the court found
contrary both to the evidence (the jury itself determined that Penn did preach on
Gracechurch Street as charged) and to the judicial instructions that such preaching
made Penn and Mead guilty under the law …

Penn's trial changed the course of jury history. Rather than pay his fine and be done
with it, juror Edward Bushel refused to pay, accepted imprisonment, and appealed
his incarceration … In a landmark decision agreed to by all the justices of England
75 save one, Chief Justice Sir John Vaughn flatly ruled that jurors may never be fined or
imprisoned for their verdicts …

Although Bushel's case did not recognize any official right of juries to decide questions of law, the upshot of the decision was that juries could never be punished for
acquitting a defendant. In this sense the case established the power of the criminal
80 jury to disregard the bench's instructions on law.

Jeffrey Abramson, *We, the Jury*, Basic Books: New York, pp. 68-73 (footnotes
omitted).

Questions on the Text

1 Explain the difference between the grand and petit juries. Give arguments
for and against the use of these two bodies. Examine the history of your own
legal system and determine whether it ever provided for the use of a jury.
When doing this research, consider the following factors relating to the petit
jury: a) does the jury deliberate alone or with a professional judge; b) how
long is the term for which a member of the jury serves; c) is this term long
enough to result in a juror's psychological identification with the court as
opposed to the criminal defendant or the parties to a private law dispute; d)
what are the qualifications for jury duty; e) do these qualifications eliminate
certain classes of people, such as the lesser educated, blue collar as opposed
to white collar workers, people in lower wage groups; f) is the selection
conducted to ensure randomness.

2 In the terminology lists in this chapter you have the *Model Penal Code* definitions of several crimes. The *Model Penal Code*, 1962 Official Draft,
American Law Institute: Philadelphia, Pennsylvania (1985), represents the
efforts of a group of scholars and practicing lawyers to codify the criminal
law in a form that could be adopted by any state legislature. It is generally
considered to be an excellent portrayal of the law, but the individual state
legislatures have not been too consistent in adopting it. Nevertheless, lawyers will refer to it and courts will consider it in reaching a decision, even
though the legislature has not adopted it. That is because they see it as stating what the common law is as it developed over the centuries. Accordingly,
it is a source of law without legislative enactment. If you were a judge in
England or the United States you would have to instruct the jury on the law
at the end of the trial, in language a layperson can understand. Attempt to
reformulate the provisions of the *Model Penal Code* you have in this chapter
into what could be useful jury instructions. Attempt to do the same with
your own criminal law provisions.

3 Read the cases in the *Suggested Reading* that follow and report on them.
Remember to include a brief statement of the facts of the case, the legal
history of the case, the issue raised on appeal, the holding and the ratio
decidendi. Note where you find this information in the various opinions.
Can you see a similarity as between cases in the organization of the judicial
opinion?

4 Read the cases in the following list of *Suggested Reading* in the chronologi-
cal sequence in which they were decided according to the issue raised of a)
right to trial by jury, b) jury size and c) discrimination in jury selection. Read
the first case and then only the statement of facts from the next case. Before
reading the full opinion in the new case, try to argue both sides of the case
based on the previous precedent. To do this exercise you will have to find
similarities and differences between the past cases and the new case in order
to argue that the new case a) should be decided the same way as a previous
case or b) should not be decided the same way. These similarities and differences should be based on aspects of the case that have relevance to considerations of justice. These considerations might be of philosophical, socio-
logical, psychological or economic nature, for example, but should be
convincing to other people. As you formulate your reasons why one case is
similar or different to the others, you in fact are developing your own theory
of what a line of precedents actually hold. This exercise represents the main
work of a common law lawyer, student or scholar.

Terminology

array	prospective jurors summoned to court for selection for jury duty, also called the **venire**, or: (U.K.) **panel** (ca. **Gesamtheit der möglichen Geschworenen**)
venire	(from the Latin meaning to come, to appear in court) another name for the **array** (ca. **Gesamtheit der möglichen Geschworenen**)
venireperson	person on the **array** or **venire**; also **venireman, venirewoman**
summons	official order calling s.o. to court to testify as a witness, to serve as a juror, etc. (**Ladung**); failure to appear can be punished as **contempt of court**
contempt of court	criminal offense of showing disrespect for the court; hindering the court in the administration of justice; can be punished with a fine or imprisonment (**Mißachtung des Gerichts**)
voir dire	(old French: to speak the truth) examination of prospective jurors for the purpose of determining who will actually serve on the petit jury; conducted by the judge but permits lawyers to question the prospective jurors and exercise challenges to have them removed
to exercise a challenge	to make use of a right to object to a prospective juror or to the entire array of prospective jurors by requesting the judge to dismiss that person or the entire array (**einen Antrag auf Ablehnung eines oder aller Geschworenen stellen**)
challenge to the array	formal request to dismiss the entire array or venire because of the jury commissioner's incorrect method of selection; also called: **motion to quash the venire, motion to quash the panel, motion to quash the array** (**Antrag auf Ablehnung der Gesamtheit der Geschworenen**)
challenge for cause	formal request by a party to a law suit that the judge dismiss a juror for certain specified reasons or causes relating to the juror's ability to be fair at the particular trial; unlimited in number (**Antrag auf Ablehnung eines Geschworenen wegen Befangenheit**)
peremptory challenge	privilege each party has to eliminate prospective jurors from service without giving any reason for the exclusion; limited in number (ca. **Antrag auf Ablehnung eines Geschworenen ohne Angabe von Gründen**)
jury box	the rows of seats, usually two in number, around which walls are constructed and where the members of the jury sit during trial (**Geschworenenbank**)
alternate juror	juror in addition to the required number to constitute the petit

jury who attends the entire trial but actually participates in deliberation only if one of the regular jurors suddenly has to be excused (**Ersatzgeschworener**)

to impanel the jury

to officially record the names of the individuals selected to serve on a petit jury (**die Geschworenenliste zusammenstellen**)

foreperson

member of the jury selected to speak for the entire body (**Obmann**); also: **foreman, forewoman**

oath

solemn promise invoking the name of God that one will do s.th., such as tell the truth or fulfill one's duties, to the best of one's abilities (**Eid**)

affirmation

substitute for the oath, omitting the name of God (**Erklärung an Eides Statt**)

deliberation

the jury's consideration of a case in an attempt to reach a verdict (**Beratung der Geschworenen**)

sequestration

isolation of the jury from any contact with the outside world; usually done when the jury goes into deliberation; judge can sequester the jury at the beginning of the trial if the case is widely publicized and the jury could be influenced by the media or other individuals' comments (ca. **Klausur der Geschworenen**)

hung jury

jury that cannot agree on a verdict; if the jury is hung, the judge will have to declare a **mistrial** and the trial has to be repeated with a new jury (**blockierte oder nicht entscheidungsfähige Geschworenenbank**)

mistrial

legally invalid trial that has no legal consequences (ca. **aus Formgründen ungültiges Verfahren**)

second-degree burglary

Model Penal Code, Section 221.1. Burglary. (**Einbruch zum Zweck der Begehung eines Verbrechens**)

(1) <u>Burglary Defined</u>. A person is guilty of burglary if he enters a building or occupied structure ... with purpose to commit a crime therein, ...

(2) <u>Grading</u>. Burglary is a felony of the second degree if it is perpetrated in the dwelling of another at night, or if, in the course of committing the offense, the actor:

(a) purposely, knowingly or recklessly inflicts or attempts to inflict bodily injury on anyone; or

(b) is armed with explosives or a deadly weapon.

Otherwise, burglary is a felony of the third degree ...

receipt of stolen goods

Model Penal Code, Section 223.6. Receiving Stolen Property. (**Hehlerei und Begünstigung**)

(1) <u>Receiving.</u> A person is guilty of theft if he purposely receives, retains, or disposes of movable property of another knowing

	that it has been stolen, or believing that it has probably been stolen, unless the property is received, retained, or disposed with purpose to restore it to the owner ...
Batson Challenge	challenge to the other party's peremptory challenge with the argument that the other party has exercised the peremptory challenge on the basis of the prospective juror's race and thus it should not be permitted (**Einspruch gegen einen Antrag auf Ablehnung eines Geschworenen mit der Begründung, der Antrag sei nur wegen der Rasse gestellt, der der Geschworene angehört**)
false imprisonment	*Model Penal Code*, Section 212.3. False Imprisonment. (**Freiheitsberaubung**) A person commits a misdemeanor if he knowingly restrains another unlawfully so as to interfere substantially with his liberty.
malicious prosecution	tort of causing criminal charges or civil proceedings to be brought against s.o. without good reason and for the purpose of harming that person
libel	tort of character defamation through writing, pictures, symbols, etc. that are published and serve to damage s.o.'s reputation
slander	tort of character defamation through oral expression
fraud	tort and crime of knowingly false representation designed to induce reliance and cause the victim of the fraud to part with his property or rights (**Betrug**)
defense counsel	lawyer representing the defendant in either a civil case (**Prozeßvertreter**) or criminal case (**Strafverteidiger**)
prima facie case	enough evidence to establish a legal claim; enough evidence so that if the other party remains silent he or she will lose to the person making the **prima facie showing**
burden of proof	obligation to offer enough evidence to prove the facts relevant to the legal claim (**Beweislast**); **the burden of proof shifts** to the other party when the person making the claim has established a prima facie case (**Umkehr der Beweislast**)
objection	formal claim to the judge that some legal error has been, or is in the process of being, committed during a judicial hearing (**Einspruch**)
summoning officer	(U.K.) public officer responsible for calling in individuals from society to be prospective jurors (ca. **Beamter, der für die Auswahl der Geschworenen zuständig ist**)
jury vetting	(U.K.) investigation into prospective jurors' personal backgrounds for the purpose of enabling a lawyer to better select them for jury service; limited to the Attorney-General, who passes the information on to the prosecutor and defense counsel;

	also limited in scope to juror's criminal conviction record and a few other matters
the right to stand by	(U.K.) right of the prosecutor to exclude a juror from the jury without giving any reason; similar to the **peremptory challenge** but reserved only to the prosecutor
jurors in waiting	(U.K.) members of the jury panel (array) who have not as yet been sworn in to serve on the jury
summing up	(U.K.) judge's instructions on the law and summary of the evidence presented during trial, including the judge's comments on this evidence; given at the end of the trial and before the jury deliberates on a verdict (**Belehrung der Geschworenen**)
jury nullification	power the jury has in a criminal case to ignore the law and acquit the defendant
double jeopardy	to be endangered twice; refers to prohibition against trying s.o. twice for the same crime (**ne bis in idem**)
to stand trial	to face formal criminal charges at a trial on the issue of guilt (ca. **sich vor Gericht in einem Strafverfahren verantworten**)
unlawful assembly	"At common law, the meeting together of three or more persons, to the disturbance of the public peace, and with the intention of co-operating in the forcible and violent execution of some unlawful private enterprise. If they take steps towards the performance of their purpose, it becomes a *rout*; and, if they put their design into actual execution, it is a *riot*." *Black's Law Dictionary*
breach of the peace	criminal offense of disturbing the public order (**Störung der öffentlichen Ruhe und Ordnung**)
warrant	formal document issued by a judge permitting a law enforcement officer, for example to arrest s.o., in which case it is referred to as an **arrest warrant** (**Haftbefehl**); or to search that person's home, in which case it is called a **search warrant** (**Durchsuchungsbefehl**)
common-law crime	criminal offense under the principles of the common law rather than under any particular statutory enactment
to establish guilt	to prove guilt (**die Schuld beweisen**)
the bench	term used to refer to a judge or to judges in general (ca. **Gesamtheit der Richter**)
landmark decision	judicial opinion that significantly changes the further development of the law (**bahnbrechendes Urteil**)

Vocabulary

to balk at	to refuse to do s.th., to drawn back from doing s.th.
cognizable	can be taken notice of, capable of being known
credibility	believability
to delve into	to dig into, to go into the depths of s.th.
dwelling	place where s.o. lives
to eradicate	to eliminate, to destroy
inference	conclusion drawn from s.th. said or done
leeway	room to manoeuver, allowable variation
mandatory	required, absolutely necessary
to rebut	to refute, to negate, to counter
routously	noisily
seditious	intending to overthrow the government
simultaneously	happening at the same time
ultimately	finally, in the last analysis
to utter	to make a sound, to say s.th.

Suggested Reading

Apodaca v. Oregon, 406 U.S. 404, 92 S.Ct. 1628, 32 L.Ed.2d 184 (1972) (jury size)

Baldwin v. New York, 399 U.S. 66, 90 S.Ct. 1886 (1970) (right to trial by jury)

Colgrove v. Battin, 413 U.S. 149, 93 S.Ct. 2448, 37 L.Ed.2d 522 (1973) (jury size)

Duncan v. Louisiana, 391 U.S. 145, 88 S.Ct. 1444, 20 L.Ed.2d 491 (1968) (right to trial by jury)

Edmonson v. Leesville Concrete Co., Inc. 111 S.Ct. 2077 (1991) (discrimination in jury selection)

Georgia v. McCollum, 112 S.Ct. 2348 (1992) (discrimination in jury selection)

J.E.B. v. Alabama ex rel. T.B. 114 S.Ct. 1419 (1994) (discrimination in jury selection)

Johnson v. Louisiana, 406 U.S. 356, 92 S.Ct. 1620, 32 L.Ed.2d 152 (1972) (jury size)

Powers v. Ohio, 111 S.Ct. 1364 (1991) (discrimination in jury selection)

Strauder v. West Virginia, 100 U.S. 303, 25 L.Ed. 664 (1880) (discrimination in jury selection)

Swain v. Alabama, 380 U.S. 202, 85 S.Ct. 824, 13 L.Ed.2d 759 (1965) (discrimination in jury selection)

United States v. Jackson, 390 U.S. 570, 88 S.Ct. 1209, 20 L.Ed.2d 138 (1968) (right to trial by jury)

Witherspoon v. State of Illinois, 391 U.S. 510, 88 S.Ct. 1770, 20 L.Ed.2d 776 (1968) (discrimination in jury selection)

Jeffrey Abramson, *We, the Jury*, New York: Basic Books (1994)

Harry Kalven, Jr. & Hans Zeisel, *The American Jury*, Chicago: University of Chicago Press (1966)

Stuart Nagel & Marian Neff, "Deductive Modeling to Determine an Optimum Jury Size and Fraction Required to Convict," 1975 *Washington University Law Quarterly* 933

Seymour Wishman, *Anatomy of a Jury*, New York: Times Books (1986), Penguin Books (1987)

Hans Zeisel, "And Then There Were None: The Diminution of the Federal Jury," 38 *University of Chicago Law Review* 710 (1971)

Chapter 3
The Adversary System of Trial

Another fundamental difference between common law and civil law systems is the method of conducting a trial. The system of trial employed in most continental European legal systems is referred to as **accusatorial** in the criminal law context and as **interrogative** in the civil law context. In a common law nation, the **adversary** system is used. The major difference between these two systems of conducting the trial lies in the roles the judge and the lawyers assume during the trial process. In continental European nations, the judge plays the more active role in the questioning of witnesses and taking of evidence. Admittedly, the judge dominates the criminal trial more so than the private law suit. Still, even in the private arena, the judge is the primary interrogator of witnesses, with the lawyers free to ask additional questions after the judge has finished. Perhaps, one reason why this system dominates in continental Europe is because it is the judge who is the factfinder at trial. Consequently, it is he who must be convinced of the truth of certain facts before being able to apply the law to those facts in reaching his judgment. Admittedly, many continental European legal systems employ lay assessors at trial. Still, these individuals can be influenced easily by the professional judge who will, at the end of the proceeding, deliberate with them. As a result, it will be the judge who will feel primarily responsible for directing the trial process in an effort to arrive at the truth.

In England and the United States it is the parties themselves, through their legal representatives, who present their conflicting views of the facts of the case. Each is permitted to portray the story behind the dispute as he or she sees it, with the jury left to determine the "real" facts of the case and to apply the law as the judge has instructed to those facts when reaching its verdict. The common law judge acts more as a referee over the courtroom debate, determining what the lawyers may and may not present as evidence to the jury and generally keeping order throughout the legal process. She does not deliberate with the jury. The only method she has of influencing the jury is through her instructions on the law, and in England through her summing up of the evidence presented during the trial. But since the jury deliberates alone, the judge's influence on the final verdict is relatively limited. Accordingly, a common law system can also be characterized in terms of the division of power over the trial process. On the one hand, power is divided between the two **advocates**, each responsible for presenting the facts most favorable for his client's position, and on the other hand, power is divided between the jury as the ultimate authority on the facts and the judge as the ultimate authority on the law.

A. Procedural Justice

Another way of describing the difference between the **adversary** and **interrogative** or **accusatorial** system is to characterize the adversary system as a system of **procedural justice** and the interrogative system as a system of **substantive** justice. Procedural justice is defined as the result of a process. Procedural rules are designed to ensure that the process runs fairly. The result reached is what the participants, by agreeing to employ that process, will accept as the just result. The process may be defined quite simply, such as the result reached by tossing a coin. Participants will agree to use this type of process when less significant matters are at stake, such as which restaurant to go to or who has to perform some simple chore around the house. Other processes, such as the trial process in a criminal case, are much more complicated. But even within the legal sphere, the participants may accept processes short of a full judicial hearing, such as **arbitration** or other **alternative dispute resolution** methods. In the trial context, the procedural rules give each party an equal opportunity to present his side of the story to an independent tribunal. The judge is responsible for conducting the process as defined by these rules. A member of a common law system accepts the result of the trial and appellate processes as the final word on justice between the parties to a law suit. **Substantive justice**, on the other hand, lives less from procedural rules than from the ability of a highly trained expert, in the person of the judge, to find the truth and establish justice in some higher sense of the word. Accordingly, it is not surprising that the common law judge acts more as a referee, mediating between the two parties in an effort to ensure that each is adequately represented before the jury as factfinder and ultimate tribunal on truth and justice. Contrarily, the civil law judge assumes the role of the professional expert on finding the truth. She does not have to be concerned about undue influence on a jury of laypersons, because even when lay assessors are present, the judge will have some control over them during deliberation. Important for the civil law judge is a feeling of certainty regarding the facts, which to some extent explains her primary control over what evidence is presented and which witnesses are called to testify.

The following two texts describe the adversary process. Both authors are U.S. Americans, and, as you will see, favor the adversary system of trial:

The adversary system has deep roots in the Anglo-American legal tradition. Its antecedent is often said to be the Norman trial by battle, wherein issues in doubt were resolved by the outcome of a duel. Perhaps more relevant is the fact that the key elements of the adversary system – the right to present evidence and the right to
5   assistance of counsel – evolved as legal controls on government absolutism in seventeenth-century England. Thus, the adversary system is not only a theory of adjudication but a constituent of our history of political liberty.

The theory of adjudication in the adversary system, as usually stated, has two linked components. One is that party presentation will result in the best presentation,
10   because each party is propelled into maximum effort in investigation and presentation by the prospect of victory; in contrast, a judge-interrogator is only interested in getting through the day and through his caseload. The other component of the theory is more complex and has to do with the psychology of decision making. It runs essentially as follows: Proof through evidence requires hypothesis; hypothesis
15   requires a preliminary mind-set; if an active judge-interrogator develops the proof, his preliminary mind-set too easily can become his final decision; therefore, it is better to have conflicting preliminary hypotheses and supporting proofs presented by the parties so that the judge's mind can be kept open until all the evidence is at hand.

20   In this version of the adversary theory, the role of the advocate is central to adjudication, because the advocate is a necessary orchestrator of the proof to be offered by a party. The prominence of the advocate in the adversary system explains in part why the legal profession as a whole strongly supports it. There are other interpretations of the adversary system, however, that attach much less significance to the role of the
25   advocate as an instrument for developing the proofs. One of these interpretations emphasizes the importance of party participation, the idea being that a party's presentation of the case on his behalf gives him a sense of involvement and control in the decision procedure. In this conception of the adversary system, counsel is and should be relegated to the role of coach rather than protagonist, because if the lawyer
30   is protagonist, his client's role is secondary and passive. This form of the adversary system appears to have actually existed in English procedure of about the thirteenth century, but it is found today only in cases, such as in small claims court, where the amount involved is too little to justify hiring a lawyer to present them. These days, if litigation is taken to a lawyer, he takes it over.

35   There is still another and more radical theory of the adversary system. On this view, trials are not quests for truth in a serious objective or empirical sense, and cannot be. This is because truth is unknowable in any objective sense, or at least because the controversies in which the issues can rationally be resolved by the evidence rarely go to trial, for parties concede what can really be proved. By exclusion, therefore, in the
40   cases that go to trial the evidence is hopelessly ambiguous according to any concept of rational proof, and decision necessarily involves important elements of intuition,

predisposition, and bias. On this analysis, a trial is necessarily theatre or ritual to an important extent.

G. Hazard, *The Adversary System*. Ethics in the Practice of Law, c. 9, Seven Springs Center, Inc. (1978), cited here from G. Hazard, Jr./C. Tait/W. Fletcher, *Pleading and Procedure: Cases and Materials*, 7th ed., The Foundation Press, Inc.:Westbury, New York (1994) 34-35.

Questions on the Text

1. List the arguments this author gives in favor of the adversary system. Some of them (lines 8-19) inherently involve a criticism of the **interrogative** system of **adjudication**. Do you agree with the author on these points? What arguments can you give in response supporting the **interrogative** system and criticizing the **adversary** system? In answering these questions assume that a) a jury is the factfinder, and b) the judge is the factfinder, i.e. there is no jury involved in the trial.

2. Does the author of the above text base his arguments on a private law dispute or a criminal procedure? Does he assume that a jury is involved or only a judge? Find the passages in the text that give you the answers to these questions.

3. The author refers to the key elements of the adversary system as being "the right to present evidence and the right to assistance of counsel" (lines 4-5). Certainly continental European legal systems also recognize these rights, but in what way might they be limited? Consider, for example, a case for which the opinion of an expert is required. In your own legal system, who selects the expert witness, the judge or the parties? Is each party permitted to call his own expert to testify, or will the judge call only one, namely a court-appointed expert? If a party is indigent and cannot pay for his own expert witness, does the state also assume these costs? Does the state pay court costs and lawyers fees for an indigent party? Does it matter whether the case is on trial or appeal? Who decides whether the costs of the appeal are covered, the party wishing to appeal or the state, assuming the state covers the costs of appeal? How are lawyers appointed for the indigent? Can the individual choose his own lawyer, or must he take the lawyer the state appoints? What other issues might arise when a system claims to guarantee the right to present evidence and the right to assistance of counsel?

A Crime of Self-Defense

The adversary system of trial, sometimes called the sporting approach to the truth, recalls our commitment to democracy as the least corruptible form of government. The system requires that two equally matched lawyers, a prosecutor and a defense counsel, joust in open court. Each lawyer makes the best case and fights as hard as he
5   can for his client, whether he thinks his client is morally right or wrong. The fight that the lawyers undertake encompasses not only the questions of guilt and innocence, but the range of evidence that the jury should be allowed to hear. The adversary system differs radically from the neutral, objective inquiry of scientists and historians, who consider all the evidence and who come to a decision only when they
10 are convinced that the evidence supports their hypothesis.

In a criminal trial, two pitted advocates urge contradictory perspectives on the truth, and a neutral judge presides over the battle; the 12 members of the jury must come to a verdict one way or another. Unlike scientific investigators, the jury cannot postpone its decision and request additional research that would clarify unresolved
15 factual questions. A trial leads to a day of judgment. The defendant must be found guilty or not guilty – for all time. The pressure of reaching a decision skews the scales of justice toward the defense; if the prosecution fails to prove guilt beyond a reasonable doubt, at least on most issues, the jury is supposed to decide for the defense.

This preference for the defense is expressed in the maxim that it is far better that ten
20 (some say a hundred) guilty defendants go free than that one innocent person be convicted. If [the defendant] were falsely convicted, his case would probably be forgotten as he disappeared behind bars. There would be no ongoing process of inquiry about his guilt as there would be about the validity of a scientific claim. And even if the error were subsequently discovered, there would be no way to replace the
25 lost years in prison and to correct the insult of having treated him as a criminal. Trial and error may be a salutary way of refining our sense about what works in the world, but in resolving accusations of crime, our greatest fear is a trial ending in error.

The adversary system may not be ideal, but our experience teaches us that it poses the fewest risks of error. The opposition between prosecutor and defense counsel insures
30 that both sides of the story are aired. Another distinctive feature of the system, separating the jury's function of deciding the facts from the judge's role of resolving questions of law, minimizes bias in the jury room as well as on the bench. Vesting the final power of judgment in laypeople, whose careers are not affected by their rejecting the state's position, contributes to an independent decision on guilt or innocence.
35

Further, if the jury and not the judge makes the decision about guilt or innocence, the lawyers remain free to argue to the judge as zealously as they like about issues of law without fear that if they alienate the judge, they will thereby influence a determination on the ultimate issue of guilt or innocence. The adversary system has resulted,
40 therefore, in a practice of criminal defense that is characteristically more vigorous than that displayed by lawyers in European legal systems that function without vesting final authority in a jury of laypersons. No one likes the thought that justice for the People or for the defendant depends, in part, on the skill of combative

lawyers. But the distortions of competition are less serious than the potential for
45   corruption when the power of judgment is concentrated in a judge who, like the
inquisitorial judge of the European past, claims the final word on the accusation, the
facts, and the law. If as Lord Acton said, power corrupts and absolute power corrupts absolutely, the safest way to run a criminal trial is to bifurcate the power of
presenting the evidence between prosecution and defense and to divide the power of
50   decision between judge and jury.

George P. Fletcher, *A Crime of Self-Defense*. Bernhard Goetz and the Law on Trial,
The Free Press: New York (1988), pp. 7-8

Questions on the Text

1. Does this author base his arguments on a private law dispute or a criminal
    trial? Does he assume that a jury is involved or only a judge? Find the pas-
    sages in the text that give you the answers to these questions.

2. In line 17, the author refers to proof of guilt **beyond a reasonable doubt** (UK:
    beyond all reasonable doubt). This phrase expresses the **standard of proof**,
    relating to the burden of proof or **burden of persuasion** placed on the pros-
    ecutor for criminal cases. The standard requires that the prosecutor exclude
    all rational doubts that the average person might have regarding the defend-
    ant's guilt. It is the highest standard of proof employed in a common law
    system. For private law disputes, the standard is expressed as proof by **a
    preponderance of the evidence** (UK: **on a balance of probabilities**). This
    standard merely requires the plaintiff to be more convincing than the de-
    fendant. What is the standard of proof in your own legal system?

3. In line 46, the author comments on the "**inquisitorial** judge of the European
    past." It is important to understand the difference between the **inquisitorial**
    system of the European past and the **accusatorial** system of today's Europe.
    In an **inquisitorial** system, one individual functions as both prosecutor and
    judge. In an **accusatorial** system, the judge and prosecutor are two different
    individuals. Still they function interdependently, because the prosecutor pre-
    pares the case against the accused and passes his file on to the judge, who
    continues with the investigation during the trial. In an **adversary** system,
    there is no interdependence between prosecutor and judge. The prosecutor,
    just like the defense attorney, prepares his case and presents it to the court
    for the court's evaluation. List the author's arguments in support of the ad-
    versary system. How many of them implicitly criticize the accusatorial sys-
    tem? What arguments can you make to counter the author's arguments?

4 This author relies very heavily on metaphorical constructions. Find the metaphors used in this text and consider how you would get the same idea across in your own native tongue.

5 In Hungarian, two words signify truth: *igazság*, also meaning justice or fairness, which indicates the truth people tell, or the truth a judge determines during the course of a trial, and *valóság*, which refers to scientific truth, or the way things really are. The author of this text draws this distinction for the trial process as opposed to the scientific laboratory. What is the purpose of a system of justice, particularly of the trial process as part of this system? Is it ever possible to determine with 100% accuracy what the truth is for any particular legal case? Reconsider lines 35-43 of the first text you read on the adversary system, where the author discusses an argument that the trial process is not intended to find the truth in any objective sense, because it cannot be found. Do you agree with this point of view? If the truth cannot be found, why not substitute tossing a coin for the expensive and tiresome trial process? What aspects of the adversary system in fact are aimed at ensuring that the truth will be discovered?

Terminology

accusatorial system	system of trial common in criminal cases in continental European nations in which the judge is the primary gatherer of evidence at trial and works from a file the prosecutor collected on the defendant's guilt before trial
interrogative system	system of trial common in civil law cases in continental European nations in which the judge is the primary gatherer of evidence at trial
adversary system	system of trial common in criminal and civil law cases in common law countries in which the parties, as opponents, present evidence most favorable to their own view of the case in an attempt to convince either judge or jury of their right to prevail (im Zivilrecht: **Parteienprozeß**)
inquisitorial system	system of trial commonly used during the Middle Ages in which one person was both prosecutor and judge (**Inquisitionsprozeß**)
advocate	a person who supports or defends s.o. or s.th.; often used for lawyers within the adversary system (**Advokat**); **to advocate**: to argue for s.th., to support or defend s.th. (**sich einsetzen für**)
substantive justice	justice defined in terms of higher truths and principles (**materiale Gerechtigkeit**)

procedural justice	justice defined in terms of the outcome of a process (**Gerechtigkeit durch Verfahren**)
arbitration	non-judicial method of resolving dispute between two parties whereby one or more **arbitrators** hear the parties' version of the problem and seek a solution based more on permitting the parties to save face and continue in their relationship toward each other rather than on determining their individual rights and providing the basis for discontinuation of the relationship; usually recognized as legally binding decision; often used for disputes between contracting companies in the international arena (**Schiedsgerichtsbarkeit**)
alternative dispute resolution	any non-judicial method of resolving disputes, such as **arbitration** (**außergerichtliche Streitbeilegung**)
adjudication	process of resolving legal dispute in a court of law where a judge presides over the hearing, as opposed to any other method of resolving a dispute, such as by arbitration (ca. **richterliche Behandlung und/oder Entscheidung eines Falles in einem streitigen Verfahren**)
standard of proof	test of when the burden of proof has been satisfied; defined measurement of how convinced the factfinder at trial has to be before deciding in favor of the party bearing the burden (**Beweismaßstab**)
burden of persuasion	another term for **burden of proof** (**Beweislast**)
beyond a reasonable doubt	standard of proof in a criminal case (U.K. **beyond all reasonable doubt**) meaning that the factfinder must be so convinced of the defendant's guilt that no rational doubt regarding that guilt remains (ca. **ohne vernünftigen Zweifel**)
preponderance of the evidence	standard of proof in a civil law dispute (U.K. **on a balance of probabilities**) meaning that the factfinder must be more convinced of the plaintiff's case than of the defendant's in order to decide in favor of plaintiff (ca. **überwiegendes Ergebnis der Beweisaufnahme**)
small claims court	simplified lower level trial court procedure for considering civil law disputes regarding a very small amount in controversy, such as $500

Vocabulary

to air	to make public, to broadcast
to alienate	to make an enemy of s.o.; to make unfriendly
ambiguous	unclear, uncertain
to bifurcate	to divide into two parts
to concede	to admit, to accept as true
constituent	component, element
to encompass	to include
indigent	poor
inherent	of the essential nature of s.th.
to joust	to battle with lances on horseback
to pit	to confront with an enemy for battle, to set into rivalry
predisposition	inclination, tendency in one direction before hearing arguments on both sides
protagonist	leading role, main character
to relegate	to assign, to entrust (as duties, responsibilities)
salutary	healthful, remedial
to skew	to tip the balance in one direction, to make biased
stake	an interest in s.th., s.th. is **at stake** if it can be won or lost
to urge	to persuade, to try to convince
to vest	to grant power, to bestow rights

B. Retaining a Lawyer

The legal profession, and the terminology accompanying it, differs markedly in the United States and England. The one term they have in common is **lawyer**, which is a very general term meaning someone who has completed a study of law regardless of what they actually do professionally. We shall consider each legal system in turn.

1. The Legal Profession in the United States

This section will describe legal education, legal practice, and legal fee arrangements in the United States.

a. Legal Education

In the United States lawyers all receive the same general legal education and therefore are all qualified for any legal profession they may later choose. To be admitted to the study of law, a student must first complete a course of **undergraduate education** at a **college** or **university** and have been awarded the **B.A.** (**Bachelor of Arts**) or the **B.S.** (**Bachelor of Science**) degree. Undergraduate education begins after completing **high school**, or secondary school through the twelfth grade, usually at the age of eighteen. The B.A. program is called **undergraduate education** because the student has not yet graduated from a university-level educational program. A student can complete a B.A. program at a **college** or **university** in four years. A **university** essentially unifies a number of colleges, or schools, such as the college of **liberal arts**, the **school of law**, the **school of medicine**, or the **school of business administration** under one educational institution. In addition, there are a number of colleges of liberal arts, or sciences, that are not within universities but rather stand alone and offer only undergraduate educational programs. Accordingly, the terms **college** and **university** are not differentiated according to the level of educational program they offer leading to the B.A. degree, but rather according to whether they are larger or smaller institutions. In a B.A. program students receive general education, but also **major** in one field in which they take considerably more courses. These fields include subjects such as mathematics, chemistry, physics, philosophy, English literature, foreign languages, economics, or any field of study that does not train one directly for a vocation or profession, as does the school of law or medicine.

On completion of the four-year bachelor's program, a student can apply for admission to **law school**. Law school admission is extremely competitive in the United States and is based primarily on the student's **GPA**, or **grade point average,** in undergraduate school and on the score the student receives on the **LSAT**, or **Law School Admission Test**. The **GPA** is computed based on the grades the student received in all courses the student took during the B.A. program weighted by the number of credits awarded for the course. The **LSAT** is a nationally administered examination, primarily oriented toward testing reading comprehension and the student's ability to think logically. Law schools are ranked in the United States according to a variety of factors and students compete not only for admission to law school in general but also for admission to the law school with the highest ranking the student can hope to achieve.

Legal education, which is considered to be **graduate education,** lasts three years and leads to the **JD,** or doctor of law, degree. The first year is devoted to basic courses, such as **contracts, torts, criminal law, constitutional law, civil** and **criminal procedure.** In the second and third years the student will take a few more basic courses in fields such as **evidence** and **remedies,** and any other **electives,** or non-required courses, the student may choose. As you probably have noticed, basic courses in a common law country such as the U.S. are strongly oriented toward teaching procedural law. First-year law students will probably take civil procedure for five hours, meaning also five **credits,** per week. In addition, they will take a separate course on **evidence,** or the rules governing the admission of proof of facts claimed in a trial, and **remedies,** or the law of what types of compensation or other relief a plaintiff can attempt to be awarded at the end of a successful trial. In contrast, in a civil law system such as Germany, students receive procedural law very late in their law school education in lectures covering only a few hours per week. Instruction in civil procedure will include the law of evidence, a very insignificant part of the **Code of Civil Procedure,** and remedies will be taught as part of the substantive law as contained in the Civil Code.

On completion of law school, the student will be ready to enter the legal profession. If the student intends to practice law in a particular state, she will have to take the **bar examination,** or the state licensing exam in that state. The term **bar** here is used to describe the group of lawyers actually licensed to practice law in a state or before the U.S. federal courts. It comes from the English practice of having lawyers in court stand behind a bar that separates the lawyers from the judges on the bench. Every state in the United States is a sovereign legal entity and each of them has its own licensing examination for lawyers. Most students take a **bar review course** to prepare for this examination. Bar review courses are offered by private companies and usually last around six weeks. The bar examination is generally a two-day exam, one day being multiple choice, which is not at all comparable to the **first state law examination** in Germany, for example. That is because the main factor determining whether and where a student is hired after law school is the student's GPA during law school and the quality of the law school she attended according to the system of law school ranking.

b. Legal Practice

As in any country, students who have finished their legal studies have a wide variety of job opportunities. They can work in a **law firm, clerk for a judge,** work as a **prosecutor** or **public defender,** work for a large company as an **in-house lawyer,** work for a **non-profit organization,** work for state or federal **administrative agencies,** or start their own legal practice, which in the United States is called **to hang out one's shingle** A **shingle** is a hanging sign outside a business indicating the name and nature of the business. Since legal education in the U.S. does not include any period of practical work experience, the first few years out of law school will function as on-the-job training. A lawyer who is actually working in the practice of law is usually called an **attorney**.

Work in a large law firm will expose the young lawyer to a variety of types of legal practice often with primarily companies, rather than individuals, as **clients**. Large law firms are divided into departments, such as **mergers and acquisitions** (*abbr* **M&A**), **banking**, **tax**, and **litigation**. Probably the most basic distinction within a law firm is that between **litigators**, attorneys who spend most of their time preparing for and being at trial or on appeal for a client, and the other lawyers, who spend most of their time at their desks drafting documents, devising tax plans, and negotiating financing arrangements. This distinction, however, is not based on any separate licensing of the lawyer, but simply on the individual's preference and talent for one type of work or the other.

Clerking for a judge is considered to be an honor for a young lawyer. How high the honor is depends on the court for which the lawyer is clerking. Most judges have only two clerks, so there are not a large number of positions available, and the judge will be very selective in the choice of lawyers to fill those positions. Lawyers clerk for two years, assisting their judge with any business before the court. This type of work exposes the young lawyer to a wide variety of legal problems and their solution by someone who is an outstanding expert on the law, the judge. Note that law students do not become judges on leaving the university. Unlike in civil law systems, students of the common law are trained to be lawyers and not for the **professional judgeship**. Judges in a common law system are either elected by the people or appointed by the **executive branch** of the **government**, meaning either the governor of a state for state courts or the President of the United States for federal courts (see Unit II, Chapter 1 on US court systems). Usually lawyers have had considerable experience practicing law before they are considered for appointment as a judge.

The **prosecutor's office** is responsible for bringing criminal charges against individuals who are suspected of having committed a crime. The **public defender's office** is a state office, similar to the prosecutor's office but responsible for defending the criminally accused who are indigent, or too poor to pay for a lawyer. Public defenders are not court-appointed lawyers, but rather full-time employees of the public defender's office, just as prosecutors are full-time employees of the prosecutor's office.

c. Legal Fee Arrangements

At one time lawyers worked according to **minimum fee schedules** established by state **bar associations,** which are responsible for monitoring the legal profession in their individual state and are organized under the umbrella of the **American Bar Association.** Minimum fee schedules fixed the minimum price a lawyer was permitted to charge for all types of legal services. The U.S. Supreme Court held that fee schedules were a violation of the **Sherman Antitrust Act** in *Goldfarb v. Virginia State Bar,* 421 U.S. 773 (1975) (see Appendix II for a description of this case). A **trust** is another word for a **cartel.** The Sherman Antitrust Act is a federal law that prohibits cartels and price fixing arrangements. After this case was decided lawyers could compete with their fees and later even price advertise. Accordingly, the market for legal services in the United States is significantly different from in Continental Europe.

A lawyer usually charges a **consulting fee** to cover the initial interview with a prospective client, regardless of whether the client decides to employ the attorney or not. If the client does **retain,** or hire, the lawyer, the client will pay her a **retainer,** which is the initial fee that essentially binds the lawyer to represent the client and thus bars the lawyer from representing anyone else with competing interests. The price of the legal services that follow can be arranged in a number of ways. The most common arrangement is the **hourly fee,** where the client pays the attorney for each hour, or part of an hour, the lawyer spends working on the case. Another arrangement is the **flat fee,** which is a set amount of money regardless of the time the lawyer needs to complete the work. This type of fee is usually agreed upon for routine matters that require a lawyer's services but do not usually vary much in the demand placed on the lawyer's time. In addition, lawyers often work on a flat-fee basis for days in court, the client paying a set amount for each day the lawyer spends in a trial. A third type of fee is the **contingency fee.** The lawyer's right to be paid is contingent, or dependent, on whether the lawyer wins the case for the client. The contingency fee is often used for cases that could result in very high awards for damage caused by torts, particularly if the defendant is a large company which will be able to pay the high damage claim and the client does not have enough money to finance the law suit otherwise. Lawyers usually receive thirty to fifty percent of the final award if they win, but they pay all of the costs of the law suit as it progresses, and they receive nothing if they lose. As you can imagine, a lawyer will not want to take a case on a contingency basis unless the lawyer is fairly certain that she will win the suit. That has the advantage that good claims will be filed, even though the client otherwise would not be able to pay a lawyer to file the suit. It also has the advantage that bad claims will not.

Regardless of the fee arrangement, the client pays his own fees. Unlike in most European nations, the loser of litigation in the United States need not pay the winner's lawyer's fees. Courts do order the loser to pay **costs,** but these are the **court costs** of the litigation and not the costs of retaining a lawyer. In cases in which a lawyer is working on a contingency, the loser in effect will pay the winner's lawyer's fees because these fees are a percentage of the total damage award in the case. Accordingly they will be deducted from what the client has been awarded in the judgment. Furthermore, legal services insurance is not available in the United States, presumably because fees can vary significantly for the same type of legal work depending on the lawyer one hires. Large **Wall Street firms** will charge far more than a small local firm, as will more experienced and well-known litigators who work on a national basis.

2. The Legal Profession in England

a. *Legal Education*

In England, students can prepare for the practice of law in two different ways. Either the student will take a three-year undergraduate program leading to the **Bachelor of Arts** (*abbr* **B.A.**) or the **Bachelor of Science** (**B.Sc.**) degree and a one-year **conversion course** of legal education, called the **Common Professional Examination** (*abbr* **CPE**) or **Diploma in Law,** or the student will take a three-year undergraduate law program leading to the **Bachelor of Laws** (*abbr* **LL.B.**) degree. Either way, the student will receive instruction in **six core subjects,** namely criminal law, constitutional and administrative law, contract law, tort law, **trusts and equity,** and **land law.**

The program of legal studies in England is then divided depending upon whether the student intends to become a **solicitor** or **barrister.** A solicitor is a lawyer who does mostly office work, as opposed to appearing in court, whereas the barrister is a litigator. Formerly, solicitors were not permitted to argue cases before the high courts of England. If a solicitor's client had to be represented in court, the solicitor would contact a barrister to take over the case. Today, although solicitors are permitted to represent their clients in the high courts of England, they still generally contact a barrister for that type of work. Litigation in a common law country is a highly complex matter and depends largely on skills that take a considerable time to acquire. It is rare that a lawyer will have that type of skills if she generally focuses on legal practice in a **law office.**

If the student intends to become a **solicitor,** she will take the **Legal Practice Course** (*abbr* **LPC**). The one-year LPC is offered as a separate program of graduate legal education at many English universities. It includes instruction in four **compulsory areas**, namely **conveyancing, wills probate and administration, business law and practice, litigation and advocacy**, and in several **optional areas** aimed at **private client work** or **corporate client work**. After completing the LPC, the student will then work in a **training establishment**, which is either a solicitor's office or an organization, as a **trainee solicitor** with a two-year **training contract**. The trainee solicitor is given a **training principal**, who is responsible for that trainee's practical education. In addition, during the two years at the training establishment, the trainee solicitor must complete the **Professional Skills Course**, a twelve-day, sixty-hour program of vocational education in three **heads: financial and business skills, advocacy and communication skills**, and **ethics and client responsibilities**. After both of these requirements are fulfilled, the trainee may apply for admission to the **Roll of Solicitors**.

If the student intends to become a **barrister**, she will proceed exactly as the solicitor until her vocational education begins. Instead of taking the LPC, however, she will take the **Bar Vocational Course** (*abbr* **BVC**), which is also a one-year course of graduate legal education offered by the **Inns of Court School of Law** (*abbr* **ICSL**) and at a number of English universities. In addition, she will have to become a member of one of the four **Inns of Court**, namely **Gray's Inn, Lincoln's Inn**, the **Inner Temple** or the **Middle Temple** and **keep term**. Keeping term at one time meant eating a specified number of dinners in one's Inn over a certain period of time. Today, the student barrister keeps term by attending twelve educational **qualifying sessions** in her Inn. The Inns of Court control the right of admission to the **Bar**, or the branch of the legal profession to which barristers belong. They also provide barristers with **sets of chambers**, or offices in which to practice their profession, and perform a number of educational, professional, and social functions for their members. After completing the BVC, the student must do one year of **pupilage**, or work in a set of chambers for a barrister. When the student has finished six months of pupilage, she will receive a **provisional practicing certificate**, permitting her to work as a barrister within her set of chambers. This certificate will become a final certificate on completion of the final six months of pupilage. The young barrister will then seek a **tenancy** as a **member of professional chambers**.

b. Legal Practice

Most solicitors practice law in law firms. Initially they are **assistant solicitors**, which means they have not become partners of the firm. A more experienced solicitor who is not yet partner is referred to as an **associate solicitor**. Solicitors cater to private and corporate clients. For private clients, they primarily do **conveyancing** work, draft and **probate wills**, handle **divorces** and **child custody**, and represent clients charged with less serious criminal offenses. Conveyancing is the legal work associated with the purchase of real property. A will, sometimes also called a **last will and testament,** is a declaration of an individual's intent for the transfer of all property remaining after death to the individual's **heirs,** or the persons who **inherit** the property. A will is **probated** when the property is actually distributed to the heirs according to the provisions in the will. For their corporate clients the work is very similar to the work undertaken in the United States in the larger law firms, namely preparing company mergers and acquisitions, drafting and arranging financing agreements, advising clients on taxation issues, but generally not representing clients in court. For this type of work, the solicitor **instructs** a barrister, meaning the solicitor passes on the documents associated with the case to the barrister, who prepares for litigation.

The profession of a barrister is divided into **Queen's Counsel** (*abbr* **QC**) or **King's Counsel** (*abbr* **KC**) depending upon whether the reigning monarch is female or male, and **junior barristers,** or **juniors**. Approximately ten percent of the profession are **QC**. QCs are considered to be the best in the profession as judged by their peers. To be appointed Queen's Counsel, the barrister will apply to the Lord Chancellor, who is the head of the British judiciary and the speaker of the House of Lords. This process is also referred to as **applying for silk** and QCs are also called **silks**. The Lord Chancellor will conduct an investigation of the applicant and recommend him to the Queen for appointment, or reject the application. Queen's Counsel usually appear in court with a **junior,** or a barrister who is not QC. The QC, also called **leader,** is then responsible for litigation strategy and advocacy, whereas juniors are responsible for drafting the pleadings and other paperwork associated with litigation.

c. Legal Fee Arrangements

Solicitors' fees are generally determined by the solicitor himself based on the type of work involved. One initial difference is between fees for **contentious** or **non-contentious work,** the former being litigation and the latter office work. Fees for litigation are **assessed** by the court at the end of the case, based on the solicitor's own statement of costs but subject to the court's control. For so-called **fast-track cases,** or cases that are expected to be litigated within one day, the costs for the solicitor's day in court are fixed. In England **costs follow the event,** meaning the loser of a law suit is required to pay the costs for both parties. The court will make a **between party assessment** after conclusion of the case to determine the winner's costs. If the client is dissatisfied with the amount his own solicitor is charging, he can ask the court to make a **solicitor and own client assessment** to determine whether he has to pay the full amount of the solicitor's charges.

Fees for non-contentious work are settled between the solicitor and his client. At one time solicitor's fees for conveyancing work were fixed as **scale fees** based on the value of the property being conveyed. Today, as in the United States, solicitors are free to charge what they like and are permitted to advertise their fees in order to compete within the profession.

Barristers' fees are determined between the barrister and the solicitor giving the instructions. For litigation work, the barrister's fee is composed of a **brief fee**, which covers the first day in court and the barrister's preparatory work, and **refreshers**, which cover each additional day in court beyond the first. QCs are paid more than juniors, and since they are usually attended by a junior as well, the client will ultimately be paying for both of their services.

Terminology

Legal Profession in the United States:

to retain a lawyer	to hire a lawyer to represent you (**einem Rechtsanwalt ein Mandat erteilen**)
undergraduate education	university-level education following high school and preceding the first university degree; contrasted to graduate education (**Ausbildung, die zu einem ersten Universitätsabschluß führt**)
college	school within a university, e.g. college of law, college of medicine; if the college offers a program of undergraduate education it is called a college of liberal arts and can exist alone as an institution, or within a university (**Fakultät**)
university	union of two or more colleges within one educational institution (**Universität**)
Bachelor of Arts / Bachelor of Science	(*abbr* **B.A.** or **B.S.**) first university-level academic degree (**Baccalaureus Artium / Baccalaureus Scientiarum**)
high school	secondary school of learning; usually includes grades 9–12 or 10-12; on graduation the student receives the high school diploma (**Gymnasium, Oberschule**)
business administration	graduate course of study that prepares students for later work in business management, marketing, personnel, etc. (**Betriebswirtschaftslehre**)
major	main field of study during undergraduate education (**Hauptfach**)

grade point average	(*abbr* **GPA**) average grade attained during an educational program; computed by multiplying the value attached to the grade (A = 4.0, B = 3.0, C = 2.0, D = 1.0, F = 0) by the number of credits given for the course (1 hour of class per week for one semester is one credit) and dividing by the total number of credits received during the program (**Notendurchschnitt**)
Law School Admission Test	(*abbr* **LSAT**) standardized test given to college graduates nationwide to determine their ability to study law; one of the more important scores on which admission to a law school is based (**Zulassungsprüfung für ein rechtswissenschaftliches Studium**)
graduate education	program of study following completion of a bachelor's program, e.g. law or medicine (**Universitätsausbildung nach einem ersten Universitätsabschluß**)
JD	(*abbr* = **juris doctor**) degree awarded after completion of law school (**Doktor der Rechte, erster juristischer Grad**)
criminal law	area of law dealing with violations of statutes for which punishment is imposed; also called **penal law** (**Strafrecht**)
constitutional law	area of law dealing with the provisions of the **constitution**, which is the fundamental law of a nation and establishes the various branches or departments of the government, their powers, and guarantees civil and human rights (**Verfassungsrecht**)
civil procedure	area of law dealing with the requirements of private litigation, e.g. how to initiate a law suit, jurisdiction of the courts, etc. (**Zivilprozeßrecht**)
criminal procedure	area of law dealing with the requirements of criminal litigation and the rights of an accused (**Strafprozeßrecht**)
evidence	title of required course in *US* law schools; teaches students the law relating to the admission of evidence at trial (**Recht der Beweisführung**)
remedies	title of required course in *US* law schools; teaches students the law determining what a plaintiff may be awarded by a court to compensate for injury caused by a defendant and the implications of suing for that remedy (**Recht der zulässigen Rechtsbehelfe**)
elective	non-required course at a university or within a course of studies (**Wahlfach**)
Code of Civil Procedure	compilation of laws relating to the permissible manner of pursuing a law suit in court (**Zivilprozeßordnung**)
bar	group or class of practicing lawyers within a particular jurisdiction, e.g. the California bar, the American bar (**die Anwaltschaft**)
bar examination	state licensing examination for lawyers who intend to practice law within the jurisdiction (**juristisches Staatsexamen**)

bar review course	privately offered cram course to help students study for and pass the bar examination (Repetitorium)
law firm	partnership of lawyers practicing together within one business organization (Rechtsanwaltskanzlei)
to clerk for a judge	to work for a judge as a young lawyer, usually immediately upon leaving law school (als wissenschaftlicher Mitarbeiter an einem Obergericht arbeiten)
public defender	public official hired to work within a state office by defending indigent persons who have been accused of having committed a crime (vom Staat gestellter Verteidiger)
in-house lawyer	lawyer who works within a company on the company's legal staff (Syndikus)
non-profit organization	charitable foundation, organization that survives on donations and does not work for profit (gemeinnütziger Verein)
administrative agency	part of the executive branch of the government which is responsible for the enforcement of the law (Verwaltungsbehörde)
to hang out a shingle	to begin working independently as a one-man law firm (sich selbständig machen)
attorney	lawyer who is actually practicing law (as opposed to e.g. a professor or judge) (Rechtsanwalt)
client	person who hires a lawyer to represent him (Mandant / Mandantin)
mergers and acquisitions	(abbr M&A) department of a law firm which focuses on preparing the documents and agreements necessary to bring about the purchase of one firm by another (acquisition) or the combination of two firms into one (merger) (Fusionen und Übernahmen)
banking	department of a law firm which focuses on negotiating financial agreements and preparing the necessary documents for financing (Abteilung für Bankwesen)
tax	department of a law firm which focuses on fiscal problems, e.g. personal and corporate income tax, and devises methods of saving taxes for its clients (Steuerabteilung)
litigator	lawyer specialized in representing clients in court
litigation	to present one's case in a court of law for resolution of a dispute (Prozeßführung)
professional judgeship	judge's position within a legal system that appoints lawyers as judges immediately after they have finished law school (Berufsrichterschaft)
executive branch	branch of the government that is responsible for enforcing laws (Exekutive)

government	the executive and legislative branches of the state, the state in general (**Staat**)
prosecutor's office	office of the government responsible for bringing individuals accused of having committed a crime to court to answer for the charges (**Staatsanwaltschaft**)
public defender's office	office of the government responsible for defending individuals accused of having committed a crime who cannot afford to pay for a private attorney (**Behörde für die öffentliche Verteidigung von Angeklagten**)
minimum fee schedules	lists of minimum amounts a lawyer is permitted to charge for specified legal services; usually established by the bar association responsible for the particular lawyer; considered to be illegal price fixing in the United States; see Appendix B for U.S. Supreme Court's decision in *Goldfarb v. Virginia State Bar* (**Bundesanwaltsgebührenordnung oder Anwaltsgebührenordnungen der Einzelstaaten**)
bar association	professional organization of lawyers, responsible for monitoring attorney's conduct (**Rechtsanwaltskammer**)
American Bar Association	umbrella organization for all bar associations in the U.S. (**amerikanische Anwaltskammer**)
Sherman Antitrust Act	antitrust act; federal statute prohibiting anticompetitive behavior (**Bundeskartellgesetz**)
trust	cartel (**Kartell**)
consulting fee	initial fee a lawyer charges for the time he expends in first meeting the client and hearing the alleged facts of the case (**Beratungsgebühr**)
retainer	fee paid to retain, or hire, a lawyer as one's own representative; this fee closes the contract between the individual and the lawyer and prohibits the lawyer from representing anyone from the opposing side of the dispute (**Honorar bei der Erteilung eines Mandats**)
hourly fee	fee a lawyer charges depending on how many "hours" she spends working on a legal problem for a client; usually recorded in terms of minutes and not full hours (**Stundenhonorar**)
flat fee	lawyer's fee that is set, rather than calculated for hours of work, for a particular job, e.g. a day of representing the client in court (**festes Honorar**)
contingency fee	lawyer's fee that is charged only if the lawyer wins the case for her client; usually a percentage, currently between 33.3 and 50 percent, of what the client is awarded at trial (**Erfolgshonorar**)
court costs	the price of having a court involved in resolving a legal dispute; usually the losing party to a law suit is required to pay the court costs for both parties (**Gerichtskosten**)

Wall Street firm	law firm located in the financial district of New York, originally on Wall Street; today a general term for any large law firm that pursues business with corporate clients (**Wall-Street Kanzlei**)

Legal Profession in England:

conversion course	one-year course of legal study to teach students who have completed a university program leading to the B.A. or the B.Sc., rather than the LL.B., the basics of law so that they can continue with practical legal education (**Umschulungskurs für den Anwaltsberuf**)
Common Professional Examination	(*abbr* CPE) name for the conclusion of the conversion course (**Abschluß des Umschulungskurses für den Anwaltsberuf**)
Diploma in Law	another name for the conclusion of the conversion course (**Abschluß des Umschulungskurses für den Anwaltsberuf**)
Bachelor of Laws	(*abbr* LL.B.) academic degree awarded at the successful completion of a three-year course of legal studies at an English university (**Baccalaureus Legum**)
core subjects	six areas of law that form the basics of first-level legal education in England (**Hauptfächer**)
trusts and equity	course offered within program of legal studies covering the trust, which is a method of passing property on to later generations or of establishing a foundation, and the field of equity (**Stiftungs- und Billigkeitsrecht**)
land law	law of real estate transfers from one person to another during life or after death (**Sachenrecht**)
solicitor	lawyer specialised in the office type of legal work rather than in litigation as the barrister
barrister	lawyer specialised in litigation rather than in the office type of legal work as the solicitor
law office	office of a number of solicitors working within one business structure (**Rechtsanwaltskanzlei**)
Legal Practice Course	(*abbr* LPC) one-year course of graduate legal education to prepare for the profession of solicitor (**juristisches Aufbaustudium**)
compulsory areas	mandatory or required subjects for the LPC; include conveyancing, wills probate and administration, business law and practice, litigation and advocacy (**Pflichtfächer**)
conveyancing	LPC course covering the law of real property transfers (**Lehre von der Eigentumsübertragung**)

wills probate and administration	LPC course covering the law of executing a will, probate court procedure, and administration of an estate (**Testamentsvollstreckung und Nachlaßverwaltung**)
business law and practice	LPC course covering the law of company organisation, organisation of a firm, commercial relations (**Wirtschaftsrecht und Wirtschaftspraxis**)
litigation and advocacy	LPC course covering the skill of presenting and arguing cases in court (**Prozeßführung und Vertretung**)
optional areas	non-required courses, electives (**Wahlfächer**)
private client work	legal services aimed at the legal problems individuals usually have (**juristische Praxis für Privatpersonen**)
corporate client work	legal services aimed at the legal problems companies usually have (**juristische Praxis für Firmen**)
training establishment	law office or organisation that gives students who have finished the LPC practical legal instruction to prepare them to become a solicitor (**Ausbildungskanzlei**)
trainee solicitor	apprentice solicitor, student working within a training establishment learning the practical skills needed to be a solicitor (**auszubildende(r) Jurist(in)**)
training contract	two-year contract entered into by the trainee solicitor and the training establishment providing for the practical legal education of the trainee (**Ausbildungsvertrag**)
training principal	solicitor within a training establishment to whom a trainee is assigned for one-on-one practical legal training (**Ausbildungsleiter**)
Professional Skills Course	twelve-day, sixty-hour program of vocational education offered to trainee solicitors at some time during their two-year training contract
heads	main areas of study or emphasis during the Professional Skills Course (**Hauptfächer**)
financial and business skills	one of three heads offered as part of the Professional Skills Course; covers commercial skills and financing arrangements (**Finanz- und Wirtschaftswesen**)
advocacy and communication skills	one of three heads offered as part of the Professional Skills Course; teaches students to formulate arguments, negotiate, get across their ideas to others (**Argumentations- und Kommunikationsfähigkeiten**)
ethics and client responsibilities	one of three heads offered as part of the Professional Skills Course; teaches students professional rules of conduct and their obligations toward clients (**Standesrecht**)
Roll of Solicitors	list of solicitors admitted to practice law

Bar Vocational Course	(*abbr* **BVC**) one-year graduate course of legal education to prepare student to become a barrister (**juristisches Aufbaustudium**)
Inns of Court	professional association of barristers responsible for providing barristers with sets of chambers, offering courses of legal education, and controlling admission to the Bar; include Gray's Inn, Lincoln's Inn, the Inner Temple, and the Middle Temple (**Vereinigungen der Barristers**)
to keep term	to attend twelve educational qualifying sessions at the barrister-student's Inn (**regelmäßig juristische Vorträge besuchen**)
set of chambers	group of individual offices within which a barrister practices law (**Bürogemeinschaft**)
pupilage	one year of practical legal training with a barrister; required to be admitted to the Bar (**Lehrlingszeit bei einem Barrister**)
provisional practising certificate	authorisation to practice law awarded to a student barrister after completing six months of pupilage (**vorläufige Zulassung als Barrister**)
tenancy	right to use an office within a set of chambers as a barrister (**Bürobenutzungsrecht**)
member of professional chambers	barrister practising law within a set of chambers (**Mitglied einer Bürogemeinschaft**)
assistant solicitor	beginning solicitor within a law firm who is not yet partner of the firm (**Solicitor bei Beginn seiner Tätigkeit**)
associate solicitor	more experienced solicitor than an assistant within a law firm before becoming partner
to probate a will	to have the validity of a will determined, pay off any remaining debts, collect the assets, and distribute them to the testator's heirs (**einen Nachlaß verwalten**)
will	document with which the testator (male) or testatrix (female) passes property on to his or her heirs after death; also called a last will and testament (**Testament**)
testator / testatrix	person who leaves a last will and testament; person who dies testate, as opposed to *s.o.* who dies without leaving a will who is said to die intestate (**Testator / -in**)
to die testate	to leave a will at death (**ein Testament hinterlassen**)
to die intestate	to die without leaving a will (**sterben, ohne ein Testament zu hinterlassen**)
heir	*s.o.* who has a right to property left after another person's death (**Erbe**)
to inherit property	to acquire ownership rights in real or personal property as a result of *s.o.'s* death (**erben**)
divorce	dissolution of marriage (**Scheidung**)

child custody	right to care, maintain, and supervise a child; on divorce the probate court will award custody rights to one of the parents (**Sorgerecht**)
to instruct a barrister	to pass a case file on to a barrister to permit the barrister to prepare the case for litigation (**einem Barrister einen Fall anvertrauen**)
Queen's Counsel	(*abbr* **QC**) outstanding barrister who is appointed by the Queen (or King, in which case the barrister is called **King's Counsel**, *abbr* **KC**) on the recommendation of the Lord Chancellor (**von der Königin / dem König bestellter Barrister**)
silks	another name for barristers who are QCs / KCs (**von der Königin / dem König bestellte Barristers**)
to apply for silk	to file a request with the Lord Chancellor to be reviewed and recommended to the reigning monarch for appointment as QC or KC (**die Bestellung durch die Königin / den König beantragen**)
junior	barrister who is not QC; less experienced, less outstanding barrister (**junger Barrister**)
contentious work	legal services involving litigation (**juristische Dienstleistungen, die mit der Führung eines Prozesses verbunden sind**)
non-contentious work	legal services not involving litigation (**juristische Dienstleistungen, die nicht mit der Führung eines Prozesses verbunden sind**)
to assess fees	to establish as a court the appropriate fees for a solicitor's work involving litigation (**Anwaltsgebühren festsetzen**)
fast-track case	case that is expected to be litigated within one day (**Schnellverfahren**)
costs follow the event	costs are borne by the loser of the law suit (**Anwaltskosten werden von der unterlegenen Partei getragen**)
between party assessment	court's assessment of the winner of a law suit's costs to be paid by the losing party (**Festsetzung der Anwaltskosten der im Prozeß obsiegenden Partei**)
solicitor and own client assessment	court's determination whether the client has to pay his solicitor the full amount of the fees the solicitor has charged the client (**Kontrolle der Anwaltsgebühren durch das Gericht**)
scale fees	fixed solicitor's fees based on the value of property conveyed (**in einer Gebührenordnung festgelegte Anwaltsgebühren**)
brief fee	barrister's fee for preparation of a case for litigation and for the first day in court (**Prozeßvorbereitungs- und Prozeßführungskosten für den ersten Tag vor Gericht**)
refresher	barrister's fee for an additional day in court after the first day (**zusätzliche Prozeßführungskosten**)

C. The Trial Process

In a system of procedural justice, the trial process plays a role that is far more significant than in a system of substantive justice. This section will acquaint you with the most important moves the parties to the law suit can make in progressing toward their goal of winning the trial.

1. Initiating a Law Suit

In order to initiate a law suit, the plaintiff must file a **complaint**. The complaint is a document that contains allegations of 1) the court's **jurisdiction** over the person of the defendant and the subject matter in dispute, 2) the facts relevant to the plaintiff's **cause of action**, and 3) a **prayer for relief**. **Personal** and **subject matter jurisdiction** will be discussed at length in Unit II, Chapter 2. Suffice it to say for the present that the plaintiff must claim in his complaint that the court has a right to require the defendant to appear and defend herself against the plaintiff's claims (personal jurisdiction) and a right to adjudicate the particular **issue in controversy** (subject matter jurisdiction). Furthermore, the plaintiff must claim a set of facts which, if true, would give the plaintiff the right under applicable law to prevail over the defendant. It is this set of legally relevant facts that make out the plaintiff's **cause of action**. The elements of the cause of action are determined by the law, meaning either case law or statutory law. If the law provides that a person who intentionally or negligently physically harms another person must pay for the damage caused, the elements of the cause of action roughly speaking would be: 1) the plaintiff's physical harm, 2) the defendant's conduct that caused this harm, 3) the defendant's intent or negligence in causing the harm. Finally, the plaintiff must indicate in the complaint what **remedy** the plaintiff is seeking. As you may recall, a remedy is what the plaintiff is suing the defendant to obtain in order to compensate for injuries the plaintiff claims the defendant has caused him. Usually, the plaintiff will be suing for money damages and the **prayer for relief**, admittedly a somewhat antiquated term, is a formal request addressed to the court asking it to order the defendant to pay a certain monetary sum to the plaintiff.

Once the complaint has been drafted, it must be filed with the court. Filing the complaint initiates the law suit and gives notice to the public that the suit is in process. In addition to filing the complaint with the court, the plaintiff must give the defendant formal notice of the pending law suit. To do so the plaintiff attaches a copy of the complaint to a **summons**, which is a formal order addressed to the defendant to appear in court to defend against the law suit. The summons notifies the defendant that if she does not respond, a **default judgment** will be entered against her. The complaint and the summons then have to be delivered to the defendant. Delivery of the summons and complaint is referred to as **service of process**. The most common method of serving process is personal service, but other methods are also available (see, Unit II, Chapter 2, B, 1 for more details on service of process).

When the defendant has been served, she will have a specified time within which to respond to the complaint. Several types of responses are available. The defendant may file a **motion to dismiss**, a **demurrer**, or an **answer**. The **motion to dismiss** claims that some procedural problem bars the law suit. The defendant may claim, for example, that the court does not have jurisdiction over her person or over the subject matter of the law suit. She could also claim that the **statute of limitations**, or the **limitation period** for filing an action, has run.

The **demurrer** claims that the plaintiff's complaint **fails to state a cause of action**. The test for determining whether the complaint states a cause of action requires the judge to assume, only for the sake of considering the demurrer, that all of the facts the plaintiff has claimed are true. Then the judge must ask whether the law would permit the plaintiff to prevail over the defendant in the law suit. If so, then the demurrer will be **dismissed** or **overruled**. If not, then the demurrer will be **sustained**, either with or without **leave to amend**. A demurrer permits the parties to the law suit to clarify what the law exactly provides before going into the trail itself with all of its expense and inconvenience. One might wonder why that would ever be necessary considering that it is usually lawyers who draft complaints and one expects lawyers to know the law. Unfortunately, the law is often unclear, particularly with respect to the question of how it applies to a new, and in some senses unique, set of facts. To give you an idea of when and why a demurrer is filed, refer back to the case *Ploof v. Putnam* in Unit I, Chapter 1, B., 2. That case went all the way to the Supreme Court for the State of Vermont on a demurrer. As you probably recall, the case involved a claim for money damages for loss of the plaintiff's sail boat and physical injury to himself and to his family. The plaintiff had tried to moor his boat at the defendant's dock during a particularly severe storm. The defendant untied the boat and prevented the plaintiff from mooring with the result that the boat sank and the plaintiff and his family were injured. When the plaintiff filed his complaint, the defendant **demurred**. It was the defendant's position that Vermont state law did not provide the plaintiff with the **justification of necessity** or the **lesser evils justification**. If available, this justification would have given the plaintiff the right to use the defendant's dock and even to damage it in order to save himself from a greater evil, namely here the loss of his boat and physical injury. If not available, the plaintiff would not have had this right with the result that the defendant would have had the right to defend his dock from the plaintiff's unlawful use of it by untying the boat. If the defendant had the right to defend his dock, then the plaintiff could not collect any money damages from him, or stated differently, the plaintiff's complaint would have failed to **state a cause of action**. Before the case was decided, Vermont law was unclear on the issue. The trial court first had to rule on the demurrer. That ruling could be appealed by the losing party to the intermediate court of appeals, and the court of appeals' decision could be appealed to the Vermont Supreme Court. Once the Vermont Supreme Court reached its decision, the law of the State of Vermont was clear, because that decision bound all lower courts in Vermont. In this case the court held that the necessity defense was available and therefore that the plaintiff had a good cause of action against the defendant. That decision, however, did not close the case in the plaintiff's favor. It merely held that the plaintiff's complaint **withstood the defendant's demurrer**, meaning that a trial indeed should take place. The parties then had to return to the trial court where the defendant had to file an **answer** to the plaintiff's complaint.

In the **answer**, the defendant can include **admissions, denials, defenses**, and **counterclaims. Admissions** mean that the defendant **admits**, or agrees to, the truth of some of the facts in the plaintiff's complaint. **Denials** indicate that the defendant disagrees with, or **denies** the truth of some of the facts in the plaintiff's complaint. In **defenses**, the defendant claims that she either had a right to do what she did or that she should be excused from paying for some or all of the plaintiff's damage. Finally, in a **counterclaim** the defendant essentially files a complaint against the plaintiff, arguing that the plaintiff in fact should be ordered to pay for damage he caused the defendant. Let us consider a very simple case in which the plaintiff **alleges** in his complaint that for no apparent reason, the defendant intentionally punched him in the nose with the result that the plaintiff had medical expenses and loss of pay for days missed at work. In an **admission** the defendant could admit that she did in fact intentionally punch the plaintiff in the nose. In a **denial** the defendant could claim that she did have a reason for doing so and that this reason was apparent to the plaintiff. The reason could have been that the plaintiff attacked the defendant first. By maintaining that the plaintiff started the fist fight, the defendant would be claiming the **justificatory defense** of self-protection or self-defense, which would have given the defendant the right to punch the plaintiff in the nose. Finally, the defendant in a **counterclaim** could contend that the plaintiff actually owes her money for medical costs and lost pay.

After the defendant has filed an **answer**, the plaintiff may **reply**. The reply, also called the **replication**, is a response to the defendant's claims in her answer, particularly if they raise a counterclaim. Generally the reply will contain admissions and/or denials. Finally the defendant can respond to the plaintiff's reply in her **rejoinder**.

The **complaint,** the **answer,** the **reply,** and the **rejoinder** constitute the **pleadings**. It is the pleadings that provide the framework for the factual and legal issues at trial. Factual issues are raised when one party denies the truth of the other party's allegations. If the parties are in dispute as to the facts, each has a right to a trial, and often a trial by jury. As discussed in Chapter 2, the main job for the jury is to determine what evidence to believe and thus what the facts really are.

If the parties are in agreement on the facts, a trial is unnecessary. The judge can resolve the legal dispute by simply applying the law to the facts the parties agree are true. In such cases, one of the parties may make a **motion for summary judgment,** asking the judge to do just that. The judge will grant the motion if no facts are in dispute or if it is clear that any factual disputes cannot be resolved through a trial, perhaps because a necessary witness cannot be found to testify or because relevant documents have been destroyed.

Even if the parties are not in agreement on the facts, one of them may try to avoid going to trial by making a **motion for judgment on the pleadings**. This motion is somewhat similar to the **demurrer,** but it can be made by either the plaintiff or the defendant after all of the pleadings have been filed. It asks the judge to believe the facts most favorable to the other party, or the **non-moving party**. Still, the **moving party** claims, the non-moving party cannot win the law suit as a matter of law. Essentially the moving party is saying: "Even if we go to trail and the jury decides all of the factual issues in favor of my opponent, I will still win the law suit if the law is correctly applied." If that is true, then of course there is no need for a trial and the judge will grant the motion.

The judge will make one final effort to avoid trial by holding a **pretrial conference** to determine whether the parties are capable of reaching a **pretrial settlement,** or a voluntary compromise of their dispute. Since a trial is expensive, slow, and an uncertain process for resolving disputes, the parties may be willing to agree to split their differences and avoid it. If a pretrial settlement cannot be reached, the trial will begin.

2. Pretrial Discovery

The **pretrial discovery process** begins as soon as the pleadings have been filed. The purpose of pretrial discovery is to permit the parties to gather the evidence they need to prove their case in order to prevent surprise at trial, to expedite the trial process, and to assist the parties in deciding whether a trial is at all worth-while. Each party has the *right* to engage in discovery and today courts generally tend to interpret this right very broadly. If one party refuses to cooperate, the other party can turn to the court for an **order to compel compliance**. To facilitate the gathering of evidence, both parties are equipped with certain **tools of discovery**, such as **interrogatories, depositions, requests for admissions, requests for the production of documents**, and **physical and mental examinations**.

An **interrogatory** is addressed to one of the parties. It is a written list of questions the other party is required to answer in writing and under oath. The parties have considerable latitude in the questions they are permitted to ask in an interrogatory. The fact that the information sought may later prove inadmissible as evidence at trial is not the question here. That question will be resolved later at the trial itself. Important is that each party have the opportunity to determine what the facts surrounding the case are.

A **deposition** is an oral interview of a party or a witness under oath. The person being deposed is referred to as the **deponent**. It is much like the taking of testimony at a trial. When one party decides **to depose** a witness, the other party must be informed and have the opportunity to be present and thus to **cross-examine** the witness. In addition, a **court reporter** must be present to prepare a certified copy of exactly what was said during the deposition. The deposition is useful not only for discovering information prior to trial, but also for use at the trial itself. It can be read to the jury, for example, if the witness cannot easily be called into court to testify, because she lives too far away from the court, is ill or otherwise inconvenienced. Since the witness's testimony was taken under oath and the other party had the opportunity to cross-examine, the preliminary requirements for admission of this testimony into evidence have been fulfilled. If either party claims that a question posed during the deposition was not permissible under the **rules of evidence** governing the trial process, the judge can rule on that party's objection before the deposition is read to the jury. If the judge sustains it, the question itself and the testimony in response to it will simply not be read to the jury. As you can probably imagine, jurors can become rather bored listening to someone read something like a deposition to them. For that reason, today a video recording of the deposition is usually made and shown to the jury when the witness does not actually come to court to testify during the trial.

Read the following text on deposition tactics:

> "The greatest advantages of a deposition over other forms of discovery are that the
> deponent is answering directly rather than through her lawyer, that the deponent
> does not know in advance what the precise questions will be, and that the questioner
> can ask follow-up questions suggested by the answers given. (Note, however, that a
> 5 careful lawyer defending a deponent will prepare him for the deposition, covering
> beforehand the questions that are likely to be asked.) The greatest disadvantage of a

deposition is its cost. At a minimum, it includes the cost of the lawyer preparing for, travelling to, and attending the deposition, and the reporter's fee for the transcript. Subtler advantages include the opportunity to assess potential witnesses – will they
10   stand up under cross-examination, will they present a sympathetic and believable figure to the jury, etc.; the opportunity to assess a lawyer for the other side – is she well prepared and skillful, etc.; the opportunity to show to the other side how well-prepared and skillful you are; and the possibility of establishing facts that might help in settlement negotiations. Subtler disadvantages include the danger of dis-
15   covering and recording information unfavorable to one's client; and tipping one's hand on possible lines of analysis or attack.

"Lawyers have certain rules of thumb about depositions. For example, a lawyer almost never deposes her own client, since she can learn everything she needs to
20   know from an informal interview. (There are exceptions. For example, the client may be in failing health.) A lawyer deposes friendly witnesses relatively infrequently. (An exception, as above, should be made if the witness will be unavailable at trial.) The lawyer usually can learn enough from a friendly witness in an informal interview; in addition, the nuisance and formality of a deposition sometimes risks alienating the
25   witness. Unless court-imposed limitations on discovery or considerations of expense preclude a lawyer from doing so, a lawyer will ordinarily depose all important unfriendly witnesses. Sometimes, in corporate litigation, the most important depo-nent is a person far down in the defendant's corporate hierarchy who really knows what happened. Sometimes the most important deponent is the highest person in the
30   hierarchy; once such a person is deposed, she may realize what an expense and embarrassment the lawsuit is going to be, and may agree to settle the case on favorable terms. Sometimes the order in which witnesses are deposed makes a dif-ference in the effectiveness with which information is discovered."

G. Hazard, Jr. /C. Tait / W. Fletcher, *Pleading and Procedure: Cases and Materials*, 7th ed., The Foundation Press, Inc.: Westbury, New York (1994) 929–30.

A somewhat indirect "tactical" advantage of using depositions is that the younger, less experienced lawyers in a law firm can be sent to take them and thereby learn how to examine witnesses in a trial setting without doing as much damage as they might do at the trial itself and in the presence of a jury.

A **request for admission** is a written question addressed to the opposing party of the form "Do you admit that ..." If the other party does admit the truth of the statement then the issue will not have to be proved at trial. In a jury trial the judge will instruct the jury that the parties agree as to the truth of the admitted statement. In a non-jury trial the judge himself will simply assume that the state-ment is true when reaching a judgment. The request for admission, as all tools of discovery, is a method of shortening the expensive trial process.

A **request for the production of documents** is addressed to a party or a witness and requires that person to do just that – turn over certain documented information. Suppose you are representing the plaintiff in a **toxic torts case**. You need to prove that the defendant company, by illegally dumping dangerous chemicals into a river, poisoned the river water, which eventually landed in the local water supply causing serious illness and injury to your client. To prove that, you could ask the defendant to hand over all invoices paid and billed out over a certain period of time. These invoices will show what the defendant was purchasing and selling, giving you insight into its production process. The invoices, or the lack thereof, will also show whether the defendant paid an approved company to dispose of any toxic wastes properly. As you can probably imagine, the other party will often not like the idea of turning over internal company documents to help you prove your case, and there are a number of ways of circumventing your request. One of them is to provide so many documents that your task becomes one of looking for a needle in a haystack. Imagine looking out the window of your law office and seeing several moving vans unloading more cartons of documents that you can fit into your entire building. On the other hand, the opposing party might have very good reasons for not wanting to release certain documents. They may contain trade secrets, for example, which the party has a right to protect. If so, the party called upon to produce certain documents may turn to the court in charge of the case and request a **protective order**, which the court may or may not grant. Sometimes a judge will require the party to turn the documents over to the court and the court will select the information that is discoverable and turn only it over to the other party.

On court order, a party may have to submit to a **mental** or **physical examination** by a doctor of the other party's choice. Normally, the tools of discovery are available and can be used by either party to the law suit without any need to get a court order to force the other party to comply. Since medical examinations by their very nature involve infringements of personal autonomy, they can be obtained only on court order and, of course, only if they are directly relevant to some issue of the law suit.

To understand how serious the duty to comply with discovery requests really is, read the following case:

National Hockey League v. Metropolitan Hockey Club, Inc.
427 U.S. 639 (1976)

PER CURIAM.

This case arises out of the dismissal, under Fed.R.Civ.P. 37, of respondents' antitrust action against petitioners for failure to timely answer written interrogatories as ordered by the District Court. The Court of Appeal for the Third Circuit reversed the judgment of dismissal, finding that the District Court had abused its discretion. The question presented is whether the Court of Appeals was correct in so concluding. Rule 37 (b) (2) provides in pertinent part as follows:

> "If a party ... fails to obey an order to provide or permit discovery ... the court in which the action is pending may make such orders in regard to the failure as are just, and among others the following:
>
> ...
>
> "(C) An order striking out pleadings or parts thereof, or staying further proceedings until the order is obeyed, or dismissing the action or proceeding or any part thereof or rendering a judgment by default against the disobedient party."

This Court held in Societe Internationale v. Rogers, 357 U.S. 197, 212 (1958), that Rule 37

> "should not be construed to authorize dismissal of [a] complaint because of petitioner's noncompliance with a pretrial production order when it has been established that failure to comply has been due to inability, and not to willfulness, bad faith, or any fault of petitioner."

While there have been amendments to the Rule since the decision in Rogers, neither the parties, the District Court, nor the Court of Appeals suggested that the changes would affect the teachings of the quoted language from that decision.

The District Court, in its memorandum opinion directing that respondents' complaint be dismissed, summarized the factual history of the discovery proceeding in these words:

> "After seventeen months where crucial interrogatories remained substantially unanswered despite numerous extensions granted at the eleventh hour and, in many instances, beyond the eleventh hour, and notwithstanding several admonitions by the Court and promises and commitments by the plaintiffs, the Court must and does conclude that the conduct of the plaintiffs demonstrates the callous disregard of responsibilities counsel owe to the Court and to their opponents. The practices of the plaintiffs exemplify flagrant bad faith when after being expressly directed to perform an act by a

date certain, viz., June 14, 1974, they failed to perform and compounded that noncompliance by waiting until five days afterwards before they filed any motions. Moreover, this action was taken in the face of warnings that their failure to provide certain information could result in the imposition of sanc-
50   tions under Fed.R.Civ.P. 37. If the sanction of dismissal is not warranted by the circumstances of this case, then the Court can envisage no set of facts whereby that sanction should ever be applied." 63 F.R.D. 641, 656 (1974).

The Court of Appeals, in reversing the order of the District Court by a divided vote,
55   stated:

"After carefully reviewing the record, we conclude that there is insufficient evidence to support a finding that M-GB's failure to file supplemental answers by June 14, 1974 was in flagrant bad faith, willful or intentional."
60   531 F.2d 1188, 1195 (1976).

The Court of Appeals did not question any of the findings of historical fact which had been made by the District Court, but simply concluded that there was in the record evidence of "extenuating factors." The Court of Appeals emphasized that
65   none of the parties had really pressed discovery until after a consent decree was entered between petitioners and all of the other original plaintiffs except the respondents approximately one year after the commencement of the litigation. It also noted that respondents' counsel took over the litigation, which previously had been managed by another attorney, after the entry of the consent decree, and that respond-
70   ents' counsel encountered difficulties in obtaining some of the requested information. The Court of Appeals also referred to a colloquy during the oral argument on petitioners' motion to dismiss in which respondents' lead counsel assured the District Court that he would not knowingly and willfully disregard the final deadline.

75   While the Court of Appeals stated that the District Court was required to consider the full record in determining whether to dismiss for failure to comply with discovery orders, ... we think that the comprehensive memorandum of the District Court supporting its order of dismissal indicates that the court did just that. That record shows that the District Court was extremely patient in its efforts to allow the re-
80   spondents ample time to comply with its discovery orders. Not only did respondents fail to file their responses on time, but the responses which they ultimately did file were found by the District Court to be grossly inadequate.

The question, of course, is not whether this Court, or whether the Court of Appeals,
85   would as an original matter have dismissed the action; it is whether the District Court abused its discretion in so doing. ... Certainly the findings contained in the memorandum opinion of the District Court quoted earlier in this opinion are fully supported by the record. We think that the lenity evidenced in the opinion of the Court of Appeals, while certainly a significant factor in considering the imposition of
90   sanctions under Rule 37, cannot be allowed to wholly supplant other and equally necessary considerations embodied in that Rule.

There is a natural tendency on the part of reviewing courts, properly employing the benefit of hindsight, to be heavily influenced by the severity of outright dismissal as a sanction for failure to comply with a discovery order. It is quite reasonable to
95 conclude that a party who has been subjected to such an order will feel duly chastened, so that even though he succeeds in having the order reversed on appeal he will nonetheless comply promptly with future discovery orders of the district court.

But here, as in other areas of the law, the most severe in the spectrum of sanctions
100 provided by statute or rule must be available to the district court in appropriate cases, not merely to penalize those whose conduct may be deemed to warrant such a sanction, but to deter those who might be tempted to such conduct in the absence of such a deterrent. If the decision of the Court of Appeals remained undisturbed in this case, it might well be that these respondents would faithfully comply with all future
105 discovery orders entered by the District Court in this case. But other parties to other lawsuits would feel freer than we think Rule 37 contemplates they should feel to flout other discovery orders of other district courts. Under the circumstances of this case, we hold that the District Judge did not abuse his discretion in finding bad faith on the part of these respondents, and concluding that the extreme sanction of dismissal was
110 appropriate in this case by reason of respondents' "flagrant bad faith" and their counsel's "callous disregard" of their responsibilities. Therefore, the petition for a writ of certiorari is granted and the judgment of the Court of Appeals is reversed.

Analysis

Note that the decision in this case was reached by the U.S. Supreme Court and announced **per curiam**. A **per curiam opinion** is usually rather short and merely announces a court's holding without providing detailed arguments in support or even indicating which judge wrote the opinion. As you can tell from the last sentence in this case, the Supreme Court here granted the writ of certiorari and reversed the decision of the court of appeals simultaneously in this one per curiam opinion. In other cases, the Supreme Court will first consider the petition for the writ of certiorari and issue a, usually very short, opinion granting or denying the writ. The writ itself is an order to the lower court to certify and send up the record in the case for review. If the writ is granted, the Supreme Court will subsequently consider the parties' written and oral arguments. Written arguments are contained in a document called an **appellate brief**. In the case that you have read, the Court apparently decided the case based only on the petition for certiorari.

The issue in this case is whether the **U.S. District Court,** or the trial court in the federal court system (see Unit II for an explanation of the U.S. court systems), **abused its discretion** by dismissing the **respondent's** law suit, here an **antitrust**

action, against **petitioner.** As you know, the petitioner is the party who petitions the Supreme Court for a writ of certiorari to have the decision of the lower court reviewed. The **respondent** is the name given to the other party. **Antitrust laws,** such as the **Sherman Act** and the **Clayton Act,** prohibit cartels and some other forms of anticompetitive behavior. In the United States, a private party can bring an action against another private party for violation of the antitrust laws, which is referred to as an **antitrust action.** In this case the U.S. District Court **dismissed the action** under Rule 37 of the **Federal Rules of Civil Procedure** (*abbr* **Fed.R.Civ.P.**). The intermediate appellate court, which in the federal system is called the **U.S. Court of Appeals** for one of eleven numbered circuits, here the third, reversed the decision of the trial court thereby **reinstating** the plaintiff's law suit.

The **pertinent,** or relevant, **part** of Rule 37 is quoted in the case and indicates that the court in which the **action is pending,** or the court in which the action has been initiated but not yet decided, "may make such orders ... as are just." This language gives the court **discretion,** or leaves it up to the court's good judgment, to decide whether to make any orders imposing **sanctions,** or penalties, in response to a party's failure to cooperate in the discovery process. In this particular case, the respondent had failed to answer **written interrogatories** on time. A court **abuses its discretion** when it makes unfair or unjust orders in the sense that they are too severe in relation to the violation committed. As you can see from part (C) of the Rule, the court is permitted to **strike out the pleadings** or parts of them. The pleadings that would be most relevant here would be the plaintiff's complaint and the defendant's answer. If, for example, the plaintiff had refused to cooperate in the discovery of certain facts relevant to one of his claims, the court could simply strike, or exclude, the factual allegations from the complaint. The court is also permitted to **stay the proceedings,** or bring them to a standstill, until the offending party cooperates in the discovery process, or even render a **judgment by default** against the offending party, meaning that the law suit would be decided in favor of the other party. Here the court in its **memorandum opinion,** which indicates only the decision the court reached and the orders it issued but does not include any reasons supporting the decision, dismissed the plaintiff's complaint.

In reviewing the trial court's order dismissing the action, the court of appeals considered the **record** in the case, which includes all of the pleadings and other relevant documents, and all **transcripts,** or verbatim reports, of depositions or courtroom proceedings in the case. The court of appeals indicated that discovery was not really pushed forward until after a **consent decree** had been entered into between the parties. A **consent decree** is an agreement between the parties that a decree, or order, justly determines their rights. We do not have enough information from the case to determine what the consent decree contained, but it is not relevant to the main issue here, namely whether the trial court abused its discretion in dismissing the plaintiff's action. Ultimately, the court of appeals decided that the appellants had not **knowingly and willfully** refused to cooperate in discovery that and therefore the trial court should not have dismissed the complaint.

The U.S. Supreme Court points out in lines 84-86, that the correct **standard of review** is not whether the court of appeals, or whether the Supreme Court itself, would have done the same as the trial court if they had the case to decide as an **original matter**, meaning as a trial court. Instead an appellate court is required to determine only whether the trial court's response was an abuse of its discretion. The Supreme Court found that the Court of Appeals showed too much **lenity**, or mercy, in reversing the trial court's order. Here the word **lenity** is used in its nonlegal meaning. It also has a legal meaning in the sense of the **lenity rule**. This rule requires a judge to resolve any ambiguity in a criminal statute in favor of the defendant.

Although dismissing an action seems like a particularly severe measure, Rule 37 authorizes it. The Supreme Court found that dismissal should be available to the trial court not only to penalize the particular plaintiff, but also to **deter** others from disobeying discovery orders. A **deterrent** is a threat of some negative consequence for misbehavior. The term **deterrence** is also used within the field of criminal law in contrast to **retribution** and **rehabilitation** or **resocialization** as a purpose of punishment. Retribution is oriented toward the **eye-for-an-eye** theory of paying the criminal offender back for his wrongful conduct through punishment. Rehabilitation is oriented toward making the offender a better person through punishment. Deterrence is divided into **general** and **specific deterrence**. The former theory states that punishing offenders will hinder others from committing similar offenses because of fear of being punished themselves. The latter theory states that punishing the offender will keep him from committing crimes, for example because he cannot while imprisoned.

Questions on the Text

1. Who was the original plaintiff in this case? What was he called on the intermediate appellate court level?

2. State in your own words a) the facts of the case, b) the legal history of the case, c) the issue raised on appeal, d) the holding, and e) the ratio decidendi of the case.

3. The text mentions some of the advantages of discovery. Nonetheless, discovery is not available to parties in Continental European legal systems. What are some arguments against it?

Terminology

prayer for relief

formal request addressed to the court asking it to declare the plaintiff's right to receive a specified remedy, e.g. money damages (**Klagebegehren**)

issue in controversy

legal question raised in a law suit, topic of dispute between the parties (**Streitfrage**)

default judgment

judgment entered against the defendant for failure to answer the plaintiff's complaint, or against either party for failure to proceed with the action as required (**Versäumnisurteil**)

service of process

delivery of complaint and summons to the defendant to put him on notice that a law suit has been filed against him and that he needs to defend (**Zustellung der Klage und der Ladung**)

motion to dismiss

formal request addressed to the court asking it to refuse to hear the plaintiff's case because of some procedural defect, such as the court's lack of jurisdiction over the defendant's person or over the subject matter of the law suit; under federal law the motion to dismiss includes the demurrer (**Antrag auf Klageabweisung wegen Unzulässigkeit**)

demurrer

motion for dismissal of the complaint because it fails to state a cause of action (**Antrag auf Klageabweisung wegen Unschlüssigkeit**)

leave to amend

permission granted by the court to a party to revise a pleading, usually the complaint after the court has sustained the defendant's demurrer (**Zulassung der Ergänzung oder Berichtigung eines Schriftsatzes**)

lesser evils justification

defense to a criminal charge based on the defendant's claim to have saved a higher-valued interest by sacrificing the lower-valued interest protected by the criminal norm he is charged with violating, also called **justification of necessity, necessity as a justification** (**rechtfertigender Notstand**)

admission

agreement to the truth of a factual claim; usually contained in the defendant's answer and relating to the plaintiff's complaint (**Zugeständnis**)

denial

claim that a factual claim is false; usually contained in the defendant's answer and relating to the plaintiff's complaint (**Bestreiten**)

counterclaim

legal claim filed by defendant in response to plaintiff's complaint; statement of a cause of action against the original plaintiff in a case (**Widerklage**)

to allege

to claim, to contend, to maintain that certain facts are true (**behaupten**)

justificatory defense	defendant's claim that he had a good and legally recognized reason for what he did; defeats a plaintiff's claim in a private law suit and a criminal charge (**Rechtfertigung als Verteidigungsvorbringen**)
reply	plaintiff's response to the defendant's counterclaim, also called **replication** (**Replik**)
rejoinder	defendant's response to plaintiff's reply (**Duplik**)
pleadings	documents filed in the initiation of a law suit which define the parties' factual claims; they include the plaintiff's complaint, the defendant's answer, the plaintiff's reply, and the defendant's rejoinder (**Schriftsätze**)
motion for summary judgment	formal request addressed to the court asking it to reach a judgment in the case without a trial because the parties are not in disagreement on the facts of the case (**Antrag auf ein Urteil im summarischen Verfahren**)
motion for judgment on the pleadings	formal request addressed to the court asking it to reach a judgment for the party making the motion, or the moving party, on the assumption that the facts most favorable to the other party, or the non-moving party, are true; this motion, unlike the motion for summary judgment, is not made because the parties agree on the facts, but because one party is of the opinion that the law does not permit the other party to prevail in the law suit even if one assumes that the facts he claims are true (**Antrag auf ein Urteil, das allein auf den Schriftsätzen beruht und auf Rechtsfragen beschränkt ist**)
moving party	party making a motion (**Antragsteller**)
non-moving party	party against whom a motion has been made (**Antragsgegner**)
pretrial conference	judge's conference with the parties to a pending law suit held before the trial begins in an effort to reach a pretrial settlement (**Besprechung vor der Eröffnung der Hauptverhandlung**)
pretrial settlement	voluntary agreement between the parties that ends their dispute before the trial has begun (**außergerichtlicher Vergleich vor der Eröffnung der Hauptverhandlung**)
pretrial discovery	process of gathering evidence before the trial begins (**Sammeln von Beweismaterial vor der Eröffnung der Hauptverhandlung**)
order to compel compliance	judicial order addressed to a party who is not cooperating in the discovery process requiring his cooperation (**Anordnung, ein Begehren zu erfüllen**)
tools of discovery	methods of gathering evidence before trial available to both parties as a matter of right; they include the interrogatory, deposition, request for admissions, request for the production of documents, and physical and mental examinations (**Mittel der Entdeckung von Beweismaterial**)

interrogatory	written list of questions addressed to a party to a law suit that have to be answered in writing under oath; one tool of discovery (**Fragenkatalog zur Aufklärung der Beweislage**)
deposition	oral interview of a witness or party to a law suit taken under oath and recorded by a court reporter in the presence of both parties (**mündliche Befragung zur Aufklärung der Beweislage**)
deponent	person being questioned during a deposition (**der Befragte**)
to depose	to take the sworn testimony of a witness or party to a law suit during the pretrial discovery process (**befragen**)
to cross-examine	to ask a witness who has been questioned by the opposing party questions related to the witness' testimony for the purpose of discrediting it (**ein Kreuzverhör vornehmen**)
court reporter	a court official responsible for recording testimony verbatim and preparing the transcript of the session (**Protokollführer**)
rules of evidence	rules governing the introduction during trial and use of various forms of proof of facts relevant for the trial (**Regeln zulässiger Beweisführung**)
settlement negotiations	discussions between the parties aimed at reaching a resolution of their dispute without going to or completing trial (**Verhandlungen zur Herbeiführung eines Vergleichs**)
friendly witness	a person who is expected to testify favorably toward the party who questions him (**Zeuge der eigenen Partei**)
unfriendly witness	a person who has been called to testify by the opposing party; a person who is expected to testify unfavorably toward the party who questions him; also called hostile witness (**Zeuge der Gegenpartei**)
hostile witness	a person who has been called to testify by the opposing party; a person who is expected to testify unfavorably toward the party who questions him; also called unfriendly witness (**Zeuge der Gegenpartei**)
corporate litigation	trial in which at least one party is a corporation (**Führung eines Prozesses für eine Gesellschaft; Gerichtsverhandlung im Namen einer Gesellschaft**)
corporate hierarchy	structure of responsibility and power within a corporation (**Hierarchie innerhalb einer Firma**)
request for admission	written question asking the opposing party to a law suit whether he agrees that a certain statement is true with the effect that if he does that fact does not have to be proved at trial; one tool of discovery (**Aufforderung, etwas zuzugestehen**)
request for the production of documents	request that the other party to the law suit or a witness turn over written records for inspection prior to trial; one tool of discovery (**Aufforderung, Urkunden vorzulegen**)

toxic torts case	law suit involving the emission into the atmosphere, the depositing into the water, or the burial into the ground of extremely poisonous substances (**Rechtsfall, der ein Umweltdelikt betrifft**)
protective order	court order stopping one party to a law suit from discovering information from the other which the latter is not under a legal obligation to release (**Anordnung einer Schutzmaßnahme**)
mental examination	medical examination conducted by a psychiatrist or psychologist to determine a person's mental capacities; one tool of discovery (**psychiatrische oder psychologische Untersuchung**)
physical examination	medical examination conducted by a physician to determine a person's physical capacities or the extent of any injuries; one tool of discovery (**medizinische Untersuchung**)
per curiam opinion	opinion of the court; usually short opinion published without extensive argumentation in support of the holding; unsigned opinion representing the opinion of the court in general rather than that of a particular judge or group of judges (**Rechtsauffassung eines Kollegialgerichts**)
appellate brief	written document containing a short statement of the legal arguments supporting one party's position on appeal (**Revisionsantrag**)
abuse of discretion	unfair or unjust exercise of a decision maker's power over a situation; misuse of leeway to decide how to deal with a situation (**Ermessensmißbrauch**)
antitrust law	law prohibiting the formation of a cartel or anticompetitive practices (**Kartellgesetz**)
Sherman Act	antitrust act; federal statute prohibiting anticompetitive practices (**Bundeskartellgesetz**)
Clayton Act	antitrust act; addition to the Sherman Act prohibiting mergers, price discrimination, exclusive dealing if effect is to reduce competition (**Gesetz zur Ergänzung des Bundeskartellgesetzes**)
antitrust action	law suit charging violation of the antitrust laws (**Klage in einer Kartellsache**)
to dismiss an action	judge's decision refusing to hear a case; court's rejection of a law suit (**eine Klage abweisen**)
to reinstate an action	to restore a law suit that has been dismissed; to revive a dismissed law suit (**Aufhebung eines die Klage abweisenden Urteils**)
Federal Rules of Civil Procedure	rules governing the pretrial, trial, and post-trial process for the federal courts (*abbr* **Fed.R.Civ.P.**) (**Zivilprozeßordnung für die Bundesgerichte**)
in pertinent part	to the extent relevant; generally used when quoting only part of a text (**soweit hier relevant**)

pending action	law suit that has been initiated but not yet decided (**anhängiges Verfahren**)
sanction	punishment, measure to discourage or punish conduct (**Sanktion**)
to strike out the pleadings	to exclude all or part of the factual claims included in the plaintiff's complaint or the defendant's answer (**Teile der Klage abweisen**)
to stay the proceedings	to postpone the trial process; to bring the law suit to a temporary standstill (**das Verfahren aussetzen**)
judgment by default	to enter judgment against one of the parties for failure to proceed as required with the law suit (**Versäumnisurteil**)
memorandum opinion	judicial opinion indicating what decision the court reached and what orders it issued but not including any argumentation for its conclusions (**verkürzte Entscheidung ohne Angabe von Gründen**)
F.R.D.	*abbr* **Federal Rules Decisions**, published collection of federal court decisions on the interpretation of the Federal Rules of Civil Procedure (**Sammlung bundesgerichtlicher Entscheidungen zur Regelung von Verfahren**)
record	all of the documents relevant to a law suit, including in particular the **transcript** (**Gerichtsakte**)
transcript	verbatim recording of everything said during a trial or on a **deposition** (**Protokoll**)
consent decree	court order to which the parties to a law suit have agreed and which they have recognized as a just determination of their rights
knowingly and willfully	with the intent to act under full awareness of the circumstances (**wissentlich und willentlich**)
standard of review	norm to be followed by an appellate court in determining whether lower court erred in reaching its decision (**Revisionsmaßstab**)
original matter	case, or issues raised in a case, on the trial, as opposed to appellate, court level (**erstinstanzliche Sache**)
lenity rule	rule requiring a judge to resolve any statutory ambiguity in favor of the defendant in a criminal case (**in dubio mitius, Gebot restriktiver Gesetzesauslegung zugunsten des Angeklagten**)
to deter	to keep *s.o.* from doing *sth*; to threaten *s.o.* with negative consequences for engaging in criminal behavior (**abschrecken**)
deterrent	*n. sth*, such as the threat of punishment, that has the effect of preventing *s.o.* from doing *sth* (**Abschreckungsmittel**); *adj* of or relating to a **deterrent**, having the effect of preventing certain conduct (**abschreckend**)
deterrence	one purpose or effect of punishment, namely preventing the commission of crimes (**Abschreckung**)

specific deterrence	deterrence of an individual from committing crimes, *e.g.* by imprisoning him so that he is not a threat to society (**Spezial-prävention**)
general deterrence	deterrence of society in general from committing crimes by punishing those who have committed them (**Generalprävention**)
retribution	one purpose or effect of punishment, namely paying the criminal offender back for the wrong he has done to the victim and to society according to the biblical "eye for an eye" theory (**Ver-geltung**)
rehabilitation	one purpose or effect of punishment, namely training the in-dividual to accept and correspond to social norms in the future (**Resozialisierung**)
resocialization	one purpose or effect of punishment, namely training the in-dividual to accept and correspond to social norms in the future (**Resozialisierung**)

Vocabulary

admonition	warning
to alienate *s.o.*	to anger *s.o.*, to put *s.o.* off, to estrange *s.o.* from yourself
ample	plenty, sufficient
callous	hard and indifferent
chastened	punished
to circumvent	to maneuver around and thus avoid (*a request, rule, law*)
colloquy	exchange of arguments, dispute
to compound	to add onto, to make stronger
to construe	to interpret
a date certain	a clearly specified day
to be deemed	to be considered as being, to be viewed in a certain way
duly	justly, according to worth, worthily
at the eleventh hour	right before the deadline, at the last minute
embodied	encased, given substance within *sth*
to encounter	to run into, to be confronted with
to envisage	imagine, to foresee
extenuating	excusing

flagrant	open and obvious
to flout	to contemptuously ignore
grossly	extremely, greatly
hindsight	view after *sth* has already happened
lenity	mercifulness
nonetheless	still, regardless
notwithstanding	regardless of
nuisance	bother, annoyance
to preclude	to hold *s.o.* back from doing *sth*, to rule out certain conduct
rules of thumb	generally applied and basic rules
to supplant	do take the place of, to exclude by taking over
to tip one's hand	to unintentionally reveal one's tactics or plan to an opponent
viz.	(Latin: videlicit) namely, that is to say

3. The Trial

After the jury has been selected and impaneled (see Unit I, Chapter 2, A, 2.), the trial process can begin. If both parties waived their right to a trial by jury, the process will be somewhat more simplified, but generally it will be conducted as described for a jury trial. As you will see from the following description of the trial itself, it is the attorneys, and not the judge, who are responsible for **presenting their case** to the court in an adversary system. Since the plaintiff initiated the law suit and bears the burden of proof, she will begin.

a. Opening Statements

The purpose of the **opening statement** is to give the jury a framework within which to understand the presentation of evidence during the trial. If the plaintiff began to present her case by simply calling her first witness, the jury would not have any idea as to why the witness was called and would not be able to evaluate the witness's **testimony** or place it into any relevant context. To avoid this disorientation, the plaintiff, or more precisely the plaintiff's lawyer, will explain in her opening statement what the trial is about. She will tell the jury why the plaintiff has sued the defendant and explain what it is that the plaintiff expects to be awarded as a remedy for whatever harm she claims the defendant has done her. She will tell the jury in advance what witnesses will be called and what it is that the jury can expect to learn from them. Furthermore, she will give a brief sketch of what the law requires her to prove to **make a prima facie case** against the defendant, meaning what the elements of her law suit are.

After the plaintiff has finished, the defendant may make an opening statement immediately, or he may postpone it until the plaintiff has **rested her case**. The plaintiff will rest after she has provided some evidence to prove each single element of her case. It is then the defendant's turn to present evidence to the jury in his defense. The purpose of the defendant's opening statement is very similar to that of the plaintiff's, namely to give the jury a framework within which to understand the testimony of the witnesses the defendant will call to testify. The defendant will explain to the jury why it is that the plaintiff does not deserve to win the law suit, what witnesses he will call to prove that, and what the jury can expect these witnesses to tell them. Whether the defendant makes his opening statement immediately following the plaintiff's or waits until it is his turn to present evidence is a matter of tactics. Speaking immediately has the advantage that the jury will acknowledge him as an important participant in the **litigation** from the beginning of the trial and will relate to him better during his cross-examination of the plaintiff's witnesses. Waiting until later when it is the defendant's turn to present his case has the advantage that the jury will better remember the defendant's analysis and description of the case when he begins to call his witnesses.

It is important to note that the judge will instruct the jury not to regard anything either lawyer says as evidence to be considered in reaching a final verdict or as a valid statement of what the law is. Accordingly, although the lawyers' opening statements will contain a description of what will follow during the trial, that description is merely a means of orientation for the jury and not at all evidentiary of the facts of the case or of their proper legal evaluation. Nonetheless, the opening statement gives the lawyer an important opportunity to appeal to the jury to get their attention and to gain their confidence for what will follow.

b. Plaintiff's Case

After the opening statement, plaintiff will **present her case**. Since the jury may only consider evidence presented at the trial and nothing the lawyer says, the lawyer must get the evidence before the jury through witnesses and their testimony. There are two types of witnesses. One is the **lay witness,** or a person who has personal knowledge of something that is relevant for the trial, usually because of what they have seen or heard. The other type of witness is the **expert witness,** or a person who has been trained in a profession and whose opinion or evaluation of a situation is important for those who are not experts in the field.

Let us assume that the plaintiff is suing the defendant for monetary compensation for injuries the plaintiff has incurred in an automobile accident the plaintiff claims the defendant was at fault for causing. Important lay witnesses would be people who actually saw the accident happen. An important expert witness would be a medical doctor who examined the plaintiff immediately after the accident and who could explain to the jury exactly in what way the plaintiff was injured and what the consequences for the plaintiff will be in the future as a result of the injury.

The plaintiff will call witnesses to the **witness stand** on **direct examination**. In a common law system, witnesses are always required to take an oath or affirmation before they testify that they will "tell the truth, the whole truth and nothing but the truth" when responding to the lawyers' questions. They sit in a chair next to the judge and elevated above the lawyers and the jury, which is called the **witness stand**. Since the witness was called by the plaintiff to respond to the plaintiff's questions, one says that the witness is testifying on **direct examination**, as opposed to **cross-examination**, when the witness is required to respond to the other party's lawyer's questions.

To introduce a lay witness to the judge and jury the plaintiff will first ask the witness questions about his or her identity and connection with the case, for example as an eye witness to an automobile accident. The plaintiff will then ask the witness to describe what he saw when the accident took place. The plaintiff is not permitted to **lead the witness**, meaning to put words in his mouth, on direct examination. Questions thus take the form of "Could you tell the court where you were on December 10 at 2:00 p.m.?" "Would you describe for the court what you observed as you stood at the pedestrian light on the corner of Broadway and 116th Street?" A **leading question**, in contrast, would take the form of "Isn't it true that you saw the defendant run the red light going at a speed in excess of the speed limit?" Leading questions on direct examination are prohibited because the witness usually is considered to be a **friendly witness** for the party who called him. One could thus assume that the witness will agree with anything the lawyer says and be glad the lawyer is saying it so well rather than have to say it himself. The **evidentiary value** of such passive statements of agreement is relatively low, however, and therefore not of much use to the jury in determining what really happened. Moreover, a lay witness is not permitted to give any opinion or evaluation of what happened, but only to describe the facts as the witness remembers them. It is the jury that is supposed to form an opinion from the evidence presented and thus the witness's opinion is irrelevant. Furthermore, the lay witness is usually not qualified to provide any evaluation of the facts. That realm is reserved for the expert.

To introduce the **expert witness**, the plaintiff will also ask the usual questions as to the witness's identity and connection with the case. In addition, however, the plaintiff will have **to qualify the witness as an expert** if the witness is to be asked to express an opinion based on his or her own filed of specialization. To qualify the witness, the plaintiff will ask him where he studied, what he is currently doing professionally, what professional organizations he belongs to, and what he has published in the field. The plaintiff will then make a motion to have the witness recognized as an expert. Defense counsel can object to this motion or accept the witness without objection. The judge will rule on the motion and if the witness is qualified, say as a medical doctor, then he will be able to express his professional evaluation of the plaintiff's injuries from the automobile accident.

To get a document or a physical object into evidence as an **exhibit,** the plaintiff will have to use a witness as well. The purpose of the witness is to identify the document or object so that its relevance to the case and authenticity can be established and also be the subject of cross-examination.

After the plaintiff has finished her direct examination, the defendant has a right to cross-examine the witness. Cross-examination is limited to the areas discussed during direct examination. Generally, the purpose of cross-examination is to discredit the witness, meaning to take away as much of the witness's impact on the jury as possible. Witnesses can be discredited by showing the jury that they do not really remember everything as clearly as they seemed to under direct examination or, in the extreme case, by showing that they were lying. They can also be discredited by showing the jury that they have not generally been that honest in the past, perhaps by comparing their statements during a deposition to what they are now saying in court. An expert witness can be discredited by showing that the witness has given incorrect evaluations in similar cases in the past, or later when the defense puts on its own case and calls other experts who convincingly contradict the plaintiff's expert. Since the witness on cross-examination was called to testify by the opposing party, the witness is considered to be **hostile** to the lawyer conducting the cross-examination. For this reason, leading questions are permitted. The idea is that the witness will not let himself be led around by the lawyer and indeed will even be difficult to question.

When the defendant has concluded his cross-examination, the plaintiff may examine the witness again on **redirect examination**. The plaintiff may conduct redirect to clarify any matter that has become murky on cross-examination, or to **rehabilitate** the witness, meaning to restore the jury's confidence in the truth of what the witness has said. Following redirect, the defendant can conduct **re-cross-examination,** limited to the issues raised on redirect examination. Theoretically, this process could go on ad infinitum, but because each time recross is limited to the issues raised on redirect, the scope for examination will be more and more limited until the examination simply stops. The plaintiff will then continue to call witnesses until she decides to **rest her case.**

c. Defendant's Case

Before defendant presents his case, he may make a **motion for non-suit**. This motion is a request addressed to the judge asking that the case be dismissed because the plaintiff has failed to make a prima facie case. The test for determining whether to grant the motion is to assume facts most favorable to the plaintiff from the evidence offered. Still, the defendant argues, plaintiff has failed to provide reasonable proof of every element of her cause of action. This motion is made not because the defendant wants the judge to make an evaluation of the facts of the case, because that would deprive plaintiff of her right to a jury trial where the jury is the ultimate evaluator of the evidence and determines what the facts of the case are. Instead, the defendant agrees to view the evidence presented in the most favorable light to the plaintiff and asks the judge to decide as a matter of law that the plaintiff has failed to make a case. As you may have noticed, this motion is similar to the demurrer and to the motion for judgment on the pleadings, but is made at a later point in the trial process. It, and motions that may be made later during the trial, attempts to stop the trial process with the argument that the law, and not the facts, determine the outcome of the case. The motion arises because the parties disagree on the correct interpretation of the law. If the defendant can convince the judge that his interpretation is correct, then the plaintiff will have failed to make a prima facie case because the plaintiff will have failed to offer proof of some element that the defendant claims is part of the cause of action. If the plaintiff can convince the judge that her interpretation of the law is correct, then the element is not a part of the cause of action and the plaintiff will prevail on the motion. Determining exactly what a plaintiff has to prove to make a prima facie case is a question of law, not of fact. If the plaintiff prevails, the trial will continue with the **defendant's case in chief**.

Similar to the plaintiff, the defendant will call lay and expert witnesses, and introduce documents and physical exhibits into evidence. The purpose of the defendant's case is to weaken the jury's belief in what they have heard from the plaintiff's witnesses, and possibly to make out a defense against the plaintiff's claims or to establish a prima facie case for a counterclaim. The defendant now conducts direct examination of his witnesses, who are subject to plaintiff's cross-examination, defendant's redirect, and plaintiff's recross-examination. When the defendant has finished, he will **rest his case**.

At this point in the law suit, either party can make a **motion for a directed verdict**. Similar to the motion for non-suit, this motion asks the judge to decide the case as a matter of law and not submit it to the jury, but it can be made by either of the parties rather than just by the defendant as for the motion for non-suit. Again, the **moving party** asks the judge to view the evidence most favorable to the **non-moving party**. Still, the moving party argues, as a matter of law the non-moving party has no right to prevail in the law suit, the plaintiff because she has failed to make a prima facie case, the defendant because he has failed to offer proof of some element of his defense or counterclaim that the plaintiff argues is essential. If the judge has ruled against the moving party previously in the trial on one of his or her similar motions, the judge is unlikely to grant the motion for a directed verdict. In general, one can say that judges are not very favorable toward a motion for a directed verdict, because the trial at this point is almost over. Granting the motion will not save much court time and it will take the case away from the jury with the result that no one will know what the jury would have decided had it had a chance to deliberate on the evidence presented. If the motion is denied then the trial will continue.

d. Plaintiff's Rebuttal and Defendant's Surrebuttal

After defendant has rested his case, the plaintiff, proceeding as she did during her case in chief, will have an opportunity to introduce new evidence to **rebut** defendant's case. Plaintiff's **rebuttal** is limited to the presentation of evidence directed toward that goal, meaning that the plaintiff cannot introduce evidence on a completely new aspect of the case. Similarly, after plaintiff has concluded her rebuttal, the defendant can present his **surrebuttal**, also limited by what the plaintiff has presented in rebuttal of the defendant's case. At the conclusion of rebuttal and surrebuttal, either party can again make a motion for a directed verdict. If denied the parties will then make their **closing arguments**.

e. Closing Arguments

Each party has an opportunity to argue the case before the jury, beginning with the plaintiff, then the defendant, and then, because the plaintiff bears the burden of proof, concluding with the plaintiff. Each lawyer will remind the jury of what certain witnesses said within an argumentative framework attempting to show why the jury should decide in their client's favor. The judge will later tell the jury, as for the opening statements, that they are not to take anything a lawyer said as evidence of what in fact happened. Still, closing arguments are important to convince the jury that your client has a good case based on what witnesses actually said during the trial.

f. Jury Instructions, Sequestration, Deliberation

Before the case is submitted to the jury for deliberation, the judge will **instruct the jury on the law**. As you know, the jurors are not trained lawyers. Their primary function at trial is to determine what the facts in a case were. The judge then explains the relevant law to them in terms a lay person can understand, and they will be instructed to apply this law to the facts of the case as they believe them to be true in order to reach a verdict. Usually, the judge will expect the jury to reach a **general verdict,** which takes the form of "We find in favor of the plaintiff in the amount of $ 10,000" or "We find in favor of the defendant." Sometimes, however the court will ask the jury to reach a **special verdict.** The special verdict can take any number of forms, depending on what exactly the court wants to find out about what facts the jury believed to be true. The judge might give the jury a list of questions to answer, or simply ask them to write a list of the facts they found to be true and on which they based their verdict. The special verdict will help the judge to determine whether the jury understood the law and applied it correctly, because once the judge knows what facts to proceed on, she can reach the correct verdict herself by accurately applying the law. If the jury did not reach that verdict, then she will be able to correct the mistake in response to **post-trial motions.** Normally, however, judges require juries to reach general verdicts, perhaps because judges generally agree with jury verdicts anyway and do not want to open the door to permit the jury to **impeach its verdict,** meaning to supply a good reason, such as an incorrect legal evaluation of the facts, not to trust the verdict.

Although the judge is responsible for instructing the jury, she will consider each party's requests on how to instruct them, and sometimes incorporate three somewhat different instructions on one legal issue, namely the judge's preference, the plaintiff's preference, and the defendant's preference. That is because jury instructions provide the best and most common basis of appeal. On appeal the losing party will argue that the judge instructed the jury incorrectly, meaning that the jury understood the relevant law incorrectly, with the result that they could not reach an accurate verdict. Accordingly, the trial court judge will attempt to accommodate both parties in order to exclude an easy appeal on the instructions. After the jury has been instructed, the judge will send them into deliberation and sometimes, but not usually in a private law dispute, sequester them until they have reached their verdict.

g. Judgment and Post-Trial Motions

The jury's verdict has no legal effect until the judge **enters judgment on the verdict.** In the normal course of events the judge will automatically enter judgment in accord with the jury's verdict. Still, the judge has the ultimate control over the outcome of a private law dispute. Consequently, the dissatisfied party after trial will often attempt to challenge it by making a **motion for judgment notwithstanding the verdict** (*abbr* **j.n.o.v.**). This motion is a formal request that the court ignore the jury's verdict and enter judgment for the other party.

A natural question to ask is why a system of law would provide for trial by jury and then permit the judge to simply ignore the jury's verdict and enter judgment for the other party. The answer to this question follows from the nature of the jury's and judge's functions at trial. The jury is responsible as the **factfinder**, whereas the judge is responsible for ensuring that the law is applied correctly. By the nature of the game, however, the jury has to apply the law, as instructed by the judge, to the facts as the jury finds them in order to reach a verdict. Consequently, it is possible for the jury to make a mistake either because they did not understand the judge's instructions and thus do not know what the law provides, or they did not understand how to apply the law correctly in the particular case although they may have understood the law itself. When a party makes a motion for judgment notwithstanding the verdict, the party essentially says that the judge should assume the facts most favorable to the other party from the evidence presented. Still, the moving party claims, no reasonable jury which understood and applied the law correctly could arrive at the verdict the jury reached. The motion therefore maintains the jury's authority over determination of the facts of the case from the evidence presented, because the test for granting it proceeds from the facts most favorable to the party in whose favor the jury decided. It permits the judge, however, who is the specialist on the law, to correct the final result attained by applying the law correctly in the case.

The motion for a j.n.o.v. can be made by either party and with regard to the general outcome of the case, meaning in favor of the plaintiff or of the defendant, and with regard to the damage award in case of a verdict in favor of the plaintiff. Assuming the jury found in favor of the plaintiff in the amount of $10 million, the defendant could make a motion for a j.n.o.v. asking the court to change the verdict to either in favor of the defendant or to change the damage award from $10 million to $ 1 million. The latter type of motion does not contest the jury's correct application the law, but rather the jury's ability to give a correct legal evaluation of the appropriate **remedy**. Juries tend to be sympathetic toward individuals who have been harmed, especially by large and powerful companies with deep pockets. It is always easy to be generous with someone else's money as well. When juries overreact to harm caused a plaintiff, one refers to them as **run-away juries,** and they are usually stopped by a defendant's successful motion for a j.n.o.v.

As you know from the materials on juries, however, there is one case in which a motion for a j.n.o.v. may not be made successfully. That is when the jury reaches a verdict of not guilty in a criminal case. As the jury in such case has the ability to ignore the law and acquit the defendant, or to **nullify the law**, the judge may not alter the verdict based on the judge's correct understanding or application of that law. Contrarily, however, if the jury in a criminal case convicts the defendant unjustly, the judge has an obligation to enter a j.n.o.v. in favor of the defendant.

Although a jury, as composed of the defendant's peers, may choose to ignore what they consider an unjust law, they may not out of animosity toward the defendant simply make up law to convict someone who is innocent.

Another common **post-trial motion** is a **motion for a new trial**. This motion is based on the claim that legal error occurred during the trial that could have affected its outcome. Such an error is referred to as **prejudicial error** and it makes the result reached in the case void. If the judge grants the motion, a new trial will be ordered. On the other hand, if the judge thinks the error could not have affected the outcome, in which case it is called **harmless error**, or if the judge does not agree that any error occurred, then the judge will deny the motion. A motion for a new trial could be based on many sources of error during the trial. The primary source lies in the instructions the judge gives the jury at the end of the trial. Of course, if the judge instructs the jury incorrectly on the law, then the jury will be unable to give the proper legal evaluation of the facts of the case and a new trial will be necessary. One might wonder how a judge could be mistaken about the law, but often issues arise during a trial that are either novel, meaning no past case has dealt with them before, or about whose treatment legal minds differ. Another question might relate to why a judge would grant a motion for a new trial based on a lawyer's argument that the judge incorrectly instructed the jury on the law, when it is one and the very same judge who did the instructing and who is being asked to grant the motion. The answer is that the judge will probably not grant the motion, but her refusal to do so provides the lawyer with the basis for an appeal. It also preserves the right to have a new trial in the future should a higher court agree that prejudicial error occurred through the instructions.

The decisions of the trial court on all of the motions discussed above, which can be made at various stages of the pretrial, trial, and post trial proceedings are appealable, as is the judgement itself. Reconsider the demurrer, for example, which a defendant may file in response to the plaintiff's complaint. Remember that the demurrer does not raise any factual questions. The defendant asks the judge to assume that all of the facts the plaintiff has alleged are true. Still as a matter of law the defendant claims the plaintiff cannot prevail in the law suit. The demurrer is filed to test the law applicable in the case because the plaintiff and defendant disagree on its interpretation. If the court overrules the demurrer, that shows that the judge does not agree with the defendant's interpretation of the applicable law. The defendant can now appeal the judge's dismissal of the demurrer, arguing to the appellate court and ultimately to the supreme court that his interpretation of the law is correct and should be controlling in the case. The higher courts then have the opportunity to clarify the law before the trial takes place, saving time and avoiding a judgment in the main proceedings that is based on an incorrect interpretation of the law.

As you can see from the above description of the trial process, common law civil procedure plays an important role in an adversary system of trial, as perhaps well it should. A system of procedural, as opposed to substantive, justice must ensure above all that the procedure is equally fair for both of the parties. As equally matched and equally treated adversaries, they should be able to present the best case for their position, so that a jury gets an optimal picture of each side of the dispute and can base its decision on the best evidence available in the case.

The following charts map the flow of the trial process in the United States:

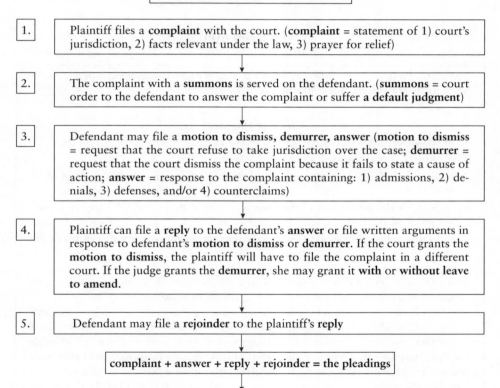

Pleadings and Pretrial Motions

1. Plaintiff files a **complaint** with the court. (**complaint** = statement of 1) court's jurisdiction, 2) facts relevant under the law, 3) prayer for relief)

2. The complaint with a **summons** is served on the defendant. (**summons** = court order to the defendant to answer the complaint or suffer **a default judgment**)

3. Defendant may file a **motion to dismiss, demurrer, answer** (**motion to dismiss** = request that the court refuse to take jurisdiction over the case; **demurrer** = request that the court dismiss the complaint because it fails to state a cause of action; **answer** = response to the complaint containing: 1) admissions, 2) denials, 3) defenses, and/or 4) counterclaims)

4. Plaintiff can file a **reply** to the defendant's **answer** or file written arguments in response to defendant's **motion to dismiss** or **demurrer**. If the court grants the **motion to dismiss**, the plaintiff will have to file the complaint in a different court. If the judge grants the **demurrer**, she may grant it **with** or **without leave to amend**.

5. Defendant may file a **rejoinder** to the plaintiff's **reply**

complaint + answer + reply + rejoinder = the pleadings

6. | Either party may file a **motion for summary judgment** or a **motion for judgment on the pleadings**. A **motion for summary judgment** claims that there are no factual issues that can be resolved at trial, either because relevant evidence is unavailable or because no factual issues are in dispute. A **motion for judgment on the pleadings** claims that even if the facts most favorable to the **non-moving party** were true still the **moving party** has a right to prevail in the law suit as a matter of law. If the judge grants either of these motions, the trial process will not take place.

7. | The judge will hold a **pretrial conference** in an effort to determine whether the parties can reach a **pretrial settlement**. If not, the trial process will begin.

Pretrial Discovery

The pretrial discovery phase begins when the pleadings have been filed. It permits each party to the law suit to gather information before the trial.

Tools of Discovery

1. **interrogatory** = list of written questions to a party
2. **deposition** = oral questioning of witness or party
3. **request for admission** = request that the other party agree to the truth of some statement
4. **request for the production of documents** = request that the other party turn over documented evidence
5. **mental or physical examination** = medical examination of party if relevant to the case

Through discovery the parties will be able to determine some of the facts of the case with certainty. As a consequence, either party may decide to abandon the law suit because it may have become obvious to the party that he cannot possibly win it in light of the facts discovered. Another consequence of discovering the certain truth of some factual claims is that they need not be proved at trial. Either way, time in court, and thus considerable expense, may be saved through discovery. Discovery also helps to ensure that both parties are optimally prepared for trial and that the ultimate decision in the case will be based on the widest range of relevant evidence and thus will more likely be the correct decision.

Jury Selection

1. **Selection of the array:** The **jury commissioner** is responsible for randomly selecting individuals for jury duty and ensuring that they are qualified for jury service. Those selected as qualified will receive a **summons** to appear in court. The group of people selected is called the **array** or **venire** and one of them is called a **venireperson.**

2. **Voir dire** = selection process to choose jurors who will actually serve at a particular trial
   a. **challenge to the array** = request that the judge dismiss the entire array because the selection process was incorrectly performed
   b. **challenge for cause** = request that the judge dismiss a particular **venireperson** because she is considered legally unfit to serve as a juror for this particular case.
   c. **peremptory challenge** = request that the judge dismiss a particular venireperson without giving any reason for the dismissal
   d. **Batson challenge** = request that the judge refuse to grant a peremptory challenge because the challenge is based on prejudice toward some characteristic of the juror.

3. **Impaneling and swearing in the jury** = recording the names of the jurors and administering an oath to them requiring them to swear that they will do their best to apply the law as instructed to the facts as they believe them to be true from the evidence presented at trial. The court is now prepared to go forward with the trial.

The Trial

1. Plaintiff's **opening statement**

2. Defendant's **opening statement** (may be reserved until defendant presents case)

3. Plaintiff's **case in chief** (plaintiff must make a **prima facie** case = reasonable proof of each element of cause of action)
   Plaintiff calls lay and expert witnesses to testify and introduces documentary and physical exhibits into evidence
   Witnesses' testimony
   a. **plaintiff's direct examination** of witnesses to get information into evidence
   b. **defendant's cross-examination** to rebut or discredit witness
   c. **plaintiff's redirect examination**
   d. **defendant's recross-examination**

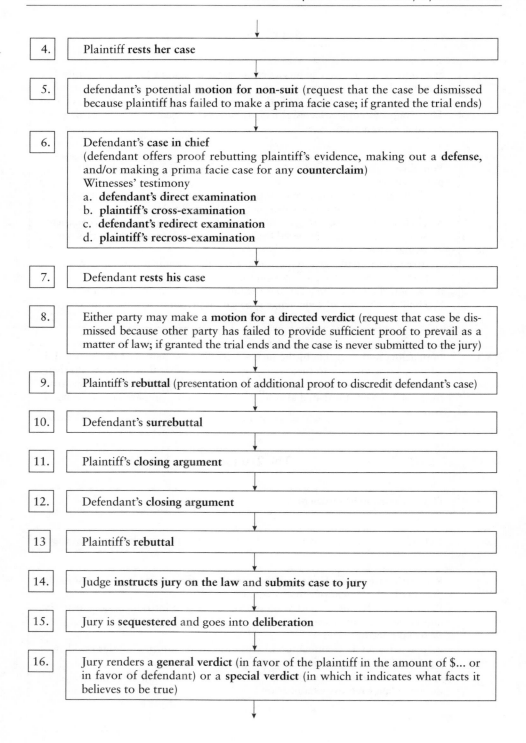

4. Plaintiff **rests her case**

5. defendant's potential **motion for non-suit** (request that the case be dismissed because plaintiff has failed to make a prima facie case; if granted the trial ends)

6. Defendant's **case in chief**
(defendant offers proof rebutting plaintiff's evidence, making out a **defense**, and/or making a prima facie case for any **counterclaim**)
Witnesses' testimony
a. **defendant's direct examination**
b. **plaintiff's cross-examination**
c. **defendant's redirect examination**
d. **plaintiff's recross-examination**

7. Defendant **rests his case**

8. Either party may make a **motion for a directed verdict** (request that case be dismissed because other party has failed to provide sufficient proof to prevail as a matter of law; if granted the trial ends and the case is never submitted to the jury)

9. Plaintiff's **rebuttal** (presentation of additional proof to discredit defendant's case)

10. Defendant's **surrebuttal**

11. Plaintiff's **closing argument**

12. Defendant's **closing argument**

13 Plaintiff's **rebuttal**

14. Judge **instructs jury on the law** and **submits case to jury**

15. Jury is **sequestered** and goes into **deliberation**

16. Jury renders a **general verdict** (in favor of the plaintiff in the amount of $... or in favor of defendant) or a **special verdict** (in which it indicates what facts it believes to be true)

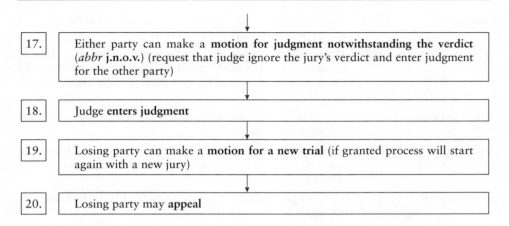

17.	Either party can make a **motion for judgment notwithstanding the verdict** (*abbr* **j.n.o.v.**) (request that judge ignore the jury's verdict and enter judgment for the other party)
18.	Judge **enters judgment**
19.	Losing party can make a **motion for a new trial** (if granted process will start again with a new jury)
20.	Losing party may **appeal**

Questions on the Text

1. What do the demurrer, motion for judgment on the pleadings, motion for non-suit, motion for directed verdict, and motion for judgment notwithstanding the verdict have in common?

2. What are the differences in the motions listed in no.1?

3. Describe the trial process in your own legal system. Do lawyers in your own system deliver opening statements and closing arguments? Are they permitted to cross-examine the other party's witnesses? Trials in England and the United States are usually open to the public. If you have the opportunity, try to attend a criminal trial with a jury where the defendant has pleaded not guilty to the charges (court clerks are usually glad to help you pick out an interesting trial to observe). If you are unfamiliar with the trial process in your own country, attend a trial and compare it to the process described above.

Terminology

to present one's case	to call witnesses and present evidence of each element of the cause of action or defense one has against the other party (**den Beweis antreten**)
opening statement	lawyer's description of the trial to come to give the jury a framework within which to understand the evidence that will be presented (**einleitender Vortrag vor dem Gericht**)

testimony	what a witness says under oath in response to either lawyer's questions (**Zeugenausage**)
to make a prima facie case	to provide reasonable evidence of each element of a cause of action such that if the other party remains silent one will win the law suit (**Beweise vortragen, die die Richtigkeit der Klage nachweisen**)
to rest one's case	to conclude presenting evidence in support of one's case (**sein Vorbringen abschliessen**)
lay witness	witness who testifies as to what she saw or heard, but who is not qualified to give an opinion upon which a jury can base a decision (**Zeuge**)
expert witness	witness who is qualified to give an opinion in a court (**Sachverständiger**)
witness stand	seat in which witness sits while testifying in court (**Zeugenbank**)
direct examination	questioning of a witness by the lawyer who called the witness to testify (**Vernehmung eines Zeugen, den der vernehmende Anwalt selbst benannt hat**)
cross-examination	questioning of a witness by the lawyer opposed to the lawyer who called the witness (**Kreuzverhör**)
to lead a witness	to put words into a witness's mouth; to ask a question in a way that suggests or already states the answer (**suggestive Fragen stellen**)
leading question	a question that is formulated to suggest or state the answer to that question (**Suggestivfrage**)
evidentiary value	value of *sth* as proof of what happened or of what the facts are (**Wert als Beweismittel**)
to qualify a witness as an expert	to show the court that a witness is a specialist and can thus express an opinion within her field of expertise (**die Fähigkeit eines Zeugen belegen, als Sachverständige(r) auszusagen**)
exhibit	physical object introduced as evidence at trial (**Beweisstück**)
redirect examination	lawyer's questioning of his own witness following the other party's cross-examination (**wiederholte Vernehmung eines Zeugen, den der vernehmende Anwalt selbst benannt hat**)
recross-examination	lawyer's questioning of the opposing party's witness following redirect examination (**nochmaliges Kreuzverhör**)
to rehabilitate a witness	to build a witness' credibility back up in the mind of the factfinder following cross-examination (**die Glaubwürdigkeit eines Zeugen wiederherstellen**)
motion for a non-suit	defendant's formal request addressed to the court to dismiss the plaintiff's law suit for failure to make a prima facie case; made following plaintiff's case in chief (**Antrag auf Klageabweisung wegen Unschlüssigkeit**)

case in chief	main part of a party's presentation of evidence (as opposed to the presentation of evidence on **rebuttal** (**Hauptvorbringen**)
motion for a directed verdict	plaintiff's or defendant's formal request addressed to the court to decide the case as a matter of law rather than give it to the jury to decide; motion asks judge to believe the evidence most favorable to the non-moving party but to still decide as a matter of law that the moving party should prevail in the law suit (**Antrag auf Klageabweisung wegen Unschlüssigkeit**)
rebuttal	plaintiff's presentation of evidence following defendant's **case in chief** that is aimed at discrediting the defendant's case (**Antwort auf das Vorbringen des Beklagten**)
surrebuttal	defendant's presentation of evidence following plaintiff's **rebuttal** that is aimed at discrediting the rebuttal (**Replik auf die Antwort des Klägers**)
closing argument	final address to the jury in an attempt to sum up the evidence that has been presented during trial and convince the jury that one's own client should prevail in the law suit (**Schlußplädoyer**)
to instruct the jury on the law	to explain the law applicable in the case to the jury in terms a lay person can understand to permit the jury to apply it to the facts of the case it believes are true, in order to be able to reach a verdict (**die Geschworenen belehren**)
general verdict	jury's final decision in a case in favor of one of the parties to the law suit (**Wahrspruch, Spruch der Geschworenen**)
special verdict	jury's indication of what facts it believes are true following a trial (**Tatsacheninterlokut**)
to impeach a verdict	to give a reason to believe that a verdict has not been reached properly (**Gründe dafür angeben, daß an einem Wahrspruch zu zweifeln ist**)
judgment on the verdict	judge's decision based on the conclusion the jury reached in a trial; when the judge enters judgment on the verdict, the verdict receives legal effect (**Urteil in Übereinstimmung mit dem Wahrspruch der Geschworenen**
judgment notwithstanding the verdict	(*abbr* **j.n.o.v.**) judge's decision contrary to the conclusion reached by the jury in a trial; the test for granting a motion for a j.n.o.v. is to assume the evidence most favorable to the non-moving party is true and still decide as a matter of law that the moving party should prevail in the law suit; permits judge to control jury verdicts (**Urteil im Gegensatz zu dem Wahrspruch der Geschworenen**)
factfinder	jury, or in a non-jury trial the judge, in its role as determining what evidence to believe represents the facts of the case (**Tatsachenrichter**)

run-away jury	jury that strongly exaggerates the seriousness of the defendant's wrong or of the plaintiff's injury by awarding excessive damages (**außer Rand und Band geratene Geschworenenbank**)
to nullify the law	to ignore the law and decide a case as a jury; permissible in criminal cases if jury acquits defendant regardless of the law
post-trial motion	formal request by either party to the law suit addressed to the judge following completion of the trial, e.g. motion for a new trial, motion for a judgment notwithstanding the verdict (**Antrag nach der Hauptverhandlung**)
motion for a new trial	post-trial motion asking the judge to void the trial and order a new trial to take place; motion is based on claim that legal error was committed which could have affected the outcome of the trial (**Antrag auf Wiederaufnahme des Verfahrens**)

Suggested Reading

U. Bentele, E. Cary, *Appellate Advocacy. Priciples and Practice* (2d ed.) Anderson Publishing Co.: Cincinnati (1995)

D. Binder, P. Bergman, S. Price, *Lawyers as Counselors,* West Publishing Co.: St. Paul, Minn. (1991)

G. Fletcher, *A Crime of Self-Defense: Bernhard Goetz and the Law on Trial,* Free Press: New York (1988)

Introduction to Advocacy: Research, Writing, and Argument (6th ed.), Board of Student Advisers Harvard Law School (eds.), Foundation Press: Westbury, N.Y. (1996)

T. Mauet, *Trial Techniques* (4th ed.) Little Brown and Co.: Boston, New York, Toronto, London (1996)

T. Mauet, W. Wolfson, *Materials in Trial Advocacy* (3rd. ed.), Little Brown and Co.: Boston/ New York/Toronto/London (1994)

La Tour, Houlden, Walker, Thibaut, "Procedure: Transnational Perspectives and Preferences," 86 *Yale Law Journal* 258 (1976)

M. Zander, *Cases and Materials on the English Legal System* (8th ed.) Butterworths: London, Edinburgh, Dublin (1999)

Chapter 4
Retroactivity: A Return to Stare Decisis

This Unit has introduced some of the fundamental characteristics of a common law system. One of the most complicated problems touched upon has been the question of when a new precedent can be applied retroactively, that is to cases that arose in the past before the new precedent was announced. As you recall, *Regina v. Shivpuri* raised the issue whether the House of Lords could apply the new precedent it announced in that case to Shivpuri himself or only to future cases arising from facts that occurred after the *Shivpuri* decision. This last Chapter will resume discussing this problem in light of a series of decisions reached by the United States Supreme Court. The purpose of this Section is not only to provide more insight on the retroactivity question, but also to review the material presented in this Chapter and to permit the reader to practice the skills already attained.

A. Retroactivity of New Precedents in Criminal Cases

The United States Supreme Court has indicated that not all of its decisions can be applied retroactively. In *Linkletter v. Walker*, 381 U.S. 618, 85 S.Ct. 1731, 14 L.Ed.2d 601 (1965), for example, the U.S. Supreme Court refused to apply retroactively the rule it had laid down earlier in *Mapp v. Ohio*, 367 U.S. 643, 81 S.Ct. 1684, 6 L.Ed.2d 1081 (1961). The *Mapp* case involved a prosecution for possession of pornography in violation of Ohio law. Police officers had conducted an illegal search of Ms. Mapp's home and had taken pornographic material they found there. Mapp's conviction rested primarily on this evidence. The U.S. Supreme Court held that evidence obtained in a **search and seizure** in violation of an individual's rights under the Fourth Amendment to the U.S. Constitution could not be used against the accused in criminal proceedings in a state court. Before *Mapp*, this **exclusionary rule** applied only to criminal proceedings in federal court (for an explanation of the court systems of the United States, see Unit II). After *Mapp*, this exclusionary rule also applied to criminal proceedings in state courts, and the Court used it to reverse Ms. Mapp's conviction on appeal. Similarly to the House of Lords in *Shivpuri*, the U.S. Supreme Court applied its new precedent to facts that had arisen before the precedent was announced. The *Linkletter* case then raised a slightly different question. If the *Mapp* precedent applied retroactively to Ms. Mapp herself, why should it not also apply retroactively to all similar cases that had been decided before *Mapp*. In *Linkletter*, the petitioner argued that the exclusionary rule announced in *Mapp* should be applied retroactively to his own case. Linkletter's state court conviction had also been based on evidence which had been seized illegally. The U.S. Supreme Court, however, refused to apply *Mapp* retroactively to Linkletter's state court conviction, which had become final before *Mapp* was decided, even though it had been based in part on evidence gained through an illegal search.

In *Gideon v. Wainwright*, 372 U.S. 335 (1963), the U.S. Supreme Court held that the Sixth Amendment to the U.S. Constitution guaranteed an indigent criminal defendant the right to the advice of legal counsel at trial in a state court. Before *Gideon*, the Sixth Amendment guarantee of right to counsel had been interpreted as applying only to trials in federal courts. Gideon had been charged with breaking and entering a poolroom in violation of Florida law. At trial, Gideon requested the Florida court to appoint a lawyer for him, as he did not have the money to hire his own lawyer. The court refused to do so because Florida law provided for appointed counsel only in death penalty cases. Gideon defended himself but was found guilty and sentenced to five years imprisonment. After Gideon's conviction was final, the U.S. Supreme Court considered the case and held that the Sixth Amendment guarantees also applied to trials in state courts. Similar to the holding in *Mapp*, this holding was applied retroactively to overturn Gideon's conviction.

Read the Fourth and Sixth Amendments to the U.S. Constitution:

> Fourth Amendment. The right of the people to be secure in their persons, houses, papers, and effects, against unreasonable searches and seizures, shall not be violated, and no Warrants shall issue, but upon probable cause, supported by Oath or affirmation, and particularly describing the place to be searched, and the persons or things to be seized.

> Sixth Amendment. In all criminal prosecutions, the accused shall enjoy the right … to have the Assistance of Counsel for his defence.

A **search** involves a police officer either examining an individual's person or looking around in a person's home, automobile or any other place containing that person's belongings when the police officer is trying to find evidence of criminal activity. If the police officer conducts a search and finds evidence, then the police can **seize** that evidence, or take it into police **custody**, for use later as evidence in a trial against the person searched. The Fourth Amendment prohibits so-called "unreasonable" searches and seizures. What exactly is unreasonable is a question that U.S. Supreme Court decisions answer over time. Very generally one can say that police officers need a warrant in order to conduct a search, particularly of a person's home. A **warrant** is a document a court can issue to permit the police to arrest an individual, in which case it is called an **arrest warrant,** or to search an individual or an area under his control, such as his home or automobile, in which case it is referred to as a **search warrant**. As the Fourth Amendment indicates, a judge may not issue a warrant unless it is based on **probable cause,** which is also a term subject to a considerable amount of judicial interpretation. Suffice it to say that probable cause is not just any reason the police officer might give, but instead a good reason for believing that an individual has committed a crime. Finally, the Fourth Amendment requires the police officer to take an oath or to solemnly affirm that the information on which the probable cause is based is true.

Returning to *Mapp* and *Gideon*, one might think at first sight that the cases are the same. In both of them, the Supreme Court applied a new precedent to facts that had occurred before the precedent was announced, namely to the cases themselves. Still in *Linkletter*, the Court refused to apply the new precedent in *Mapp* retroactively to a case in which the conviction had become final before *Mapp* was handed down. Suppose you are a state attorney and you have a case similar to *Gideon*. Like Gideon, your hypothetical defendant was convicted in a trial in which he was refused state appointed counsel. Like Linkletter, he has appealed his conviction through the courts and no longer has any **avenue of appeal** open to him. His conviction is thus final. On learning of the U.S. Supreme Court's decision in *Gideon*, he petitions to the Court with the argument that *Gideon* should apply retroactively to his own case. You now are preparing for oral argumentation before the U.S. Supreme Court and, since you are representing the state, you want the Court to refuse to apply *Gideon* retroactively to your case and instead uphold the conviction.

The essence of legal practice in a common law jurisdiction is finding arguments that show similarities and differences between cases. Only through this exercise can a lawyer represent his client in a new case. The lawyer will try to argue that the new case is more similar to a former case announcing a precedent favorable to his client and different from any case announcing a precedent unfavorable to his client. In order to make the argument as state attorney in our hypothetical case, let us first consider the nature of the constitutional defect found in each *Mapp* and *Gideon*. Both of the relevant amendments guarantee basic rights for a person suspected or accused of having committed a crime. But the Fourth Amendment seems even more fundamental than the Sixth. At the time a Fourth Amendment violation occurs, the person whose rights are violated may not yet have been formally accused of having engaged in criminal activity. In fact, it is often the product of the unreasonable search that gives police the reason for arresting the person. The Sixth Amendment guarantee, however, applies only to those who have already been criminally accused.

On the basis of this distinction and using *Linkletter* as a favorable precedent for your case as state attorney, you could argue as follows:

1. Fourth Amendment rights are more fundamental than Sixth Amendment rights because Fourth Amendment rights protect citizens generally from state action and Sixth Amendment rights protect only those citizens for whom we already have good reason to believe they have committed a crime.

2. In *Linkletter*, the Supreme Court held that even judgments based on violations of the more fundamental Fourth Amendment rights could not be reversed retroactively in cases in which the conviction had already become final.

3. The judgment in *Gideon* was based on a violation of the less fundamental Sixth Amendment rights.

4. Therefore, under the precedent announced in *Linkletter*, *Gideon* should not be applied retroactively to cases in which the conviction has already become final.

5. My case is a case like *Gideon* and the defendant's conviction has become final.

6. Therefore *Gideon* should not be applied retroactively to my case and the defendant's conviction should be upheld.

The argument may sound convincing and the case seem simple, but suppose you are the defense lawyer. What arguments can be found for your client? Remember what the issue is. We have three precedents to work from: *Mapp*, *Gideon* and *Linkletter*. *Linkletter* is a bad precedent for you as defense counsel, because it held that *Mapp* could not be applied retroactively to convictions which had become final before *Mapp* was announced. Your task is now a little more complex than the one facing the state attorney, because you need two arguments. One argument has to convince the Supreme Court that your case is in some way significantly different from *Linkletter* so that *Linkletter* does not bind the Court in your case. The second argument has to convince the Court that your case is in some way significantly different from *Mapp*, so that the Court sees the need to arrive at a new precedent to govern your type of case.

To make the first argument it is important to understand more fully one difference between *Mapp* and *Gideon*, namely that *Mapp* went to the U.S. Supreme Court on appeal, whereas *Gideon* petitioned for a **writ of habeas corpus**. The fact that *Mapp* was on appeal means that Ms. Mapp's conviction was not yet final. A conviction does not become final until all **avenues of appeal** have been exhausted, which means that the appellant has already appealed to the highest court available in his case or that although he could have filed another appeal he failed to do so within the time period allotted for the appeal. When an attack is made through the normal appellate process it is referred to as a **direct attack** and one says that the case is **on direct review**. The **writ of habeas corpus** (Lat. "you may have the body"), sometimes referred to as the "great writ of liberty," originated in England and has been incorporated in the U.S. Constitution in Article I Section 9: "The Privilege of the Writ of Habeas Corpus shall not be suspended, unless when in Cases of Rebellion or Invasion the public Safety may require it." This writ permits a person whose criminal conviction is final to challenge the legality of his detention in prison. Since the prisoner's conviction has already been finally determined, the **habeas corpus challenge** does not relate to the person's guilt or innocence. Instead it raises the question of whether his confinement violates constitutional principles. The writ can be used, for example, to have someone released from a prison on the grounds that prison conditions are in violation of the Constitution's **prohibition against cruel and unusual punishment**. Gideon did not use the writ to argue that he was not guilty of the offense charged, but that his confinement in prison was due to a violation of the constitutionally guaranteed right to be represented by an attorney. The **petition for a writ of habeas corpus** is a form of so-called **collateral attack**, which means that the possibility to file it runs alongside the regular trial and appellate processes for determining guilt. When a court considers a **collateral attack** it does so on so-called **collateral review**.

With this distinction in mind, consider the following first argument for your client:

1. Ms. Mapp's conviction was not final because Ms. Mapp won on *appeal* to the U.S. Supreme Court.
2. The decision in *Mapp* to apply the new precedent retroactively to reverse Ms. Mapp's conviction was merely a decision, like the *Shivpuri* decision, to apply a new precedent to the case in which it was announced, or to *facts* that arose before the precedent.
3. Linkletter's conviction, on the other hand, was final and came to the U.S. Supreme Court on collateral review, namely on a writ of habeas corpus.
4. Applying *Mapp* to Linkletter would involve applying a retroactive decision in a case on appeal retroactively to a case on collateral review.
5. *Linkletter* merely holds that retroactive application of a new precedent to cases on appeal does not necessarily mean that the precedent will be applied retroactively to cases on collateral review.
6. In contrast to *Mapp*, *Gideon* was on collateral review to the U.S. Supreme Court because his conviction was already final.
7. Still, the Court held that the new precedent announced in *Gideon* applied retroactively to Gideon himself.

8. The *Linkletter* holding applies only to cases seeking retroactive application of precedents announced on direct review (*Mapp*) and not to cases seeking retroactive application of precedents announced in cases on collateral review.

9. My case seeks retroactive application of a precedent announced in a case on collateral review.

10. Therefore, the precedent in *Linkletter* does not apply to my case.

This argument is good as far as it goes, because it could convince the Court that *Linkletter* is not binding precedent in your case, and that in fact is quite a bit. What remains, however, is the task of convincing the Court to establish a new precedent in your favor. In trying to solve this problem, consider that both Mapp and Gideon could be retried for the criminal offenses they had originally been accused of. That is because the U.S. Supreme Court held that the trial leading to their conviction was conducted in a manner inconsistent with the U.S. Constitution. Accordingly, the trial process itself was defective and thus void of any legal effect. To cure the constitutional defect in *Mapp*, the trial court would have to exclude the evidence the police had obtained illegally. Without that evidence it is fairly certain that Ms. Mapp would be acquitted. To cure the constitutional defect in *Gideon*, the trial court would have to appoint a lawyer to represent Gideon. Whether Gideon would be convicted or acquitted would depend on whether this legal assistance really does make a difference in the way the jury will evaluate the evidence against him. This comparison may seem to work against you in your position as defense counsel, because it is pretty obvious that Mapp will be acquitted but not at all obvious that Gideon will be acquitted (in fact Gideon was retried and acquitted). Consider, however, the purpose of the two rules, namely what the Supreme Court is trying to achieve with each. Is the Court in *Mapp* concerned that Mapp was convicted without sufficient proof of her guilt? Clearly not. Instead the Court intends to deter the police from conducting illegal searches and seizures. What better way to deter them than to exclude the evidence from trial thus making it totally useless for them to conduct such a search? On the other hand, in *Gideon* the Court seems more concerned that Gideon might be innocent, but that the trial process was insufficient for actually determining the answer to the question of guilt. On the basis of this distinction, your second argument could take the following form:

1. The rule in *Mapp* was not intended to improve the trial process in the sense of avoiding mistakes about a defendant's guilt, but instead to establish a new means of controlling the police in their investigations.

2. Past police conduct cannot be controlled.

3. Therefore, it makes no sense to apply *Mapp* retroactively in *Linkletter* and all other cases in which the police have already conducted illegal searches and the trial court has used that evidence.

4. The purpose of the rule in *Gideon* is to ensure that the trial process leads us to a correct conclusion, which presumably is more likely when both parties, the state and the defendant, have the assistance of legal advice.
5. Gideon may have been convicted not because he really committed the crime, but instead because he was not given legal representation.
6. If Gideon was convicted only because he did not have adequate legal representation, he may be innocent.
7. Therefore, it is imperative that he, and everyone else like him, have a new trial so that the issue of guilt can be adequately resolved.
8. My client did not have the assistance of counsel and therefore is like Gideon.
9. Therefore my client should have a new trial.

In fact, the U.S. Supreme Court has applied *Gideon* retroactively to cases on collateral review (e.g. *Burgett v. Texas*, 389 U.S. 109 (1967); *Kitchens v. Smith*, 401 U.S. 847, 91 S.Ct. 1089 (1971); *Loper v. Beto*, 405 U.S. 473, 92 S.Ct. 1014, 31 L.Ed.2d 374 (1972)), so if the above line of argumentation has not convinced you, you may want to take a look at those cases. Important is developing the ability to argue new cases from precedents. In the section on the ratio decidendi of a case, we discussed formulating the holding of a case, or series of cases. In this section, the emphasis is placed on formulating a holding in a way that can be used to solve future cases, regardless of which side of the case one might be arguing. In a common law country, this exercise is the essence of legal education, because a law school in a common law country trains students to be lawyers in an adversary system.

Questions on the Text

Re-read *Batson v. Kentucky* in Chapter 2 and then attempt to argue:

1. The new precedent announced in *Batson* should be applied retroactively to similar cases on direct review.
2. The new precedent announced in *Batson* should not be applied retroactively to similar cases on direct review.
3. The new precedent announced in *Batson* should be applied retroactively to similar cases on collateral review.
4. The new precedent announced in *Batson* should not be applied retroactively to similar cases on collateral review.

In 1989, the U.S. Supreme Court clarified when a new rule could be applied retroactively in a criminal case in which the conviction had already become final and the issue was approached on **collateral attack**. Read the following case:

Teague v. Lane
489 U.S. 288, 109 S.Ct. 1061, 103 L.Ed.2d 334 (1989)

Justice O'CONNOR announced the judgment of the Court ...

5

I

Petitioner, a black man, was convicted by an all-white Illinois jury of three counts of attempted murder, two counts of armed robbery, and one count of aggravated battery. During jury selection for petitioner's trial, the prosecutor used all 10 of his
10   peremptory challenges to exclude blacks. Petitioner's counsel used one of his 10 peremptory challenges to exclude a black woman who was married to a police officer. After the prosecutor had struck six blacks, petitioner's counsel moved for a mistrial. The trial court denied the motion ... When the prosecutor struck four more blacks, petitioner's counsel again moved for a mistrial, arguing that petitioner was
15   "entitled to a jury of his peers." ... The prosecutor defended the challenges by stating that he was trying to achieve a balance of men and women on the jury. The trial court denied the motion, reasoning that the jury "appear[ed] to be a fair [one]." ...

On appeal, petitioner argued that the prosecutor's use of peremptory challenges denied him the right to be tried by a jury that was representative of the community.
20   The Illinois Appellate Court rejected petitioner's fair cross section claim ... . The Illinois Supreme Court denied leave to appeal, and we denied certiorari. 464 U.S. 867, 104 S.Ct. 206, 78 L.Ed.2d 179 (1983).

Petitioner then filed a petition for a writ of habeas corpus ...

25   II

Petitioner's first contention is that he should receive the benefit of our decision in *Batson* even though his conviction became final before *Batson* was decided. ...

A

30   In the past, the Court has, without discussion, often applied a new constitutional rule of criminal procedure to the defendant in the case announcing the new rule, and has confronted the question of retroactivity later when a different defendant sought the benefit of that rule ... In several cases, however, the Court has addressed the retroactivity question in the very case announcing the new rule ... These two lines of cases
35   do not have a unifying theme, and we think it is time to clarify how the question of retroactivity should be resolved for cases on collateral review ...

Not all new rules have been uniformly treated for retroactivity purposes. Nearly a quarter of a century ago, in *Linkletter*, the Court attempted to set some standards by which to determine the retroactivity of new rules. The question in *Linkletter* was
40 whether *Mapp v. Ohio*, which made the exclusionary rule applicable to the States, should be applied retroactively to cases on collateral review. The Court determined that the retroactivity of *Mapp* should be determined by examining the purpose of the exclusionary rule, the reliance of the States on prior law, and the effect on the administration of justice of a retroactive application of the exclusionary rule ...

45 The *Linkletter* retroactivity standard has not led to consistent results. Instead, it has been used to limit application of certain new rules to cases on direct review, other new rules only to the defendants in the cases announcing such rules, and still other new rules to cases in which trials have not yet commenced ...

Dissatisfied with the *Linkletter* standard, Justice Harlan advocated a different ap-
50 proach to retroactivity. He argued that new rules should always be applied retroactively to cases on direct review, but that generally they should not be applied retroactively to criminal cases on collateral review. See *Mackey v. United States*, 401 U.S. 667, 675, 91 S.Ct. 1160, 1164, 28 L.Ed.2d 404 (1971) (opinion concurring in judgment in part and dissenting in part); *Desist*, 394 U.S. at 256, 89 S.Ct., at 1037
55 (dissenting opinion).

In *Griffith v. Kentucky*, 479 U.S. 314, 107 S.Ct. 708, 93 L.Ed.2d 649 (1987), we rejected as unprincipled and inequitable the *Linkletter* standard for cases pending on direct review at the time a new rule is announced, and adopted the first part of the retroactivity approach advocated by Justice Harlan ... [W]e held that "a new rule for
60 the conduct of criminal prosecutions is to be applied retroactively to all cases, state or federal, pending on direct review or not yet final, ...

Justice Harlan believed that new rules generally should not be applied retroactively to cases on collateral review ...

Justice Harlan identified only two exceptions to his general rule of nonretroactivity
65 for cases on collateral review. First, a new rule should be applied retroactively if it places "certain kinds of primary, private individual conduct beyond the power of the criminal law-making authority to proscribe." ... Second, a new rule should be applied retroactively if it requires the observance of "those procedures that ... are 'implicit in the concept of ordered liberty.'" ...

70 [W]e now adopt Justice Harlan's view of retroactivity for cases on collateral review. Unless they fall within an exception to the general rule, new constitutional rules of criminal procedure will not be applicable to those cases which have become final before the new rules are announced ...

Justice Harlan had reasoned that one of the two principal functions of habeas corpus
75 was "to assure that no man has been incarcerated under a procedure which creates an impermissibly large risk that the innocent will be convicted," and concluded "from this that all 'new' constitutional rules which significantly improve the pre-existing fact-finding procedures are to be retroactively applied on habeas." ...

We therefore hold that, implicit in the retroactivity approach we adopt today, is the
80 principle that habeas corpus cannot be used as a vehicle to create new constitutional

rules of criminal procedure unless those rules would be applied retroactively to *all* defendants on collateral review through one of the two exceptions we have articulated ...

Questions on the Text

1. Give a statement of a) the facts of the case, b) the legal history of the case, c) the issue raised on collateral review

2. Try to formulate the U.S. Supreme Court's position on the retroactivity of new precedents in criminal cases. What is the rule for cases on direct review? What is the rule for cases on collateral review?

3. The *Teague* holding articulates two exceptions to the general rule on retroactivity for cases on collateral review. What are they? To answer this question you need to understand the language in lines 65-69. What kinds of cases involve the announcement of a new rule that "places 'certain kinds of primary, private individual conduct beyond the power of the criminal law-making authority to proscribe.'"? Consider the case of *Roe v. Wade* 410 U.S. 113, 93 S.Ct. 705, 35 L.Ed.2d 147 (1973). Here the U.S. Supreme Court held that any law providing for criminal punishment of a woman who obtained an abortion was unconstitutional, because such a law violated the woman's constitutionally protected right to privacy. Is this the type of new rule that would fit under Justice Harlan's first exception? The second exception is somewhat more difficult to understand because expressions like "procedures ... implicit in the concept of ordered liberty" suffer from a lack of specificity. This exception, however, is clarified to a certain extent in lines 74-78 where the Court refers to habeas corpus as a means of ensuring that no one has been imprisoned "under a procedure which creates an impermissibly large risk that the innocent will be convicted" and states that new rules will be applied retroactively to cases on collateral review if they "significantly improve the pre-existing fact-finding procedures." To determine which cases those are, reconsider *Mapp v. Ohio* and Linkletter's attempt to have the exclusionary rule applied retroactively to his case on collateral review. Does the exclusionary rule improve the fact-finding process significantly, or at all? Is the purpose of the exclusionary rule to improve the fact-finding process or does it have a completely different purpose? Also reconsider *Gideon v. Wainwright*. Does being represented by a lawyer at trial improve the fact-finding process? Can you now distinguish between the holdings in *Mapp* and *Gideon* based on the Supreme Court's holding in *Teague*?

4 What do you think the result was in *Teague v. Lane*? Does the use of peremptory challenges to exclude members of the defendant's race negatively affect the fact-finding process? Is there any reason to believe that individuals of the same race as the defendant are better at determining what the facts are than members of a different race? Do you think that black jurors will automatically decide in favor of a black defendant? If so, would not the fact-finding process indeed be improved by the exclusion of blacks from the jury? Does that seem like a position the U.S. Supreme Court would want to adopt? Indeed the Court in *Batson* noted that "the Equal Protection Clause forbids the prosecutor to challenge potential jurors solely ... on the assumption that black jurors as a group will be unable impartially to consider the State's case against a black defendant" (lines 32-35). On the other hand, could one make an argument that whites may not be free from racial prejudice in judging a black defendant? If so, would the fact-finding process be improved by also including members of the defendant's race? Does the constitutional guarantee of a trial by a jury of one's peers mean that members of the defendant's own race should not be purposefully excluded? Although there is certainly language in the *Batson* decision indicating that position, review the development of cases on this issue that followed *Batson*, which are discussed in Chapter 2. In those cases the Supreme Court focused more on the denial of the prospective jurors' rights to equal protection rather than on the defendant's right to a trial by a jury of his peers. Reconsider in particular *Powers v. Ohio*, where a *white* defendant successfully objected to the exclusion of *black* jurors from the venire. Could Powers have been successful if the ratio decidendi of these cases had been that a defendant had a right to a jury of his peers in the sense that members of his own race could not be excluded? In fact, the U.S. Supreme Court held in *Teague* that *Batson* did not apply retroactively and Teague's conviction was upheld.

Terminology

custody	security of and control over a person (**Haft**) or a thing (**Gewahrsam**)
exclusionary rule	rule of evidence prohibiting the admission at trial of proof of the commission of a crime when the evidence has been gathered in an unreasonable search and seizure in violation of constitutional guarantees (**Beweisverwertungsverbot wegen unzulässiger Durchsuchung und Beschlagnahme**)

probable cause	reasonable grounds for a belief; used often in connection with the standard applied when deciding whether to issue an arrest warrant or a search warrant (ca. **dringender Tatverdacht**)
search and seizure	looking through s.o.'s belongings and taking into custody those things that may prove criminal activity (**Durchsuchung und Beschlagnahme von Beweismaterial**)
avenue of appeal	possibility to go to a higher court with a claim that a legal error has occurred in a lower court (**Rechtsweg**)
habeas corpus	(Latin: you may have the body)
writ of habeas corpus	also called the Great Writ; court order that s.o. be released from prison because confinement involves the potential violation of a constitutionally guaranteed right; does not revolve around question of guilt (**richterliche Haftprüfung**)
petition for a writ of habeas corpus	a form of **collateral attack** that can be filed after the person's conviction has become final and all **avenues of appeal have been exhausted** (**Antrag auf richterliche Haftprüfung**)
habeas corpus challenge	legal attack against constitutionality of a person's confinement in prison (ca. **Antrag auf richterliches Gehör wegen der Verfassungswidrigkeit einer Inhaftierung**)
prohibition against cruel and unusual punishment	prohibition contained in the Eighth Amendment to the U.S. Constitution prohibiting inhumane, unreasonable forms of punishment (**Verbot unmenschlicher oder erniedrigender Strafe**)
direct attack	an appeal from a judgment within the normal appellate process (ca. **Anfechtung eines Urteils**)
direct review	a court's consideration of a **direct attack** within the normal trial-appellate process, for example on appeal
to be pending	to be within the judicial process waiting for a judgment (**anhängig sein**)
cases pending on direct review	law suits in which the parties are still involved in appealing the decisions of lower courts(**anhängige Verfahren**); cases that are not yet final or **res judicata** (**rechtskräftig**)
cases on collateral review	law suits in which a party attacks a court judgment outside the normal appellate process (**wiederaufgenommene Verfahren**)
collateral attack	means of challenging a court's decision that is separate from the normal trial-appellate process, e.g. through a petition for a **writ of habeas corpus** (**Antrag auf Wiederaufnahme eines Verfahrens**)
collateral review	court's consideration of a collateral attack (**Wiederaufnahmeverfahren**)

retroactive application of a new precedent	application of a legal rule newly announced in a case to facts or law suits that arose before that rule was announced (**rückwirkende Anwendung einer neuen Rechtsregel**)
armed robbery	robbery committed with the use of a weapon (**Raub mit Waffen**)
aggravated battery	"An unlawful act of violent injury to the person of another, accompanied by circumstances of aggravation, such as the use of deadly weapon, great disparity between the ages and physical conditions of the parties, or the purposeful infliction of shame and disgrace" *Black's Law Dictionary* (vgl.: **gefährliche Körperverletzung**)
to proscribe	to prohibit (**verbieten**); opposite of: **to prescribe**: to require (**gebieten**)

B. Retroactivity of New Precedents in Civil Cases

In some sense the issue of retroactivity of new precedents is less complicated in civil than in criminal cases because collateral attack of final judgments is relatively rare in the civil law arena. The following case relates to this issue. Although it will be followed by an analysis and a list of terminology and general vocabulary, the case will not be interrupted before you reach the end of it. That, however, is no reason for you not to occasionally interrupt your own reading and try to analyze the case yourself in the manner to which you have become accustomed in this Unit. You should fully understand the facts of the case, the legal history of the case, the issue raised on appeal, the holding and the ratio decidendi on a level that would permit you to explain it to someone else.

James B. Beam Distilling Co. v. Georgia
501 U.S. 529, 111 S.Ct. 2439 (1991)

Justice SOUTER announced the judgment of the Court, and delivered an opinion in
5 which Justice STEVENS joins.

The question presented is whether our ruling in *Bacchus Imports, Ltd. v. Dias*, 468 U.S. 263, 104 S.Ct. 3049, 82 L.Ed.2d 200 (1984), should apply retroactively to claims arising on facts antedating that decision. We hold that application of the rule in that case requires its application retroactively in later cases.

10 Prior to its amendment in 1985, Georgia state law imposed an excise tax on imported alcohol and distilled spirits at a rate double that imposed on alcohol and distilled spirits manufactured from Georgia-grown products. See Ga.Code Ann. § 3-4-60 (1982). In

1984, a Hawaii statute that similarly distinguished between imported and local alcoholic products was held in *Bacchus* to violate the Commerce Clause ...

15   In *Bacchus'* wake, petitioner, a Delaware corporation and Kentucky bourbon manu-
      facturer, claimed Georgia's law likewise inconsistent with the Commerce Clause, and
      sought a refund of $2.4 million ... for the years 1982, 1983, and 1984. Georgia's
      Department of Revenue failed to respond to the request, and Beam thereafter
      brought a refund action against the State in the Superior Court of Fulton County ...

20   [T]he trial court agreed that § 3-4-60 could not withstand a *Bacchus* attack for the
      years in question, and that the tax had therefore been unconstitutional. Using the
      analysis described in this Court's decision in *Chevron Oil Co. v. Huson*, 404 U.S. 97,
      92 S.Ct. 349, 30 L.Ed.2d, 296 (1971), the court nonetheless refused to apply its
      ruling retroactively. It therefore denied petitioner's refund request. The Supreme

25   Court of Georgia affirmed the trial court in both respects. The court held the pre-
      1985 version of the statute to have violated the Commerce Clause as, in its words, an
      act of "simple economic protectionism." ... But it, too, applied that finding on a
      prospective basis only, in the sense that it declined to declare the State's application
      of the statute unconstitutional for the years in question. The court concluded that

30   but for *Bacchus* its decision on the constitutional question would have established a
      new rule of law by overruling past precedent ... upon which the litigants may justifi-
      ably have relied ...

      Beam sought a writ of certiorari from the Court on the retroactivity question. We
      granted the petition ... and now reverse ...

35   It is only when the law changes in some respect that an assertion of nonretroactivity
      may be entertained, the paradigm case arising when a court expressly overrules a
      precedent upon which the contest would otherwise be decided differently and by
      which the parties may previously have regulated their conduct. Since the question is
      whether the court should apply the old rule or the new one, retroactivity is properly

40   seen in the first instance as a matter of choice of law, "a choice ... between the
      principle of forward operation and that of relation backward." ...

      As a matter purely of judicial mechanics, there are three ways in which the choice-of-
      law problem may be resolved. First, a decision may be made fully retroactive, ap-
      plying both to the parties before the court and to all others by and against whom

45   claims may be pressed, consistent with res judicata and procedural barriers such as
      statutes of limitations. This practice is overwhelmingly the norm ... and is in keeping
      with the traditional function of the courts to decide cases before them based upon
      their best current understanding of the law ... But in some circumstances retroactive
      application may prompt difficulties of a practical sort. However much it comports

50   with our received notions of the judicial role, the practice has been attacked for its
      failure to take account of reliance on cases subsequently abandoned, a fact of life if
      not always one of jurisprudential recognition ...

      Second, there is the purely prospective method of overruling, under which a new rule
      is applied neither to the parties in the law-making decision nor to those others

55   against or by whom it might be applied to conduct or events occurring before that
      decision. The case is decided under the old law but becomes a vehicle for announcing

the new, effective with respect to all conduct occurring after the date of that decision. This Court has, albeit infrequently, resorted to pure prospectivity ... This approach claims justification in its appreciation that "[t]he past cannot always be erased by a
60 new judicial declaration," ... and that to apply the new rule to parties who relied on the old would offend basic notions of justice and fairness. But this equitable method has its own drawback: It tends to relax the force of precedent, by minimizing the costs of overruling, and thereby allows the courts to act with a freedom comparable to that of legislatures ...

65 Finally, a court may apply a new rule in the case in which it is pronounced, then return to the old one with respect to all others arising on facts predating the pronouncement. This method, which we may call modified, or selective, prospectivity, enjoyed its temporary ascendancy in the criminal law during a period in which the Court formulated new rules, prophylactic or otherwise, to insure protection of the
70 rights of the accused ...

But selective prospectivity also breaches the principle that litigants in similar situations should be treated the same, a fundamental component of *stare decisis* and the rule of law generally ... For this reason, we abandoned the possibility of selective prospectivity in the criminal context in *Griffith v. Kentucky* ..., even where the new
75 rule constituted a "clear break" with previous law, in favor of completely retroactive application of all decisions to cases pending on direct review. Though *Griffith* was held not to dispose of the matter of civil retroactivity, ... selective prospectivity appears never to have been endorsed in the civil context ... This case presents the issue.

80 Both parties have assumed the applicability of the *Chevron Oil* test, under which the Court has accepted prospectivity ... where a decision displaces a principle of law on which reliance may reasonably have been placed, and where prospectivity is on balance warranted by its effect on the operation of the new rule and by the inequities that might otherwise result from retroactive application ... But we have never em-
85 ployed *Chevron Oil* to the end of modified civil prospectivity ...

Griffith cannot be confined to the criminal law. Its equality principle, that similarly situated litigants should be treated the same, carries comparable force in the civil context ... Its strength is in fact greater in the latter sphere. With respect to retroactivity in criminal cases, there remains even now the disparate treatment of those cases
90 that come to the Court directly and those that come here in collateral proceedings ... Whereas *Griffith* held that new rules must apply retroactively to all criminal cases pending on direct review, we have since concluded that new rules will not relate back to convictions challenged on habeas corpus. *Teague v. Lane*, 489 U.S. 288, 109 S.Ct. 1060, 103 L.Ed.2d 334 (1989). No such difficulty exists in the civil arena, in which
95 there is little opportunity for collateral attack of final judgments.

Nor is selective prospectivity necessary to maintain incentives to litigate in the civil context as it may have been in the criminal before *Griffith*'s rule of absolute retroactivity. In the civil context, "even a party who is deprived of the full retroactive benefit of a new decision may receive some relief." ... Had the petitioners in *Bacchus*
100 lost their bid for retroactivity, for example, they would nonetheless have won protec-

tion from the future imposition of discriminatory taxes, and the same goes for the petitioner here. Assuming that pure prospectivity may be had at all, moreover, its scope must necessarily be limited to a small number of cases; its possibility is therefore unlikely to deter the broad class of prospective challengers of civil prece-
105 dent ...

Of course, retroactivity in civil cases must be limited by the need for finality ... once suit is barred by res judicata or by statutes of limitation or repose, a new rule cannot reopen the door already closed. It is true that one might deem the distinction arbitrary, just as some have done in the criminal context with respect to the distinction
110 between direct review and habeas: why should someone whose failure has otherwise become final not enjoy the next day's new rule from which victory would otherwise spring? It is also objected that in civil cases unlike criminal there is more potential for litigants to freeload on those without whose labor the new rule would never have come into being. (Criminal defendants are already potential litigants by virtue of
115 their offense, and invoke retroactivity only by way of defense; civil beneficiaries of new rules may become litigants as a result of the law change alone, and use it as a weapon.) That is true of the petitioner now before us, which did not challenge the Georgia law until after its fellow liquor distributors had won their battle in *Bacchus*. To apply the rule of *Bacchus* to the parties in that case but not in this one would not,
120 therefore, provoke Justice Harlan's attack on modified prospectivity as "[s]imply fishing one case from the stream of appellate review, using it as a vehicle for pronouncing new constitutional standards, and then permitting a stream of similar cases to flow by unaffected by that new rule." ... Beam had yet to enter the waters at the time of our decision in *Bacchus*, and yet we give it *Bacchus*' benefit. Insofar as
125 equality drives us, it might be argued that the new rule should be applied to those who had toiled and failed, but whose claims are now precluded by res judicata; and that it should not be applied to those who only exploit others' efforts by litigating in the new rule's wake.

Nor, finally, are litigants to be distinguished for choice-of-law purposes on the
130 particular equities of their claims to prospectivity: whether they actually relied on the old rule and how they would suffer from retroactive application of the new. It is simply in the nature of precedent, as a necessary component of any system that aspires to fairness and equality, that the substantive law will not shift and spring on such a basis ... .Once retroactive application is chosen for any assertedly new rule, it
135 is chosen for all others who might seek its prospective application ...

The grounds for our decision today are narrow. They are confined entirely to an issue of choice of law: when the Court has applied a rule of law to the litigants in one case it must do so with respect to all others not barred by procedural requirements or res judicata. We do not speculate as to the bounds or propriety of pure prospectivity ...

140 The judgment is reversed, and the case is remanded for further proceedings.

Analysis

This case involves an **excise tax,** which the State of Georgia imposed on alcohol imported from other states. An **excise tax** is defined by *Black's Law Dictionary* as follows:

> A tax imposed on the performance of an act, the engaging in an occupation, or the enjoyment of a privilege ... A tax on the manufacture, sale, or use of goods or on the carrying on of an occupation or activity, or a tax on the transfer of property. In current usage the term has been extended to include various license fees and practically every internal revenue tax except the income tax.

The administrative office responsible for collecting federal taxes is called the **Internal Revenue Service (IRS), revenues** being money received either from the operation of a business or as the government in the collection of taxes. In lines 17-18 of the *Beam* opinion, the Court refers to the Georgia **Department of Revenue,** which is the tax authority for the State of Georgia. A **refund action** is a law suit against the tax authority demanding a refund or return of taxes paid that are claimed not to have been due. In this case the plaintiff is a **corporation,** which is a legal entity with its own **legal personality,** by virtue of which it can sue and be sued. The corporation's legal personality is separate from that of its **shareholders** and it continues in existence regardless of who those shareholders are. When the Court states that it is a **Delaware corporation,** that means that the corporation was formed under the laws of the State of Delaware.

The case relies on the U.S. Supreme Court's decision in *Bacchus,* which involved an interpretation of the **Commerce Clause.** The **Commerce Clause** is contained in Article I Section 8 of the U.S. Constitution and reads as follows:

> The Congress shall have Power ... To regulate Commerce with foreign Nations, and among the several States, and with the Indian Tribes; ...

Furthermore, Article I Section 9 provides:

> No tax or duty shall be laid on Articles exported from any State.
> No preference shall be given by any Regulation of Commerce or Revenue to the Ports of one State over those of another; nor shall Vessels bound to, or from, one State be obliged to enter, clear, or pay Duties in another.

Compare these provisions to the *Treaty establishing the European Economic Community,* Articles 2 and 3:

> Article 2. The Community shall have as its task, by establishing a common market and progressively approximating the economic policies of Member States, to promote throughout the Community a harmonious development of economic activities, a continuous and balanced expansion, an increase in stability, an accelerated raising of the standard of living and closed relations between the States belonging to it.

> Article 3. For the purposes set out in Article 2, the activities of the Community shall include, as provided in this Treaty and in accordance with the time-table set out therein (a) the elimination, as between Member States, of customs duties and of quantitative restrictions on the import and export of goods, and of all other measures having equivalent effect ...

It is helpful to imagine the organization of the U.S. government as being more similar to the organization of the European Union than to the organization of the Federal Republic of Germany.

The *Teague* case involves retroactive application of new precedents to criminal cases on collateral review in cases in which the defendant's conviction has already become final. The *Beam* case discusses a similar question but with respect to civil disputes. When the judgment in a civil case becomes final, we say that the decision is **res judicata**. Consider the definition in *Black's Law Dictionary* of "**res judicata**":

> A matter adjudged; a thing judicially acted upon or decided; a thing or matter settled by judgment. Rule that a final judgment rendered by a court of competent jurisdiction on the merits is conclusive as to the rights of the parties and their privies, and, as to them, constitutes an absolute bar to a subsequent action involving the same claim, demand or cause of action ... And to be applicable, requires identity in thing sued for as well as identity of cause of action, of persons and parties to action, and of quality in persons for or against whom claim is made. The sum and substance of the whole rule is that a matter once judicially decided is finally decided.

When the Court refers in line 45 to **claims pressed consistent with res judicata**, it means that law suits may be filed based on a new rule as long as there has not already been a final judgment regarding that same claim. As you can see from the above definition, a case is only **res judicata** if a **court of competent jurisdiction** reached a **judgment on the merits** in that case. The word "jurisdiction" means the authority of a court to decide a case. A **court of competent jurisdiction** is a court that indeed does have this authority over the particular case in question. A **decision on the merits** is the resolution of a legal dispute based on the substantive value of the claim in light of the evidence presented, and not a judgment based merely on some technical or procedural defect. If a case is **res judicata,** then it cannot be retried, which means that a **subsequent action** is prohibited, or **barred**. To be barred, the subsequent action, or law suit, must involve the same **cause of action**, which means the legal basis for the claim.

The Court also refers to other "procedural barriers," such as **statutes of limitations** (lines 45; 107) and **statutes of repose** (line 107). A **statute of limitations** establishes the time period within which a person can bring a law suit after the basis for the law suit has arisen. If, for example, A runs into B's automobile causing damage, B must file his action within a specified amount of time after the accident or he will lose his right to file it under the **statute of limitations**. **Statutes of repose** limit the time in which an **actionable** injury may occur, for

example to a certain number of years after the sale of a product or the performance of services. If A performs services for B and B is injured as a result of A's
negligence in performing those services, B may only file an action based on those
injuries if they occurred within the time period established by a **statute of repose.**
If B is injured after the **statute of repose** has elapsed, then he no longer may file
a law suit based on that injury. The *Beam* decision makes clear that new rules
may not be the basis for a law suit that is otherwise barred by these various
procedural barriers.

Questions on the Text

1. State the facts of the *Beam* case, the legal history of the case, the issue on
appeal, the holding and the ratio decidendi in your own words.
2. In what three ways can a court resolve the problem of applying a new precedent? To which one of these possibilities is the *Beam* case addressed? Does
Beam say anything about the other two? If so, would the statement be part
of the holding or merely dicta? Do you think that the Court might be willing
to overrule the *Chevron Oil* case if it had the opportunity? Without having
read *Chevron Oil*, do you think that the new rule announced in it applied to
the parties to that suit?
3. In what ways does the problem of retroactivity arise in a civil law country
such as Germany within the European Union?

Terminology

excise tax	any one of a number of taxes imposed on sales, property trans-fers, the manufacture of goods
Commerce Clause	contained in Article I Section 8 of the U.S. Constitution; permits the U.S. Congress to regulate trade between the individual states
corporation	legal entity organized under law with legal personality distinct from the personalities of its shareholders (**Aktiengesellschaft**)
Delaware corporation	corporation organized under the laws of the State of Delaware, a state which has particularly beneficial laws for corporations and thus a common state of incorporation
legal personality	entity's ability to act with legal effect such that the entity is then subject to duties and can be attributed with violations of those

	duties; feature of a legal or juridical person (**Rechtspersönlichkeit**)
shareholder	person or legal entity holding shares of a company (**Aktionär**)
Department of Revenue	tax authority for the State of Georgia
Internal Revenue Service	federal tax authority (**Finanzamt**); commonly referred to as the IRS
refund action	law suit for return of taxes paid based on the claim that the taxes were not due (**Klage auf Rückzahlung einer Steuer**)
to press a claim	to sue for s.th. (**klagen**)
res judicata	case that has already been finally judged (**rechtskräftig entschiedene Sache**); used to mean that law suits which have already reached a final judgment may not be filed again
statute of limitations	(UK **limitation period**) period within which a law suit may be initiated after a violation of rights has occurred (**Verjährungsfrist**)
the rule of law	principle that cases should be decided in accordance with established principles of law and not by s.o.'s arbitrary determination (**Rechtsstaatsprinzip**); to be contrasted with **a rule of law**, which means any legal rule (**Rechtsregel**)
statute of repose	period within which damage must occur in order to be the basis for a law suit (**Frist, nach deren Ablauf ein Anspruch erloschen ist**)
actionable	of or relating to an injury for which a law suit may be maintained (ca. **einklagbar, gerichtlich verfolgbar**)
to bar	to hinder, to prohibit (**ausschließen**); **to be barred**: to be prohibited (**ausgeschlossen sein**), as in:
	claim barred by res judicata (**die Rechtskraft steht der Klage entgegen**)
	claim barred by procedural requirements (**die Klage ist unzulässig**)
	claim barred by the statute of limitations (**der Anspruch ist verjährt**)
	claim barred by a statute of repose (**Anspruch, der erloschen ist**)
court of competent jurisdiction	court with the power to decide a law suit; a court that has authority to decide a case (**zuständiges Gericht**)
judgment on the merits decision on the merits	a judgment that resolves the substantive claims of the parties and not one based on some procedural defect, such as lack of jurisdiction (**Sachurteil**)

Vocabulary

albeit	although
to aggravate	to make worse, to make more serious
ascendancy	peak, dominance, superiority
assertion	claim
to comport with	to agree with
to be confined to	to be limited to, to be restricted to
disparate	different, unequal, dissimilar
drawback	disadvantage
to endorse	to approve, to accept
to freeload	to take advantage of s.th. that s.o. else has had to pay for
to incorporate	to embody, to comprise
notion	idea, concept
paradigm	model, prime example
subsequent	later in time, following
to toil	to labor, to work hard
wake	aftermath; from the expression used for the water tracks created through the movement of a boat; used figuratively means s.th. that follows or results from s.th. else
to be warranted	to have a good reason supporting s.th., to be justified

Final Exercise in Unit I

In the selected readings below you will find a list of cases on the retroactivity of certain precedents, which are also in this list. Read the case announcing the new precedent and make arguments in the style introduced in this Chapter a) for the appellant and b) for the appellee/state attorney. All of these cases were decided before *Teague v. Lane*, so they will permit you to see a development in the law on this issue and thus give you an insight into the real life of the common law.

Suggested Reading

1. Cases for exercise:

Miranda v. Arizona, 384 U.S. 436 (1966) (announces new precedent)
    Johnson v. New Jersey, 384 U.S. 719 (1966) (addresses retroactivity issue)
    Jenkins v. Delaware, 395 U.S. 213 (1969) (addresses retroactivity issue)
Witherspoon v. Illinois, 391 U.S. 510 (1968) (announces new precedent)
    Witherspoon v. Illinois fn. 22 (addresses retroactivity issue)
Katz v. United States, 389 U.S. 347 (1967) (announces new precedent)
    Desist v. United States, 394 U.S. 244 (1969) (addresses retroactivity issue)
Douglas v. California, 372 U.S. 353 (1963) (announces new precedent)
    Stovall v. Denno, 388 U.S. 293 (1967)(addresses retroactivity issue)

2. Additional cases of interest:

Caspari v. Bohlen, 114 S.Ct. 948 (1994)
Gilmore v. Taylor, 113 S.Ct. 2112 (1993)
Graham v. Collins, 113 S.Ct. 892, 122 L.Ed.2d 260 (1993)
Harper v. Virginia Dept. of Taxation, 113 S.Ct. 2510 (1993)

Language Exercises
Unit I

I. Fill in the blanks with the correct verb. (The German verbs used for expressing the ideas in the following sentences are indicated in the infinitive form. The fact that the same German verb is used in more than one of these sentences does not mean that the English verb will be the same!):

1. The legislature ___ statutes. (verabschieden)
2. The German Civil Code ___ into a general part and four specific parts. (teilen)
3. The common law in the United States ___ from the common or unwritten law of England. (ableiten)
4. Judges in a common law system ___ by their previous decisions, referred to as precedents. (binden)
5. In an 1898 case, the House of Lords ___ that it was ___ by its own decisions and could not ___ from them, or ___ them, in future cases. (entscheiden [not: to decide!]; binden; abweichen; außer Kraft setzen)
6. In 1966 this decision ___ in an official announcement. (zurücknehmen)
7. The Lord Chancellor ___ this announcement. (bekanntgeben)
8. The doctrine of stare decisis ___ at least some degree of certainty in the law. (liefern)
9. On the other hand, one should not ___ to this doctrine too rigidly. (sich halten an)
10. Ms. Anderton ___ for attempting to handle stolen goods. (verfolgen)
11. She was only ___ for the attempt, because the crime ___. (verfolgen; nicht vollenden)
12. The trial court ___ the charges against Ms. Anderton, but its decision ___ by the court of appeal. (abweisen; aufheben)
13. On appeal to the Hours of Lords, the decision of the trial court ___ and Ms. Anderton ___ . (aufrechterhalten, bestätigen; freisprechen)
14. In contrast, Mr. Shivpuri ___ of an impossible attempt to deal with heroin. (verurteilen)
15. Mr. Shivpuri claimed that he ___ on the law ___ in *Anderton*. (sich verlassen auf; darstellen)

II. *Fill in the blanks with one or more terms:*

The person initiating a law suit is called the 1 . In order to initiate a law suit, one has to file a 2 or 3 , which contains 4 or 5 or 6 , all of which are words for "claims". The person against whom the law suit is initiated is called the 7 . A law suit is filed with the 8 . A party who is dissatisfied with the decision of this court can 9 to a higher court. The party doing that is called the 10 and the other party is called the 11 . In a common law system, judicial opinions contain principles of law in the 12 , which function as binding 13 for future similar cases. In a civil law system, the primary source of law is contained in 14 . A common law system also has written laws called 15 . The highest court in England is the 16 , which is headed by the 17 , who is also the head of the British 18 . The other judges on this court are called 19 . A higher court's opinion contains a description of the 20 , which tells you what happened, and a statement of the 21 , which tells you how the lower courts decided the case. Furthermore, the opinion contains a statement of the 22 , which is the legal problem raised for the court's decision and the 23 , which is the solution to this problem. Anything the court says that is not necessary for its decision in the case is called 24 . Another way to say that someone is responsible for paying for the damage he has caused is to say that he was held 25 for 26 . Responsibility in a torts case is often based on 27 , which means the failure to exercise 28 care under the circumstances.

III. *Which of the following forms of action are actions ex contractu and which are actions ex delicto?*

assumpsit – covenant – debt – replevin – trespass – trespass on the case – trover

IV. *Match the following definitions to the above terms:*

a. form of action to recover damages to compensate for injury caused by the defendant's unlawful interference with the plaintiff's person, property or rights

b. form of action to recover a specific sum of money the defendant owes the plaintiff

c. form of action to recover damages to compensate for the value of personal property which the defendant has wrongfully converted to his own use, such as by finding the plaintiff's property and keeping it for himself

d. form of action for damages to compensate for the defendant's failure to perform as promised under a simple contract, whereby the promise may be implied by law or expressly made by the defendant

e. form of action to recover personal property from defendant who unlawfully detains it, whereby the plaintiff may secure possession of that property on the posting of a bond or security at any time before judgment

f. form of action to recover damages to compensate for injury resulting from the defendant's wrongful act which was not an act of direct or immediate force but instead which caused the harm indirectly or as a secondary consequence

g. form of action for damages to compensate for the defendant's failure to perform as promised under a contract which is written and has been signed, sealed and delivered to the plaintiff

V. Fill in the blanks (some could require more than one word):

In the United States, two types of jury are used, the _1_ and the _2_. The former is responsible for handing down the _3_, which contains the criminal charges against the accused. The latter is also referred to as the _4_ and is classically composed of twelve members. The members of this _5_ are selected from the _6_, or the group of people who are qualified for and neither excused nor exempt from service. If a lawyer suspects that the jury commissioner has exercised discrimination in selecting this body, she may exercise a _7_. The actual selection process for the twelve who will serve is called the _8_. Lawyers can affect the composition of the _9_ by exercising a _10_ if there is good reason to believe that the person is unfit to serve. In addition, each of the lawyers has a certain limited number of _11_ with which they may exclude persons without giving any reason for the exclusion. After the twelve have been chosen they are _12_ and sworn in.

VI. Select the correct verb to complete the sentences. (The German verbs used for expressing the ideas in the following sentences are indicated in the infinitive form. The fact that the same German verb is used in more than one of these sentences does not mean that the English verb will be the same!):

1. The court ___ that discrimination in jury selection was unconstitutional. (entscheiden)
2. The lawyer ___ a peremptory challenge. (ausüben)
3. The defendant ___ for a writ of certiorari. The Supreme Court ___ the writ. (beantragen; stattgeben/ablehnen)
4. The lawyer ___ to impanel a twelve-person jury. The judge ___ the motion and impaneled six. (beantragen; ablehnen)
5. The defendant ___ by a jury of his peers. (beurteilen)
6. The grand jury ___ to determine the validity of the indictment. (zusammentreffen)
7. The trial jury ___ the defendant as charged. (verurteilen)

8. The trial court judge ___ the defendant to life imprisonment. (verurteilen)
9. Mr. Justice White ___ the opinion of the Court, in which Mr. Justice Stevens ___. (verkünden; zustimmen)
10. The prosecutor ___ the accused to trial. (anklagen)
11. The judge ___ the jury on the law. The jury was then ___. It ___ only 30 minutes before it ___a verdict. (belehren; isolieren; beraten; [zu einer Entscheidung] kommen)
12. The witness ___ as to what she saw on the night of the crime. (bezeugen)
13. The Court of Appeals ___ the decision of the trial court, but the Supreme Court disagreed, so they ___. (aufrechterhalten; [Entscheidung] aufheben)
14. Florida law ___ for a jury of six persons. (vorsehen)
15. After the plaintiff ___ a prima facie case, the burden of proof ___ to the defense. (darlegen; Umkehr der Beweislast)

VII. *Explain the difference between the following terms*:

1. judgment – verdict – sentence
2. felony – misdemeanor – petty offense – capital crime
3. to overrule – to reverse – to remand
4. citation – quotation
5. deliberation – sequestration

VIII. *Insert the correct prepositions*:

The theory _1_ adjudication _2_ the adversary system, as usually stated, has two linked components. One is that party presentation will result _3_ the best presentation, because each party is propelled _4_ maximum effort in investigation and presentation _5_ the prospect of victory; _6_ contrast, a judge-interrogator is only interested in getting _7_ the day and through his caseload. The other component of the theory is more complex and has to do _8_ the psychology of decision making. It runs essentially as follows: Proof through evidence requires hypothesis; hypothesis requires a preliminary mind-set; if an active judge-interrogator develops the proof, his preliminary mind-set too easily can become his final decision; therefore, it is better to have conflicting preliminary hypotheses and supporting proofs presented _9_ the parties so that the judge's mind can be kept open until all the evidence is _10_ hand.

IX. *Explain the difference between the following terms*:

1. beyond a reasonable doubt – by a preponderance of the evidence
2. alternative dispute resolution – adjudication

X. *Explain the difference between the following terms:*

1. lawyer – attorney – litigator
2. solicitor – barrister – junior – QC – silk
3. in-house lawyer – Wall Street lawyer – judge's clerk – public defender
4. consulting fee – retainer – hourly fee – flat fee – contingency fee – brief fee – refresher
5. interrogatory – deposition – request for admissions
6. deterrence – rehabilitation – retribution
7. record – transcript
8. motion for a non-suit – motion for a directed verdict – motion for judgment notwithstanding the verdict
9. prejudicial error – harmless error
10. general verdict – special verdict

XI. *Answer the following questions on terminology:*

1. What are the names of the three branches of the government?
2. What are the names of the persons who work within each of these branches?
3. What adjectives are used for each of these branches of government?
4. What is the difference between the term **government** in English and **Regierung** in German?

XII. *Fill in the blanks, some of which may require more than one term:*

In order to initiate a law suit the _1_ must file a _2_ . The _2_ contains allegations of the court's _3_ over the person of the _4_ and over the subject matter of the law suit. It also contains allegations of facts that make out a _5_ , and a _6_ , asking the court to award the _1_ compensation for the injury the _4_ has caused him. A _7_ is attached to the _2_ , which is a formal order addressed to the _4_ telling her to appear in court to defend against the law suit. If the _4_ fails to do so, the court will enter a _8_ against her. The _2_ and _7_ must be served on the _4_ , which is called _9_ . The _4_ must respond to the _2_ by filing either a _10_ , which asks the court to refuse to hear the suit because of procedural error, or a _11_ , which claims that the _2_ fails to state a _5_ , or an _12_ . The _12_ may contain _13_ , _14_ , _15_ , or _16_ . The _1_ may respond to the _4_'s _12_ in his _17_ , and the _4_ may in

turn respond to the 1's 17 in her 18 . The 2 , the 12 , the 17 , and the 18
constitute the 19 . After they have all been filed either party may make a 20 .

XIII. Fill in the blanks with the correct terminology:

Ms. Mapp was 1 for possession of pornography in violation of Ohio law. The
 2 had been gathered in an illegal 3 and 4 and used against her at 5 . The U.S.
Supreme Court held that 6 gathered in violation of a person's Fourth Amendment rights could not be used against that person. It thus extended the 7 to
apply to criminal proceedings in a state court. The Supreme Court, however,
refused to apply its 8 in *Mapp* 9 to overturn Linkletter's 10 . That was because
Linkletter came to the Court on 11 rather than on 12 as did *Mapp*.

For the police to be permitted to take someone into 13 , they must first obtain
an 14 . If they want to inspect a person's home for proof that the person committed a crime, they must first obtain a 15 . A judge may not issue one of these
 16 unless it is based on 17 , meaning there is good reason to think the person
actually committed a crime.

XIV. Explain the relationship and distinction between the following terms:

1. direct attack – direct review – appeal – collateral attack – collateral review –
   petition for a writ of habeas corpus
2. statute of limitations – statute of repose – res judicata

Unit II
The Courts and their Jurisdiction

Chapter 1
Court Systems in the United States

A. General Structure

Very generally stated, court systems in the United States are three-tiered systems, which include **trial courts**, intermediate **appellate courts** and a **supreme court**.

1. Trial Courts

It is in the **trial court** that a **plaintiff** initiates a law suit against a **defendant**. **Trial courts** are called **courts of first impression**, because a case is heard for the first time in these courts. A trial court is headed by one judge and convenes with or without a jury. Here **issues of fact** and **issues of law** can be raised for judicial determination. **Issues of fact** are questions about what actually happened in a case. To answer these questions, the **factfinder** needs **evidence** or proof of the facts the parties claim are true. The **factfinder** is either a jury or the **trial court judge**. It is the jury if one of the **parties to the law suit** exercises her right to trial by jury. It is the judge if both parties waive their rights to trial by jury. Thus either a jury or judge will hear the evidence the parties present and decide, as **factfinder,** what to believe in a particular case. **Issues of law** are questions about what rules of law to apply to the case and how to interpret those rules. It is always the judge who is the final authority on the law and who is thus responsible for resolving the **issues of law**. As you know from Chapter 2, in a jury trial the judge will instruct the jury on the law at the end of the trial. Consequently, it is up to the jury to apply that law to the facts the jury believes to be true from the evidence presented. Still, it is the judge who will decide what instructions to give the jury and how to formulate these instructions. This decision rests on the judge's determination of what rules of law to apply to the particular case and on how to interpret those rules.

We say that trial courts have **original jurisdiction**. **Jurisdiction** is the power of a court to hear a case. **Original jurisdiction** is the power of a court to hear a case in the first instance, or as a trial court. If the jurisdiction of a court is unlimited, meaning that it has the power to hear any case as a trial court, regardless of the subject matter of the dispute or the amount in controversy, we say that the court has **general jurisdiction**. Many continental European nations have courts which are specialized according to the types of cases they hear, such as **administrative courts** or **labor courts**, or are divided into separate chambers or senates for criminal or civil law disputes. Most trial courts in the United States, however, hear cases regardless of whether they raise questions of criminal, civil or public law, and therefore are considered to be **courts of general jurisdiction**. There are, however, also **courts of limited jurisdiction**. So, for example, a **juvenile court** may hear only cases involving **minors** and a **municipal court** may hear only cases in which the **amount in controversy** is rather low (e.g. $20,000 or less). A court of limited jurisdiction, however, does not fit within our major three-tiered hierarchy of courts but is auxiliary to it. In some sense the decision it reaches as a trial court does not supply the final word on the facts of a case either. Instead, a party dissatisfied with the result a **trial court of limited jurisdiction** has reached may often turn to the **trial court of general jurisdiction** and request a **trial de novo**, or a completely new trial with a new determination of the issues of fact raised in the case.

Most trial courts are also said to be **courts of record**, meaning that they keep a detailed record of their proceedings. The most informative part of the **record** is the **transcript**, a verbatim documentation of every word uttered during the trial. In addition the record includes the **pleadings**, which are the formals documents filed by the parties to initiate the law suit, physical exhibits introduced into evidence during the trial, the jury's verdict, the judgment the trial court entered, and any other orders the trial court issued or documents relating to the law suit.

2. Intermediate Appellate Courts

A party dissatisfied with the decision of a trial court of general jurisdiction can **appeal** to an intermediate **appellate court**. The party filing the appeal is called the **appellant** and the other party is called the **appellee**. In a **court of appeals** only **issues of law** may be raised. The appellate court does *not* conduct a second trial and hear evidence of the facts of a case on appeal as a trial court of general jurisdiction does in a **trial de novo**. The appellate court is responsible only for legal error that may have occurred during the trial. The **appellate court** is headed by a panel of judges, usually three in number, and since there are no factual decisions to be made, no jury is ever present on appeal. Generally, individuals have a right to appeal once, meaning that the intermediate appellate court is obliged to hear the case. Appellate courts are said to have **appellate jurisdiction**, the power to hear a case after it has already been decided by a lower court. When a court of appeals reaches a decision, the decision will be published in a **reporter**. It is these decisions and the decisions of the supreme courts that give the common law lawyer information on the status of the law. It is also these decisions that a student of law reads during law school, and that you have been reading in this book.

3. Supreme Court

Finally, a party dissatisfied with the decision of the appellate court may **petition** to the **supreme court** to have that court review the decision. Again only **issues of law** may be raised and no issues of fact. Supreme courts are usually headed by seven to nine **justices** who hear each case **in banc,** or as a whole court, rather than in panels as the intermediate appellate court. A party to a law suit has no right to have a case heard by the **supreme court**. Instead, the party must **petition** the court and the **supreme court** itself will decide whether to hear the appeal. As you should recall from Unit I, this petition is referred to as a **petition for a writ of certiorari**. If the supreme court decides to hear the case it will grant the **writ of certiorari**. This writ is then addressed to the court of appeals ordering it to certify the **record** in the case and send it up to the supreme court for review. So although it is the dissatisfied party to the law suit who petitions for the writ, it is the court of appeals which receives it if it is issued. Since the supreme court hears a case after it has been decided by a lower court, the supreme court is also said to have **appellate jurisdiction**. On this level, the party petitioning is referred to as the **petitioner** and the other party as the **respondent**. The supreme courts are referred to as **courts of last resort**, because there is no place to turn after they have reached their decision. Consequently, the supreme court has the final word on what the law is, and its precedents bind all courts of appeals and trial courts within its jurisdiction.

4. Unique Characteristics of the U.S. Judiciary

Each state in the United States has its own court system and the federal government also has a court system, making the United States judiciary very different from the judiciaries of European nations. It is important to realize that each state in the United States is a self-contained legal system. Accordingly, it has its own state constitution, a governor as the head of the executive branch, a state legislature, which is usually divided into a house of representatives and a senate, and a judiciary comprising trial courts, appellate courts and one state supreme court. The state courts are responsible for interpreting and applying law that the state legislature has adopted. This law governs legal areas over which the state has jurisdiction, which include criminal law, civil law and public law. Indeed the lives of most U.S. citizens are governed primarily by state law. If an individual commits a crime, closes a contract or causes an automobile accident, most likely his conduct will be subject to state and not federal law and his case will be tried by a state court and not a federal court. The state supreme court will have the final word on the law in his case and he will not be able to turn to the U.S. courts for assistance. It is only in a specifically limited number of cases that the federal legal system comes into play, for example for crimes in violation of federal law such as kidnapping where the victim has been transported across a state border, for contracts involving interstate commerce, under certain circumstances for accidents caused by a citizen of one state which injure a citizen of another state, and in general for any case arising under U.S. law, including the Constitution and international treaties.

The federal system will be discussed first in more detail, but before moving on consider the following chart characterizing the general structure of a court system coupled with the relevant terminology:

Supreme Court

petitioner v. respondent
grants or denies petition for a writ of certiorari as a matter of discretion
has appellate jurisdiction
considers issues of law and not of fact
hears cases in banc (7-9 justices)
court of last resort

|

Court of Appeals

appellant v. appellee
appeal generally as a matter of right
has appellate jurisdiction
considers issues of law and not of fact
hears cases in panels of three judges
intermediate appellate court

|

Trial Court

plaintiff v. defendant
has general jurisdiction
has original jurisdiction
is a court of record
considers issues of fact and of law
hears cases with one judge and perhaps a jury
court of first impression

B. Federal Courts: Organization

The judicial power of the United States is defined in Article III of the United States Constitution. (See Appendix I for the text of Article III). Article III, Section 1 provides directly for one supreme court and "such inferior Courts as the Congress may from time to time ordain and establish." Accordingly, the existence of all of the federal courts, with the exception of the United States Supreme Court, depends on legislative enactment. Congress may increase or decrease the number of federal courts, or indeed abolish them altogether. The President of the United States, with the "advice and consent of the Senate," appoints the judges for all federal courts. They serve life terms and can only be dismissed for misbehavior in office.

1. U.S. District Courts

The federal court system includes trial courts, called **U.S. District Courts**, which are scattered throughout the United States and its territories. States with a comparatively low population have only one. As the population of an individual state increases, so do the number of **district courts** in that state. The largest number of **district courts** in any single state is four, in the states of California, New York and Texas. As any trial court, the **U.S. District Court** is a court of **original jurisdiction**. Its jurisdiction, however, is **limited** since it may hear only cases over which the Constitution or federal law specifically grants it jurisdiction. The U.S. District Court is also a **court of record**. For private law disputes and criminal cases, the **U.S. District Court** convenes with one judge and possibly a jury. For some rare cases, the U.S. District Court convenes as a three-judge panel with no jury (see for example, *Brown v. Board of Education* in Unit III on constitutional law). In addition to the U.S. District Courts, there are several specialized trial courts in the federal system, such as the **United States Court of Federal Claims** and the **Court of International Trade**. The specialization of these courts usually relates to the subject matter of the law suits they are empowered to hear. The **Claims Court,** for example, has jurisdiction over cases involving legal claims against the United States, over some cases involving patent or copyright infringements and over some claims filed by Native Americans, the American Indians. The **Court of International Trade** has jurisdiction, for example, over claims filed against the United States under laws relating to tariffs and trade, to imports, to embargoes or other quantitative restrictions on importation.

2. U.S. Courts of Appeals

The intermediate court of appeals in the federal system is referred to as the **U.S. Court of Appeals**. There are thirteen courts of appeals in the federal system. First, the United States is divided into eleven numbered **circuits**, or areas, each of which has one circuit court of appeals. These courts hear appeals from final decisions of the district courts located in their particular circuit. The eleven numbered circuits are organized as follows:

U.S. Court of Appeals for the:	hears appeals from the district courts located in:
First Circuit	Maine, Massachusetts, New Hampshire, Puerto Rico, Rhode Island
Second Circuit	Connecticut, New York, Vermont
Third Circuit	Delaware, New Jersey, Pennsylvania, Virgin Islands
Fourth Circuit	Maryland, North Carolina, South Carolina, Virginia, West Virginia
Fifth Circuit	District of the Canal Zone, Louisiana, Mississippi, Texas
Sixth Circuit	Kentucky, Michigan, Ohio, Tennessee
Seventh Circuit	Illinois, Indiana, Wisconsin
Eighth Circuit	Arkansas, Iowa, Minnesota, Missouri, Nebraska, North Dakota, South Dakota
Ninth Circuit	Alaska, Arizona, California, Idaho, Montana, Nevada, Oregon, Washington, Guam, Hawaii
Tenth Circuit	Colorado, Kansas, New Mexico, Oklahoma, Utah, Wyoming
Eleventh Circuit	Alabama, Florida, Georgia

In addition there is a circuit for the District of Columbia (Washington D.C.), which is referred to as the D.C. Circuit, and a so-called **Federal Circuit**. The **U.S. Court of Appeals for the Federal Circuit** hears appeals, for example, from final decisions of the **Court of Federal Claims** and the **Court of International Trade**.

A **U.S. Court of Appeals** generally convenes in three-judge panels. After hearing an appeal, the judges will reach a decision in the case by a simple majority. They will also write a **majority opinion** indicating their **holding** and giving reasons for this holding. If a judge disagrees with the majority, he is in the **dissent** and may write a **dissenting opinion**. These opinions are published and signed by the judge or judges who agree with the particular opinion.

3. U.S. Supreme Court

The **United States Supreme Court** consists of one **chief justice** and eight **associate justices**. The U.S. Supreme Court has both **original jurisdiction** and **appellate jurisdiction**. Consider the following section from the **United States Code**, containing the laws of the United States, on the Supreme Court's **original jurisdiction**:

UNITED STATES CODE

TITLE 28

JUDICIARY AND JUDICIAL PROCEDURE

PART IV – JURISDICTION AND VENUE

CHAPTER 81 – SUPREME COURT

§ 1251. Original jurisdiction

(a) The Supreme Court shall have original and exclusive jurisdiction of all controversies between two or more States.

(b) The Supreme Court shall have original but not exclusive jurisdiction of:

(1) All actions or proceedings to which ambassadors, other public ministers, consuls, or vice consuls of foreign states are parties;

(2) All controversies between the United States and a State;

(3) All actions or proceedings by a State against the citizens of another State or against aliens.

According to 1251(a), the U.S. Supreme Court has both **original** and **exclusive jurisdiction** over all cases in which the parties are states of the United States. **Exclusive jurisdiction** is the power to hear a case to the exclusion of all other courts. Accordingly, it is the U.S. Supreme Court, and it alone, that will convene as a trial court when, for example, the State of California files an action against the State of Oregon. In addition 1251(b) grants the U.S. Supreme Court **original** but *not* **exclusive jurisdiction** over three other types of cases. Here the U.S. Supreme Court shares jurisdiction as a trial court with other courts, primarily the U.S. District Courts.

In addition, the U.S. Supreme Court has **appellate jurisdiction** over so-called **direct appeals** from the decisions of the federal district courts when the judges hear a case as a three-judge panel. These appeals are called "direct" because the parties skip over the intermediate court of appeals and take their appeal directly to the U.S. Supreme Court.

By far the most common type of appeal to the U.S. Supreme Court is via the **writ of certiorari**. A party may petition for a writ of certiorari from the final decision of a U.S. Court of Appeals, because it is the U.S. Supreme Court that is the court of last resort for cases initiated in the federal court system. A party may also petition for a writ of certiorari from the judgment of the highest court of a state if the appeal raises questions under the U.S. Constitution, treaties or laws of the United States. Consider the following section of the U.S.Code:

UNITED STATES CODE

TITLE 28

JUDICIARY AND JUDICIAL PROCEDURE

PART IV – JURISDICTION AND VENUE

CHAPTER 81 – SUPREME COURT

§ 1257. State Courts; certiorari

(a) Final judgments or decrees rendered by the highest court of a State in which a decision could be had, may be reviewed by the Supreme Court by writ of certiorari where the validity of a treaty or statute of the United States is drawn in question or where the validity of a statute of any State is drawn in question on the ground of its being repugnant to the Constitution, treaties, or laws of the United States, ...

Again the overlapping jurisdiction of the state and federal courts may be a source of confusion. A party who claims, for example, that a state law violates his rights under the United States Constitution may file his law suit in a U.S. District Court, because that court has jurisdiction over issues raised under the U.S. Constitution. But he may also file the law suit in a state trial court, because all courts in the United States are bound by and have jurisdiction to interpret the U.S.Constitution. If he files it in a state trial court and loses, he may appeal to the intermediate appellate court in the state. If he loses on appeal, he may petition to that state's supreme court. If the state supreme court hears the appeal and he again loses, 28 U.S.C. 1257 permits him to petition for a writ of certiorari to the United States Supreme Court. This form of appellate jurisdiction is available to give the U.S.Supreme Court the final say on matters raised under the Constitution, federal law or U.S. treaties, regardless of where the law suit was originally filed.

As indicated, the U.S. Supreme Court actually hears only a small fraction of the cases for which a petition has been filed. One of the most likely types of cases to be granted certiorari is a case raising an issue of law over which the various circuits disagree. Recall the *Batson* decision in which the Supreme Court held that the use of peremptory challenges to exclude people of a particular race was unconstitutional. *Batson* was in fact a criminal case and the prosecutor was the one to use his peremptory challenges discriminatorily to exclude members of the defendant's race. After the Supreme Court decided *Batson*, cases came to the various U.S. Courts of Appeals raising a whole range of questions not directly answered in *Batson*: Did *Batson* apply to defense counsel as well? Did it apply for civil law disputes, or only criminal? Did it apply when the discrimination was directed against a race other than the defendant's? Or the plaintiff's? Did it apply to discrimination based on gender? religion? age? As these cases came to the various U.S. Courts of Appeals, the results they reached varied. Remember a judicial precedent binds only the court which reached the decision and all lower courts over which that court has appellate jurisdiction. Accordingly, if the Court of Appeals for the Second Circuit answered one of these questions in the affirmative, that decision bound that court in all future cases and also bound the district courts in the second circuit, namely those located in the states of Connecticut, New York and Vermont. It did not bind the other courts of appeals in the other circuits or the district courts in those circuits. The Court of Appeals for the Seventh Circuit, for example, was free to answer the same question negatively, thus binding only itself and the courts in the various districts in the seventh circuit. As time passes in a situation such as this, and the various courts of appeals come down differently on new issues of law raised by a Supreme Court decision, uncertainty creeps into the interpretation and application of federal law. It is in this type of situation that the U.S. Supreme Court will step in by granting a writ of certiorari in the next case raising the disputed issue. The Supreme Court's holding will then be final and bind all federal courts throughout the United States.

A simple majority (5 to 4) is sufficient for deciding a case. One member of the majority of Supreme Court justices will write the **majority opinion**, and as many justices who agree in both the **holding** and the reasons for that holding will join in the opinion and sign their names to it. Some justices may agree with the holding but disagree on the reasons for it. If so, they may write a **concurring opinion**, spelling out their own reasons for the holding they reached as part of the majority. Justices who disagree with the holding may write a **dissenting opinion**. In some cases, the Supreme Court does not write any full opinion at all, but rather merely publishes its disposition of the case in a **per curiam** opinion, which is a short statement of the holding without any explanation of the reasons for it.

Perhaps because judges in the United States always sign their opinions, thus permitting lawyers to follow their general views on legal issues and prepare themselves accordingly for future argument before these justices, lawyers generally know their names. Indeed, many people in the United States who have nothing to do with the legal profession know their names. That may be attributable to the fact that we have only nine of these justices, that their appointments are usually surrounded by a good deal of popular press coverage, that their appointments are for life rather than only a few years and that the appointments have some political overtones because the President of the United States, as representative of a particular political party, makes them, albeit under the approval of a simple majority of the Senate.

The current justices, the year of their appointment, the president who appointed them and the president's party affiliation are:

1. Chief Justice William H. Rehnquist   1986   President Ronald Reagan (Republican)
2. Justice John Paul Stevens   1975   President Gerald Ford (Republican)
3. Justice Sandra Day O'Connor   1981   President Ronald Reagan
4. Justice Antonin Scalia   1986   President Ronald Reagan
5. Justice Anthony M. Kennedy   1988   President Ronald Reagan
6. Justice David H. Souter   1990   President George Bush (Republican)
7. Justice Clarence Thomas   1991   President George Bush
8. Justice Ruth Bader Ginsburg   1993   President William Clinton (Democrat)
9. Justice Steven Breyer   1994   President William Clinton

Questions on the Text

1. Describe your own court system using the general terminology from this section. Does your system also have three tiers? Are your courts distinguished on the basis of the types of cases they hear? Does your system have courts of limited and general jurisdiction? Does it provide for trials de novo and for appeals? Is an appeal to your highest court a matter of right, or can the court refuse to hear the case as a matter of its own discretion?

2. Do you know the names of any of your higher court justices? Do you have only one highest court to hear appeals for all types of cases, or a number of higher courts? Do your justices serve life terms, or are they appointed for a limited term? How are they appointed? Are their appointments also politically influenced?

3. Is your judicial system, or legal system in general, divided into individual states which are members of a federal union? If so, do you have state, as opposed to federal, courts?

Terminology

trial court	first court to hear a case, considers both issues of fact and issues of law, convenes with one judge and possibly a jury (**Tatsacheninstanz**)
appellate court	intermediate court; considers only issues of law on appeal, namely errors that it is claimed the trial court made in the law; convenes with a panel of judges (usually three) and no jury; also called the **court of appeals** (U.S.: **Revisionsgericht** [and *not* **Berufungsgericht!**]; U.K.: **Berufungs- oder Revisionsgericht**)
supreme court	highest court in a court system; considers only issues of law on appeal; decision to hear a case is within the discretion of the court; convenes in banc; usually has seven to nine judges (**oberstes Revisionsgericht**)
court of first impression	term used to describe a trial court because it is the first court to hear a case (**erstinstanzliches Gericht**)
court of last resort	final court in a hierarchy of courts to which a party can turn on appeal (**letztinstanzliches Gericht**)
court of record	court that keeps a detailed protocol of exactly what happened in a case
issue of fact	question about what actually happened in a case (**Tatfrage**)
issue of law	question about what law to apply in a case and how to interpret that law (**Rechtsfrage**)
original jurisdiction	the power to hear a case as a trial court (**Zuständigkeit als Tatsacheninstanz; Zuständigkeit in erster Instanz**)
general jurisdiction	power of a court to hear any type of case as a trial court, regardless of the subject matter or amount in controversy (**unbeschränkte Zuständigkeit**)
limited jurisdiction	power of a court to hear a case as a trial court which is restricted according to subject matter of the case or the amount in controversy (**beschränkte Zuständigkeit**)
appellate jurisdiction	power of a court to hear cases after they have been decided by a lower court; power of review of lower court decisions for errors of law (**Zuständigkeit als Revisionsgericht**)
exclusive jurisdiction	power of a court alone to hear a case to the exclusion of all other courts (**ausschließliche Zuständigkeit**)
respondent	party against whom an appeal to a supreme court has been taken by the **petitioner** via a **writ of certiorari** (**Revisionsbeklagter** [Zivilrecht]; **Revisionsgegner** [Strafrecht]); (U.K.) term used to indicate person against whom appeal has been taken, or what in

	U.S. could also be called the **appellee** if the appeal is not to the supreme court
justice	judge, usually used for judges on a supreme court (**Richter**)
in banc	as a whole court, describes method of hearing cases whereby all judges on the court convene together rather than in panels or groups of judges
juvenile court	court of limited jurisdiction with the power to hear only cases involving **minors** (those under eighteen years of age) and usually relating to juvenile delinquency problems (**Jugendgericht**)
trial de novo	a second trial held by a court of general jurisdiction of a case already decided by a trial court of limited jurisdiction (**Verfahren in der Berufungsinstanz**); (U.K.) also called **appeal** on points of fact
reporter	collection of complete decisions of a court or courts (see Appendix II for a list of reporters in the U.S. and U.K.) (**Entscheidungssammlung**)
U.S. District Court	trial court in the federal court system (**Bundesbezirksgericht**)
U.S. Court of Appeals	intermediate appellate court in the federal court system (**Bundesrevisionsgericht**)
U.S. Supreme Court	highest court in the federal court system (combination of all the **oberste Bundesgerichte** and the **Bundesverfassungsgericht**)
U.S. Court of Federal Claims	trial court in the federal court system with jurisdiction over some claims because of their subject matter, such as claims against the United States
Court of International Trade	trial court in the federal system with jurisdiction over claims relating to tariffs and trade, imports, embargoes and other quantitative restrictions on imports
district	an area of a state over which a U.S. District Court has jurisdiction; each state comprises at least one and currently at most four districts (**Gerichtsbezirk**)
circuit	an area including a number of districts over which a U.S. Court of Appeals has jurisdiction to hear appeals from its district courts; there are 13 circuits: 11 numbered circuits, which cover the 50 states and the U.S. territories; the D.C. Circuit, and the Federal Circuit (**Kreis, der aus mehreren Gerichtsbezirken besteht**)
majority opinion	the written decision of the simple majority of judges who hear an appeal; the majority opinion contains the holding of the case and the reasons for that holding; it is the majority opinion that is decisive for the precedent of the case (**Mehrheitsvotum**)
concurring opinion	the opinion of one or more judges who agree on the holding but

	not on the reasons for that holding (**Sondervotum, das eine in der Begründung abweichende Meinung eines Richters enthält**)
dissenting opinion	the opinion of one or more judges in the minority of the court of judges hearing an appeal who do not agree on the holding the majority reached in the case (**Sondervotum, das eine im Ergebnis abweichende Meinung eines Richters enthält**)
per curiam opinion	decision of the court, indicates a decision containing only the holding of the case without any lengthy discussion of the reasons for that holding
chief justice	the head judge of a supreme court (**Gerichtspräsident**)
associate justices	all judges on a court of appeals other than the head judge (**beisitzende Richter**)
United States Code	multi-volume collection of the laws of the United States; abbreviated **U.S.C.**; also comes in an annotated edition: **United States Code Annotated (U.S.C.A.)** which includes comments on the legal history of the section, case decisions relating to the various legal provisions, etc.
direct appeal	appeal from the decision of a trial court to a supreme court without first appealing to the intermediate court of appeals (**Sprungrevision**)
copyright	intellectual property right protecting an author's ownership of his or her own creations from unauthorized use (**Urheberrecht**)
patent	intellectual property right protecting an individual's inventions from unauthorized use (**Patent**)
infringement	violation, usually of s.o.'s rights (**Verletzung, Rechtsverletzung**)
administrative court	court with jurisdiction over cases arising under public law, executive orders or regulations; most common law systems do not have separate courts for administrative matters (**Verwaltungsgericht**)
labor court	court with jurisdiction over disputes arising between employer and employee within the employment relationship (**Arbeitsgericht**)

Vocabulary

affiliation	membership
alien	foreign resident
auxiliary	in addition to s.th., not main part of s.th. but in support of it

decree	formal order
to ordain	to establish by law or decree
repugnant	conflicting, offensive
tier	level
verbatim	word-for-word repetition of what someone said

C. State Courts: Organization

Most states in the United States also have a three-tiered court system of trial courts of general jurisdiction, intermediate courts of appeals and supreme courts. Many also have some inferior courts of limited jurisdiction and a few have only a trial court and one appellate court, usually then called the supreme court, without any intermediate court of appeals. Indeed the court structures of the individual states, and particularly the names given to these courts, vary drastically. Consequently, this section will indicate the general judicial scheme in the states without going into extensive details on any particular state.

Read the following description of the state courts:

a. Trial Courts. (1) Courts of Limited Jurisdiction. Most states have courts of limited jurisdiction, i.e. courts that are authorized to hear and determine cases involving a relatively small amount in controversy and (ordinarily) simple issues. ...

5   The names and authority of courts of limited jurisdiction vary from state to state. Most states still have courts known as justice courts, some have a court analogous to the municipal court, and many have a court of limited jurisdiction known as the "county" court ...

A word should be said about "small claims courts." A "small claims court" is not a
10   separate court at all. Rather, the term refers to a simplified form of procedure available in courts of limited jurisdiction, such as the justice or municipal court, for the trial of cases involving a relatively small amount, $250 to $2,500 or so according to the particular state.

(2) Courts of General Jurisdiction. All states have courts, usually organized along
15   county lines, for hearing cases of all types, unlimited by subject matter or amount in controversy. Such a court is referred to as the trial court of general jurisdiction. The court of general jurisdiction is known by different names in different states: in California it is the Superior Court; in New York, it is the Supreme Court; in many states it is the Circuit Court; in other states it is known as the District Court, the
20   County Court, the Court of Common Pleas, or by other names. Whatever its name,

this is the court in which are heard all cases that are not channelled elsewhere, i.e., either to an administrative agency or to a court of limited jurisdiction ...

In some states, the jurisdiction of the court of general jurisdiction is concurrent with that of the courts of limited jurisdiction, so that a case of a size and kind cognizable
25 in a court of limited jurisdiction may nevertheless be brought at plaintiff's option in the court of general jurisdiction. In other states the jurisdiction of the court of general jurisdiction is exclusive of that of the inferior courts: if a case is within the authority of an inferior court it must be brought there and not in the court of general jurisdiction ...

30 The hearing of cases in trial courts, whether of limited or general jurisdiction, is ordinarily conducted by a single judge. The trial bench in urban areas usually has more than one judge, and in such courts different judges may be called upon to hear various phases of a particular case. Thus one judge may pass upon preliminary pleading questions, another on questions arising in discovery matters, and yet an-
35 other preside at trial. But at any hearing only one judge ordinarily sits and decides. This is to be contrasted with the practice in continental civil procedure, where many hearings (at least in trial courts of general jurisdiction) are before a panel of three judges.

States also have specialized types of "courts," such as the "probate" court, the
40 "domestic relations" court and others. In some states, these are indeed separate courts staffed by separate judges. Thus, in New York there is a separate tribunal known as the Surrogate's Court which has probate jurisdiction, i.e., authority to hear matters pertaining to decedents' estates. In many states, however, the terms "probate court" or "domestic relations court" do not refer to separate courts but to spe-
45 cialized procedures applied in the court of general jurisdiction to these particular types of cases.

b. Appellate Courts. (1) Appeals from Courts of Limited Jurisdiction. Most states permit appeal of the determinations made by courts of limited jurisdiction. In some states, the mode of appeal is by trial de novo in the court of general jurisdiction, so
50 that a litigant dissatisfied with the result of the disposition by the inferior court may by appropriate procedure request that the case be retried in the court of general jurisdiction. Retrial is usually limited to the issues framed in the lower court, but additional evidence as well as additional argument may be presented. In other states, the mode of appeal is strictly review. That is, the record of the proceedings in the
55 inferior court is presented to the court of general jurisdiction for consideration of the correctness of the disposition of the case as it was presented below. In some states, the appeal to the court of general jurisdiction is the final appeal and no further review may be obtained. In others, under some circumstances, the disposition of the court of general jurisdiction may itself be reviewed by further appeal ...

60 (2) Appeals from Courts of General Jurisdiction. All states permit appellate review of the disposition of cases in courts of general jurisdiction. In a few states there is but one appellate court for appeals from the trial courts of general jurisdiction. Such an appellate court is usually known as the Supreme Court of the state, but in some jurisdictions it is known as the Court of Appeals or by some other name. Most states

65   have intermediate appellate courts as well. Their organization varies from state to
     state, as do their names, but the usual title is Court of Appeals. In New York, the
     intermediate appellate court is the Appellate Division of the Supreme Court; in
     California, it is the Court of Appeal. The intermediate appellate courts in almost all
     states are several in number, organized along geographical lines by groups of coun-
70   ties.

     The subject matter jurisdiction of intermediate appellate courts also varies from state
     to state. The typical pattern is that all types of appeals from the trial courts are taken
     to the intermediate appellate court; further appellate review in the state supreme
     court is obtainable only in the discretion of the supreme court or upon special request
75   of the intermediate appellate court. The procedural device for such further review
     may be simply an "appeal"; more often it is known as certiorari. In California,
     review by the Supreme Court of a decision of the Court of Appeal is obtained by
     "application for hearing," which if granted is followed by a "transfer" of the case
     from the Court of Appeal to the Supreme Court ...

80   The highest appellate court of a state consists of several judges, the number varying
     from state to state but typically being seven, as in California, Illinois and New York.
     The intermediate appellate courts usually consist of a number of judges who sit in
     panels of three. In the New York Appellate Division five judges sit on any particular
     appeal.

     G. Hazard, Jr./C. Tait/W. Fletcher, *Pleading and Procedure: Cases and Materials*, 7th
     ed., The Foundation Press, Inc.: Westbury, New York (1994) 14-16

                                      Analysis

As you can see from the above text, it is almost impossible to say anything generally
true of all of the state court systems. Indeed most lawyers in the United States will
be familiar only with the court system in the state or states within which they are
licensed to practice law and with the federal system. One aspect of the individual
state court systems particularly worthy of notice for the continental European lawyer is the review procedure for decisions reached by trial courts of limited jurisdiction. As you read (lines 47-53), the trial de novo is one method of review. This is
truly a new trial of the case, and is a rather unusual procedure in the United States,
albeit not so unusual in continental European nations. In Germany, the corre-
sponding procedure is the *Berufung*, also a new trial of a case already decided by a
lower trial court. But in a civil law dispute in Germany, for example, one may have
a trial de novo from the decision of a court of limited jurisdiction, the *Amtsgericht*,
or from the decision of a court of general jurisdiction, the *Landgericht*. In the
United States, a party may not have a trial de novo from the decision of a court of

general jurisdiction. Perhaps the reason for this difference is that most cases brought before a trial court of general jurisdiction in the United States are cases for which the right to trial by jury is ensured. Once a jury has reached a verdict in a case, a trial de novo following that verdict would require either a new jury trial or a hearing by a judge or panel of judges. A new jury trial presumably would be a waste of time and money, because there is no reason to assume that the second jury will do a better job than the first. A second trial by a judge or panel of judges would contradict the right to trial by jury, because it would permit professional judges to cancel the effectiveness of the jury verdict. A trial de novo might fit nicely into the judicial framework of continental European nations which do not use lay juries. It is only compatible with a common law system regarding the decisions of courts of limited jurisdiction where the right to trial by jury most likely is not guaranteed because of the relative insignificance of the case.

The text refers to **concurrent jurisdiction** (line 23) as between the courts of limited and of general jurisdiction. **Concurrent jurisdiction** refers to a situation in which two or more courts have jurisdiction over one and the same case. As you have seen from the text, when that occurs, the plaintiff may choose whichever court he prefers and file the action there. **Concurrent jurisdiction** may also arise as between state courts and federal courts, as will be discussed more thoroughly in the next section.

In lines 33-35 the text discusses the various duties a trial judge has in a case and points out that different judges may fulfill these individual duties in any particular case, the duties being passing on **preliminary pleading** questions, on questions arising in **discovery** matters and **presiding at trial**. **Preliminary pleading** matters relate to the various documents the parties may file before the trial actually begins, such as the plaintiff's **complaint**, which is the document initiating the law suit, the defendant's **answer**, which is his response to the plaintiff's claims in the complaint, the plaintiff's **reply**, a response to the answer, and others. **Discovery** is the term used to describe the evidence gathering phase, which extends from the time the plaintiff files the complaint to the beginning of the trial. According to the text, various judges may be involved in different phases of one and the same trial, but at each phase only one judge will make the decisions.

The State of New York is especially worthy of notice for the confusing names it has given its courts, confusing at least with respect to the names most other states use for theirs. The trial court of general jurisdiction in New York is the "Supreme Court" (line 18), the intermediate appellate court is the "Appellate Division" (line 67) and the supreme court is the "Court of Appeals."

The text refers to **subject matter jurisdiction** (line 71). This term will be discussed in the following sections, but it generally refers to the court's authority to hear a case raising a certain type of legal issue or issues. The term is contrasted to

personal jurisdiction, or the authority of the court to decide a case involving a particular defendant. Accordingly, a California trial court, for example, may have **subject matter jurisdiction** over any civil law dispute regarding an amount in controversy of at least $20,000 or over any criminal case for which the punishment threatened exceeds six months. Still this trial court may not have **personal jurisdiction** over a defendant residing in Nevada, for example. In order for a court to decide a case it must have both jurisdiction over the subject matter of the dispute and over the person of the defendant.

Terminology

justice court municipal court county court	several names for a state trial court of limited jurisdiction (**Gericht mit beschränkter Zuständigkeit** e.g. **Amtsgericht**); as an adjective "**municipal**" is primarily used to mean city or town (**Stadt**); a "**county**" is a subdivision of a state (**Verwaltungsbezirk**); **county lines** refers to the borders of the county (**Verwaltungsbezirksgrenzen**)
Superior Court **Circuit Court** **District Court** **County Court** **Court of Common Pleas**	several names for state trial courts of general jurisdiction (**Landgericht**); "circuit" and "district," like "county" all refer to a geographical area, but "county" also designates a governmental unit in the sense of **Kreis** or **Landkreis**; the **Court of Common Pleas** was the original name of the court that heard legal disputes arising between the King's subjects; a **plea** (**Gesuch**), like **pleadings** (**Schriftsätze**), is a request addressed to a court in a formal document
administrative agency	a governmental body responsible for implementing legislation (**Verwaltungsbehörde**)
concurrent jurisdiction	the power to decide a case as one of several courts with that same power over the subject matter of the case; a plaintiff may decide to initiate the law suit in any one of these several courts (**konkurrierende Zuständigkeit**)
subject matter jurisdiction	authority of a court to decide a particular type of case according to the legal issues it raises and the amount in controversy (**sachliche Zuständigkeit**)
personal jurisdiction	authority of a court to reach decisions binding on the defendant in the case (**Gerichtshoheit über eine Person**)
to preside at trial	to act as the authority over a trial; to direct or control proceedings, as a judge (**den Vorsitz führen**)
preliminary pleading	document filed with a court in preparation and initiation of a law suit; includes: **complaint** (**Klageschrift**), **answer** (**Klageerwiderung**), **reply** (**Replik**)

discovery	also called **pretrial discovery**; evidence gathering phase which extends from the filing of the complaint to the beginning of the trial; gives each party the right to evidence in the possession of the other party (**Beweiserhebungsverfahren, in dem jede Partei ein Recht hat, Beweise durch Zeugenvernehmungen, Vorlage von Urkunden usw. zu erheben**)
probate court	special court, or special type of court procedure, for inheritance, and in some states also for family law problems, such as adoption of minor children (**Nachlaß- und Familiengericht**)
probate jurisdiction	the authority as a court to hear cases involving inheritance, and perhaps also family law problems (**Zuständigkeit als Nachlaß- und Familiengericht**)
domestic relations court	court with jurisdiction over family law issues (**Familiengericht**)
Surrogate's Court	one name for a probate or domestic relations court
decedents' estates	"**decedent**" is the commonly used legal term for someone who has died, e.g. within the context of the law of inheritance (**Erblasser**); and in this context "**estate**" is the total amount of property left after death (**Nachlaß**); used together they identify an area of law relating to the administration of the estate after death but before it is distributed to the decedent's heirs and to the legal rules governing that distribution, including the law of last wills and testaments (**Erbrecht**)

D. Jurisdiction

Not every court can adjudicate any case that is brought to it. As should be clear by now, some courts have limited jurisdiction in the sense that they may reach a legally effective decision only up to a maximum amount in controversy. Other courts have jurisdiction over only some types of cases, such as those involving juveniles. These limits relate to the court's **subject matter jurisdiction**. To hear a case, a court has to have **jurisdiction over the subject matter** in dispute. In addition, a court has to have the authority to reach decisions binding on the particular defendant. By filing a law suit in some court, the plaintiff cannot simply determine that the defendant has to appear and defend himself in that court. The court itself must have a legal basis for forcing the defendant to appear before it and heed its judgments. This second type of jurisdiction might be based on the court's **jurisdiction over the person of the defendant**, referred to as **in personam jurisdiction**; or, if the dispute relates to property rights, over the property in dispute, namely **in rem jurisdiction**; or over the defendant by virtue of the fact that the defendant owns property located within the court's jurisdiction, namely **quasi in rem jurisdiction**. Taken together, all of these various forms of jurisdiction are sometimes referred to as **territorial jurisdiction**. Accordingly, the first question is: Is the court empowered to hear the particular type of case for the amount in controversy involved? And the second question is: Is the court empowered to reach a judgment binding with respect to the particular defendant or the particular property involved? A simple automobile accident case can illustrate the difference between these two jurisdictional requirements. Suppose a citizen of the State of Alaska (A) injures a citizen of the State of Wyoming (W) while both are vacationing in the State of North Dakota. W intends to file a tort claim against A for $50,000 in a state court in Wyoming. The first question is whether the state court in Wyoming has jurisdiction to adjudicate tort claims for as much as $50,000. If so, the second question is whether the state court in Wyoming can adjudicate the claim against the defendant A. Since the subject matter jurisdiction of the individual state courts is fairly straightforward and has been discussed in connection with the organization of these courts, the next section will deal with the somewhat more unusual subject matter jurisdiction of the federal courts.

1. Subject Matter Jurisdiction

The federal district courts are courts of limited jurisdiction, because they have the power to hear only cases over which federal law grants them jurisdiction. When speaking of jurisdiction in this context, one means **subject matter jurisdiction**. Consider the following sections of the *United States Code* granting **subject matter jurisdiction** to the district courts:

UNITED STATES CODE

TITLE 28

JUDICIARY AND JUDICIAL PROCEDURE

PART IV – JURISDICTION AND VENUE

CHAPTER 85 – DISTRICT COURTS; JURISDICTION

§ 1330. Actions against foreign states

(a) The district courts shall have original jurisdiction without regard to amount in controversy of any nonjury civil action against a foreign state …

§ 1331. Federal question

The district courts shall have original jurisdiction of all civil actions arising under the Constitution, laws, or treaties of the United States.

§ 1332. Diversity of citizenship; amount in controversy; costs

(a) The district courts shall have original jurisdiction of all civil actions where the matter in controversy exceeds the sum or value of $50,000, exclusive of interest and costs, and is between -

(1) citizens of different States;

(2) citizens of a State and citizens or subjects of a foreign state;

(3) citizens of different States and in which citizens or subjects or a foreign state are additional parties; and

(4) a foreign state ... as plaintiff and citizens of a State or of different States ...

§ 1333. Admiralty, maritime ...

The district courts shall have original jurisdiction, exclusive of the courts of the States, of:

(1) Any civil case of admiralty or maritime jurisdiction ...

§ 1345. United States as plaintiff

Except as otherwise provided by Act of Congress, the district courts shall have original jurisdiction of all civil actions, suits or proceedings commenced by the United States, or by any agency or officer thereof expressly authorized to sue by Act of Congress.

All of these sections grant the district courts **original jurisdiction,** or the jurisdiction to hear the case as a trial court, but only one, § 1333 grants the district courts **original** and **exclusive jurisdiction** in **maritime** or **admiralty cases,** namely cases arising on the high seas, great lakes or other bodies of water. Otherwise, the district courts share original jurisdiction over the cases listed above with either other federal courts or with the state courts.

Two of the most important grants of subject matter jurisdiction are contained in § 1331, relating to **federal question jurisdiction,** and § 1332(1) relating to **diversity jurisdiction.** Section 1331 on **federal question jurisdiction** grants the district courts original jurisdiction over any case arising under federal law, including the U.S. Constitution and any treaties the United States closed with other nations. As noted, the jurisdiction of the federal courts is not exclusive over cases raising federal questions. Therefore, a plaintiff may bring such an action in either a federal district court or in a state court. Section 1331 merely opens the federal court system to a plaintiff, but does not hinder the plaintiff in bringing his action elsewhere. Section 1332(1) grants the district courts original jurisdiction over cases between the **citizens of different States,** so-called "**diversity jurisdiction.**" In this context, "States" refers to the individual states in the United States. The federal courts have jurisdiction over "**diversity cases**" to protect one party from being unfairly treated by the judges of a different state. Although at one time it may have been sensible to worry about a Virginia defendant being unfairly treated by the courts of the plaintiff's state of New York, for example, today this concern seems to be somewhat misplaced. Still, the courts have retained this area of jurisdiction. Note that unlike federal question jurisdiction, diversity jurisdiction depends on the amount in controversy being more than $50,000. If it is less, the plaintiff may file his action in a state court only. If it is more, the plaintiff may choose between the U.S. District Court and a state court.

As you can see, several courts may have jurisdiction over one and the same case, and it is at least initially up to the plaintiff to choose between them when filing the complaint. There are a number of reasons why a plaintiff may prefer one court over another. He may prefer to litigate at home rather than in another state or another part of the same state. The procedural rules in a federal court may be more advantageous to him than those applicable in any state court. It may even be that one court is faster in reaching decisions than another court. The judicial system in the United States permits what is referred to as **forum shopping,** or looking around to find the court most desirable and filing the complaint in that court.

Of course, the plaintiff is not the only party who will have a word on which court will hear the case. If the plaintiff chooses a state court over a federal court, for example, the defendant may **remove** the case to a federal district court under certain circumstances:

UNITED STATES CODE

TITLE 28

JUDICIARY AND JUDICIAL PROCEDURE

PART IV – JURISDICTION AND VENUE

CHAPTER 89 – DISTRICT COURTS; REMOVAL OF CASES FROM STATE COURTS

§ 1441. Actions removable generally

(a) Except as otherwise expressly provided by Act of Congress, any civil action brought in a State court of which the district courts of the United States have original jurisdiction, may be removed by the defendant or the defendants, to the district court of the United States for the district and division embracing the place where such action is pending. ...

(b) Any civil action of which the district courts have original jurisdiction founded on a claim or right arising under the Constitution, treaties or laws of the United States shall be removable without regard to the citizenship or residence of the parties. Any other such action shall be removable only if none of the parties in interest properly joined and served as defendants is a citizen of the State in which such action is brought ...

Section 1441(a) generally permits a defendant to **remove** a case from a state court to a federal district court if the district court has original jurisdiction over the case. The case can be removed to the federal district in which the state court where the plaintiff originally brought the action is located, or where the state court action is **pending**. A case is **pending** after it has been filed and before a final judgment has been reached. Accordingly, if a plaintiff files an action in a state court in Rhode Island, a state with only one federal district, the defendant may have the case removed to the U.S. District Court for the District of Rhode Island. If the plaintiff files an action in a state court in San Diego, California, the defendant may have it removed to the U.S. District Court for the Southern District of California.

Section 1441(b) differentiates between cases which have been filed in a state court over which the district courts have original jurisdiction by virtue of § 1331 on **federal question jurisdiction** and other cases over which the district courts have original jurisdiction. Cases of **federal question jurisdiction** may be removed regardless of the parties' state citizenship. Consequently, if a New Mexico plaintiff has filed an action in a New Mexico state court and the action raises a question of law under the "Constitution, treaties or laws of the United States" then the defendant may have the action removed to the U.S. District Court for the District of New Mexico even though the defendant is also a citizen of the State of New Mexico. For all other cases over which the district courts have original jurisdiction, the action may be removed only if the defendant, or in the case of multiple defendants *all* of the defendants, are not citizens of the state in which the action is pending. If one defendant is a citizen of the state where the plaintiff filed the complaint, the action may not be removed to federal court even if all other defendants are citizens of a different state or states.

2. Jurisdiction: in personam, in rem, quasi in rem

A court must be able to assert its jurisdiction over the person of the defendant or over property in dispute in order to reach a binding judgment as to that defendant or property. Whether the court can assert this jurisdiction depends initially on whether the defendant has been notified sufficiently of the law suit filed against him. In addition, it depends on whether the court has the right in light of **due process** requirements to force the notified defendant to come to the court to defend himself. We shall first deal with the notification requirement and then turn to the due process requirement.

a. Service of Process

Notification is referred to as **service of process**. Read the following text on **service of process** under the Federal Rules of Civil Procedure 4:

> Service of process to commence a lawsuit requires delivery of both a "summons" (a command to appear in court) and a copy of the complaint. 4(c)(1).
>
> **(1) Service on individuals.** Service on competent adults may be accomplished in a variety of ways.

5

> (a) Personal service. The most reliable method of service on an individual defendant is personal delivery of the summons and complaint 4(e)(1). Ordinarily, the summons and complaint are handed to the defendant personally. If a defendant attempts to evade personal service, it is sufficient that the papers be left near the person so long
>
> 10   as it is made clear what they are. In Errion v. Connell, 236 F.2d 447, 457 (9th Cir. 1956), the sheriff testified that he saw the defendant and spoke to her, and when she ducked behind a door, he "pitched" the papers through a hold in the screendoor and told her brother he was serving process. The testimony was in conflict, but the court believed the sheriff and found service properly made. However, in Weiss v. Glemp,
>
> 15   792 F.Supp. 215 (S.D.N.Y. 1992), service was attempted on Polish Cardinal Jozef Glemp in a libel suit brought by Rabbi Avi Weiss ... When Glemp was in Albany, New York, on a visit to the United States, he led an out-door procession in which service was attempted. The testimony was in conflict, but the District Court found that although a private process server thrust the papers toward Glemp, the papers
>
> 20   never touched him, and he did not know what they were. The court quashed service, and, because *in personam* jurisdiction was premised on the service of process, dismissed for lack of jurisdiction ...

> (b) **"Dwelling house or usual place of abode."** A process server may also leave the
>
> 25   summons and complaint "at the individual's dwelling house or usual place of abode with some person of suitable age and discretion then residing therein." 4(e)(2). In National Development Co. v. Triad Holding Corp., 930 F.2d 253 (2d Cir. 1991), the court upheld service when papers were left at the New York apartment of a Saudi Arabian national who was ... temporarily residing in New York ...

30

> (c) **Mail.** Under a 1993 amendment to the Rule, plaintiff may mail two copies of the summons, together with the complaint to the defendant, and request that the defendant return a "waiver" of service. 4(d). The defendant has a duty to minimize the costs of serving process. Accordingly, if the defendant fails to comply with the request by
>
> 35   returning the waiver of service, she will be liable for all costs subsequently incurred in effecting service. 4(d)(2)(G) ...

(f) **Individuals in a foreign country.** Service on an individual in a foreign country may be made by obtaining a waiver of service of process under Rule 4(d), [or] by com-
40   plying with an internationally agreed means of serving process such as the Hague Convention, …

(5) *In rem* **and** *quasi in rem* **jurisdiction. (a) Actions relating to title to property.** A District Court may assert jurisdiction over, and adjudicate interests in, property in accordance
45   with applicable federal statutes. 4(n)(1). The statute contemplated by (but not mentioned in) Rule 4 is 28 U.S.C. § 1655, which governs actions to enforce or to remove liens or encumbrances, or to remove clouds on title, for property within the district. Under § 1655, an order to appear "shall be served on the absent defendant personally if practicable, wherever found, and also on the person or persons in possession of such
50   property, if any. Where personal service is not practicable, the order shall be published as the court may direct, not less than once a week for six consecutive weeks." **(b) Other actions.** In other cases where personal jurisdiction cannot be obtained over a defendant, the federal court may assert *quasi in rem* jurisdiction based on seizure of defendant's assets within the jurisdiction, in accordance with the law of the state in which the federal
55   District Court sits. 4(n)(2). This provision has limited applicability, given the extensive reach of most state's long-arm statutes …

G. Hazard, Jr./C. Tait/W. Fletcher, *Pleading and Procedure: Cases and Materials*, 7th ed., The Foundation Press, Inc.: Westbury, New York (1994) 281-283

Analysis

Note that the text considers **service of process** for all three types of jurisdiction: *in personam*, *in rem*, and *quasi in rem*. Personal service can be made by the **sheriff**. Although a reader might associate this term with the Wild West, consider the definition of "**sheriff**" in *Black's Law Dictionary*:

> **Sheriff.** … The chief executive and administrative officer of a county, being chosen by popular election. His principal duties are in aid of the criminal courts and civil courts of record; such as serving process, summoning juries, executing judgments, holding judicial sales and the like. He is also the chief conservator of the peace within his territorial jurisdiction. When used in statutes, the term may include a deputy sheriff. He is in general charge of the county jail in most states.

One of a sheriff's duties, as you read in this definition, is **serving process**. The text defines "**process**" (lines 1-2) as consisting of the **summons**, which is a court order addressed to the defendant to a law suit ordering him to answer to the complaint filed against him and to appear in court to defend himself against the plaintiff's charges. Furthermore, **serving process** includes giving the defendant a copy of the plaintiff's complaint. The sheriff's further duties include **summoning juries,** a job a jury commissioner usually performs; **executing judgments,** which can also be stated as **enforcing judgments,** meaning to force the defendant who has lost a law suit to do what he is ordered to do in the judgment, usually to pay the plaintiff a certain amount of money; **holding judicial sales,** which is often the means of enforcing a judgment, namely by confiscating the defendant's property and selling it to obtain the money necessary to pay the plaintiff what is owed to her.

As you may note from the text (line 19) private individuals, rather than a public official like the sheriff, can also serve process. Often lawyers will use their clerks or other employees as process servers, but if a lawyer in Mississippi needs to serve a defendant in Oklahoma, she will hire a process server in Oklahoma, rather than send someone from her office. One purpose a process server has is to be a witness to the fact that the defendant actually received process. The best way to ensure that the defendant receive process is to actually put the documents in the defendant's hand after determining the defendant's identity. As you read (lines 24-26), however, it is also sufficient under the Federal Rules of Civil Procedure to leave process at the defendant's place of residence, which is where someone **dwells** or his **place of abode.** Note that as late as 1993, the Federal Rules started to permit service by mail. Actually service by mail is not really service in the traditional sense. Instead, for reasons of convenience and cutting costs, the Rules allow for a **waiver of service,** which the defendant is obliged to give or pay the costs of service himself. A **waiver** is a sacrifice of one's right to something, here actual service of process. As you can see, service of process in the United States is a good deal more difficult than it is in Germany, where service by registered mail is permitted.

An **action *in rem*** is really an action against a thing, rather than against a person. Usually, however, it means a claim to establish ownership rights in land. The court has jurisdiction over the claim if the property is located within the area over which the court generally has jurisdiction, such as within an individual state's boundaries, or for the federal courts within the district in which the U.S. District Court is located where the action is brought. The terms **lien, encumbrance** and **cloud** all relate to someone's, other than the owner's, rights to that property. A **lien** is usually a claim to property as security for a debt, such as a **mortgage. Encumbrance** can be used synonymously for **lien,** but includes also leases and rights of way. A **cloud** is a very general term for any claim that affects or restricts one's ownership rights, including both liens and encumbrances. Accordingly, an **action *in rem*** may be filed by the owner of property to have a **lien** or **cloud** or **encumbrance** removed from the owner's **title,** or his legal right to ownership of the property. An **action *in rem*** may also be brought by the holder of the **lien** to enforce the payment of a debt that has been secured with the property. In either event, the court derives its jurisdiction from the location of the property rather than from its power over any particular person as defendant. As you have read (lines 48-51), process is still to be served on the defendant personally, but an exception can be made if service is not practicable. In such case it is sufficient to publish notification of the law suit, usually in a newspaper, for at least six consecutive weeks.

An **action** *quasi in rem* permits a court to assert jurisdiction because some of the defendant's property is within the state or federal district. The action is not against the property, but rather against the defendant's interest in the property as a means of satisfying the plaintiff's personal claim against the defendant. The text indicates that the usefulness of this type of action has been obviated by **long-arm statutes**. A **long-arm statute** is a law granting a court the right to extend its jurisdiction beyond the borders of the state or federal district in which it is located. Whether a long-arm statute is really effective depends on its constitutionality under the **due process clause** of the Fifth Amendment for federal courts or of the Fourteenth Amendment for the state courts. We turn to this problem in the next section.

b. Due Process

The term "**due process**" is a very general term into which the United States Supreme Court has interpreted a considerable amount of constitutional meaning. The actual wording of the due process amendments – "No person shall ... be deprived of life, liberty, or property, without due process of law" – is not exceptionally illuminating. Very generally one can say that the **due process guarantees** contained in the Fifth Amendment for the federal government and in the Fourteenth Amendment for the state governments ensure a fair trial, or a fair "process," when the defendant's life, liberty or property is at stake.

Assume that a law suit has been filed against you in Alaska. The plaintiff has managed to notify you adequately of the pending suit by serving you process at your place of residence. The plaintiff is also a citizen of your home state, but likes the idea of litigating in Alaska. The **due process** requirement would prevent the plaintiff from terrorizing you in this manner, unless of course you had some relation to the **forum state**, or the state in which the court is located where the action was filed – here Alaska.

Any study of the **due process** requirement requires reading a significant number of U.S. Supreme Court decisions on this issue. One case is included in this Chapter to familiarize the reader with the relevant terminology and types of argumentation employed. But for those who are particularly interested in this field of law, it is advised that you read the cases suggested at the end of this Unit.

World-Wide Volkswagen Corp. v. Woodson

444 U.S. 286, 100 S.Ct. 559, 62 L.Ed.2d 490 (1980)

MR. JUSTICE WHITE delivered the opinion of the Court.

5

The issue before us is whether, consistently with the Due Process Clause of the Fourteenth Amendment, an Oklahoma court may exercise *in personam* jurisdiction over a nonresident automobile retailer and its wholesale distributor in a products-liability action, when the defendants' only connection with Oklahoma is the fact that
10   an automobile sold in New York to New York residents became involved in an accident in Oklahoma.

I

Respondents Harry and Kay Robinson purchased a new Audi automobile from petitioner Seaway Volkswagen, Inc. (Seaway), in Massena, N.Y., in 1976. The following year
15   the Robinson family, who resided in New York, left that State for a new home in Arizona. As they passed through the State of Oklahoma, another car struck their Audi in the rear, causing a fire which severely burned Kay Robinson and her two children.

The Robinsons subsequently brought a products-liability action in the District Court
20   for Creek County, Okla., claiming that their injuries resulted from defective design and placement of the Audi's gas tank and fuel system. They joined as defendants the automobile's manufacturer, Audi NSU Auto Union Aktiengesellschaft (Audi); its importer Volkswagen of America, Inc. (Volkswagen); its regional distributor, petitioner World-Wide Volkswagen Corp. (World-Wide); and its retail dealer, peti-
25   tioner Seaway. Seaway and World-Wide entered special appearances, claiming that Oklahoma's exercise of jurisdiction over them would offend the limitations on the State's jurisdiction imposed by the Due Process Clause of the Fourteenth Amendment.

The facts presented to the District Court showed that World-Wide is incorporated
30   and has its business office in New York. It distributes vehicles, parts, and accessories, under contract with Volkswagen, to retail dealers in New York, New Jersey, and Connecticut. Seaway, one of these retail dealers, is incorporated and has its place of business in New York. Insofar as the record reveals, Seaway and World-Wide are fully independent corporations whose relations with each other and with Volks-
35   wagen and Audi are contractual only. Respondents adduced no evidence that either World-Wide or Seaway does any business in Oklahoma, ships or sells any products to or in that State, has an agent to receive process there, or purchases advertisements in any media calculated to reach Oklahoma. In fact, as respondents' counsel conceded at oral argument, … there was no showing that any automobile sold by
40   World-Wide or Seaway has ever entered Oklahoma with the single exception of the vehicle involved in the present case.

Despite the apparent paucity of contacts between petitioners and Oklahoma, the District Court rejected their constitutional claim and reaffirmed that ruling in denying petitioners' motion for reconsideration. Petitioners then sought a writ of

45 prohibition in the Supreme Court of Oklahoma to restrain the District Judge, respondent Charles S. Woodson, from exercising *in personam* jurisdiction over
them ...

The Supreme Court of Oklahoma denied the writ, ... holding that personal jurisdiction over petitioners was authorized by Oklahoma's "long-arm" statute ... Although
50 the court noted that the proper approach was to test jurisdiction against both
statutory and constitutional standards, its analysis did not distinguish these questions, probably because [Oklahoma's long-arm statute] has been interpreted as conferring jurisdiction to the limits permitted by the United States Constitution. ...

We granted certiorari ... to consider an important constitutional question with re-
55 spect to state-court jurisdiction and to resolve a conflict between the Supreme Court
of Oklahoma and the highest courts of at least four other States. We reverse.

Analysis

The original plaintiffs in this case, the Robinsons, bought a **products-liability
action** against four defendants. A **products-liability action** is a tort claim for
injury caused by a defective product. One of the defendants, World-Wide, is a
wholesaler or **distributor** of Audis, which means that World-Wide does not sell
Audis to final consumers, but rather to **retailers**, who then sell to the public. The
retailer in the case is Seaway. The action was filed in the **District Court for Creek
County**, a *state court* in Oklahoma. You can tell this is a state, and not a federal
court, because as you know, all federal district courts have names like (U.S.)
District Court for the District of Rhode Island, or District Court for the Southern
District of California, or names including the name of the state in which the
federal district is located. As you also know, many states use the name "District
Court" for their trial courts of general jurisdiction and states are divided into
counties. Accordingly a District Court for some county will always be a state
court.

Seaway, the retailer, and World-Wide, the wholesale distributor, **entered special
appearances** (line 25). Consider the following definition of "appearance" in
Black's Law Dictionary:

> An appearance may be either *general* or *special*; the former is a simple and unquali-
> fied or unrestricted submission to the jurisdiction of the court, the latter a submission
> to the jurisdiction for some specific purpose only, not for all the purposes of the suit.
> A special appearance is for the purpose of testing or objecting to the sufficiency of
> service or the jurisdiction of the court over defendant without submitting to such
> jurisdiction; a general appearance is made where the defendant waives defects of
> service and submits to the jurisdiction of court ...

Accordingly, World-Wide and Seaway appeared in court, but only for the purpose of objecting to, in this case, the Oklahoma state court's *in personam* jurisdiction over them and not for the purpose of defending the tort claims filed against them. The basis of their objection was not that they had not been served process, but rather that the constitutional limits expressed in the Fourteenth Amendment's due process clause would be violated if they were forced to defend in the State of Oklahoma.

Both World-Wide and Seaway are **incorporated** in New York, meaning that they were both formed as a corporation under the laws of the State of New York. Furthermore, both have their main business offices in New York. They are fully independent from each other and from the two other defendants, Volkswagen and Audi, meaning that none of these companies holds shares in either World-Wide or Seaway. Instead, their relation is **contractual,** meaning they do business with each other only by closing contracts rather than by any shared management or ownership arrangement. Neither World-Wide nor Seaway has an **agent to receive process** in Oklahoma. A **process agent** is someone a company appoints, often a lawyer who represents the company, to receive process when it is served in a state where the company or corporation does business.

Note the legal history of the case. The action was filed in the Oklahoma trial court of general jurisdiction. That court rejected the defendants' claims of constitutional violation and refused to grant the defendants' **motion for reconsideration,** meaning their formal request that the District Court rethink its position and possibly change it. The defendants then sought **a writ of prohibition** from the Oklahoma Supreme Court, the highest court in the State of Oklahoma. A **writ of prohibition** is an order issued by a superior court to an inferior court to **restrain,** or stop, a judge in the inferior court from exercising his judicial power beyond the limits imposed on this power. In this case, the defendants wanted the Supreme Court of Oklahoma to prevent the trial court judge from hearing the case because they claimed he had no jurisdiction over their persons. The Supreme Court of Oklahoma denied the writ based on Oklahoma's **long-arm statute.** This statute, which is included in the footnotes to the U.S. Supreme Court's decision, reads as follows:

> A court may exercise personal jurisdiction over a person, who acts directly or by an agent, as to a cause of action or claim for relief arising from the person's ... causing tortious injury in this state by an act or omission outside this state if he regularly does or solicits business or engages in any other persistent course of conduct, or derives substantial revenue from goods used or consumed or services rendered, in this state ...

Of course, this statute is valid only if it is in accord with the United States Constitution's due process guarantee. The Supreme Court of Oklahoma implicitly affirmed its constitutionality, however, by denying the **writ of prohibition.** The defendants then **petitioned** to the U.S. Supreme Court for a **writ of certiorari**. At that point they became the "**petitioners**" and the plaintiffs became the "**respondents**," as they are called in the decision you have been reading. The U.S. Supreme Court granted the **writ,** thereby ordering the Oklahoma Supreme Court to send up the record in the case for review. As you read above, the U.S. Supreme Court will grant a writ of certiorari to clarify the law when several federal courts of appeals disagree. Note here that the U.S. Supreme Court explains its reason for granting certiorari with the comment that it wishes to "resolve a conflict between the Supreme Court of Oklahoma" and other state supreme courts (lines 54-56). Here the conflict is on the state, rather than the federal, level. But the conflict involves the correct interpretation of the U.S. Constitution. Although the individual state courts have the authority to consider claims under the U.S. Constitution, still the U.S. Supreme Court has the final authority over these issues and also the responsibility to avoid inconsistent state court decisions.

Continue reading the case:

II

The Due Process Clause of the Fourteenth Amendment limits the power of a state court to render a valid personal judgment against a nonresident defendant ... A
60   judgment rendered in violation of due process is void in the rendering State and is not entitled to full faith and credit elsewhere ... Due process requires that the defendant be given adequate notice of the suit, ... and be subject to the personal jurisdiction of the court, ... In the present case, it is not contended that notice was inadequate; the only question is whether these particular petitioners were subject to the jurisdiction
65   of the Oklahoma courts.

As has long been settled, and as we reaffirm today, a state court may exercise personal jurisdiction over a nonresident defendant only so long as there exist "minimum contacts" between the defendant and the forum State ... The concept of minimum contacts, in turn, can be seen to perform two related, but distinguishable, functions. It protects the defendant against the burdens of litigating in a distant or
70   inconvenient forum. And it acts to ensure that the States through their courts, do not reach out beyond the limits imposed on them by their status as coequal sovereigns in a federal system.

The protection against inconvenient litigation is typically described in terms of "reasonableness" or "fairness." We have said that the defendant's contacts with the
75   forum State must be such that maintenance of the suit "does not offend 'traditional notions of fair play and substantial justice.'" ...

The limits imposed on state jurisdiction by the Due Process Clause in its role as a guarantor against inconvenient litigation, have been substantially relaxed over the years. As we noted in *McGee v. International Life Ins. Co.,* ... [355 U.S. 220, at
80   222-223, 78 S.Ct. 199, at 201, 2 L.Ed.2d 223 (1957)] this trend is largely attributable to a fundamental transformation in the American economy:

"Today many commercial transactions touch two or more States and may involve parties separated by the full continent. With this increasing nationalization of commerce has come a great increase in the amount of business conducted by mail across
85 state lines. At the same time modern transportation and communication have made it much less burdensome for a party sued to defend himself in a State where he engages in economic activity."

The historical developments noted in *McGee*, of course, have only accelerated in the generation since that case was decided.

90 Nevertheless, we have never accepted the proposition that state lines are irrelevant for jurisdictional purposes, nor could we, and remain faithful to the principles of interstate federalism embodied in the Constitution. The economic interdependence of the States was foreseen and desired by the Framers. In the Commerce Clause, they provided that the Nation was to be a common market, a "free trade unit" in which
95 the States are debarred from acting as separable economic entities ... But the Framers also intended that the States retain many essential attributes of sovereignty, including, in particular, the sovereign power to try causes in their courts. The sovereignty of each State, in turn, implied a limitation on the sovereignty of all of its sister States – a limitation express or implicit in both the original scheme of the Constitu-
100 tion and the Fourteenth Amendment. ...

III

Applying these principles to the case at hand, we find in the record before us a total absence of those affiliating circumstances that are a necessary predicate to any exercise of state-court jurisdiction. Petitioners carry on no activity whatsoever in
105 Oklahoma. They close no sales and perform no services there. They avail themselves of none of the privileges and benefits of Oklahoma law. They solicit no business there either through salespersons or through advertising reasonably calculated to reach the State. Nor does the record show that they regularly sell cars at wholesale or retail to Oklahoma customers or residents or that they indirectly, through others, serve or
110 seek to serve the Oklahoma market. In short, respondents seek to base jurisdiction on one, isolated occurrence and whatever inferences can be drawn therefrom: the fortuitous circumstance that a single Audi automobile, sold in New York to New York residents, happened to suffer an accident while passing through Oklahoma.

It is argued, however, that because an automobile is mobile by its very design and
115 purpose it was "foreseeable" that the Robinsons' Audi would cause injury in Oklahoma. Yet "foreseeability" alone has never been a sufficient benchmark for personal jurisdiction under the Due Process Clause ...

This is not to say, of course, that foreseeability is wholly irrelevant. But the foreseeability that is critical to due process analysis is not the mere likelihood that a product
120 will find its way into the forum State. Rather, it is that the defendant's conduct and connection with the forum State are such that he should reasonably anticipate being haled into court there ... The Due Process Clause, by ensuring the "orderly administration of the laws," ... gives a degree of predictability to the legal system that allows potential defendants to structure their primary conduct with some minimum assur-
125 ance as to where that conduct will and will not render them liable to suit.

When a corporation "purposefully avails itself of the privilege of conducting activities within the forum State," ... it has clear notice that it is subject to suit there, and can act to alleviate the risk of burdensome litigation by procuring insurance, passing the expected costs on to customers, or, if the risks are too great, severing its connec-
130 tion with the State. Hence if the sale of a product of a manufacturer or distributor such as Audi or Volkswagen is not simply an isolated occurrence, but arises from the efforts of the manufacturer or distributor to serve directly or indirectly, the market for its product in other States, it is not unreasonable to subject it to suit in one of those States if its allegedly defective merchandise has there been the source of injury
135 to its owner or to others. The forum State does not exceed its powers under the Due Process Clause if it asserts personal jurisdiction over a corporation that delivers its products into the stream of commerce with the expectation that they will be purchased by consumers in the forum State ...

In a variant on the previous argument, it is contended that jurisdiction can be
140 supported by the fact that petitioners earn substantial revenue from goods used in Oklahoma ...

This argument seems to make the point that the purchase of automobiles in New York, from which the petitioners earn substantial revenue, would not occur *but for* the fact that the automobiles are capable of use in distant States like Oklahoma.
145 Respondents observe that the very purpose of an automobile is to travel, and that travel of automobiles sold by petitioners is facilitated by an extensive chain of Volkswagen service centers throughout the country, including some in Oklahoma. However, financial benefits accruing to the defendant from a collateral relation to the forum State will not support jurisdiction if they do not stem from a constitution-
150 ally cognizable contact with that State ... In our view, whatever marginal revenues petitioners may receive by virtue of the fact that their products are capable of use in Oklahoma is far too attenuated a contact to justify that State's exercise of *in personam* jurisdiction over them.

Because we find that petitioners have no "contacts, ties, or relations" with the State
155 of Oklahoma, ... the judgment of the Supreme Court of Oklahoma is

Reversed.

Analysis

In section II of the opinion, the Court discusses the Due Process guarantee in terms of state sovereignty and a defendant's protection against usurpations of power by a state with which he has no "minimum contacts." The Court indicates (lines 59-61) that a decision of a state court in violation of the due process clause is void and "not entitled to full faith and credit elsewhere." The **full faith and credit** clause is contained in Art. IV, Section 1. of the U.S. Constitution: " Full Faith and Credit shall be given in each State to the public Acts, Records, and judicial Proceedings of every other State ... " Consider the definition of "full faith and credit" in the *Merriam Webster's Dictionary of Law*:

> the recognition and enforcement of the public acts, records, and judicial proceedings of one state by another ... A public law or a judicial decision may not, however, be entitled to full faith and credit for specific reasons (as for having been decided by a court not having jurisdiction) ...

Giving full faith and credit to a decision reached by an Oklahoma court would mean, for example, that the State of New York, where the petitioners had their business office, would recognize that judgment as a valid and final determination of the parties' rights and would be willing to use its judicial and executive machinery to enforce it in New York. If the judgment is void for lack of jurisdiction over the petitioners, then it would not receive full faith and credit in New York. In section III of the opinion, the Court discusses the actual facts of the case and refutes the arguments the respondents had advanced in their own favor.

Questions on the Text

1. State in your own words a) the facts of the case; b) the legal history of the case; c) the issue raised on appeal to the U.S. Supreme Court; d) the holding, and e) the ratio decidendi. In formulating the ratio decidendi, consider the balance between state sovereignty, defendant's convenience in litigating, and the practicality of doing business across state borders (in particular the passage quoted from *McGee*).

2. Note the similarity of the structure of the United States to the European Union (lines 92-95). Are French judicial decisions given "full faith and credit" in Germany? Is this a particularity of the fact that both Germany and France are in the EU? Do the decisions of a Hungarian court have full faith and credit in Germany? Hungary is not in the EU. Does that mean that Germany and Hungary would have to close an international treaty regarding their mutual recognition and enforcement of each other's judgments for those judgments to have full faith and credit in each of the two states? Do the decisions of a Bavarian court have full faith and credit in Thuringia?

3. How would you translate **personal jurisdiction** into your own language? For a German reader, the first reaction might be "örtliche Zuständigkeit." As you have seen from the terminology list at the end of the last Chapter, the term has been explained more than it has been translated (**Gerichtshoheit über eine Person**). That is because this term, as is true for many legal terms, does not correspond exactly to any term commonly used within the German

legal system. The term **örtliche Zuständigkeit** is often used as a translation of the English "**venue**," a term that you have seen in the headings of the U.S. Code sections in these two chapters: "PART IV – JURISDICTION AND VENUE." Consider the following definition of "**venue**" in *Black's Law Dictionary*:

> The particular county, or geographical area, in which a court with jurisdiction may hear and determine a case. Venue deals with locality of suit, that is, with question of which court, or courts, of those that possess adequate personal and subject matter jurisdiction may hear the specific suit in question ...

> Venue does not refer to jurisdiction at all ... "Jurisdiction" of the court means the inherent power to decide a case, whereas "venue" designates the particular county or city in which a court with jurisdiction may hear and determine the case.

The problem raised here relates to where a plaintiff may file a suit, assuming that several courts have jurisdiction over the subject matter in dispute and over the person of the defendant. This problem can be explained most easily by considering an example regarding the federal court system. For some cases, all of the federal district courts have subject matter and personal jurisdiction. That is not surprising because the federal district courts are all subject to the same federal statute granting all of them subject matter jurisdiction over certain types of cases, such as those brought under the U.S. Constitution, federal law or U.S. treaties. Furthermore, they may all have personal jurisdiction over a U.S. citizen, or over a company doing business in all fifty states. Still, a plaintiff will have to file her law suit in a federal district court where, for example, the defendant resides or where the events giving rise to the action occurred, and not just in any district court the plaintiff chooses. This latter problem relates to **venue**, which is also statutorily regulated for the federal district courts. Do you agree that "**örtliche Zuständigkeit**" captures the meaning of "**venue**"?

Terminology

territorial jurisdiction	term that includes:
personal jurisdiction	a court's power over the person of the defendant (**Gerichtshoheit über eine Person**)
in rem jurisdiction	a court's power over property in dispute (**Gerichtshoheit über eine Sache**)

quasi in rem jurisdiction	a court's power over the person of the defendant by virtue of the fact that he owns property within the court's geographical area of jurisdiction (**fingierte in rem-Zuständigkeit, Gerichtshoheit über eine Person, die von der Belegenheit einer Sache abgeleitet wird**)
to assert jurisdiction to exercise jurisdiction	to take control over a case and over the parties to the case as a court of law (**die eigene Zuständigkeit annehmen**)
federal question jurisdiction	power granted to the federal district courts to decide cases raising legal questions under the Constitution, laws or treaties of the United States (**Zuständigkeit eines Bundesgerichts, weil sich eine Rechtsfrage mit Bezug auf das Bundesrecht stellt**); cases raising such issues are referred to as **federal question cases**
diversity jurisdiction	power granted to the federal district courts to hear civil law disputes between citizens of different states, assuming the amount in controversy is more than $50,000 (**Zuständigkeit eines Bundesgerichts, weil die Parteien Einwohner verschiedener Bundesstaaten sind**); cases brought to the federal district courts on this basis are called **diversity cases**
admiralty jurisdiction maritime jurisdiction	exclusive power granted to the federal district courts to hear cases that arose on the high seas, great lakes, or other navigable bodies of water (ca. **Seegerichtsbarkeit**); **admiralty cases**
forum	court (**Gericht**)
forum state	state in which a court is located
forum shopping	looking around and choosing among several courts with **concurrent jurisdiction** to find the court most suitable for filing one's own cause of action
removal	taking a civil action filed in a state court out of that court and putting it into a federal district court; can be done at the defendant's option (**Verweisung an ein anderes Gericht**)
service of process	delivery of a **summons** and a copy of the plaintiff's **complaint** to the defendant for the purpose of notifying the defendant that an action has been filed against him (**Klagezustellung**)
process server	person who delivers the summons and copy of the plaintiff's complaint to the defendant (**Zusteller von Klage und Ladung**)
sheriff	chief executive and administrative officer of a county; may be required to **serve process** within the county over which he is responsible
private process server	private party who is hired to serve process on a defendant
agent to receive process process agent	person appointed to accept process for another person; mostly agents for companies doing business in various states (**Zustellungsbevollmächtigter**)

personal service	delivery of process to the defendant by handing it over, or in some other way placing it within his reach
waiver of service	substitute for personal service of process by mailing process to the defendant and requesting that the defendant give up his right to personal service (**Verzicht auf Zustellung von Klage und Ladung**)
summons	formal court order to a person to appear before that court; attached to a complaint ordering the defendant to answer the complaint and appear in court to defend himself against the plaintiff's claims (**Ladung**)
title	ownership right to property (**Eigentumsrecht** [and *not* **Titel**(!), meaning in German the right one acquires through a final judicial judgment in a case])
lien **encumbrance** **cloud**	all terms indicating a claim against another person's property, such as to secure a debt, or because one holds a lease on the property or right of way across the property (**Pfandrecht** [lien]; **Belastung** [encumbrance]; **Belastung** [cloud])
mortgage	type of **lien** against property; security for creditor's claim for repayment of a debt; secured by giving the creditor a right to sell the property to satisfy the debt if the debtor defaults (**Hypothek**)
assets	total of one's property rights and claims against others (**Vermögen**); contrasted to **liabilities**, which are the property rights and claims of others against oneself (**Verbindlichkeiten**)
long-arm statute	law granting a court personal jurisdiction over individuals who are not physically within the court's geographical area of jurisdiction
judgment enforcement **judgment execution**	forcing a defendant to do what he is ordered to do in a final judicial decision (**Vollstreckung**)
judicial sale	method of enforcing a judgment by selling the defendant's property to satisfy the plaintiff's claims (**Zwangsversteigerung**)
products liability	responsibility of a manufacturer, producer, distributor, retailer for defects in a product sold to the public which cause injury (**Produkthaftung**); (U.K.) **product liability**
wholesaler **distributor**	intermediate seller, sells to other wholesalers or to retailers, but not to the consumer (**Zwischen- oder Großhändler**)
retailer	seller to the final consumer (**Einzelhändler**)
general appearance	coming to a court for the purpose of litigating a case, usually used to refer to a defendant who comes to court to defend against the substantive claims contained in the plaintiff's complaint and who thereby submits himself to the court's jurisdiction (ca. **vorbehaltlose Einlassung**); contrast to: **special appear-**

	ance (ca. **beschränkte Einlassung zum Zweck der Rüge formeller Mängel**)
special appearance	coming to court for the limited purpose of objecting to the court's jurisdiction; not an appearance to defend against substantive claims, but rather to argue that the court has no jurisdiction over one's person (ca. **beschränkte Einlassung zum Zweck der Rüge formeller Mängel**), contrast to: **general appearance** (ca. **vorbehaltlose Einlassung**)
incorporated	to be organized under law as a corporation (**als Aktiengesellschaft eingetragen**)
motion for reconsideration	formal request that a court rethink a ruling it has made and possibly change that ruling
writ of prohibition	order issued by a higher court to stop a lower court judge from asserting jurisdiction over a case because the lower court judge would be exceeding the power granted to him (**gerichtliche Feststellung, daß ein unteres Gericht die Grenzen seiner Zuständigkeit überschritten hat**)
full faith and credit	clause in Article IV of the U.S. Constitution requiring each state in the United States to recognize and enforce all public acts, records, and judicial proceedings issued or conducted in one of the other states
venue	location of a court with subject matter and personal jurisdiction; relates to where the court is and not to the power of the court to hear the case (**örtliche Zuständigkeit**)

Vocabulary

to accrue	to come about by addition (as in: **interest accrues** at 6% per annum); to come into being, to arise as a benefit
to adduce	to bring forward, to present for consideration
to advance an argument	to put forward for consideration
to alleviate	to lighten, to make easier
affiliating	accompanying, joining
attenuated	weak, not central, lessened in importance
collateral	not central, running alongside
to confer	to grant (usually authority or power)
to confiscate	to take away from s.o., to seize as a public authority

to contemplate	to consider, to think about, to have in mind
to debar	to prohibit
to evade	to avoid
fortuitous	by chance
to hale	to pull, to compel s.o. to go somewhere
to heed	to pay attention to, to follow (as advice)
illuminating	enlightening, informative
to incur	to suffer, to become liable for (an expense)
marginal	insignificant, not central, of profits: low in amount
paucity	scarcity, smallness of amount
predicate	characteristic property of s.th.
to be premised on	to be based on
to procure	to purchase, to acquire
to restrain	to hold back, to stop s.o. from doing s.th.
to sever	to cut

Chapter 2
Court System in England

The English court system is perhaps best described as a four-tier system, although the two bottom levels perform the same function and are differentiated only through the cases they hear, and the very top level, the House of Lords is rarely reached.

A. Trial Courts of Limited Jurisdiction

The **magistrates' courts** and the **county courts** are trial courts of limited jurisdiction. The former are responsible primarily for criminal and family law matters, whereas the latter are responsible for private law disputes. Perhaps the most unusual aspect of the **magistrates' courts** for someone from a Continental European legal system is that most of the judges who serve on them are lay persons, meaning that they have not been trained in the law. The magistrates do have a **court clerk**, who is a trained lawyer and who will advise them on the law and procedure to be followed in a case. Some of the magistrates are professionals, meaning that they are paid as full-time judges and hear cases sitting alone. Most of them are not. The lay magistrate is not paid for her work and usually hears cases with at least one other colleague. The magistrates' courts handle over 95 percent of all criminal cases in England. As they are courts of limited jurisdiction, the maximum punishment they may impose is six months imprisonment or a fine of up to £ 5,000. Criminal offences are divided into **summary-only offences, either-way offences** or **hybrid offences**, and **indictable offences**. The magistrates' court has exclusive jurisdiction over the first, the **crown court** over the third, and the defendant can choose between **trial summarily** or **summary trial** in the magistrates' court, or trial by jury in the crown court, for the second. The **crown court** is the court of general jurisdiction for criminal offences and will be discussed below. If the magistrates' court is of the opinion that a defendant who chose summary trial for an either-way offence should be tried in the crown court, or if the offence is an indictable offence, then the magistrates' court will hold **committal proceedings** to **commit the defendant for trial** at the crown court. As noted in Unit I on the jury, England has abolished its grand jury. Still, committal proceedings are held, which in effect are very similar in that lay persons decide whether the prosecutor can make out a prima facie case against the defendant.

The **county courts** primarily deal with contract, tort, and land law cases. At one time their jurisdiction in these cases was limited by the amount in controversy, but today the county courts have concurrent jurisdiction with the **High Court of Justice**. Their jurisdiction, however, was limited in the past and still is limited with respect to equity matters. Furthermore, the High Court, which will be discussed below, will not hear cases with an amount in controversy of less than £ 25,000, so the less significant cases always are heard by the county court.

B. Trial Courts of General Jurisdiction

The trial court of general jurisdiction for criminal cases is the **crown court** and for private law and other areas the **High Court of Justice.** The crown court is the traditional criminal court in the common law sense. It hears the more serious criminal cases with one judge and a jury. The High Court of Justice is divided into the **Queen's Bench Division** (*abbr* **QBD**) or **King's Bench Division** (*abbr* **KBD**) depending on whether the reigning monarch is female or male, the **Family Division,** and the **Chancery Division.** The QBD sitting as a trial court hears primarily contract and tort law cases, but only if the amount involved is at least £ 25,000. It also has jurisdiction over **admiralty** and **commercial cases.** The **Family Division** exercises jurisdiction over **contested** or **defended divorce cases.** The **Chancery Division** has jurisdiction over **intellectual property,** meaning **copyright** and **patent** claims, **equity** matters, **insolvency cases, company law cases,** and **probate.**

C. Courts of Appeal

Appeals from decisions of the county courts go directly to the **Court of Appeal,** which is composed of a **Civil Division** and a **Criminal Division.** Appeals from decisions of the magistrates' courts go to the crown court if the appeal is taken on issues of fact. The appeal is then heard by one judge and several magistrates and is essentially a new trial of the case. If the appeal is taken on issues of law, or **by way of case stated,** then it will go to the **Divisional Court of the Queen's Bench Division** of the High Court of Justice. Appeals from decisions of the various divisions of the High Court of Justice and from the crown courts go to the appropriate division of the Court of Appeal. The Court of Appeal hears appeals in two to five-judge panels. The Criminal Division is presided over by the **Lord Chief Justice.** The **Master of the Rolls** presides over the Civil Division. The final court in the appellate system is the **House of Lords** sitting as a court with five to seven judges, or law lords.

Generally the appellant needs **leave to appeal,** or permission to file the appeal with the higher court. Leave is granted either by the lower court which heard the trial or previous appeal or by the court to which the party appeals. Leave is not required from a judgement of the magistrates' court in a criminal case, but is in almost all civil law cases and in criminal cases where the crown court heard the trial. If the **appeal is allowed,** then the appellant was successful; if the **appeal is dismissed,** then he was not.

Consider the following diagram of the English court system:

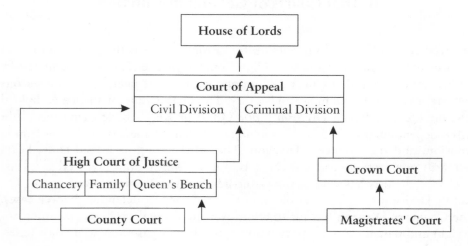

Terminology

magistrates' court	trial court of limited jurisdiction responsible primarily for hearing criminal cases involving less serious crimes and family law cases that are uncontested (**erstinstanzliches Gericht mit beschränkter Zuständigkeit**)
county court	trial court of limited jurisdiction responsible primarily for hearing private law disputes (**erstinstanzliches Gericht mit beschränkter Zuständigkeit**)
court clerk	trained lawyer who advises the magistrates on the law (**juristischer Berater für die Laien Richter am magistrates' court**)
summary-only offence	criminal offence over which the magistrates' courts have exclusive jurisdiction (**in einem summarischen Verfahren zu beurteilende Straftat**)

either-way offence	criminal offence for which the defendant can decide whether to have the trial in the magistrates' court or in the crown court, also called hybrid offence (**Straftat, die entweder durch summarisches Verfahren oder durch Eröffnung einer Hauptverhandlung vor dem crown court zu beurteilen ist**)
hybrid offence	criminal offence for which the defendant can decide whether to have the trial in the magistrates' court or in the crown court, also called either-way offence (**Straftat, die entweder durch summarisches Verfahren oder durch Eröffnung einer Hauptverhandlung vor dem crown court zu beurteilen ist**)
indictable offence	criminal offence over which the crown court has exclusive jurisdiction; more serious criminal offence (**Straftat, die nur vor dem crown court angeklagt werden kann**)
crown court	criminal court of general jurisdiction (**erstinstanzliches Gericht für Strafsachen mit unbeschränkter Zuständigkeit**)
summary trial	shortened version of a trial; common in the magistrates' courts; also called trial summarily (**erstinstanzlicher Prozeß im summarischen Verfahren**)
trial summarily	shortened version of a trial; common in the magistrates' courts; also called summary trial (**erstinstanzlicher Prozeß im summarischen Verfahren**)
committal proceedings	proceedings in the magistrates' court to determine whether a defendant should be indicted for trial in the crown court (**Verfahren zur Klärung der Frage, ob der Angeklagte an den crown court überwiesen werden soll**)
to commit the defendant for trial	to indict a defendant for trial at the crown court (**eine Anklage erheben und den Angeklagten an den crown court überweisen**)
High Court of Justice	court of general jurisdiction that hears private and public law cases; divided into three divisions, namely the Queen's (or King's) Bench Division, the Family Division, and the Chancery Division (**erstinstanzliches Gericht mit unbeschränkter Zuständigkeit**)
Queen's Bench Division	(*abbr* **QBD**) one of three divisions of the High Court of Justice; court of general jurisdiction over private law disputes, admiralty, and commercial cases (**Abteilung des High Court of Justice für Zivilsachen**)
Family Division	court of general jurisdiction over family law cases, particularly contested divorce cases (**Abteilung des High Court of Justice für Familienrechtssachen**)
Chancery Division	court of general jurisdiction over intellectual property cases, equity, insolvency, company law, and probate cases (**Abteilung des High Court of Justice für geistiges Eigentum, Billigkeitsentscheidungen, Insolvenzfälle, Gesellschaftsrecht und Nachlaßsachen**)
commercial cases	law suits between merchants, or those who are in the business of selling goods or services (**wirtschaftsrechtliche Fälle**)

contested divorce	dissolution of marriage when partners are not in agreement over the division of their property or the custody of their children; also called defended divorce (**streitige Scheidung**)
defended divorce	dissolution of marriage when partners are not in agreement over the division of their property or the custody of their children; also called contested divorce (**streitige Scheidung**)
intellectual property	ownership rights over ideas, as opposed to physical objects; includes copyrights and patents (**geistiges Eigentum**)
copyright	intellectual property right over a written work, screen play, multimedia programme, etc. (**Urheberrecht**)
patent	intellectual property right over a design, production process, material, etc. (**Patent**)
insolvency	condition of having more debts than assets; results in dissolution of property and distribution to creditors (**Insolvenz**)
company law	law governing business associations, i.e. firms, companies (**Gesellschaftsrecht**)
Court of Appeal	intermediate court of appeal in England composed of a civil division and a criminal division (**Revisionsgericht**)
Civil Division	the half of the Court of Appeal responsible for hearing appeals from the trial courts of general and limited jurisdiction in private and public law suits, namely from the county courts and from the High Court of Justice (**Zivilsenat des Revisionsgerichts**)
Criminal Division	the half of the Court of Appeal responsible for hearing appeals in criminal cases from the crown court (**Strafsenat des Revisionsgerichts**)
Lord Chief Justice	judge who presides over the Criminal Division of the Court of Appeal
Master of the Rolls	judge who presides over the Civil Division of the Court of Appeal
leave to appeal	permission to file an appeal in a case granted by the court whose decision is being appealed or by the court to which the appeal is taken (**Zulassung der Revision**)
to allow an appeal	to decide an appeal in favour of the appellant (**der Revision stattgeben**)
to dismiss an appeal	to decide an appeal in favour of the appellee (**die Revision abweisen**)

Suggested Reading

G. Hazard, Jr./C. Tait/W. Fletcher, *Pleading and Procedure: Cases and Materials*, 7th ed., The Foundation Press, Inc.: Westbury, New York (1994) 14-16

Milliken v. Meyer, 311 U.S. 457, 61 S.Ct. 339, 85 L.Ed. 278 (1940)

International Shoe Co. v. Washington 326 U.S. 310, 66 S.Ct. 154, 90 L.Ed. 95 (1945)

Schaffer v. Heitner, 433 U.S. 186, 97 S.Ct. 2569, 53 L.Ed.2d 683 (1977)

Burger King Corp. v. Rudzewicz, 471 U.S. 462, 105 S.Ct. 2174, 85 L.Ed.2d 528 (1985)

Asahi Metal Industry Co. v. Superior Court, 480 U.S. 102, 107 S.Ct. 1026, 94 L.Ed.2d 92 (1987)

Burnham v. Superior Court of California, 495 U.S. 604, 110 S.Ct. 2105, 109 L.Ed.2d 631 (1990)

J. Langbein, The German Advantage in Civil Procedure, 52 *University of Chicago Law Review* 823 (1986)

Language Exercises
Unit II

I. Translate the following terms into English:

1. Kläger
2. Beklagter
3. Tatsacheninstanz
4. Revisionsgericht
5. Tatfrage
6. Rechtsfrage
7. Zuständigkeit eines Gerichts
8. Revisionskläger
9. Revisionsbeklagter
10. Berufungsinstanz
11. Sprungrevision
12. Verwaltungsgericht
13. Arbeitsgericht
14. Jugendgericht
15. Nachlaß- und Familiengericht
16. Familiengericht
17. Verwaltungsbehörde

II. Fill in the blanks with the correct terminology:

Most states have courts of _1_, i.e. courts that are authorized to hear and determine cases involving a relatively small amount in controversy and (ordinarily)
simple issues. All states have courts for hearing cases of all types, unlimited by
subject matter or amount in controversy. Such a court is referred to as the trial
court of _2_. Sometimes these two courts share _3_ over one and the same case, in
which case they have _4_. Sometimes the _5_ of the one court bars the other court
from hearing the case, in which case the first court has _6_. If the losing party
disagrees with the decision of a court which is authorized to hear only cases
involving a relatively small amount in controversy, the party sometimes can turn
to the other court and have a new trial called a _7_

*III. Match the following U.S. court names with the type of court they most likely
are:*

trial court – intermediate appellate court – highest appellate court

Municipal Court Superior Court   County Court U.S. Court of Appeals
Supreme Court   U.S. District Court Justice Court Court of Common Pleas

IV. Fill in the blanks with the correct terminology:

The U.S. District Courts are the only courts where cases arising on the high seas, or _1_ cases may be filed. Thus we say the court has _2_ over these cases. Since the district courts hear cases as a trial court, we also say they have _3_. The authority of a district court to hear a case involving a question under a law adopted by the U.S. Congress is called _4_. The authority of these courts to hear cases between parties who reside in different states is called _5_. In both of these latter two types of cases, the state courts may also hear the case, which permits the plaintiff to look around and choose the most favorable court, which is called _6_. Under certain circumstances, a defendant who is unhappy about the choice of a state court may have the action _7_ to federal court. The authority of a court over a particular defendant is called _8_, which in part depends on whether the defendant received notice of the law suit, or was properly _9_. The authority of a court over property that is the subject of dispute is called _10_, and over the defendant's assets which have been seized within the state where the court sits is _11_. A law permitting a court to extend its authority beyond its own state borders is called a _12_. The state where the court is located is called the _13_.

Unit III
Constitutional Law

Unit II discussed some aspects of the United States Constitution, particularly in relation to the federal court system. Unit I discussed the Fifth, Sixth and Seventh Amendment provisions on the right to have a trial by jury. It also considered the Fourteenth Amendment extension of these rights to the individual states of the United States. Finally, it touched upon the Fourth Amendment guarantees against unlawful searches and seizures.

This Unit on constitutional law first considers **judicial review** and the famous *Marbury v. Madison* decision, which laid the foundation for the U.S. Supreme Court to review acts of the legislature for their unconstitutionality. It then highlights one case in order to familiarize the reader with U.S. Supreme Court opinions interpreting the U.S. Constitution. This case, *Brown v. Board of Education*, returns to the Fourteenth Amendment, but focuses on the **equal protection clause** of that amendment in the school desegregation cases.

In Appendix I you will find the complete text of the U.S. Constitution. The Constitution itself contains less than five thousand words. It establishes the three branches of the federal government, contains prohibitions against, for example **ex post facto** laws, defines the amending process and the status of international treaties, and enumerates the rights granted to the federal government, such as the right to regulate interstate commerce, which was discussed in the *James Beam* case in Unit I on retroactivity of new judicial precedents.

The U.S. Constitution is the oldest living written constitution in the world. It has been amended only twenty-seven times, whereby two of those amendments cancel each other out: the Eighteenth Amendment, introducing the prohibition of alcoholic beverages, and the Twenty-First Amendment, repealing the Eighteenth. Hence today only twenty-five changes have been added to the original text and ten of those, the **Bill of Rights**, were adopted only four years after the Constitution was ratified. Consider the text of the U.S. Constitution and the Amendments in Appendix I and compare the general appearance of your own constitution to this one before proceeding with Chapter 1 on judicial review.

Chapter 1
Judicial Review

The power of judicial review is the power a court has to declare legislative enactments void because of their incompatibility with the Constitution. Most U.S. Americans and Germans take this power for granted, because they live in legal systems where the highest court of the land exercises it regularly. But the House of Lords in England does not have the power to declare acts of Parliament unconstitutional. Instead, the British Parliament is considered to be the safekeeper of the British constitution.

It is important to realize that vesting the power to protect the constitution in the judiciary, rather than in the executive or legislative branches of the government, is not an obvious move. Certainly the philosophical literature of eighteenth century Europe provided the foundation for this decision, but the U.S. Constitution itself does not provide for judicial review. As you have seen from Unit II, the Constitution is in many respects vague on the role of the courts, and even on what courts, other than the U.S. Supreme Court, there shall be. Article III, Section 1 provides for one Supreme Court and grants the power to establish any other federal courts to the U.S. Congress. Section 2 and the Eleventh Amendment define the jurisdiction of the federal courts. Section 3 relates merely to the crime of **treason**. The power of judicial review indeed was not established until 1803.

In 1800 Thomas Jefferson, of the State of Virginia and the Republican party (now the Democrats), was elected to be the third president of the United States. Before that time the federal government had been under the control of the Federalist party (now the Republicans) and presidents George Washington and John Adams. When Jefferson defeated Adams in 1800, Adams and his closer associates feared that the federal government would lose power to the individual state governments, a position Jefferson favored. Indeed, Jefferson tended to favor vesting the power of guarding the constitution in the individual state legislatures. To stave off this development, Adams and his Federalist Congress collaborated to strengthen the position of the federal courts and be sure that they were staffed with judges who agreed with the Federalist position. To accomplish this goal, Congress, under the authority granted in Article 3, first created a significant number of new judicial posts before Jefferson actually took office on March 4,

1801. John Adams, still president, had the power to nominate and appoint federal judges, with the advice and consent of the Senate. Adams essentially packed the courts with Federalist judges before leaving office.

The appointments had to be signed by Adams and then turned over to his Secretary of State, John Marshall, who was to seal and deliver them before the government changed hands. Although Marshall worked late into the night sealing judicial commissions, he was unable to deliver all of them before the deadline. Accordingly, Marshall passed on the commissions that had been sealed but not yet delivered to his successor James Madison, Thomas Jefferson's Secretary of State. On taking office, Jefferson instructed Madison not to deliver seventeen of the commissions, all appointing Federalists to the position of **justice of the peace** in Washington, D.C. One of these appointments was William Marbury. Marbury, naturally dissatisfied when he did not receive his commission, filed a petition with the U.S. Supreme Court for a **writ of mandamus** against Madison. A writ of mandamus is a court order that can be addressed to a public official directing him to perform some act which it is his duty to perform. Here, Marbury wanted the Supreme Court to force Madison to deliver Marbury's commission. The Supreme Court was authorized to issue these writs by Section 13 of the Judiciary Act of 1789, a Congressional enactment.

John Marshall, whom Adams had appointed to be the new Chief Justice of the U.S. Supreme Court as of March 4, 1801, was now faced with a dilemma. If he issued the writ, Jefferson and Madison might simply ignore it, and Marshall's and the Supreme Court's power would be seriously diminished. If Marshall failed to issue the writ, he would be exhibiting weakness himself by refusing to tackle the executive, and thus playing right into the hands of the Jeffersonian Republicans. What would you have done in Marshall's position? Read the following excerpts from *Marbury v. Madison* to find out why John Marshall is considered to be one of the greatest legal minds in the history of the United States:

Marbury v. Madison

5 U.S. (1 Cranch) 137, 2 L.Ed. 60 (1803)

5 [O]n the 24th February, the following opinion of the Court was delivered by the
   Chief Justice.

   Opinion of the Court.

   At the last term on the affidavits then read and filed with the clerk, a rule was granted
   in this case, requiring the secretary of state to show cause why a mandamus should
   not issue, directing him to deliver to William Marbury his commission as a justice of
10 the peace for the county of Washington, in the District of Columbia.

No cause has been shown, and the present motion is for a mandamus. The peculiar delicacy of this case, the novelty of some of its circumstances, and the real difficulty attending the points which occur in it, require a complete exposition of the principles on which the opinion to be given by the court is founded ... In the order in which the
15 court has viewed this subject, the following questions have been considered and decided.

1st. Has the applicant a right to the commission he demands?

2d. If he has a right, and that right has been violated, do the laws of his country afford him a remedy?

20 3d. If they do afford him a remedy, is it a mandamus issuing from this court? ... [After answering the first two questions in the affirmative, John Marshall continues with the third inquiry, first discussing the nature of the writ of mandamus and then turning to the question of the power of the Supreme Court to issue it.]

The act to establish the judicial courts of the United States authorizes the Supreme
25 Court "to issue writs of mandamus in cases warranted by the principles and usages of law, to any courts appointed, or persons holding office, under the authority of the United States." [Judiciary Act of 1789, Section 13].

The Secretary of State, being a person holding an office under the authority of the United States, is precisely within the letter of the description, and if this court is not
30 authorized to issue a writ of mandamus to such an officer, it must be because the law is unconstitutional, and therefore absolutely incapable of conferring the authority, and assigning the duties which its words purport to confer and assign.

The constitution vests the whole judicial power of the United States in one Supreme Court, and such inferior courts as congress shall, from time to time, ordain and
35 establish. This power is expressly extended to all cases arising under the laws of the Unites States; and, consequently, in some form, may be exercised over the present case; because the right claimed is given by a law of the United States.

In the distribution of this power it is declared that "the Supreme Court shall have original jurisdiction in all cases affecting ambassadors, other public ministers and
40 consuls, and those in which a state shall be a party. In all other cases, the Supreme Court shall have appellate jurisdiction." [Article III, Section 2 of the U.S. Constitution]

If it had been intended to leave it in the discretion of the legislature to apportion the judicial power between the supreme and inferior courts according to the will of that
45 body, it would certainly have been useless to have proceeded further than to have defined the judicial power and the tribunals in which it should be vested. The subsequent part of the section is mere surplusage, is entirely without meaning, if such is to be the construction. If congress remains at liberty to give this court appellate jurisdiction, where the constitution has declared their jurisdiction shall be original;
50 and original jurisdiction where the constitution has declared it shall be appellate; the distribution of jurisdiction, made in the constitution, is form without substance. ...

To enable this court, then, to issue a mandamus, it must be shown to be an exercise of appellate jurisdiction, ...

It is the essential criterion of appellate jurisdiction, that it revises and corrects the
55   proceedings in a cause already instituted, and does not create that cause. Although,
therefore, a mandamus may be directed to courts, yet to issue such a writ to an officer
for the delivery of a paper, is in effect the same as to sustain an original action for that
paper, and, therefore, seems not to belong to appellate but to original jurisdiction. ...

The authority, therefore, given to the Supreme Court, by the act establishing the
60   judicial courts of the United States, to issue writs of mandamus to public officers,
appears not to be warranted by the constitution; and it becomes necessary to inquire
whether a jurisdiction so conferred can be exercised.

Analysis

The legal history of this case is somewhat difficult to understand, but it is contained in lines 7-10. The Court points out that during its last **term,** or the period within which the Supreme Court hears cases, a **rule** was granted on the basis of **affidavits** that had been read to the Court. An **affidavit** is a statement of facts declared under oath. The **rule** the Court refers to is the **rule nisi**, which is also called a **rule to show cause.** Consider the definition of a **rule nisi** from *Black's Law Dictionary*:

> A rule which will become imperative and final *unless* cause can be shown against it.
> This rule commands the party to show cause why he should not be compelled to do
> the act required, or why the object of the rule should not be enforced. ...

To **show cause** is to give a good argument or reason for something. A **rule nisi** requires the person against whom it is directed to give a good reason why the "object of the rule," here the **writ of mandamus** should not be issued. Accordingly, the legal history of the case is that during the previous term of court, Marbury had petitioned for a **writ of mandamus** to order Madison to deliver Marbury's commission as justice of the peace. He supported his petition for mandamus with an **affidavit**, a sworn statement of the facts of the case, namely that he had been appointed by President Adams and approved by the Senate, that his commission had been signed by Adams and sealed by John Marshall, then Secretary of State, but that the new Secretary of State, James Madison, had not delivered it to him. Since Madison had the official duty to deliver the commission, Marbury has petitioned the Court to force him to do so. The Court then issued the **rule nisi**, ordering Madison to give a good reason why he should not be ordered to deliver the commission. Madison failed to **show cause** and now the Court must determine whether to issue the **writ of mandamus** or not. This question is the main issue in the case. Consider the following definition of the **writ of mandamus** from *Black's Law Dictionary*:

> We command. This is the name of a writ … which issues from a court of superior jurisdiction, and is directed to … an executive, administrative or judicial officer, or to an inferior court, commanding the performance of a particular act therein specified, and belonging to his or their public, official, or ministerial duty, …

In the part of the opinion omitted here, the Court determines that Marbury has a right to his commission and that the laws of the United States provide him with a remedy, or a means of enforcing this right. The question is whether the remedy can be a writ of mandamus issued by the U.S. Supreme Court. The answer to that question depends on Section 13 of the Judiciary Act of 1789, which indeed does grant the Supreme Court the power to issue writs of mandamus in this type of case (lines 24-27). But Marshall does not stop here. He then moves on to the Supreme Court's judicial power under the Constitution. The Constitution grants the Supreme Court judicial power in all cases arising under the laws of the United States, and since the Judiciary Act of 1789 is a law of the United States, the Supreme Court has judicial power over cases brought under it (lines 33-37). Still, the Constitution distinguishes between the Supreme Court's **original** and **appellate jurisdiction**. The Supreme Court has original jurisdiction, or jurisdiction as a **court of first impression**, in cases "affecting ambassadors, other public ministers and consuls" (lines 38-40), which does not include someone like Marbury, but rather only *foreign* ambassadors, ministers and consuls. Therefore, the Court cannot have **original jurisdiction** in this case. Accordingly, the Court concludes that if it has jurisdiction to issue a writ of mandamus, it must be **appellate jurisdiction**. Marshall then shows that issuing a writ of mandamus, at least to a public officer, is *not* an exercise of appellate jurisdiction (lines 54-58). Marshall notes that a writ of mandamus also may be directed to a lower court, ordering the court to fulfill one of its official duties. In such case, the Supreme Court's jurisdiction might be appellate, because the **cause**, meaning the **cause of action**, would have been initiated in that lower court. On the other hand, if mandamus is to be directed to a public officer, the petition for the writ of mandamus institutes the cause of action and granting the writ would be an exercise of **original jurisdiction**. Note the manner in which the argument is set up and pursued step-by-step. If you are having problems understanding **original** and **appellate jurisdiction**, review the materials in Unit II on the courts and their jurisdiction before proceeding.

Marshall has established the dilemma he needs to continue with his analysis of the constitutionality of the Judiciary Act of 1789. In that Act, Congress granted the Supreme Court original jurisdiction to issue writs of mandamus directed to public officials. The Constitution, however, limits the Supreme Court's original jurisdiction to a different set of cases. The question now becomes what to do when a legislative enactment is contradictory to the Constitution.

Continue reading the case:

The question, whether an act, repugnant to the constitution, can become the law of the land, is a question deeply interesting to the United States; but, happily, not of an
65 intricacy proportioned to its interest. It seems only necessary to recognize certain principles, supposed to have been long and well established, to decide it.

That the people have an original right to establish, for their future government, such principles, as, in their opinion, shall most conduct to their own happiness is the basis on which the whole American fabric has been erected. The exercise of this original
70 right is a very great exertion; nor can it, nor ought it to be frequently repeated. The principles, therefore, so established, are deemed fundamental. And as the authority from which they proceed is supreme, ... they are designed to be permanent.

This original and supreme will organizes the government, and assigns to different departments their respective powers. It may either stop here, or establish certain
75 limits not to be transcended by those departments.

The government of the United States is of the latter description. The powers of the legislature are defined and limited; and that those limits may not be mistaken, or forgotten, the constitution is written. To what purpose are powers limited, and to what purpose is that limitation committed to writing, if these limits may, at any time,
80 be passed by those intended to be restrained? The distinction between a government with limited and unlimited powers is abolished, if those limits do not confine the persons on whom they are imposed, and if acts prohibited and acts allowed, are of equal obligation. It is a proposition too plain to be contested, that the constitution controls any legislative act repugnant to it; ...

85 ... The constitution is either a superior paramount law, unchangeable by ordinary means, or it is on a level with ordinary legislative acts, and, like other acts, is alterable when the legislature shall please to alter it.

If the former part of the alternative be true, then a legislative act contrary to the constitution is not law; if the latter part be true, then written constitutions are absurd
90 attempts, on the part of the people, to limit a power in its own nature illimitable.

Certainly all those who have framed written constitutions contemplate them as forming the fundamental and paramount law of the nation, and, consequently, the theory of every such government must be, that an act of the legislature, repugnant to the constitution, is void. ...

95 If an act of the legislature, repugnant to the constitution, is void, does it, notwith-standing its invalidity, bind the courts, and oblige them to give it effect? Or, in other words, though it be not law, does it constitute a rule as operative as if it was a law? This would be to overthrow in fact what was established in theory; and would seem, at first view, an absurdity too gross to be insisted on. It shall, however, receive a more
100 attentive consideration.

It is emphatically the province and duty of the judicial department to say what the law is. Those who apply the rule to particular cases, must of necessity expound and interpret that rule. If two laws conflict with each other, the courts must decide on the operation of each.

105 So if a law be in opposition to the constitution; if both the law and the constitution apply to a particular case, so that the court must either decide that case conformably to the law, disregarding the constitution; or conformably to the constitution, disregarding the law; the court must determine which of these conflicting rules governs the case. This is of the very essence of judicial duty.

110 If, then, the courts are to regard the constitution, and the constitution is superior to any ordinary act of the legislature, the constitution, and not such ordinary act, must govern the case to which they both apply.

Those, then, who controvert the principle that the constitution is to be considered, in court, as a paramount law, are reduced to the necessity of maintaining that courts
115 must close their eyes on the constitution, and see only the law.

This doctrine would subvert the very foundation of all written constitutions. It would declare that an act which, according to the principles and theory of our government, is entirely void, is yet, in practice, completely obligatory. It would declare that if the legislature shall do what is expressly forbidden, such act, notwith-
120 standing the express prohibition, is in reality effectual. It would be given to the legislature a practical and real omnipotence, with the same breath which professes to restrict their powers within narrow limits. It is prescribing limits, and declaring that those limits may be passed at pleasure.

That it thus reduces to nothing what we have deemed the greatest improvement on
125 political institutions, a written constitution, would of itself be sufficient, in America, where written constitutions have been viewed with so much reverence, for rejecting the construction. But the peculiar expressions of the constitution of the United States furnish additional arguments in favour of its rejection.

The judicial power of the United State is extended to all cases arising under the
130 constitution.

Could it be the intention of those who gave this power, to say that in using it the constitution should not be looked into? That a case arising under the constitution should be decided without examining the instrument under which it arises?

This is too extravagant to be maintained. ...

135 There are many other parts of the constitution which serve to illustrate this subject.

It is declared that "no tax or duty shall be laid on articles exported from any state." Suppose a duty on the export of cotton, of tobacco, or of flour; and a suit instituted to recover it. Ought judgment to be rendered in such a case? Ought the judges to close their eyes on the constitution, and only see the law? ...

140 From these, and many other selections which might be made, it is apparent, that the framers of the constitution contemplated that instrument as a rule for the government of courts, as well as of the legislature.

Why otherwise does it direct the judges to take an oath to support it? This oath certainly applies in an especial manner, to their conduct in their official character.
145 How immoral to impose it on them, if they were to be used as the instruments, and the knowing instruments, for violating what they swear to support! ...

If such be the real state of things, this is worse than solemn mockery. To prescribe, or to take this oath, becomes equally a crime ...

Thus, the particular phraseology of the constitution of the United States confirms
150 and strengthens the principle, supposed to be essential to all written constitutions, that a law repugnant to the constitution is void; and that courts, as well as other departments, are bound by that instrument.

The rule must be discharged.

Questions on the Text

1. John Marshall was not only a great legal thinker and politically a good tactician, he was also quite talented rhetorically. He often uses some form of the *reductio ad absurdum* in his argumentation. Such an argument proceeds by assuming that what one wants to prove is false and then showing that the falsity of the statement leads to incorrect or absurd results. Accordingly, one concludes that it must be true. Consider in particular lines 85-90 for an example of this type of argument. Marshall's argumentation, although often using the tools of rhetoric, is extremely clear because he approaches problems in sequence. Write a diagram of the flow of his argument, reducing the decision to outline form.

2. Although when one reads the opinion, it seems clear and convincing, John Marshall's position here was certainly a break with the past, and with English legal traditions. As indicated above, the supreme court of England, the House of Lords sitting as a court, does not have the power of judicial review. However, another difference between the U.S. Constitution and the English constitution is that there is no single written document that constitutes the English constitution. Instead, the English constitution is composed of an entire body of principles which are expressed in a variety of documents. How does Marshall use this difference to his benefit in writing the opinion? Does it matter whether a constitution is written in the sense that one document is called "the constitution"? What examples can you think of in German constitutional law, where constitutional principles are not directly expressed in the Basic Law itself? Does the Basic Law grant the *Bundesverfassungsgericht* the power of judicial review?

Terminology

judicial review	court's exercise of its power to consider the decisions of a lower court or of any branch of the government, in particular in light of their correspondence with the Constitution but also with established law (**gerichtliche Überprüfung**)
ex post facto law	a law passed after the fact, meaning after an act has been committed or an event occurred, which changes the legal evaluation of the circumstances retroactively; Art. I, Section 9 of the Constitution prohibits the federal government, and Art. I, Section 10 prohibits the individual state governments from passing any **ex post facto law** (**Gesetz mit Rückwirkung**)
treason	"Treason against the United States, shall consist only in levying war against them, or in adhering to their enemies, giving them aid and comfort. No person shall be convicted of treason unless on the testimony of two witnesses to the same overt act, or on confession in open court ... " Art. III, Section 3 U.S. Constitution (ca. **Landesverrat, Hochverrat**)
justice of the peace	lower level court judge; judge on a court of limited jurisdiction (**Friedensrichter**), usually empowered to perform marriages (**Standesbeamter**)
writ of mandamus	court order directed to a lower court or to a public officer ordering him to perform some act which he is legally obligated to perform as part of his official duties (ca. **gerichtliche Anweisung, eine Amtshandlung vorzunehmen**)
term	period during which a court hears cases (ca. **Sitzungsperiode**); the U.S. Supreme Court's term begins on the first Monday in October
affidavit	sworn statement of facts (ca. **eidesstattliche Erklärung**)
rule nisi **rule to show cause**	order to give a good reason why a court ruling should not become final and enforced (ca. **Ladung mit Aufforderung, etwaige Einwendungen vorzubringen**)
to show cause	to give a good reason for s.th. (**Behauptungen substantiieren**)

Vocabulary

to apportion	to divide and assign parts of s.th. to different individuals, to share
to controvert	to deny, to dispute, to oppose by arguments

emphatic	stressed, forceful
exertion	use of great effort to accomplish s.th.
to expound	to clarify the meaning of s.th., to explain
gross	large, unrefined, obvious
intricate	detailed and complicated, complex
mockery	insulting or ridiculing conduct or speech
omnipotence	total power
operative	functional, effective
paramount	supreme, highest ranked
to profess	to openly declare, to acknowledge
proposition	statement, assertion
province	area of authority, jurisdiction
to stave off	to fight off, to ward off
repugnant	incompatible, contrary to, objectionable
to subvert	to undercut, to overthrow
surplusage	in excess of what is essential
transcend	to exceed the limits of, to go beyond or above s.th.
vague	not completely clear or specific

Chapter 2
Equal Protection

Following the Civil War, three amendments were adopted, the Thirteenth Amendment prohibiting **involuntary servitude**, the Fourteenth Amendment guaranteeing the **equal protection of the laws**, and the Fifteenth Amendment granting African-Americans the right to vote. These amendments are often referred to as the **post-War Amendments**. The war was over in 1865 but whites and blacks remained socially separated in most parts of the United States for the century that followed. Sometimes this separation, or in this context usually called **segregation**, was required by law, in which case one refers to it as **de jure segregation**. Sometimes it just happened without the force of law, because whites and blacks were not accustomed to socializing with each other and most people did not make any effort to change the situation. In this latter type of case we speak of **de facto segregation**. In 1954, the following cases came to the U.S. Supreme Court with the argument that laws requiring segregated schools were unconstitutional because they were a violation of the **equal protection clause** of the Fourteenth Amendment.

Brown v. Board of Education
Briggs v. Elliott
Davis v. County School Board
Gebhart v. Belton

5   347 U.S. 483, 74 Sup. Ct. 686, 98 L.Ed. 873 (1954)

Mr. Chief Justice WARREN delivered the opinion of the Court.

These cases come to us from the States of Kansas, South Carolina, Virginia, and Delaware. They are premised on different facts and different local conditions, but a
10   common legal question justifies their consideration together in this consolidated opinion.*

---

* [Court's footnote 1] In the Kansas case, Brown v. Board of Education, the plaintiffs are Negro children of elementary school age residing in Topeka. They brought this
15   action in the United States District Court for the District of Kansas to enjoin enforce-

ment of a Kansas statute which permits, but does not require, cities of more than
125,000 population to maintain separate school facilities for Negro and white students. Kan. Gen. Stat. § 72-1724 (1949). Pursuant to that authority, the Topeka
Board of Education elected to establish segregated elementary schools. Other public
20   schools in the community, however, are operated on a nonsegregated basis. The
three-judge District Court, convened under 28 U.S.C. §§ 2281 and 2284, found that
segregation in public education has a detrimental effect upon Negro children, but
denied relief on the ground that the Negro and white schools were substantially
equal with respect to buildings, transportation, curricula, and educational qualifica-
25   tions of teachers. 98 F.Supp. 797. The case is here on direct appeal under 28 U.S.C.
§ 1253.

Analysis

This short passage refers to the Supreme Court's opinion in two ways, as the
opinion of the Court (line 7) and as a **consolidated opinion** (line 10). The reference to the **opinion of the Court** means the opinion of the majority of the justices
on the U.S. Supreme Court, referred to as the **majority opinion**. This opinion is
also a **consolidated opinion** because it contains one holding and one opinion for
four different cases, namely the cases listed at the beginning of the opinion. The
facts of each of these cases are discussed in the Court's footnote 1, the first of
which, *Brown v. Board of Education*, you have just read.

The plaintiffs filed their law suit with, or **brought this action in**, the **U.S. District
Court for the District of Kansas** (lines 14-15). As you should recall from the
discussion in Unit II, the U.S. District Courts are the lowest level courts in the
federal court system. They serve as **trial courts** in certain cases. In this particular
case, the District Court's trial court jurisdiction is called **federal question jurisdiction** because the law suit raises a question under federal law, namely the
United States Constitution. Accordingly, the U. S. District Court has the authority to decide the case or **has jurisdiction over the case**. As was pointed out in Unit
II, federal district courts are scattered throughout the United States. States with
a higher population have several district courts, but every state in the United
States has at least one district court. Since the U.S. District Court here is for the
District of Kansas, rather than, for example, for some geographically divided
area of Kansas, such as the Eastern or Western District of Kansas, you can tell
that there is only one District Court in the State of Kansas. The plaintiffs here
also could have brought their action in a Kansas state court, because they are
challenging a Kansas statute that the Kansas state legislature **enacted**, or adopted
and put into force as law. The fact that the plaintiffs are basing their legal claim
on the United States Constitution does not mean that a Kansas state court cannot

hear the case. State courts in the United States are bound by the United States Constitution and by the United States Supreme Court's interpretation of it, so there is no reason why they should not be empowered to interpret the U.S. Constitution and apply former U.S. Supreme Court precedents when doing so. As a result, in this case the U.S. District Court and the Kansas state court had **concurrent jurisdiction** and the plaintiff was free to choose between them.

The text states that the plaintiffs brought the action "**to enjoin** enforcement of a Kansas statute" (line 15). In other words, the plaintiffs were suing the school board in Topeka, Kansas, and the **remedy** they sought was an **injunction**. A **remedy**, which is the object of the law suit, is whatever the court can grant the plaintiff to protect the plaintiff's rights. We often use the saying "where there is a right, there is a remedy" (*Ubi jus, ibi remedium*) to mean that if the violation of which the plaintiff is complaining actually relates to a right the plaintiff has, then there must be something a court can do about that violation, namely grant a remedy. Conversely, if the court refuses to award the plaintiff any remedy, then the plaintiff actually had no right that could have been violated by the defendant to start with. Hence the word "remedy" designates the class of possible awards one can bring action to receive. An **injunction** is one example of a remedy. There are several types of **injunctions**. Consider the following definitions from *Black's Law Dictionary*:

Types of Injunctions

Injunction. A court order prohibiting someone from doing some specified act or commanding someone to undo some wrong or injury. A prohibitive, equitable remedy issued or granted by a court at the suit of a party complainant, directed to a party defendant in the action, ... forbidding the latter from doing some act which he
5 is threatening or attempting to commit, or restraining him in the continuance thereof, such act being unjust and inequitable, injurious to the plaintiff, and not such as can be adequately redressed by an action at law. ...

Interlocutory injunction. Interlocutory injunctions are those issued at any time dur-
10 ing the pendency of the litigation for the short-term purpose of preventing irreparable injury to the petitioner prior to the time that the court will be in a position to either grant or deny permanent relief on the merits. In accordance with their purpose, interlocutory injunctions are limited in duration to some specified length of time, or at the very outside, to the time of conclusion of the case on the merits. Within the
15 category of interlocutory injunctions there are two distinct types which must be considered individually. The first is generally referred to as a preliminary injunction, and includes any interlocutory injunction granted after the respondent has been given notice and the opportunity to participate in a hearing on whether or not that injunction should issue. The second is generally referred to as a temporary restrain-

20   ing order, and differs from a preliminary injunction primarily in that it is issued ex
      parte, with no notice or opportunity to be heard granted to the respondent. Tempo-
      rary restraining orders supply the need for relief in those situations in which the
      petitioner will suffer irreparable injury if relief is not granted immediately, and time
      simply does not permit either the delivery of notice or the holding of a hearing.
25   Fed.R.Civil P. 65 …

      Permanent injunction. One intended to remain in force until the final termination of
      the particular suit.

30   *Perpetual injunction.* An injunction which finally disposes of the suit, and is indefi-
      nite in point of time.

      Preliminary injunction. An injunction granted at the institution of a suit, to restrain
      the defendant from doing or continuing some act, the right to which is in dispute, and
35   which may either be discharged or made perpetual, according to the result of the
      controversy, as soon as the rights of the parties are determined. Fed.R.Civil P. 65.

      Temporary injunction. A preliminary or provisional injunction, or one granted
      pendente lite; as opposed to a final or perpetual injunction. A provisional remedy to
40   preserve subject matter of controversy pending trial …

As you can see, some of these terms overlap. A preliminary injunction, for
example, is a type of interlocutory injunction, and a temporary injunction is
another name for a preliminary injunction.

In *Brown v. Board of Education*, the plaintiffs sought **to enjoin** the Topeka Board
of Education from enforcing a statute (**Kansas General Statute** § 72-1724,
adopted in 1949) which permitted racial segregation of children in public
schools. In other words, they wanted the U.S. District Court to prohibit the
defendant from segregating public schools **pursuant to**, or according to, the
authority of the statute.

The three-judge District Court convened under 28 U.S.C. §§ 2281 and 2284. For
a private law dispute, the U.S. District Court acts as a trial court, with one judge
and possibly a jury of twelve individuals. As you should recall from the discussion of the Seventh Amendment right to trial by jury "in suits **at common
law**," the U.S. Constitution does not guarantee the right to trial by jury for suits
in equity. Since an injunction is an **equitable remedy**, as you read in the above
definitions (line 2), the court does not use a jury. In this case, the court convened
as a three-judge panel as authorized by the laws of the United States. The citation: **28 U.S.C. §§ 2281 and 2284** refers to Title 28 of the **United States Code**,

containing laws adopted by the United States Congress. Read these sections as they appear today in Title 28:

UNITED STATES CODE ANNOTATED
TITLE 28
JUDICIARY AND JUDICIAL PROCEDURE
PART VI – PARTICULAR PROCEEDINGS
5   CHAPTER 155 – INJUNCTIONS; THREE-JUDGE COURTS

[§ 2281. Repealed. Pub.L. 94-381, § 1, Aug. 12, 1976, 90 Stat. 1119]

HISTORICAL AND STATUTORY NOTES

10

Section 2281, Act June 25, 1948, c. 646, 62 Stat. 968, provided that an interlocutory or permanent injunction restraining the enforcement, operation or execution of a State statute on grounds of unconstitutionality should not be granted unless the application has been heard and determined by a three-judge district court.

Effective Date of Repeal

Repeal by Pub.L. 94-381 not applicable to any action commenced on or before Aug. 12, 1976, see section 7 of Pub.L. 94-381, set out as an Effective Date of 1976 Amendment note under section 2284 of this title.

§ 2284. Three-judge court; when required; composition; procedure

(a) A district court of three judges shall be convened when otherwise required by Act of Congress, or when an action is filed challenging the constitutionality of the apportionment of congressional districts or the apportionment of any statewide legislative body.

(b) In any action required to be heard and determined by a district court of three judges under subsection (a) of this section, the composition and procedure of the court shall be as follows:

(1) Upon the filing of a request for three judges, the judge to whom the request is presented shall, unless he determines that three judges are not required, immediately notify the chief judge of the circuit, who shall designate two other judges, at least one of whom shall be a circuit judge. The judges so designated, and the judge to whom

the request was presented, shall serve as members of the court to hear and determine the action or proceeding. ...

As you can see from the text, § 2281 provided for a three-judge district court when a plaintiff brought action for an injunction to restrain someone from enforcing a state statute on the grounds of unconstitutionality. This section was enacted in 1948 and **repealed,** or put out of force, in 1976. Accordingly, it was applicable in 1954 to the cases here.

The District Court **denied relief** (line 23), which means that it refused to grant the plaintiffs the remedy, or relief, they requested, namely the injunction. The citation 98 F.Supp. 797 refers to the place where one can find the decision of the U.S. District Court denying the relief requested. The opinion of the District Court in *Brown* can be found in vol. 98 of the Federal Supplement on page 797. (See Appendix II for a list of citations).

The decision of the U.S. District Court was appealed directly to the U.S. Supreme Court, or it was on **direct appeal** to the U.S. Supreme Court under **28 U.S.C. § 1253** (lines 25-26). Normally, when a District Court decision is appealed, it is appealed to the intermediate federal court, the United States Court of Appeals. If it is appealed directly to the U.S. Supreme Court, then the appellant did not first turn to the intermediate court, but jumped over it to the Supreme Court. The authority for a direct appeal is stated in 28 U.S.C. § 1253:

§ 1253. Direct appeals from decisions of three-judge courts

Except as otherwise provided by law, any party may appeal to the Supreme Court from an order granting or denying, after notice and hearing, an interlocutory or permanent injunction in any civil action, suit or proceeding required by any Act of Congress to be heard and determined by a district court of three judges.

(June 25, 1948, c. 646, 62 Stat. 928)

A note on politically correct speech: The modern reader will be somewhat surprised to see the Court refer to the plaintiffs as Negroes. In 1954, when this case was decided, that was the proper way to refer to members of the black race. During the 1960s, this expression was rejected, partly because of disparaging slang expressions associated with it, and the designation "blacks" was adopted, as opposed to "whites." Today the correct expression is "African-American." For American Indians the correct expression is "Native Americans," for people from the Far East "Asian-Americans," or more specifically "Chinese-Americans" or "Japanese-Americans." One also speaks of a "man" or "woman of color" to refer to a member of any one of the non-white races.

Questions on the Text

1. Why do you think that the plaintiffs brought their action in the United States District Court, rather than in a Kansas state court? What tactical advantage did they hope to get? If you were being discriminated against by a state statute, would you prefer to try your chances with a court in the state that adopted the statute or with a different court?

2. If the plaintiffs had brought the action in a Kansas state court, but the defendants preferred the U.S. District Court, what could they have done to get the case in federal court? If you cannot answer this question, refer to Unit II).

3. Were the plaintiffs seeking to enjoin the defendant perpetually or only temporarily? Do you think the court granted a temporary injunction in this case? What would be the arguments in favor and opposed to granting a temporary injunction here?

4. Why did the U.S. District Court deny the relief the plaintiffs requested? What difference could it make that the facilities, namely the buildings, transportation (by school bus), curricula and educational qualifications of teachers, in the black and white schools were equal? Based on provisions of the German Basic Law, what arguments could you make in favor and opposed to granting the injunction the plaintiffs sought?

Continue reading the case (Court's footnote 1):

> In the South Carolina case, Briggs v. Elliott, the plaintiffs are Negro children of both elementary and high school age residing in Clarendon County. They brought this action in the United States District Court for the Eastern District of South Carolina
> 30   to enjoin enforcement of provisions in the state constitution and statutory code which require the segregation of Negroes and whites in public schools. S.C. Const., Art. XI, § 7; S.C. Code § 5377 (1942). The three-judge District Court, convened under 28 U.S.C. §§ 2281 and 2284, denied the requested relief. The court found that the Negro schools were inferior to the white schools and ordered the defendants to
> 35   begin immediately to equalize the facilities. But the court sustained the validity of the contested provisions and denied the plaintiffs admission to the white schools during the equalization program. 98 F.Supp. 529. This Court vacated the District Court's judgment and remanded the case for the purpose of obtaining the court's views on a report filed by the defendants concerning the progress made in the equalization
> 40   program. 342 U.S. 350. On remand, the District Court found that substantial

equality had been achieved except for buildings and that the defendants were proceeding to rectify this inequality as well. 103 F.Supp. 920. The case is again here on
direct appeal under 28 U.S.C. § 1253.

Analysis

Most of the terminology in the second paragraph of the footnote is the same as
in the first. Perhaps initially confusing is the expression "**to enjoin enforcement
of provisions** in the state constitution and statutory code ... " (line 30).
The word "provisions" refers to what the law provides (*vorsieht*, as in the
German "*das Gesetz sieht vor*"). "To enjoin enforcement of provisions of
the state constitution and statutory code ... " means that the state constitution
(Art. XI § 7) and a statute (§ 5377) in South Carolina provided for segregation
of public schools, and the plaintiffs wanted the court to prohibit the defendant
from segregating the schools based on the authority granted in those legal provisions.

The District Court **sustained the validity of the contested provisions** (lines 35-
36), meaning the court upheld the state constitutional and statutory provisions
against the plaintiffs' constitutional attack

This Court vacated the District Court's judgment and remanded the case ... "
(lines 37-38). "This Court" refers to the court whose decision you are reading,
namely the U.S. Supreme Court. To **vacate a judgment** means to make the judgment empty of meaning or to invalidate the judgment with the result that it no
longer has any legal effect. To **remand a case** is to hand it back to the lower court
with an order to take some specified measures in the case. Here the U.S. Supreme
Court wanted information on the progress made in the equalization program.
The U.S. Supreme Court's decision **vacating** the District Court's decision and
remanding the case can be found in volume 342 of the **U.S. Reports** on page 350
(line 40).

Questions on the Text

1. How many U.S. District Courts were there (at least) in South Carolina in
   1954?
2. What are the relevant factual differences and similarities between the Kansas
   case and the South Carolina case?

3 Do you think that the U.S. District Court in South Carolina granted the plaintiffs a temporary injunction? Why or why not?

4 Describe in your own words the legal history of *Briggs v. Elliott*.

Continue reading the case (Court's footnote 1):

In the Virginia case, Davis v. County School Board, the plaintiffs are Negro children
45 of high school age residing in Prince Edward County. They brought this action in the United States District Court for the Eastern District of Virginia to enjoin enforcement of provisions in the state constitution and statutory code which require the segregation of Negroes and whites in public schools. Va. Const. § 140; Va. Code § 22-221 (1950). The three-judge District Court, convened under 28 U.S.C. §§ 2281
50 and 2284, denied the requested relief. The court found the Negro school inferior in physical plant, curricula, and transportation, and ordered the defendants forthwith to provide substantially equal curricula and transportation and to "proceed with all reasonable diligence and dispatch to remove" the inequality in physical plant. But, as in the South Carolina case, the court sustained the validity of the contested provi-
55 sions and denied the plaintiffs admission to the white schools during the equalization program. 103 F.Supp. 337. The case is here on direct appeal under 28 U.S.C. § 1253.

In the Delaware case, Gebhart v. Belton, the plaintiffs are Negro children of both elementary and high school age residing in New Castle County. They brought this action in the Delaware Court of Chancery to enjoin enforcement of provisions in the
60 state constitution and statutory code which require the segregation of Negroes and whites in public schools Del. Const., Art. X, § 2; Del. Rev. Code § 2631 (1935). The Chancellor gave judgment for the plaintiffs and ordered their immediate admission to schools previously attended only by white children, on the ground that the Negro schools were inferior with respect to teacher training, pupil-teacher ratio, extra-cur-
65 ricular activities, physical plant, and time and distance involved in travel. 87 A.2d 862. The Chancellor also found that segregation itself results in an inferior education for Negro children (see note 10, infra), but did not rest his decision on that ground. Id. at 865. The Chancellor's decree was affirmed by the Supreme Court of Delaware, which intimated, however, that the defendants might be able to obtain a modifica-
70 tion of the decree after equalization of the Negro and white schools had been accomplished, 91 A.2d 137, 152. The defendants, contending only that the Delaware courts had erred in ordering the immediate admission of the Negro plaintiffs to the white schools, applied to this Court for certiorari. The writ was granted, 344 U.S. 891. The plaintiffs, who were successful below, did not submit a cross-petition.

Analysis

The Delaware case is significantly different from the other three. First, the original action was brought in a state court, the Delaware Court of Chancery, rather than in the U.S. District Court. As you should recall from the section on **equity** in Unit I, the original English Court of Chancery was a court of equity headed by the King's Chancellor, a higher member of the clergy. Although most courts of equity have been abolished in the United States, the State of Delaware still appears to have had a court of equity in 1954. Notice also that the judge in the state action is referred to as the Chancellor.

Citation form: The decision of the Delaware Court of Chancery is reported in vol. 87 of the Atlantic Reporter, second series on page 862: **87 A.2d 862** (lines 65-66). Refer to Appendix II for an explanation of case citations. In line 67 you see the reference: (see note 10 **infra**). This reference refers to a footnote in the U.S. Supreme Court's decision, footnote 10, which comes later in the opinion [renumbered as **]. To refer to something stated later or below, courts and lawyers generally use the Latin "**infra.**" To refer to something previously stated or above, one uses "**supra.**" The Court also uses "**Id. at 865**" (line 68). This refers back to the Delaware Court of Chancery's opinion reported in 87 A.2d 862. Page 862 is the first page of the opinion, and the Court here is referring to page 865. Note the later citation **91 A.2d 137, 152** (line 71). This is a citation of the Supreme Court of Delaware's opinion affirming the Chancellor's decree. This opinion starts on page 137, but the U.S. Supreme Court's specific reference is to page 152. We also read this reference "137 **at** 152." Finally, note the citation 344 U.S. 891 (lines 73-74). Here the U.S. Supreme Court is citing its own opinion where it **granted certiorari** to hear the defendants' appeal in the Delaware case. If you looked in vol. 344 of the United States Reports on page 891 you would see the following:

> No. 448. FRANCIS B. GEBHART, William B. Horner, Eugene H. Shallcross, et al., Petitioners, v. ETHEL LOUISE BELTON, an Infant, by Her Guardian ad litem, Ethel Belton, et al.
>
> Petition for Writ of Certiorari to the Supreme Court of Delaware.
>
> See same case below, – Del –, 91 A2d 137.
>
> H. Albert Young, Attorney General of Delaware, for petitioners.
>
> Louis L. Redding, of Wilmington, Delaware, and Thurgood Marshall, of New York City, for respondents.
>
> November 24, 1952. Granted. The motion of respondents to advance is granted and the case is advanced and assigned for argument immediately following No. 413. Brief for petitioners is to be filed not later than three weeks after argument.

In the Delaware case, the plaintiffs were successful and the defendants appealed the decision, first to the Delaware Supreme Court and then by means of a **petition for a writ of certiorari,** to the United States Supreme Court. The plaintiffs could have **filed a cross-petition,** for example arguing that they should be permitted to remain in white schools even after the equalization program had been completed. The **cross-petition** here would also be a petition for a writ of certiorari, but to have the U.S. Supreme Court consider the plaintiffs' arguments as a point of appeal as well.

Continue reading the case:

75   In each of these cases, minors of the Negro race, through their legal representatives,
      seek the aid of the courts in obtaining admission to the public schools of their
      community on a nonsegregated basis. In each instance, they had been denied ad-
      mission to schools attended by white children under laws requiring or permitting
      segregation according to race. This segregation was alleged to deprive the plaintiffs
80   of the equal protection of the laws under the Fourteenth Amendment. In each of the
      cases other than the Delaware case, a three-judge federal district court denied relief
      to the plaintiffs on the so-called "separate but equal" doctrine announced by this
      Court in Plessy v. Ferguson, 163 U.S. 537. Under that doctrine, equality of treatment
      is accorded when the races are provided substantially equal facilities, even though
85   these facilities be separate. In the Delaware case, the Supreme Court of Delaware
      adhered to that doctrine, but ordered that the plaintiffs be admitted to the white
      schools because of their superiority to the Negro schools.

Analysis

The plaintiffs here are **minors,** or below **the age of legal majority,** which means that they are not yet old enough to vote and to enter into legal relations without their **legal guardian**'s permission. A child's legal guardian is usually its parents, but could be some other person appointed by a court. Although we say "**minor**" for someone below the age of legal majority, we do *not* say "major" for someone above that age. A "major" is an officer in the military!

The plaintiffs have based their case on the **equal protection clause of the Fourteenth Amendment to the U.S. Constitution.** This amendment was discussed in Unit 1 in relation to discrimination in jury selection. For the full text, see Appendix I. The lower courts, however, applied the U.S. Supreme Court's precedent in *Plessy v. Ferguson*, where the "separate but equal" doctrine was announced. *Plessy v. Ferguson* involved a state statute criminally prohibiting African-Americans from riding in railway cars reserved for white passengers and vice versa. The appellant had sat in a white car and refused to move when ordered to do so by railway personnel. He was prosecuted under the criminal statute in the State of Louisiana and eventually appealed to the U.S. Supreme Court arguing that the state statute violated his rights under the **equal protection clause**. Then (1896), the U.S. Supreme Court held that the equal protection clause did not require **integration** of the races, but rather only that members of one race receive treatment equal to that given to members of another race. Accordingly, as long as the cars for African-Americans were just as good as the cars for whites, there was no violation of the Fourteenth Amendment guarantee, at least in 1896.

Continue reading the case:

> The plaintiffs contend that segregated public schools are not "equal" and cannot be made "equal," and that hence they are deprived of the equal protection of the laws.
> 90 Because of the obvious importance of the question presented, the Court took jurisdiction. Argument was heard in the 1952 Term, and reargument was heard this Term on certain questions propounded by the Court.
>
> Reargument was largely devoted to the circumstances surrounding the adoption of the Fourteenth Amendment in 1868. It covered exhaustively consideration of the
> 95 Amendment in Congress, ratification by the states, then existing practices in racial segregation, and the views of proponents and opponents of the Amendment. This discussion and our own investigation convince us that, although these sources cast some light, it is not enough to resolve the problem with which we are faced. At best, they are inconclusive. The most avid proponents of the post-War Amendments
> 100 undoubtedly intended them to remove all legal distinctions among "all persons born or naturalized in the United States." Their opponents, just as certainly, were antagonistic to both the letter and the spirit of the Amendments and wished them to have the most limited effect. What others in Congress and the state legislatures had in mind cannot be determined with any degree of certainty ...

Analysis

The U.S. Supreme Court hears oral arguments in cases over which it **takes jurisdiction** (lines 90-91), meaning cases for which it **grants a writ of certiorari** or, still in 1954, cases on direct appeal. Oral arguments are heard during the **term** when the Court is in session and the terms are distinguished by year, as in the **1952 Term** (line 91). As you notice from the opinion, the Court heard oral arguments, but still had some questions that the parties could not answer adequately. Accordingly, a date for reargumentation was set and the Court heard oral arguments again during a later term.

Questions on the Text

1. In the passage above, the Court considers the **legislative history** of the Fourteenth Amendment. Why would a court consider the legislative history of a constitutional provision? Do your own courts do the same? Do you think that legislative history, in the sense of what the legislature intended to accomplish when it adopted the particular provision, casts much light on the way courts should interpret constitutional provisions? Does the Supreme Court think that it does? Would legislative history be more important when interpreting a statute that related to administrative or policy matters than when interpreting something like the equal protection clause? Suppose the Bill of Rights had already contained an equal protection clause. As we know, slavery was permitted in 1791 when the Bill of Rights was adopted. Accordingly, the assumption from the viewpoint of legislative history would be that the Framers of the Bill of Rights did not mean to include African-Americans within the equal protection guarantee. Should the intent of the Framers of the Constitution make much difference in the way a court interprets that clause in attempting to determine the rights of African-Americans in the United States in 1954?

2. The defendants in these cases relied on the separate but equal doctrine of *Plessy v. Ferguson.* Indeed the lower courts seemed to have done so as well. Were these courts bound by that decision? Is the U.S. Supreme Court bound by that decision? If you were a lawyer devoted to furthering the rights of racial minorities in the United States and you had the *Plessy v. Ferguson* precedent to work with, how could you use it to your benefit? How could you formulate its holding so that it would support you in *Brown v. Board of Education*?

Continue reading the case:

105   In the first cases in this Court construing the Fourteenth Amendment, decided shortly after its adoption, the Court interpreted it as proscribing all state-imposed discriminations against the Negro race. The doctrine of "separate but equal" did not make its appearance in this Court until 1896 in the case of Plessy v. Ferguson, supra, involving not education but transportation. American courts have since labored
110   with the doctrine for over half a century. In this Court, there have been six cases involving the "separate but equal" doctrine in the field of public education. In Cumming v. County Board of Education, 175 U.S. 528, and Gong Lum v. Rice, 275 U.S. 78, the validity of the doctrine itself was not challenged. In more recent cases, all on the graduate school level, inequality was found in that specific benefits enjoyed by
115   white students were denied to Negro students of the same educational qualifications. Missouri ex rel. Gaines v. Canada, 305 U.S. 337; Sipuel v. Oklahoma, 332 U.S. 631;

Sweatt v. Painter, 339 U.S. 629; McLaurin v. Oklahoma State Regents, 339 U.S. 637.
In none of these cases was it necessary to reexamine the doctrine to grant relief to the
Negro plaintiff. And in Sweatt v. Painter, supra, the Court expressly reserved decision
120 on the question whether Plessy v. Ferguson should be held inapplicable to public
education.

In the instant cases, that question is directly presented. Here, unlike Sweatt v. Painter,
there are findings below that the Negro and white schools involved have been
equalized, or are being equalized, with respect to buildings, curricula, qualifications
125 and salaries of teachers, and other "tangible" factors. Our decision, therefore, cannot turn on merely a comparison of these tangible factors in the Negro and white
schools involved in each of the cases. We must look instead to the effect of segregation itself on public education.

In approaching this problem, we cannot turn the clock back to 1868 when the Amend-
130 ment was adopted, or even to 1896 when Plessy v. Ferguson was written. We must
consider public education in the light of its full development and its present place in
American life throughout the Nation. Only in this way can it be determined if segregation
in public schools deprives these plaintiffs of the equal protection of the laws. ...

Questions on the Text

1 It should now be clear to you a) how to formulate the *Plessy v. Ferguson*
separate but equal doctrine so that it does not apply to you as a plaintiff in
Brown v. Board of Education (limit the holding to the field of transportation); and b) how to use the doctrine to your benefit (take cases involving
unequal facilities as between blacks and whites). What arguments can you
now make for overruling *Plessy v. Ferguson*?

2 In lines 119-120, the Court states that in *Sweatt v. Painter*, it "expressly
reserved decision on the question ... " How do you think the Court did that?
What would it have written in its opinion to indicate express reservation of
decision on some issue?

Continue reading the case:

We come then to the question presented: Does segregation of children in public
135 schools solely on the basis of race, even though the physical facilities and other
"tangible" factors may be equal, deprive the children of the minority group of equal
educational opportunities? We believe that it does.

In Sweatt v. Painter, supra, in finding that a segregated law school for Negroes could
not provide them equal educational opportunities, this Court relied in large part on
140 "those qualities which are incapable of objective measurement but which make for
greatness in a law school." In McLaurin v. Oklahoma State Regents, supra, the Court,

in requiring that a Negro admitted to a white graduate school be treated like all other students, again resorted to intangible considerations: " ... his ability to study, to engage in discussions and exchange views with other students, and, in general, to learn
145 his profession." Such considerations apply with added force to children in grade and high schools. To separate them from others of similar age and qualifications solely because of their race generates a feeling of inferiority as to their status in the community that may affect their hearts and minds in a way unlikely ever to be undone. The effect of this separation on their educational opportunities was well stated by a finding
150 in the Kansas case by a court which nevertheless felt compelled to rule against the Negro plaintiffs: "Segregation of white and colored children in public schools has a detrimental effect upon the colored children. The impact is greater when it has the sanction of the law; for the policy of separating the races is usually interpreted as denoting the inferiority of the Negro group. A sense of inferiority affects the motiva-
155 tion of a child to learn. Segregation with the sanction of law, therefore, has a tendency to retard the educational and mental development of Negro children and to deprive them of some of the benefits they would receive in a racially integrated school system."** Whatever may have been the extent of psychological knowledge at the time of Plessy v. Ferguson, this finding is amply supported by modern authority. Any
160 language in Plessy v. Ferguson contrary to this finding is rejected.

We conclude that in the field of public education the doctrine of "separate but equal" has no place.

Separate educational facilities are inherently unequal. Therefore, we hold that the plaintiffs and others similarly situated for whom the actions have been brought are,
165 by reason of the segregation complained of, deprived of the equal protection of the laws guaranteed by the Fourteenth Amendment. This disposition makes unnecessary any discussion whether such segregation also violates the Due Process Clause of the Fourteenth Amendment.

Because these are class actions, because of the wide applicability of this decision, and
170 because of the great variety of local conditions, the formulation of decrees in these cases presents problems of considerable complexity. On reargument, the consideration of appropriate relief was necessarily subordinated to the primary question – the constitutionality of segregation in public education. We have now announced that
175 such segregation is a denial of the equal protection of the laws. In order that we may have the full assistance of the parties in formulating decrees, the cases will be restored to the docket, and the parties are requested to present further argument on Questions 4 and 5 previously propounded by the Court for the reargument this Term. The Attorney General of the United States is again invited to participate. The Attorneys
180 General of the states requiring or permitting segregation in public education will also be permitted to appear as amici curiae upon request to do so by September 15, 1954, and submission of briefs by October 1, 1954.

It is so ordered.

---

185 ** [Court's footnote 10] A similar finding was made in the Delaware case: "I conclude from the testimony that in our Delaware society, State-imposed segregation

in education itself results in the Negro children, as a class, receiving educational opportunities which are substantially inferior to those available to white children otherwise similarly situated." 87 A.2d 862, 865.

Analysis

Note in line 160 the Court's statement: "Any language in Plessy v. Ferguson contrary to this finding is rejected." This language indicates that the Supreme Court is **overruling** its own precedent as established in *Plessy v. Ferguson.*

Note in line 164: **"plaintiffs and others similarly situated for whom the actions have been brought."** The expression **"others similarly situated"** is a key phrase indicating that *Brown v. Board of Education* was a **class action**. The plaintiffs here brought suit not only so that they personally would be admitted to public schools on a non-segregated basis, but also so that all others like them, namely all black children of elementary and high school age living within the Topeka school district, would be admitted to public schools on a non-segregated basis. Indeed all of the four cases were class actions as the Court expressly states in line 169. The **class action** permits all individuals who are in a similar situation to file one single law suit to pursue a remedy for everyone. It thus makes litigation cheaper and ensures that everyone, and not just the individual plaintiff in the case, benefits from the court's decision.

The plaintiffs brought their action on the basis of the Fourteenth Amendment which contains a so-called **equal protection clause** and a **due process clause**. The holding in *Brown* is based on the equal protection clause and, as the Court indicates in lines 166-168, not on the basis of the due process clause. Since the Court was able to reach the decision it did on the basis of the equal protection clause, it did not have to consider the due process clause of the Fourteenth Amendment.

In lines 176-177, the Court states that the **cases will be restored to the docket** for further argumentation. The **docket** is the Court's calendar of official business in the sense of the date on which it will hear cases in the future. The cases were put back on the calendar for reargumentation. The **Attorney General of the United States** and the **Attorneys General of the states** affected by the *Brown* holding were invited to appear as **amici curiae** (sing. **amicus curiae**), meaning friends of the Court (lines 179-181). When the Supreme Court needs more information to decide a case than the parties most likely could provide on their own, the Court can invite other individuals, organizations, legal representatives, etc. to provide that information if they like. Here the various attorneys general, who are the legal representatives of the United States and of each of the individual states, are invited to appear, because they will most likely be of assistance to the Court in resolving legal issues relating to the formulation of the Court's planned decrees, or orders, which will finally resolve the problem presented here. In order to participate as amici curiae, the attorneys general were required to **submit briefs** by October 1, 1954. A **brief** is a document containing legal argumentation. If the appellant submits one, it is called an **appellate brief**, and it contains the arguments and legal authorities supporting the appellant's point of view. If an **amicus curiae** submits one it is called an **amicus brief** and it contains perhaps statistics or legal argumentation relevant to the case and in support of the organization's or individual's point of view who is filing it as an amicus curiae.

Questions on the Text

1. Read the due process clause of the Fourteenth Amendment. How could you argue that segregated schools violate the right a member of a minority race has to due process?
2. Read *Bolling v. Sharpe*, 347 U.S. 497, 74 Sup.Ct. 693, 98 L.Ed. 884 (1954). This case dealt with black children's rights to be admitted to public schools in the District of Columbia on a non-segregated basis. It was decided immediately following *Brown v. Board of Education*. Here the plaintiffs made a due process argument rather than an equal protection argument. Why? Remember that Washington D.C. is not a state of the United States but rather federal territory. Do you think they relied on the Fourteenth Amendment? On what other amendment could they have relied? Does this amendment contain an equal protection clause? Why could they not have relied on the Fourteenth Amendment? If you cannot answer this question reconsider the constitutional law cases in Unit I which employed the Fourteenth Amendment to apply rights guaranteed in the Bill of Rights to the individual states. Why was that necessary?
3. State the a) facts of the cases; b) legal history of the cases; c) question raised on appeal; d) the holding; and the e) ratio decidendi in your own words. You should be able to do this in less than ten sentences!

Terminology

de jure segregation	separation of the races as required by law (**rechtlich vorgeschriebene Trennung der Rassen**)
de facto segregation	separation of the races in fact, but not because separation is required by law (**tatsächliche, aber nicht rechtlich vorgeschriebene Trennung der Rassen**)
consolidated opinion	a court's decision for a group of cases that have been joined together and for which the court writes only one opinion (**Entscheidung in verbundenen Verfahren**)
to enjoin	to prohibit s.o. from doing s.th. (**eine einstweilige Verfügung erlassen**); the remedy is an **injunction** (**einstweilige Verfügung**)
interlocutory injunction	interim measure a court can take to prohibit a party to a law suit from engaging in some type of conduct until the court can reach a final judgment (**einstweilige Verfügung**)
preliminary injunction	interlocutory injunction granted after the party to be restrained has had the opportunity to be heard (**einstweilige Verfügung**)
temporary restraining order	interlocutory injunction granted without a hearing of the party to be restrained
permanent injunction	injunction granted until the final disposition of a law suit
perpetual injunction	injunction granted as the final disposition of a law suit (**Leistungsurteil auf Unterlassung**)
temporary injunction	another name for a **preliminary injunction**
ex parte	in the absence of a party to a law suit
pendente lite	pending the law suit, awaiting the final outcome of the litigation
permanent relief	final remedy granted for unlimited amount of time
to deny relief	to refuse to give the plaintiff the remedy she has filed suit to get (**das Klagebegehren ablehnen**)
pursuant to	according to, under (the authority of) (**gemäß**)
party complainant	party filing a complaint, plaintiff (**Kläger**)
party defendant	party against whom a complaint has been filed, defendant (**Beklagter**)
to repeal a law	to cancel the effectiveness of a law, to put a law out of force (**ein Gesetz aufheben**)
to vacate	to declare void or empty of effect, as in: **to vacate the lower court's judgment** (**das Urteil der Vorinstanz aufheben**)
infra	see below; contrasted to **supra**, meaning see above
cross-petition	petition filed by the respondent to an appeal to a supreme court; the petitioner is the party filing the appeal, or petitioning for the

writ of certiorari, and the respondent is the party against whom the appeal is filed, who may also raise a point to be considered on appeal in a **cross-petition** (ca. **Anschlußrevision**); the same terminological construction is also used for the **complaint** and **cross-complaint**

cross-complaint	complaint filed by the defendant to a law suit against either the plaintiff or against any other person who is directly involved in the controversy (**Widerklage, Drittwiderklage, bzw. Streitverkündung**)
legal guardian	someone who is responsible for the legal affairs of a person who does not have the capacity, because of age or any other reason, to govern his own legal affairs (**gesetzlicher Vertreter**)
separate but equal doctrine	principle for interpreting the equal protection clause of the Fourteenth Amendment whereby "equality of treatment is accorded when the races are provided substantially equal facilities, even though these facilities be separate"; doctrine rejected in *Brown v. Board of Education*
ratification	approval of an amendment to a constitution (**Verabschiedung einer Verfassungsänderung**)
post-War Amendments	Thirteenth, Fourteenth and Fifteenth Amendments to the U.S. Constitution, which were ratified following the Civil War
involuntary servitude	slavery, prohibited by the Thirteenth Amendment (**Sklaverei**)
legislative history	events, attitudes, cultural context surrounding the adoption of a law (**Gesetzgebungsgeschichte**)
instant case	term used to refer to the case the court is considering at the moment; the actual case for which it is writing the opinion; also: **the case at bar** (**der vorliegende Fall**)
to reserve decision	to not make a decision at the moment but to postpone it to a later time (**sich die Entscheidung vorbehalten**)
findings below	refers to determinations made by a lower court before the case reached a higher court on appeal (**die Feststellungen der Vorinstanz**)
others similarly situated	term used to describe class of individuals who are all like the plaintiff to a law suit in a legally significant way; used for **class actions**
class action	law suit filed by one or more plaintiffs on behalf of themselves and all individuals like them in the sense that they too have suffered from the same violation of their rights
docket	court's calendar of official business; calendar of dates set for hearing cases (**Terminkalender eines Gerichts**); a case is **docketed** when it is registered in this calendar and thus given a specific time and day for a judicial hearing; a case is **restored to**

	the docket when it is rescheduled for an additional hearing at a later date
Attorney General	the lawyer who represents a state or nation, as the **Attorney General of the United States**, who is also the head of the Justice Department, and the **Attorneys General** of the individual states in the U.S. (ca. **Justizminister und Generalstaatsanwalt**)
brief	document containing legal argumentation of a case submitted to an appellate court when an appeal is filed or a petition for a writ of certiorari is made (**Revisionsbegründung**)
amicus curiae	friend of the court (pl. **amici curiae**); term used to refer to individuals, organizations, public officials, etc. who are not parties to a law suit but who may have information of value to the court when considering an appeal; **amici curiae** are invited by the court to submit briefs, referred to as **amicus briefs** and to participate in oral argumentation

Vocabulary

amply	more than sufficiently, strongly
avid	most enthusiastic, strongly supportive or interested
to construe	to interpret
curriculum	educational program, classes offered to students (pl. **curricula**)
detrimental	harmful, negative
diligence	care, serious effort
disparaging	derogatory, tending to make s.o. or s.th. look inferior or bad
dispatch	promptness, speed in dealing with s.th.
to err	to make a mistake
extra-curricular	in addition to the normal educational program or curricula, such athletic team training, instruction for debating teams, a school newspaper, etc.
forthwith	immediately
pupil-teacher ratio	the relationship between the total number of pupils attending the school to the total number of teachers offering instruction in the school; the lower this ratio, the smaller classes will be and the more attention any one pupil will receive from a teacher
to rectify	to make right, to correct so that something is right
tangible	s.th. that can be touched, or measured exactly; as opposed to **intangible**, meaning s.th. that cannot be touched or measured exactly

Chapter 3
Freedom of Speech

The First Amendment states that "Congress shall make no law ... abridging the freedom of speech, ... " The Founders were primarily concerned with **prior restraints** on speech, such as licensing laws for publishers, which permitted the state to select what literature its citizenry could read. Such restraints are called **prior restraints** because the law controls the speech before it is expressed. This constitutional guarantee, however, was expanded upon considerably and there are a wealth of cases dealing with all aspects of it. One initial expansion of the free-speech guarantee came from constitutional review of restraints in the form of criminal punishment imposed after the fact. An early, but still applied, test of the constitutionality of such statutes was the **clear and present danger test**, announced in *Schenck v. United States* (see Appendix II for a summary of this case): "The question in every case is whether the words used are used in such circumstances and are of such a nature as to create a clear and present danger that they will bring about the substantive evils that Congress has a right to prevent." In other words, if the state has a right to prohibit certain conduct, then it also has a right to prohibit speech that **incites**, or encourages, someone to engage in this conduct. Contrarily, if the state does not have the right to prohibit the conduct, or if the speech does not encourage people to engage in properly prohibited conduct, the state may not prohibit the speech. Another expansion of the free-speech guarantee came in cases raising the question whether the state could prohibit conduct, as opposed to the written or spoken word, if the conduct expressed a message. The following case relates to this issue.

Texas v. Johnson
491 U.S. 397, 109 S.Ct. 2533, 105 L.Ed.2d 342 (1989)

Justice BRENNAN delivered the opinion of the Court ...

5

I. While the Republican National Convention was taking place in Dallas in 1984, respondent Johnson participated in a political demonstration dubbed the "Republican War Chest Tour." ... [T]he purpose of this event was to protest the policies of the

Reagan administration and of certain Dallas-based corporations ... The demonstra-
10   tion ended in front of Dallas City Hall, where Johnson unfurled [an] American flag,
doused it with kerosene, and set it on fire. While the flag burned, the protestors
chanted: "America, the red, white, and blue, we spit on you." After the demonstrators dispersed, a witness to the flag burning collected the flag's remains and buried
them in his backyard. No one was physically injured or threatened with injury,
15   though several witnesses testified that they had been seriously offended by the flag
burning.

Of the approximately 100 demonstrators, Johnson alone was charged with a crime.
The only criminal offense with which he was charged was the desecration of a
20   venerated object in violation of Tex. Penal Code Ann. § 42.09(a)(3) (1989).* After a
trial, he was convicted, sentenced to one year in prison, and fined $2,000. The Court
of Appeals for the Fifth District of Texas at Dallas affirmed Johnson's conviction,
706 S.W.2d 120 (1986), but the Texas Court of Criminal Appeals reversed, 755
S.W.2d 92 (1988), holding that the State could not, consistent with the First Amend-
25   ment, punish Johnson for burning the flag in these circumstances ...

Because it reversed Johnson's conviction on the ground that § 42.09 was unconstitutional as applied to him, the state court did not address Johnson's argument that the
statute was, on its face, unconstitutionally vague and overbroad. We granted certio-
30   rari, 488 U.S. 907, 109 S.Ct. 257, 102 L.Ed.2d 245(1988), and now affirm.

* Texas Penal Code Ann. § 42.09 (1989) provides in full:
     "§ 42.09. Desecration of Venerated Object
        "(a) A person commits an offense if he intentionally or knowingly desecrates:
35   "(1) a public monument;
        "(2) a place of worship or burial; or
        "(3) a state or national flag.
        "(b) For purposes of this section, 'desecrate' means deface, damage, or other-
        wise physically mistreat in a way that the actor knows will seriously offend
40   one or more persons likely to observe or discover his action.
        "(c) An offense under this section is a Class A misdemeanor."

II. Johnson was convicted of flag desecration for burning the flag rather than for
uttering insulting words. This fact somewhat complicates our consideration of his
45   conviction under the First Amendment. We must first determine whether Johnson's
burning of the flag constituted expressive conduct, permitting him to invoke the First
Amendment in challenging his conviction. See, *e.g., Spence v. Washington*, 418 U.S.
405 ... (1974). If his conduct was expressive, we next decide whether the State's
regulation is related to the suppression of free expression ... If the State's regulation
50   is not related to expression, then the less stringent standard we announced in *United
States v. O'Brien* 391 U.S. 367 ... (1968) for regulations of noncommunicative
conduct controls ... If it is, then we are outside of *O'Brien's* test, and we must ask
whether this interest justifies Johnson's conviction under a more demanding standard ...

55   In deciding whether particular conduct possesses sufficient communicative elements
     to bring the First Amendment into play, we have asked whether "[a]n intent to
     convey a particularized message was present, and [whether] the likelihood was great
     that the message would be understood by those who viewed it." ... Hence, we have
     recognized the expressive nature of students' wearing of black armbands to protest
60   American military involvement in Vietnam ... ; of a sit-in by blacks in a "whites
     only" area to protest segregation ... ; of the wearing of American military uniforms
     in a dramatic presentation criticizing American involvement in Vietnam ... ; and of
     picketing about a wide variety of causes That we have had little difficulty identifying
     an expressive element in conduct relating to flags should not be surprising. The very
65   purpose of a national flag is to serve as a symbol of our country; it is, one might say,
     "the one visible manifestation of two hundred years of nationhood." ...

     The State of Texas conceded for purposes of its oral argument in this case that
     Johnson's conduct was expressive conduct, ... Johnson burned an American flag as
70   part - indeed, as the culmination - of political demonstration that coincided with the
     convening of the Republican Party and its renomination of Ronald Reagan for
     President. The expressive, overtly political nature of this conduct was both inten-
     tional and overwhelmingly apparent ...

Analysis

The original defendant in this case was convicted of **flag desecration** because he
burned a U.S. flag during a demonstration against the policies of the Reagan **administration**. The Reagan administration refers to the period of time during which
Ronald Reagan was President of the United States. Flag desecration is any form of
physical mistreatment of the flag. As you can see from the * footnote, it is a **Class
A misdemeanor**. Criminal Codes in the United States usually classify criminal offenses depending upon their seriousness and the amount of punishment with
which they are threatened. In a separate section of the code, one will then find the
range of punishment for each class of offense. A Class A misdemeanor is in the highest category of misdemeanors, which are less serious than felonies.

In lines 27-30, the Court notes that the intermediate court of appeal in this case
determined that the Texas statute was unconstitutional as applied to Johnson
and did not consider the question whether the statute was unconstitutional **on
its face**. A court will determine that a statute is unconstitutional on its face, if
every conceivable application of the statute violates the Constitution. Here the
lower court simply determined that the statute was unconstitutional in its application in Johnson's case.

Johnson has relied on the First Amendment's **freedom of speech clause** in challenging his conviction. This clause refers merely to speech, but it has been extended to

cover expressive conduct as well. In lines 43-54, the Court explains the correct approach to take in determining whether conduct, as opposed to the written or spoken word, can be prohibited without violating the First Amendment's freedom of speech clause. The first question that must be asked is whether the conduct was expressive. If not, then the First Amendment may not be relied upon in challenging the law. If the conduct was expressive the First Amendment applies, but not necessarily to the same extent as it would if pure speech were involved. For expressive conduct, the next question is whether the law is related to suppressing free expression. If it is not then the milder standard announced by the Court in *O'Brien* applies in determining the law's constitutionality. *O'Brien's test* is:

> "... a government regulation is sufficiently justified if it is within the constitutional power of the Government; if it furthers an important or substantial governmental interest; if the governmental interest is unrelated to the suppression of free expression; and if the incidental restriction on alleged First Amendment freedoms is no greater than is essential to the furtherance of that interest."

If the law is related to suppressing free expression, then the more demanding standard, or the **strict scrutiny test** will apply. The strict scrutiny test of constitutionality requires that the law in question serve a **compelling state interest** and be the **least intrusive means** of attaining the state's goal. Generally, the strict scrutiny test is applied when **fundamental rights** are in question or when the law draws a **suspect classification**. Freedom of speech is the epitome of a fundamental right, as opposed to economic rights such as freedom of contract for which the strict scrutiny test will not be applied. A suspect classification is drawn when the law distinguishes in its application based on a characteristic that is immutable, has no relation to an individual's abilities or rights, and has been used as the basis of discrimination in the past. A person's race, for example, is a suspect classification and laws that differentiate in the treatment afforded members of different races will be subjected to the strict scrutiny test. A milder test of constitutionality is the **rational basis test**. It requires simply that the law in question serve a **legitimate state interest** and be a **rational means** of attaining the state's goal. If an economic right is involved, then the question is simply whether the goal the state is pursuing with the law in question is something the state generally has a right to pursue, e.g. the development and maintenance of state parks, and whether the method employed to pursue this goal is one of many possible ways of attaining it. *O'Brien's* test lies somewhere in between the two.

In the last paragraph of the opinion, the Court notes that the State of Texas has conceded, or admitted, for the purpose of oral arguments before the Court that Johnson's conduct was expressive. Accordingly, the first requirement of the Court's test has been fulfilled and the First Amendment is applicable in this case. The next question for the Court is whether the law is or is not related to the suppression of speech.

Continue reading the case:

III. The government generally has a freer hand in restricting expressive conduct than
75 it has in restricting the written or spoken word ... It may not, however, proscribe
particular conduct because it has expressive elements ... It is ... not simply the verbal
or nonverbal nature of the expression, but the governmental interest at stake, that
helps to determine whether a restriction on that expression is valid.

80 Thus, although we have recognized that where "'speech' and 'nonspeech' elements
are combined in the same course of conduct, a sufficiently important governmental
interest in regulating the nonspeech element can justify incidental limitations on First
Amendment freedoms," ... we have limited the applicability of *O'Brien's* relatively
lenient standard to those cases in which "the governmental interest is unrelated to
85 the suppression of free expression." ...

In order to decide whether *O'Brien's* test applies here, therefore, we must decide
whether Texas has asserted an interest in support of Johnson's conviction that is
unrelated to the suppression of expression ... The State offers two separate interests
90 to justify this conviction: preventing breaches of the peace and preserving the flag as
a symbol of nationhood and national unity. We hold that the first interest is not
implicated on this record and that the second is related to the suppression of expression.

95 **A.** Texas claims that its interest in preventing breaches of the peace justifies Johnson's
conviction for flag desecration. However, no disturbance of the peace actually occurred or threatened to occur because of Johnson's burning of the flag ... The State's
emphasis on the protestors' disorderly actions prior to arriving at City Hall is not
only somewhat surprising given that no charges were brought on the basis of this
100 conduct, but it also fails to show that a disturbance of the peace was a likely reaction
to Johnson's conduct ...

The State's position, therefore, amounts to a claim that an audience that takes serious
offense at particular expression is necessarily likely to disturb the peace and that the
105 expression may be prohibited on this basis. Our precedents do not countenance such
a presumption. On the contrary, they recognize that a principal "function of free
speech under our system of government is to invite dispute. It may indeed best serve
its high purpose when it induces a condition of unrest, creates dissatisfaction with
conditions as they are, or even stirs people to anger." ... It would be odd indeed to
110 conclude both that "if it is the speaker's opinion that gives offense, that consequence
is a reason for according it constitutional protection," ... and that the government
may ban the expression of certain disagreeable ideas on the unsupported presumption that their very disagreeableness will provoke violence ...

115 We thus conclude that the State's interest in maintaining order is not implicated on
these facts. The State need not worry that our holding will disable it from preserving
the peace ... And, in fact, Texas already has a statute specifically prohibiting

breaches of the peace, ... which tends to confirm that Texas need not punish this flag
desecration in order to keep the peace ...

120

B. The State also asserts an interest in preserving the flag as a symbol of nationhood
and national unity. In *Spence*, we acknowledged that the government's interest in
preserving the flag's special symbolic value "is directly related to expression in the
context of activity" such as affixing a peace symbol to a flag ... We are equally
125 persuaded that this interest is related to expression in the case of Johnson's burning
of the flag. The State, apparently, is concerned that such conduct will lead people to
believe either that the flag does not stand for nationhood and national unity, but
instead reflects other, less positive concepts, or that the concepts reflected in the flag
do not in fact exist, that is, that we do not enjoy unity as a Nation. These concerns
130 blossom only when a person's treatment of the flag communicates some message,
and thus are related "to the suppression of free expression" within the meaning of
O'Brien. We are thus outside of *O'Brien's* test altogether.

IV. It remains to consider whether the State's interest in preserving the flag as a
135 symbol of nationhood and national unity justifies Johnson's conviction.

As in *Spence*, "[w]e are confronted with a case of prosecution for the expression of
an idea through activity," and "[a]ccordingly, we must examine with particular care
the interests advanced by [petitioner] to support its prosecution." ... Johnson was
140 not, we add, prosecuted for the expression of just any idea; he was prosecuted for his
expression of dissatisfaction with the policies of this country, expression situated at
the core of our First Amendment values ...

Johnson's political expression was restricted because of the content of the message he
145 conveyed. We must therefore subject the State's asserted interest in preserving the
special symbolic character of the flag to "the most exacting scrutiny." ...

Texas argues that its interest in preserving the flag as a symbol of nationhood and
national unity survives this close analysis ... The State's argument is not that it has an
150 interest simply in maintaining the flag as a symbol of something, no matter what it
symbolizes; ... Rather, the State's claim is that it has an interest in preserving the flag
as a symbol of nationhood and national unity, a symbol with a determinate range of
meanings ... According to Texas, if one physically treats the flag in a way that would
tend to cast doubt on either the idea that nationhood and national unity are the flag's
155 referents or that national unity actually exists, the message conveyed thereby is a
harmful one and therefore may be prohibited.

If there is a bedrock principle underlying the First Amendment, it is that the government may not prohibit the expression of an idea simply because society finds the idea
160 itself offensive or disagreeable ... We never before have held that the Government
may ensure that a symbol be used to express only one view of that symbol or its
referents ... To conclude that the government may permit designated symbols to be
used to communicate only a limited set of messages would be to enter territory

having no discernible or defensible boundaries. Could the government, on this the-
165 ory, prohibit the burning of state flags? Of copies of the Presidential seal? Of the
Constitution? In evaluating these choices under the First Amendment, how would
we decide which symbols were sufficiently special to warrant this unique status? To
do so, we would be forced to consult our own political preferences, and impose them
on the citizenry, in the very way that the First Amendment forbids us to do ...
170

There is, moreover, no indication - either in the text of the Constitution or in our
cases interpreting it - that a separate juridical category exists for the American flag
alone ... The First amendment does not guarantee that other concepts virtually
sacred to our Nation as a whole - such as the principle that discrimination on the
175 basis of race is odious and destructive - will go unquestioned in the marketplace of
ideas ... We decline, therefore, to create for the flag an exception to the joust of
principles protected by the First Amendment.

It is not the State's ends, but its means, to which we object. It cannot be gainsaid that
180 there is a special place reserved for the flag in this Nation, and thus we do not doubt
that the government has a legitimate interest in making efforts to "preserv[e] the
national flag as an unalloyed symbol of our country." ... To say that the government
has an interest in encouraging proper treatment of the flag, however, is not to say that
it may criminally punish a person for burning a flag as a means of political protest ...
185

We are fortified in today's conclusion by our conviction that forbidding criminal
punishment for conduct such as Johnson's will not endanger the special role played
by our flag or the feelings it inspires. To paraphrase Justice Holmes, we submit that
nobody can suppose that this one gesture of an unknown man will change our
190 Nation's attitude towards its flag ... Indeed, Texas' argument that the burning of an
American flag "is an act having a high likelihood to cause a breach of the peace," ...
and its statute's implicit assumption that physical mistreatment of the flag will lead
to "serious offense," tend to confirm that the flag's special role is not in danger; if it
were, no one would riot or take offense because a flag had been burned.
195

We are tempted to say, in fact, that the flag's deservedly cherished place in our
community will be strengthened, not weakened, by our holding today. Our decision
is a reaffirmation of the principles of freedom and inclusiveness that the flag best
reflects, and of the conviction that our toleration of criticism such as Johnson's is a
200 sign and source or our strength ...

The way to preserve the flag's special role is not to punish those who feel differently
about these matters. It is to persuade them that they are wrong. "To courageous,
self-reliant men, with confidence in the power of free and fearless reasoning applied
205 through the processes of popular government, no danger flowing from speech can be
deemed clear and present, unless the incidence of the evil apprehended is so imminent
that it may befall before there is opportunity for full discussion. If there be time to
expose through discussion the falsehood and fallacies, to avert the evil by the processes of education, the remedy to be applied is more speech, not enforced silence."

210 ... We can imagine no more appropriate response to burning a flag than waving one's
own, no better way to counter a flag burner's message than by saluting the flag that
burns, no surer means of preserving the dignity even of the flag that burned than by
- as one witness here did - according its remains a respectful burial. We do not
consecrate the flag by punishing its desecration, for in doing so we dilute the freedom
215 that this cherished emblem represents.

V. Johnson was convicted for engaging in expressive conduct. The State's interest in
preventing breaches of the peace does not support his conviction because Johnson's
conduct did not threaten to disturb the peace. Nor does the State's interest in preserv-
220 ing the flag as a symbol of nationhood and national unity justify his criminal conviction for engaging in political expression. The judgment of the Texas Court of Criminal Appeals is therefore ... Affirmed

Questions on the Text

[1] State the a) facts of the case; b) legal history of the case; c) issue raised on
appeal; d) holding; e) ratio decidendi in your own words.
[2] The U.S. Supreme Court affirmed the decision of the Texas Court of Criminal Appeals in this case, but the Court of Appeals had only determined that
the Texas statute was unconstitutional in its application to Johnson and not
on its face. Can you imagine how any law similar to the Texas statute could
survive constitutional attack?
[3] Consider § 90a of the German Criminal Code (*see Language Exercises
p. 261 for the full text of the section*). Would this section be unconstitutional
under *Texas v. Johnson*? Do you think it should or should not be declared
unconstitutional? For an argument against the holding in *Texas v. Johnson*,
see Chief Justice Rehnquist's dissent in that case. This dissenting opinion
also contains a history of the U.S. flag, poetry regarding the flag, including
Frances Scott Key's famous poem that later provided the words to the U.S.
national anthem, and a variety of arguments.
[4] Read the cases cited in the opinion, particularly *O'Brien* and *Spence*, and
report more exactly on the rule developed in U.S. Supreme Court precedents
regarding symbolic speech and First Amendment rights. What test did the
Supreme Court ultimately apply in *Texas v. Johnson*? Why? Refer back to
the beginning of the case and follow the line of the Court's reasoning in
answering this question.

Terminology

prior restraints	controls imposed on free speech that take effect before the word is spoken or written as opposed to statutes imposing punishment for expression after the fact (**Genehmigungsvorbehalt**)
clear and present danger test	test of constitutionality of a statute restricting speech that asks whether the state has a right to prevent the occurrence of some harm and whether the speech in question is likely to incite someone to cause that harm; if so then the speech can also be prohibited (**Test, ob eine Rede eine nicht bezweifelbare und gegenwärtige Gefahr für die Begehung von Straftaten schafft**)
to incite	to encourage *s.o.* to do *sth* (**anstiften**)
to incite a riot	to encourage people to revolt or become very unruly (**zum Landfriedensbruch anstiften**)
flag desecration	physical destruction or maltreatment of a state flag (**Verunglimpfung der Flagge**)
Republican National Convention	meeting of members of the Republic (or other) Party for the purpose of nominating a candidate for president (**Parteitag der Republikaner**)
administration	management of the executive branch of the government; collection of all persons working in the executive branch of government (**Verwaltung**)
Bush administration	management of the executive branch of the government under the leadership of President George W. Bush (**die Bush-Regierung**)
City Hall	the building which houses the administration of a city (**Rathaus**)
annotated	commented on by including relevant cases, legislative history, etc., (**kommentiert, mit Anmerkungen**), e.g. **Texas Penal Code Annotated**, (*abbr* **Ann.**) (**Kommentar zum Strafgesetzbuch von Texas**)
unconstitutional as applied to *s.o.*	in violation of the Constitution in the particular case, but not in other cases
unconstitutional on its face	in violation of the constitution regardless of how applied (**verfassungswidrig bei jeder denkbaren Anwendung**)
to provide in full	to state in its full and complete text (as opposed to: **to provide in pertinent part**)
Class A offense	offense in highest category of seriousness with respect to punishment threatened, e.g. **Class A misdemeanor, Class A felony** (**Straftat der Kategorie A**)
freedom of speech clause	clause in the First Amendment guaranteeing that the state shall not enact laws that restrict a person's right to say what he wants (**Klausel in der Verfassung, die die Redefreiheit schützt**)

strict scrutiny test	test of constitutionality of a law requiring that the state be pursuing a compelling state interest and employing the least intrusive means of attaining its goal; applied in cases involving fundamental rights, e.g. freedom of speech, or where the law distinguishes on the basis of a suspect classification, e.g. race, gender, age (**strenge Prüfung der Verfassungsmäßigkeit eines Gesetzes bei schrankenlos gewährleisteten Grundrechten und bei der Verwendung von diskriminierenden Unterscheidungsmerkmalen**)
compelling state interest	state goal that is absolutely necessary to pursue, state interest that is absolutely necessary to protect, e.g. public health (**zwingendes, übergeordnetes Staatsinteresse**)
least intrusive means	method employed to pursue state interest that is drawn as narrowly as possible to attain its goal (**mildestes Mittel**)
fundamental right	basic right, which enjoys the highest level of constitutional protection, e.g. freedom of speech (**schrankenlos gewährleistetes Grundrecht**)
suspect classification	statutory distinction drawn on the basis of a characteristic that is immutable, has no relation to an individual's abilities or rights, and has been used as the basis of discrimination in the past (**diskriminierendes Unterscheidungsmerkmal**)
rational basis test	test of constitutionality of a law requiring that the state be pursuing a legitimate state interest and employing a reasonable means of attaining its goal; applied in cases involving non-fundamental rights, e.g. economic rights, or distinctions not considered suspect (**allgemeiner Maßstab für die Legitimation eines Grundrechtseingriffs, Verhältnismäßigkeitsprüfung im weiteren Sinne**)
legitimate state interest	some goal or purpose that states generally have a right to pursue (**berechtigtes Staatsinteresse**)
reasonable means	one of several possible ways of pursuing an interest that is likely to be successful (**geeignetes Mittel**)
abridgement of speech	prohibition against free speech (**Beeinträchtigung der Redefreiheit**)
oral argument	oral presentation of arguments on appeal (**Plädoyer, mündlicher Vortrag**)
implicated on the record	involved in a case as can be seen from reading the record (**ergibt sich aus den Gerichtsakten**)
to countenance a presumption	to permit one to conclude *sth*, to support an inference (**den Schluß erlauben, daß**)

Vocabulary

to affix	to attach, to fasten (*sth* to)
to assert	to claim, to affirm
to avert	to ward off, to turn away from
to ban	to prohibit
bedrock	very basic
to blossom	to open up, to come into full dimension
to chant	to talk musically in a monotone
to cherish	to care dearly about
to coincide	to happen at the same time, to be at the same place at the same time
to concede	to give in, to admit
to convene	to come together, to meet
to convey	to transfer, to get across (*a meaning*)
core	most central position, heart
to culminate	to climax, to rise to the highest point
to deface	to disfigure, to destroy the appearance of *sth*
determinate	fixed, set, clearly defined
discernible	perceivable, capable of being seen or felt as distinct
to disperse	to separate from each other, to scatter, to spread out
to douse	to pour liquid over *sth*, to immerse into liquid
to dub	to give a name or nickname to
to fortify	to strengthen
to gainsay	to contradict
incidental	inessential, unimportant
to induce	to bring about, to bring forth, to cause
to inspire	to fill with emotion, to bring to life
to invoke	to call upon, to summon forth
joust	range, extent
lenient	mild, gentle, tolerant
odious	repulsive, offensive, hated
overwhelming	overcoming, overpowering
to picket	to demonstrate

referent	what *sth* else refers to, that which is closely associated with *sth*
at stake	at issue, to be won or lost
stringent	strict, severe
unalloyed	unmixed with anything else, pure
to unfurl	to open up to the wind
to utter	to say, to express
venerated	honored, revered

Suggested Reading

California v. Bakke 438 U.S. 265, 57 L.Ed.2d 750, 98 S.Ct. 2733 (1978) [reverse discrimination]

Price Waterhouse v. Hopkins 490 U.S. 228, 109 S.Ct. 1775, 104 L.Ed.2d 268 (1989) [sex discrimination]

Frontiero v. Richardson 411 U.S. 677, 93 S.Ct. 1764, 36 L.Ed.2d 583 (1973) [sex discrimination]

Roe v. Wade 410 U.S. 113, 93 S.Ct. 705, 35 L.Ed.2d 147 (1973) [abortion]

Allegheny v. American Civil Liberties Union 492 U.S. 573, 109 S.Ct. 3086, 106 L.Ed.2d 472 (1989) [freedom of religion]

Reynolds v. United States, 98 U.S. 145, 25 L.Ed. 244 (1878) [freedom of religion]

Furman v. Georgia 408 U.S. 238, 92 S.Ct. 2726, 33 L.Ed.2d 346 (1972) [death penalty]

Gregg v. Georgia 428 U.S. 153, 96 S.Ct. 2909, 49 L.Ed.2d 859 (1976) [death penalty]

Penry v. Lynaugh 492 U.S. 302, 109 S.Ct. 2934, 106 L.Ed.2d 256 (1989) [death penalty]

New York Times v. Sullivan 376 U.S. 254, 84 S.Ct. 710, 11 L.Ed.2d 686 (1964) [freedom of speech]

Bates v. State Bar of Arizona 433 U.S. 350, 97 S.Ct. 2691, 53 L.Ed.2d 810 (1977) [freedom of speech]

Chaplinsky v. New Hampshire, 315 U.S. 568 (1942) [freedom of speech]

Gitlow v. New York, 268 U.S. 652, 45 S.Ct. 625, 69 L.Ed. 1138 (1925) [freedom of speech]

National Association for the Advancement of Colored People v. Button, 371 U.S. 415 (1963) [freedom of speech, freedom of association]

Cox v. Louisiana, 379 U.S. 536 (1965) [freedom of speech]

Ward v. Rock Against Racism, 491 U.S. 781 (1989) [freedom of speech]

United States v. Eichman, 496 U.S. 310 (1990) [freedom of speech]

City of Ladue v. Gilleo, 512 U.S. 43, 114 S.Ct. 2038, 129 L.Ed.2d 36 (1994) [freedom of speech]

Capitol Square Review and Advisory Board et al. v. Pinette et al., 115 S.Ct. 2440, 132 L.Ed.2d 650 (1995) [freedom of speech, freedom of religion]

Rosenberger v. University of Virginia, 115 S.Ct. 2510, 132 L.Ed.2d 700 (1995) [freedom of speech, freedom of religion]

United States v. Eichman, 496 U.S. 310 (1990) [freedom of speech]

Winfried Brugger, *Einführung in das öffentliche Recht der USA*, 2. Auflage, Beck Verlag: München (2000)

G. Gunther/K. Sullivan, *Constitutional Law* (13th ed. 1997)

Laurence H. Tribe, *Constitutional Choices*, Harvard University Press: Cambridge, Massachusetts/London, England (1985)

Laurence H. Tribe, *American Constitutional Law* (2d ed.) Foundation Press: Mineola, New York (1988)

Language Exercises
Unit III

I. Fill in the blanks with the correct preposition or prepositional phrase:

The case was _1_ direct appeal to the U.S. Supreme Court _2_ 28 U.S.C. § 1253. The plaintiffs originally brought action _3_ themselves and others similarly situated _4_ the U.S. District Court _5_ the District _6_ Kansas to enjoin enforcement _7_ a Kansas statute. _8_ that authority, the Topeka Board of Education maintained segregated schools. The three-judge District Court convened _9_ 28 U.S.C. §§ 2281 and 2284. The District Court denied relief _10_ the ground that the schools were substantially equal _11_ buildings, transportation and other tangible factors. _12_ the South Carolina case, the District Court found that the black schools were inferior _13_ the white schools, and ordered the defendants to equalize the facilities. But the court denied the plaintiffs admission _14_ the white schools _15_ the equalization program. The Supreme Court vacated the District Court's judgment and remanded the case. _16_ remand, the District Court found that substantial equality had already been achieved _17_ buildings and that the defendants were proceeding to rectify this inequality as well. _18_ each of these cases, minors _19_ the black race, _20_ their legal representatives, seek the aid _21_ the courts _22_ obtaining admission _23_ the public schools _24_ their community _25_ a nonsegregated basis. They had been denied admission _26_ laws requiring or permitting segregation _27_ race.

II. Fill in the blanks with the correct terminology:

1. It is the opinion of 5 of the 9 justices on the court; it is the _.
2. It is a separate opinion of 1 of these 5 justices, agreeing in the result but not on the reasons for that result; it is a _.
3. It is an opinion of one of the other 4 justices on the court disagreeing with the result; it is a _.
4. It is one opinion that resolves four cases; it is a _.
5. The case was put on the court's calendar of official business; the case was _.
6. The attorney general was invited to submit arguments to assist the court; he was invited to submit an _.

7. The plaintiffs brought a class action; they brought it for themselves and _.
8. It is the case the court is currently considering; it is the _.
9. The court did not reach a final decision but stated it would postpone decision to a later date; the court _ decision to a later date.
10. The plaintiffs wanted to prevent the school authorities from using the law to keep black children in separate schools; the plaintiffs brought action _ enforcement of _ of the statutory code. In other words, the remedy they sought was an _.
11. The trial court had made determinations of fact, which the higher court referred to as the _.
12. The legislature canceled the effectiveness of the law; it _ the law.
13. The Fourteenth Amendment was adopted in 1868; it was _ in that year.
14. See below; see _. See above; see _.
15. The supreme court granted the petitioners a hearing; it granted them a _.
16. The court's decision was taken in the absence of a party to the suit; it was taken _.

III. *Translate the following text into English:*

§ 90a. **Verunglimpfung des Staates und seiner Symbole.** (1) Wer öffentlich, in einer Versammlung oder durch Verbreiten von Schriften (§ 11 Abs. 3)
1. die Bundesrepublik Deutschland oder eines ihrer Länder oder ihre verfassungsmäßige Ordnung beschimpft oder böswillig verächtlich macht oder
2. die Farben, die Flagge, das Wappen oder die Hymne der Bundesrepublik Deutschland oder eines ihrer Länder verunglimpft,
wird mit Freiheitsstrafe bis zu drei Jahren oder mit Geldstrafe bestraft.

(2) Ebenso wird bestraft, wer eine öffentlich gezeigte Flagge der Bundesrepublik Deutschland oder eines ihrer Länder oder ein von einer Behörde öffentlich angebrachtes Hoheitszeichen der Bundesrepublik Deutschland oder eines ihrer Länder entfernt, zerstört, beschädigt, unbrauchbar oder unkenntlich macht oder beschimpfenden Unfug daran verübt. Der Versuch ist strafbar.

(3) Die Strafe ist Freiheitsstrafe bis zu fünf Jahren oder Geldstrafe, wenn der Täter sich durch die Tat absichtlich für Bestrebungen gegen den Bestand der Bundesrepublik Deutschland oder gegen Verfassungsgrundsätze einsetzt.

Strafgesetzbuch i.d.F. v. 1999.

Appendix I
Constitution of the United States of America [1787]

Preamble

We the People of the United States, in Order to form a more perfect Union, establish Justice, insure domestic Tranquility, provide for the common defence, promote the general Welfare, and secure the Blessings of Liberty to ourselves and our Posterity, do ordain and establish this Constitution for the United States of America.

Article I

Section 1. All legislative Powers herein granted shall be vested in a Congress of the United States, which shall consist of a Senate and House of Representatives.

Section 2. The House of Representatives shall be composed of Members chosen every second Year by the People of the several States, and the Electors in each State shall have the Qualifications requisite for Electors of the most numerous Branch of the State Legislature.

No Person shall be a Representative who shall not have attained to the Age of twenty five Years, and been seven Years a Citizen of the United States, and who shall not, when elected, be an Inhabitant of that State in which he shall be chosen.

Representatives and direct Taxes shall be apportioned among the several States which may be included within this Union, according to their respective Numbers, which shall be determined by adding to the whole Number of free Persons, including those bound to Service for a Term of Years, and excluding Indians not taxed, three fifths of all other Persons. The actual Enumeration shall be made within three Years after the first Meeting of the Congress of the United States, and within every subsequent Term of ten Years, in such Manner as they shall by Law direct. The Number of Representatives shall not exceed one for every thirty Thousand, but each State shall have at Least one Representative; and until such enumeration shall be made, the State of New Hampshire shall be entitled to choose three, Massachusetts eight, Rhode-Island and Providence Plantations one, Connecticut five, New-York six, New Jersey four, Pennsylvania eight, Delaware one, Maryland six, Virginia ten, North Carolina five, South Carolina five, and Georgia three.

When vacancies happen in the Representation from any State, the Executive Authority thereof shall issue Writs of Election to fill such Vacancies.

The House of Representatives shall choose their speaker and other Officers; and shall have the sole Power of Impeachment.

Section 3. The Senate of the United States shall be composed of two Senators from each State, chosen by the Legislature thereof, for six Years; and each Senator shall have one Vote.

Immediately after they shall be assembled in Consequence of the first Election, they shall be divided as equally as may be into three Classes. The Seats of the Senators of the first Class shall be vacated at the Expiration of the second Year, of the second Class at the Expiration of the fourth Year, and of the third Class at the Expiration of the sixth Year, so that one third may be chosen every second Year; and if Vacancies happen by Resignation, or otherwise, during the Recess of the Legislature of any State, the Executive thereof may make temporary Appointments until the next Meeting of the Legislature, which shall then fill such Vacancies.

No Person shall be a Senator who shall not have attained to the Age of thirty Years, and been nine Years a Citizen of the United States, and who shall not, when elected, be an Inhabitant of that State for which he shall be chosen.

The Vice President of the United States shall be President of the Senate, but shall have no Vote, unless they be equally divided.

The Senate shall choose their other Officers, and also a President pro tempore, in the Absence of the Vice President, or when he shall exercise the Office of President of the United States.

The Senate shall have the sole Power to try all Impeachments. When sitting for that Purpose, they shall be on Oath or Affirmation. When the President of the United States is tried, the Chief Justice shall preside: And no Person shall be convicted without the Concurrence of two thirds of the Members present.

Judgment in Cases of Impeachment shall not extend further than to removal from Office, and disqualification to hold and enjoy any Office of honor, Trust or Profit under the United States: but the Party convicted shall nevertheless be liable and subject to Indictment, Trial, Judgment and Punishment, according to Law.

Section 4. The Times, Places, and Manner of holding Elections for Senators and Representatives, shall be prescribed in each State by the Legislature thereof; but the Congress may at any time by Law make or alter such Regulations, except as to the Places of choosing Senators.

The Congress shall assemble at least once in every Year, and such Meeting shall be on the first Monday in December, unless they shall by Law appoint a different Day.

Section 5. Each House shall be the Judge of the Elections, Returns, and Qualifications of its own Members, and a Majority of each shall constitute a Quorum to do Business; but a smaller Number may adjourn from day to day, and may be authorized to compel the Attendance of absent Members, in such Manner, and under such Penalties as each House may provide.

Each House may determine the Rules of its Proceedings, punish its Members for disorderly Behaviour, and, with the Concurrence of two thirds, expel a Member.

Each House shall keep a journal of its Proceedings, and from time to time publish the same, excepting such Parts as may in their Judgment require Secrecy; and the Yeas and Nays of the

Members of either House on any question shall, at the Desire of one fifth of those Present, be entered on the Journal.

Neither House, during the Session of Congress, shall, without the Consent of the other, adjourn for more than three days, nor to any other Place than that in which the two Houses shall be sitting.

Section 6. The Senators and Representatives shall receive a Compensation for their Services, to be ascertained by Law, and paid out of the Treasury of the United States. They shall in all Cases, except Treason, Felony and Breach of the Peace, be privileged from Arrest during their Attendance at the Session of their respective Houses, and in going to and returning from the same; and for any Speech or Debate in either House, they shall not be questioned in any other Place.

No Senator or Representative shall, during the Time for which he was elected, be appointed to any civil Office under the Authority of the United States, which shall have been created, or the Emoluments whereof shall have been increased during such time and no Person holding any Office under the United States, shall be a Member of either House during his Continuance in Office.

Section 7. All Bills for raising Revenue shall originate in the House of Representatives; but the Senate may propose or concur with Amendments as on other Bills.

Every Bill which shall have passed the House of Representatives and the Senate, shall, before it become a Law, be presented to the President of the United States; If he approve he shall sign it, but if not he shall return it, with his Objections to that House in which it shall have originated, who shall enter the Objections at large on their Journal, and proceed to reconsider it. If after such Reconsideration two thirds of that House shall agree to pass the Bill, it shall be sent, together with the Objections, to the other House, by which it shall likewise be reconsidered, and if approved by two thirds of that House, it shall become a Law. But in all such Cases the Votes of both Houses shall be determined by Yeas and Nays, and the Names of the Persons voting for and against the Bill shall be entered on the Journal of each House respectively. If any Bill shall not be returned by the President within ten Days (Sundays excepted) after it shall have been presented to him, the Same shall be a Law, in like Manner as if he had signed it, unless the Congress by their Adjournment prevent its Return, in which Case it shall not be a Law.

Every Order, Resolution, or Vote to which the Concurrence of the Senate and House of Representatives may be necessary (except on a question of Adjournment) shall be presented to the President of the United States; and before the Same shall take Effect, shall be approved by him, or being disapproved by him, shall be repassed by two thirds of the Senate and House of Representatives, according to the Rules and Limitations prescribed in the Case of a Bill.

Section 8. The Congress shall have Power To lay and collect Taxes, Duties, Imposts and Excises, to pay the Debts and provide for the common Defence and general Welfare of the United States; but all Duties, Imposts and Excises shall be uniform throughout the United States;

To borrow Money on the Credit of the United States;

To regulate Commerce with foreign Nations, and among the several States, and with the Indian Tribes;

To establish an uniform Rule of Naturalization, and uniform Laws on the subject of Bankruptcies throughout the United States;

To coin Money, regulate the Value thereof, and of foreign Coin, and fix the Standard of Weights and Measures;

To provide for the Punishment of counterfeiting the Securities and current Coin of the United States;

To establish Post Offices and Post Roads;

To promote the Progress of Science and useful Arts, by securing for limited Times to Authors and Inventors the exclusive Right to their respective Writings and Discoveries;

To constitute Tribunals inferior to the supreme Court;

To define and punish Piracies and Felonies committed on the high Seas, and Offences against the Law of Nations;

To declare War, grant Letters of Marque and Reprisal, and make Rules concerning Captures on Land and Water;

To raise and support Armies, but no Appropriation of Money to that Use shall be for a longer Term than two Years;

To provide and maintain a Navy;

To make Rules for the Government and Regulation of the land and naval Forces;

To provide for calling forth the Militia to execute the Laws of the Union, suppress Insurrections and repel Invasions;

To provide for organizing, arming, and disciplining, the Militia, and for governing such Part of them as may be employed in the Service of the United States, reserving to the States respectively, the Appointment of the Officers, and the Authority of training the Militia according to the discipline prescribed by Congress;

To exercise exclusive Legislation in all Cases whatsoever, over such District (not exceeding ten Miles square) as may, by Cession of particular States, and the Acceptance of Congress, become the Seat of the Government of the United States, and to exercise like Authority over all Places purchased by the Consent of the Legislature of the State in which the Same shall be, for the Erection of Forts, Magazines, Arsenals, dock-Yards, and other needful Buildings; And

To make all Laws which shall be necessary and proper for carrying into Execution the foregoing Powers, and all other Powers vested by this Constitution in the Government of the United States, or in any Department or Officer thereof.

Section 9. The Migration of Importation of such Persons as any of the States now existing shall think proper to admit, shall not be prohibited by the Congress prior to the Year one thousand eight hundred and eight, but a Tax or duty may be imposed on such Importation, not exceeding ten dollars for each Person.

The Privilege of the Writ of Habeas Corpus shall not be suspended, unless when in Cases of Rebellion or Invasion the public Safety may require it.

No Bill of Attainder or ex post facto Law shall be passed.

No Capitation, or other direct, Tax shall be laid, unless in Proportion to the Census or Enumeration herein before directed to be taken.

No Tax or Duty shall be laid on Articles exported from any State.

No preference shall be given by any Regulation of Commerce or Revenue to the Ports of one State over those of another: nor shall Vessels bound to, or from, one State, be obliged to enter, clear, or pay Duties in another.

No money shall be drawn from the Treasury, but in Consequence of Appropriations made by Law; and a regular Statement and Account of the Receipts and Expenditures of all public Money shall be published from time to time.

No Title of Nobility shall be granted by the United States: And no Person holding any Office of Profit or Trust under them, shall, without the Consent of the Congress, accept of any present, Emolument, Office, or Title, of any kind whatever, from any King, Prince, or foreign State.

Section 10. No State shall enter into any Treaty, Alliance, or Confederation; grant Letters of Marque and Reprisal; coin Money; emit Bills of Credit; make any Thing but gold and silver Coin a Tender in Payment of Debts; pass any Bill of Attainder, ex post facto Law, or Law impairing the Obligation of Contracts, or grant any Title of Nobility.

No State shall, without the Consent of the Congress, lay any Imposts or Duties on Imports or Exports, except what may be absolutely necessary for executing its inspection Laws: and the net Produce of all Duties and Imposts, laid by any State on Imports or Exports, shall be for the Use of the Treasury of the United States; and all such Laws shall be subject to the Revision and Control of the Congress.

No State shall, without the Consent of the Congress, lay any Duty of Tonnage, keep Troops, or Ships of War in time of Peace, enter into any Agreement or Compact with another State, or with a foreign Power, or engage in War, unless actually invaded, or in such imminent Danger as will not admit of delay.

Article II

Section 1. The executive Power shall be vested in a President of the United States of America. He shall hold his Office during the Term of four Years, and, together with the Vice President, chosen for the same term, be elected, as follows:

Each State shall appoint, in such Manner as the Legislature thereof may direct, a Number of Electors, equal to the whole Number of Senators and Representatives to which the State may be entitled in the Congress; but no Senator or Representative, or Person holding an Office of Trust or Profit under the United States, shall be appointed an Elector.

The Electors shall meet in their respective States, and vote by Ballot for two Persons, of whom one at least shall not be an Inhabitant of the same State with themselves. And they shall make a List of all the Persons voted for, and of the Number of Votes for each; which List they shall sign and certify, and transmit sealed to the Seat of the Government of the United States, directed to the President of the Senate. The President of the Senate shall, in the Presence of the Senate and House of Representatives, open all the Certificates, and the Votes shall then be counted. The Person having the greatest Number of Votes shall be the President, if such Number be a Majority of the whole Number of Electors appointed; and if there be more than one who have such Majority, and have an equal Number of Votes, then the House of Representatives shall immediately choose by Ballot one of them for President; and if no Person have a Majority, then from the five highest on the List the said House shall in like Manner choose the President. But in choosing the President, the Votes shall be taken by States, the Representation from each State having one Vote; A quorum for this Purpose shall consist of a Member or Members from two thirds of the States, and a Majority of all the States shall be necessary to a Choice. In every Case, after the Choice of the President, the Person having the greatest Number of Votes of the Electors shall be the Vice President. But if there should remain two or more who have equal Votes, the Senate shall choose from them by Ballot the Vice President.

The Congress may determine the Time of choosing the Electors, and the Day on which they shall give their Votes; which Day shall be the same throughout the United States.

No Person except a natural born Citizen, or a Citizen of the United States, at the time of the Adoption of this Constitution, shall be eligible to the Office of President; neither shall any Person be eligible to that Office who shall not have attained to the Age of thirty five Years, and been fourteen Years a Resident within the United States.

In case of the Removal of the President from Office, or of his Death, Resignation, or Inability to discharge the Powers and Duties of the said Office, the Same shall devolve on the Vice President, and the Congress may by Law provide for the Case of Removal, Death, Resignation or Inability, both of the President and Vice President, declaring what Officer shall then act as President, and such Officer shall act accordingly, until the Disability be removed, or a President shall be elected.

The President shall, at stated Times, receive for his Services, a Compensation, which shall neither be increased nor diminished during the Period for which he shall have been elected, and he shall not receive within that Period any other Emolument from the United States, or any of them.

Before he enter on the Execution of his Office, he shall take the following Oath or Affirmation: – "I do solemnly swear (or affirm) that I will faithfully execute the Office of President of the United States, and will to the best of my Ability, preserve, protect and defend the Constitution of the United States."

Section 2. The President shall be Commander in Chief of the Army and Navy of the United States, and of the Militia of the several States, when called into the actual Service of the United States; he may require the Opinion, in writing, of the principal Officer in each of the Executive Departments, upon any Subject relating to the Duties of their respective Offices, and he shall have Power to grant Reprieves and Pardons for Offences against the United States, except in Cases of Impeachment.

He shall have Power, by and with the Advice and Consent of the Senate, to make Treaties, provided two thirds of the Senators present concur; and he shall nominate, and by and with the Advice and Consent of the Senate, shall appoint Ambassadors, other public Ministers and Consuls, Judges of the Supreme Court, and all other Officers of the United States, whose Appointments are not herein otherwise provided for, and which shall be established by Law; but the Congress may by Law vest the Appointment of such inferior Officers, as they think proper, in the President alone, in the Courts of Law, or in the Heads of Departments.

The President shall have Power to fill up all Vacancies that may happen during the Recess of the Senate, by granting Commissions which shall expire at the End of their next Session.

Section 3. He shall from time to time give to the Congress Information of the State of the Union, and recommend to their Consideration such Measures as he shall judge necessary and expedient; he may, on extraordinary Occasions, convene both Houses, or either of them, and in Case of Disagreement between them, with Respect to the Time of Adjournment, he may adjourn them to such Time as he shall think proper; he shall receive Ambassadors and other public Ministers; he shall take Care that the Laws be faithfully executed, and shall Commission all the Officers of the United States.

Section 4. The President, Vice President, and all civil Officers of the United States, shall be removed from Office on Impeachment for, and Conviction of, Treason, Bribery, or other High Crimes and Misdemeanors.

Article III

Section 1. The judicial Power of the United States, shall be vested in one supreme Court, and in such inferior Courts as the Congress may from time to time ordain and establish. The Judges, both of the supreme and inferior Courts, shall hold their Offices during good Behaviour, and shall, at stated Times, receive for their Services, a Compensation, which shall not be diminished during their Continuance in Office.

Section 2. The judicial Power shall extend to all Cases, in Law and Equity, arising under this Constitution, the Laws of the United States, and Treaties made, or which shall be made, under their Authority; to all Cases affecting Ambassadors, other public Ministers and Consuls; to all Cases of admiralty and maritime Jurisdiction; to Controversies to which the United States shall be a Party; to Controversies between two or more States; between a State and Citizens of another state; between Citizens of different States; between Citizens of the same State claiming Lands under the Grants of different States, and between a State, or the Citizens thereof, and foreign States, Citizens or Subjects.

In all Cases affecting Ambassadors, other public Ministers and Consuls, and those in which a State shall be Party, the supreme Court shall have original Jurisdiction. In all the other Cases before mentioned, the supreme Court shall have appellate Jurisdiction, both as to Law and Fact, with such Exceptions, and under such Regulations as the Congress shall make.

The Trial of all Crimes, except in Cases of Impeachment, shall be by Jury; and such Trial shall be held in the State where the said Crimes shall have been committed; but when not committed within any State, the Trial shall be at such Place or Places as the Congress may by Law have directed.

Section 3. Treason against the United States, shall consist only in levying War against them, or, in adhering to their Enemies, giving them Aid and Comfort. No Person shall be convicted of Treason unless on the Testimony of two Witnesses to the same overt Act, or on Confession in open Court.

The Congress shall have Power to declare the Punishment of Treason, but no Attainder of Treason shall work Corruption of Blood, or Forfeiture except during the Life of the Person attainted.

Article IV

Section 1. Full Faith and Credit shall be given in each State to the public Acts, Records, and judicial Proceedings of every other State. And the Congress may by general Laws prescribe the Manner in which such Acts, Records and Proceedings shall be proved, and the Effect thereof.

Section 2. The Citizens of each State shall be entitled to all Privileges and Immunities of Citizens in the several States.

A Person charged in any State with Treason, Felony, or other Crime, who shall flee from Justice, and be found in another State, shall on demand of the executive Authority of the State from which he fled, be delivered up, to be removed to the State having Jurisdiction of the Crime.

No Person held to Service or Labour in one State, under the Laws thereof, escaping into another, shall, in Consequence of any Law or Regulation therein, be discharged from such Service or Labour, but shall be delivered up on Claim of the Party to whom such Service or Labour may be due.

Section 3. New States may be admitted by the Congress into this Union; but no new State shall be formed or erected within the Jurisdiction of any other State; nor any State be formed by the Junction of two or more States, or Parts of States, without the Consent of the Legislatures of the States concerned as well as of the Congress.

The Congress shall have Power to dispose of and make all needful Rules and Regulations respecting the Territory or other Property belonging to the United States; and nothing in this Constitution shall be so construed as to Prejudice any Claims of the United States, or of any particular State.

Section 4. The United States shall guarantee to every State in this Union a Republican Form of Government, and shall protect each of them against Invasion; and on Application of the Legislature, or of the Executive (when the Legislature cannot be convened) against domestic Violence.

Article V

The Congress, whenever two thirds of both Houses shall deem it necessary, shall propose Amendments to this Constitution, or, on the Application of the Legislatures of two thirds of the several States, shall call a Convention for proposing Amendments, which, in either Case, shall be valid to all Intents and Purposes, as Part of this Constitution, when ratified by the

Legislatures of three fourths of the several States, or by Conventions in three fourths thereof, as the one or the other Mode of Ratification may be proposed by the Congress; Provided that no Amendment which may be made prior to the Year One Thousand eight hundred and eight shall in any Manner affect the first and fourth Clauses in the Ninth Section of the first Article; and that no State, without its Consent, shall be deprived of its equal Suffrage in the Senate.

Article VI

All Debts contracted and Engagements entered into, before the Adoption of this Constitution, shall be as valid against the United States under this Constitution, as under the Confederation.

This Constitution, and the Laws of the United States which shall be made in Pursuance thereof; and all Treaties made, or which shall be made, under the Authority of the United States, shall be the supreme Law of the Land; and the Judges in every State shall be bound thereby, any Thing in the Constitution or Laws of any State to the Contrary notwithstanding.

The Senators and Representatives before mentioned, and the Members of the several State Legislatures, and all executive and judicial Officers, both of the United States and of the several States, shall be bound by Oath or Affirmation, to support this Constitution; but no religious Test shall ever be required as a Qualification to any Office or public Trust under the United States.

Article VII

The Ratification of the Conventions of nine States shall be sufficient for the Establishment of this Constitution between the States so ratifying the Same.

ARTICLES IN ADDITION TO, AND AMENDMENT OF, THE CONSTITUTION OF THE UNITED STATES OF AMERICA, PROPOSED BY CONGRESS, AND RATIFIED BY THE LEGISLATURES OF THE SEVERAL STATES PURSUANT TO THE FIFTH ARTICLE OF THE ORIGINAL CONSTITUTION.

Amendment I [1791]

Congress shall make no law respecting an establishment of religion, or prohibiting the free exercise thereof; or abridging the freedom of speech, or of the press; or the right of the people peaceably to assemble, and to petition the Government for a redress of grievances.

Amendment II [1791]

A well regulated Militia, being necessary to the security of a free State, the right of the people to keep and bear Arms, shall not be infringed.

Amendment III [1791]

No Soldier shall, in time of peace be quartered in any house, without the consent of the Owner, nor in time of war, but in a manner to be prescribed by law.

Amendment IV [1791]

The right of the people to be secure in their persons, houses, papers, and effects, against unreasonable searches and seizures, shall not be violated, and no Warrants shall issue, but upon probable cause, supported by Oath or affirmation, and particularly describing the place to be searched, and the persons or things to be seized.

Amendment V [1791]

No person shall be held to answer for a capital, or otherwise infamous crime, unless on a presentment or indictment of a Grand Jury, except in cases arising in the land or naval forces, or in the Militia, when in actual service in time of War or public danger; nor shall any person be subject for the same offence to be twice put in jeopardy of life or limb; nor shall be compelled in any criminal case to be a witness against himself, nor be deprived of life, liberty, or property, without due process of law; nor shall private property be taken for public use, without just compensation.

Amendment VI [1791]

In all criminal prosecutions, the accused shall enjoy the right to a speedy and public trial, by an impartial jury of the State and district wherein the crime shall have been committed, which district shall have been previously ascertained by law, and to be informed of the nature and cause of the accusation; to be confronted with the witnesses against him; to have compulsory process for obtaining witnesses in his favor, and to have the Assistance of Counsel for his defence.

Amendment VII [1791]

In Suits at common law, where the value in controversy shall exceed twenty dollars, the right of trial by jury shall be preserved, and no fact tried by a jury, shall be otherwise re-examined in any Court of the United States, than according to the rules of the common law.

Amendment VIII [1791]

Excessive bail shall not be required, nor excessive fines imposed, nor cruel and unusual punishments inflicted.

Amendment IX [1791]

The enumeration in the Constitution, of certain rights, shall not be construed to deny or disparage others retained by the people.

Amendment X [1791]

The powers not delegated to the United States by the Constitution, nor prohibited by it to the States, are reserved to the States respectively, or to the people.

Amendment XI [1798]

The Judicial power of the United States shall not be construed to extend to any suit in law or equity, commenced or prosecuted against one of the United States by Citizens of another State, or by Citizens or Subjects of any Foreign State.

Amendment XII [1804]

The Electors shall meet in their respective states and vote by ballot for President and Vice President, one of whom, at least, shall not be an inhabitant of the same State with themselves; they shall name in their ballots the person voted for as President, and in distinct ballots the person voted for as Vice President, and they shall make distinct lists of all persons voted for as President, and of all persons voted for as Vice President, and of the number of votes for each, which lists they shall sign and certify, and transmit sealed to the seat of the government of the United States, directed to the President of the Senate; The President of the Senate shall, in the presence of the Senate and House of Representatives, open all the certificates and the votes shall then be counted; The person having the greatest number of votes for President, shall be the President, if such number be a majority of the whole number of Electors appointed; and if no person have such majority, then from the persons having the highest numbers not exceeding three on the list of those voted for as President, the House of Representatives shall choose immediately, by ballot, the President. But in choosing the President, the votes shall be taken by states, the representation from each state having one vote; a quorum for this purpose shall consist of a member or members from two-thirds of the states, and a majority of all the states shall be necessary to a choice. And if the House of Representatives shall not choose a President whenever the right of choice shall devolve upon them, before the fourth day of March next following, then the Vice President shall act as President, as in the case of the death or other constitutional disability of the President. The person having the greatest number of votes as Vice President, shall be the Vice President, if such number be a majority of the whole number of Electors appointed, and if no person have a majority, then from the two highest numbers on the list, the Senate shall choose the Vice President; a quorum for the purpose shall consist of two-thirds of the whole number of Senators, and a majority of the whole number shall be necessary to a choice. But no person constitutionally ineligible to the office of President shall be eligible to that of Vice President of the United States.

Amendment XIII [1865]

Section 1. Neither Slavery, nor involuntary servitude, except as a punishment for crime whereof the party shall have been duly convicted, shall exist within the United States, or any place subject to their jurisdiction.

Section 2. Congress shall have power to enforce this article by appropriate legislation.

Amendment XIV [1868]

Section 1. All persons born or naturalized in the United States, and subject to the jurisdiction thereof, are citizens of the United States and of the State wherein they reside. No State shall make or enforce any law which shall abridge the privileges or immunities of citizens of the United States; nor shall any State deprive any person of life, liberty, or property, without due process of law; nor deny to any person within its jurisdiction the equal protection of the laws.

Section 2. Representatives shall be apportioned among the several States according to their respective numbers, counting the whole number of persons in each State excluding Indians not taxed. But when the right to vote at any election for the choice of electors for President and Vice President of the United States, Representatives in Congress, the Executive and Judicial officers of a State, or the members of the Legislature thereof, is denied to any of the male inhabitants of such State, being twenty-one years of age, and citizens of the United States, or in any way abridged, except for participation in rebellion, or other crime, the basis of representation therein shall be reduced in the proportion which the number of such male citizens shall bear to the whole number of male citizens twenty-one years of age in such State.

Section 3. No person shall be a Senator or Representative in Congress, or elector of President and Vice President, or hold any office, civil or military, under the United States, or under any State, who having previously taken an oath, as a member of Congress, or as an officer of the United States, or as a member of any State legislature, or as an executive or judicial officer of any State, to support the Constitution of the United States, shall have engaged in insurrection or rebellion against the same, or given aid or comfort to the enemies thereof. But Congress may by a vote of two-thirds of each House remove such disability.

Section 4. The validity of the public debt of the United States, authorized by law, including debts incurred for payment of pensions and bounties for services in suppressing insurrection or rebellion, shall not be questioned. But neither the United States nor any State shall assume or pay any debt or obligation incurred in aid of insurrection or rebellion against the United States, or any claim for the loss or emancipation of any slave; but all such debts, obligations and claims shall be held illegal and void.

Section 5. The Congress shall have power to enforce, by appropriate legislation, the provisions of this article.

Amendment XV [1870]

Section 1. The right of citizens of the United States to vote shall not be denied or abridged by the United States or by any State on account of race, color or previous condition of servitude.

Section 2. The Congress shall have power to enforce this article by appropriate legislation.

Amendment XVI [1913]

The Congress shall have power to lay and collect taxes on incomes, from whatever source derived, without apportionment among the several States, and without regard to any census or enumeration.

Amendment XVII [1913]

The Senate of the United States shall be composed of two Senators from each State, elected by the people thereof, for six years; and each Senator shall have one vote. The electors in each State shall have the qualifications requisite for electors of the most numerous branch of the State legislatures.

When vacancies happen in the representation of any State in the Senate, the executive authority of such State shall issue writs of election to fill such vacancies: *Provided*, That the legislature of any State may empower the executive thereof to make temporary appointments until the people fill the vacancies by election as the legislature may direct.

This amendment shall not be so construed as to affect the election or term of any Senator chosen before it becomes valid as part of the Constitution.

Amendment XVIII [1919]

Section 1. After one year from the ratification of this article the manufacture, sale, or transportation of intoxicating liquors within, the importation thereof into, or the exportation thereof from the United States and all territory subject to the jurisdiction thereof for beverage purposes is hereby prohibited.

Section 2. The Congress and the several States shall have concurrent power to enforce this article by appropriate legislation.

Section 3. This article shall be inoperative unless it shall have been ratified as an amendment to the Constitution by the legislatures of the several States, as provided in the Constitution, within seven years from the date of the submission hereof to the States by the Congress.

Amendment XIX [1920]

The right of citizens of the United States to vote shall not be denied or abridged by the United States or by any State on account of sex.

Congress shall have power to enforce this article by appropriate legislation.

Amendment XX [1933]

Section 1. The terms of the President and Vice President shall end at noon on the 20th day of January, and the terms of Senators and Representatives at noon on the third day of January, of the years in which such terms would have ended if this article had not been ratified; and the terms of their successors shall then begin.

Section 2. The Congress shall assemble at least once in every year, and such meeting shall begin at noon on the 3d day of January, unless they shall by law appoint a different day.

Section 3. If, at the time fixed for the beginning of the term of the President, the President elect shall have died, the Vice President elect shall become President. If a President shall not have been chosen before the time fixed for the beginning of his term, or if the President elect shall have failed to qualify, then the Vice President elect shall act as President until a President shall have qualified; and the Congress may by law provide for the case wherein neither a President elect nor a Vice President elect shall have qualified, declaring who shall then act as President, or the manner in which one who is to act shall be selected, and such person shall act accordingly until a President or Vice President shall have qualified.

Section 4. The Congress may by law provide for the case of the death of any of the persons from whom the House of Representatives may choose a President whenever the right of choice shall have devolved upon them, and for the case of the death of any of the persons from whom the Senate may choose a Vice President whenever the right of choice shall have devolved upon them.

Section 5. Sections 1 and 2 shall take effect on the 15th day of October following the ratification of this article.

Section 6. This article shall be inoperative unless it shall have been ratified as an amendment to the Constitution by the legislatures of three-fourths of the several States within seven years from the date of its submission.

Amendment XXI [1933]

Section 1. The eighteenth article of amendment to the Constitution of the United States is hereby repealed.

Section 2. The transportation or importation into any State, Territory, or possession of the United States for delivery or use therein of intoxicating liquors, in violation of the laws thereof, is hereby prohibited.

Section 3. This article shall be inoperative unless it shall have been ratified as an amendment to the Constitution by conventions in the several States, as provided in the Constitution, within seven years from the date of the submission hereof to the States by the Congress.

Amendment XXII [1951]

Section 1. No person shall be elected to the office of the President more than twice, and no person who has held the office of President, or acted as President, for more than two years of a term to which some other person was elected President shall be elected to the office of President more than once. But this Article shall not apply to any person holding the office of President when this Article was proposed by the Congress, and shall not prevent any person who may be holding the office of President, or acting as President, during the term within which this Article becomes operative from holding the office of President or acting as President during the remainder of such term.

Section 2. This article shall be inoperative unless it shall have been ratified as an amendment to the Constitution by the legislatures of three-fourths of the several States within seven years from the date of its submission to the States by the Congress.

Amendment XXIII [1961]

Section 1. The District constituting the seat of Government of the United States shall appoint in such manner as the Congress may direct:

A number of electors of President and Vice President equal to the whole number of Senators and Representatives in Congress to which the District would be entitled if it were a State, but in no event more than the least populous State; they shall be in addition to those appointed by the States, but they shall be considered, for the purposes of the election of President and Vice President, to be electors appointed by a State; and they shall meet in the District and perform such duties as provided by the twelfth article of amendment.

Section 2. The Congress shall have power to enforce this article by appropriate legislation.

Amendment XXIV [1964]

Section 1. The right of citizens of the United States to vote in any primary or other election for President or Vice President, for electors for President or Vice President, or for Senator or Representative in Congress, shall not be denied or abridged by the United States or any State by reason of failure to pay any poll tax or other tax.

Section 2. The Congress shall have power to enforce this article by appropriate legislation.

Amendment XXV [1967]

Section 1. In case of the removal of the President from office or of his death or resignation, the Vice President shall become President.

Section 2. Whenever there is a vacancy in the office of the Vice President, the President shall nominate a Vice President who shall take office upon confirmation by a majority vote of both Houses of Congress.

Section 3. Whenever the President transmits to the President pro tempore of the Senate and the Speaker of the House of Representatives his written declaration that he is unable to discharge the powers and duties of his office, and until he transmits to them a written declaration to the contrary, such powers and duties shall be discharged by the Vice President as Acting President.

Section 4. Whenever the Vice President and a majority of either the principal officers of the executive departments or of such other body as Congress may by law provide, transmit to the President pro tempore of the Senate and the Speaker of the House of Representatives their written declaration that the President is unable to discharge the powers and duties of his office, the Vice President shall immediately assume the powers and duties of the office as Acting President.

Thereafter, when the President transmits to the President pro tempore of the Senate and the Speaker of the House of Representatives his written declaration that no inability exists, he shall resume the powers and duties of his office unless the Vice President and a majority of either the principal officers of the executive department or of such other body as Congress may by law provide, transmit within four days to the President pro tempore of the Senate and the Speaker of the House of Representatives their written declaration that the President is unable to discharge the powers and duties of his office. Thereupon Congress shall decide the issue, assembling within forty-eight hours for that purpose if not in session. If the Congress, within twenty-one days after receipt of the latter written declaration, or, if Congress is not in session, within twenty-one days after Congress is required to assemble, determines by two-thirds vote of both Houses that the President is unable to discharge the powers and duties of his office, the Vice President shall continue to discharge the same as Acting President; otherwise, the President shall resume the powers and duties of his office.

Amendment XXVI [1971]

Section 1. The right of citizens of the United States, who are eighteen years of age or older, to vote shall not be denied or abridged by the United States or by any State on account of age.

Section 2. The Congress shall have power to enforce this article by appropriate legislation.

Amendment XXVII [1992]

No law, varying the compensation for the services of the Senators and Representatives, shall take effect, until an election of Representatives shall have intervened.

Appendix II
Table of U.S. Supreme Court Cases

Any table of U.S. Supreme Court cases of this length is bound to be rather selective and just cover the surface of some areas of law. The cases included in this table have been chosen primarily because of their general interest, their relation to topics considered in this book, or simply because they are very recent. An excellent website for U.S. Supreme Court cases is: http://supct.law.cornell.edu/supct/.

The Amistad, U.S. v. The Libellants and Claimants of the Schooner Amistad, 40 U.S. 518 (1841) held that Africans who had mutinied while being transported from Havana to a port in Principe, Cuba, and who later had been picked up by the U.S. coast guard off the coast of Long Island were not "the property of Spanish citizens" within the meaning of a U.S. treaty with Spain. The treaty required "all ships and merchandize of what nature soever, which shall be rescued out of the hands of any pirates or robbers, on the high seas, shall be brought into some port of either state, and shall be delivered into the custody of the officers of that port, in order to be taken care of and restored entire to the true proprietor, as soon as due and sufficient proof shall be made concerning the property thereof." The Africans had been kidnapped in their home country and illegally transported to Cuba to be sold as slaves. They were ostensibly purchased by two Spanish citizens. The United States intervened for the sole purpose of procuring restitution of the property, as Spanish property, pursuant to the treaty. As slave trading was illegal in Spain, the Court held that the Africans were free even under the law of Spain. The United States had argued that as the governor-general of Cuba had certified the Africans to be the property of the Spanish nationals, the Court had to give full faith and credit to that document. The Court rejected the full-faith-and-credit argument indicating that the document was fraudulent. As the Africans had the same rights to appeal to the courts of the United States as the nationals of any other state, they could contest the legitimacy of the governor-general's documentation.

Baker v. Carr, 369 U.S. 186, 82 S.Ct. 691, 7 L.Ed.2d 663 (1962) involved a claim under the Equal Protection Clause of the 14th Amendment against the apportionment of the State of Tennessee's legislature. The claimants argued that apportionment was based on census figures from 1901 although considerable population growth and redistribution within the state had occurred since that date. Consequently they claimed that their votes were not being counted on an equal basis with those of other voters from less populous election districts. The main issue facing the U.S. Supreme Court was whether this case raised a nonjusticiable "political question." Traditionally the Court had refused to address challenges to congressional districting schemes based on the Guaranty Clause of Art. IV, § 4, which guarantees a republican form of government. In *Baker v. Carr* the Court broke with that tradition, basing its decision on the equal protection claim, a claim clearly justiciable. The Court pointed out that resolving the claim would not require it to violate the separation of powers, or to risk embarrassment of the government abroad or serious disturbance at home, or to make policy determinations for which judicially manageable standards were lacking - all standards used to determine whether a case raised a political question. *Baker v. Carr* opened the door for an onslaught of law suits challenging apportionment schemes throughout the United States.

Batson v. Kentucky, 476 U.S. 79 (1986) [see Unit I, Chapter 2, A, 2, c for the opinion] held that the prosecutor could not use peremptory challenges to remove black jurors in a criminal case against a black defendant. This holding was later extended in *Edmonson v. Leesville Concrete Co., Inc., 111 S.Ct. 2077 (1991)* to prohibit private parties to a law suit from exercising peremptory challenges to exclude prospective jurors on the basis of race; in *Powers v. Ohio, 111 S.Ct. 1364 (1991)* to prohibit the prosecutor from exercising peremptory challenges to exclude black jurors in a criminal case against a white defendant; in *Georgia v. McCollum, 112 S.Ct. 2348 (1992)* to prohibit the defendant in a criminal case from exercising peremptory challenges on the basis of race; and in *J.E.B. v. Alabama ex rel. T.B., 114 S.Ct. 1419 (1994)* to prohibit exercising peremptory challenges on the basis of gender.

Brown v. Board of Education, 347 U.S. 483 (1954) [see Unit III, Chapter 2 for the opinion] held that maintaining public schools segregated on the basis of race violated the equal protection clause of the Fourteenth Amendment. It thus overruled the standard of "separate but equal" announced by the Court in *Plessy v. Ferguson*, 163 U.S. 537 (1896), and paved the way for an integrated public school system in the United States.

Bush v. Gore, 531 U. S. ____ (December 12, 2000) in a per curiam opinion reversed the decision of the Florida Supreme Court that mandated a manual recount of ballots in several Florida counties during the 2000 presidential election. The US Supreme Court relied on *McPherson v. Blacker*, 146 U. S. 1 (1892), which held that the Constitution vested the right to select presidential electors in the state legislature and not in the people. Still, it noted that once the legislature had enfranchised the people, the people were vested with a fundamental right. This right had to be allocated to all and exercisable by all equally. The question the US Supreme Court had to resolve, therefore, was whether the Florida Supreme Court's recount procedures were consistent with its obligation to avoid arbitrary and unequal treatment of the members of its electorate. The Court held that the absence of any definition of what should be counted as a vote, other than "giving effect to the voter's intent," was fatal to the Florida recount. Noting differences in treatment of similarly marked ballots between one county and another, but also within one and the same county, the Court held that the requirements of the Fourteenth Amendment's Equal Protection clause were not met, because some persons' votes were given more weight than others. This ruling put an end to the election contest five weeks after voters had cast their ballots on November 7, 2000 and just in time for the December 12 deadline for electors to cast their votes in the electoral college.

Clinton v. Jones, 117 S.Ct. 1636 (1997), held that the President of the United States was not entitled to temporary immunity from civil damages litigation arising out of events that occurred before he took office if the conduct which was the basis for the litigation was unofficial conduct. The Supreme Court further held that the separation of powers doctrine did not require federal courts to stay all private actions against a President in office. In this case the original plaintiff, Paula Jones, claimed that Clinton had sexually harassed her while he was governor of Arkansas and she was a state employee. Clinton petitioned the court to stay the action temporarily until he left office. In response to Clinton's argument that defending litigation while in office would pose an unreasonable burden on his time and interfere with exercising his official duties, the Court stated: "As for the case at hand, ... it appears to us highly unlikely to occupy any substantial amount of petitioner's time." The Paula Jones case and the evidence gathered in preparation for litigating it ultimately resulted in Clinton's impeachment.

Erie Railroad Co. v. Thompkins, 304 U.S. 64 (1938), held that federal courts in diversity cases had to apply the law of the state, including the common law of that state, and not any body of legal principles then known as "general law," or "federal common law." It thereby overruled

Swift v. Tyson, 41 U.S. 1 (1842), which had held that federal courts exercising jurisdiction on the ground of diversity of citizenship need not, in matters of general jurisprudence, apply the unwritten law of the state as declared by its highest court; that they were free to exercise an independent judgment as to what the common law of the state is or should be. One main criticism of *Swift* was that it permitted the federal courts, in developing federal common law, to do what the U.S. Congress was clearly unable to do, namely adopt law in areas reserved to the individual states. Another problem was that the rule in *Swift* permitted the out-of-state plaintiff to decide whether to accept state law if more favorable to his position and bring the action in the defendant's home state court, or reject unfavorable state law and bring the action in a federal court.

Furman v. Georgia, 408 U.S. 238 (1972) held (5-4) that statutes providing for the death penalty in 39 of 40 states were unconstitutional. The holding in the case is contained in a short per curiam opinion accompanied by 9 concurring and dissenting opinions. Accordingly, the ratio decidendi is not entirely clear. Two justices were of the opinion that the death penalty was per se unconstitutional as a violation of the Eight Amendment prohibition against cruel and unusual punishment. A third justice was of the opinion that the death penalty as imposed under these statutes was unconstitutional because it was in fact discriminatorily imposed against blacks, the poor and the uneducated. A further two justices were of the opinion that it was unconstitutional as imposed because it was very rare and thus not necessary in the eyes of the legislatures of the various states, because it did not fulfill any purpose beyond what was served by a sentence of life imprisonment, and because it was imposed arbitraily. See also *Gregg v. Georgia infra,* which later upheld a death penalty statute enacted following *Furman.*

Gideon v. Wainwright, 372 U.S. 335 (1963) held that an indigent defendant to a felony prosecution in a state court had a constitutionally guaranteed right under the Sixth Amendment to the assistance of court-appointed counsel. The Court used the Fourteenth Amendment due process clause to extend the Sixth Amendment right to assistance of counsel to the individual states. Gideon had been charged with breaking and entering a poolroom in violation of Florida criminal law. At trial he requested court-appointed legal assistance because he could not afford a lawyer. This request was denied because under Florida law only defendants in death penalty cases had a right to court-appointed counsel. Gideon represented himself, was found guilty and sentenced to prison for five years. He later turned to the US Supreme Court, which overruled the contrary precedent it had set in *Betts v. Brady*, 316 U.S. 455 (1942) and upheld Gideon's right to court-appointed legal representation.

Goldfarb v. Virginia State Bar, 421 U.S. 773 (1975) held that the state bar association's establishment of a minimum fee schedule violated the Sherman Antitrust Act's prohibition against price fixing. Lawyers who undercut the minimum fee in Virginia, as in most states in the United States, were subject to disciplinary proceedings and could be disbarred. The state thus had the means necessary to ensure that price competition among lawyers would not take place. The Court rejected the argument that the provision of lawyers' services was not subject to the Sherman Antitrust Act because they were professional services rather than normal trade or commerce. It also rejected the argument that the fee schedule constituted state action, which was exempt from the Sherman Act prohibitions. This case opened the legal profession to competition and has resulted in significantly lower legal fees, particularly for rather straightforward legal services.

Gregg v. Georgia, 428 U.S. 153 (1976) held (7-2) that Georgia's death penalty statute satisfied the constitutional requirements laid down in *Furman v. Georgia, supra,* in murder cases. The newly enacted Georgia statute listed specific aggravating circumstances that would permit a jury to impose the death penalty, established the burden of proof of the existence of these aggravating circumstances at "beyond a reasonable doubt," provided for direct review of a death penalty sentence to the Georgia state supreme court, and required the supreme court to review the case in light of other death penalty cases to determine whether the death penalty was being consistently and not discriminatorily imposed.

Griswold v. Connecticut, 381 U.S. 479 (1965), held that Connecticut's statute prohibiting the use of contraceptives, even by married people, was unconstitutional as a violation of an individual's constitutionally guaranteed right to privacy. The Court derived the right to privacy, which is not specifically guaranteed in the Constitution, from the penumbra of the First Amendment rights of freedom of speech, press and assembly; the Third Amendment right not to have soldiers quartered in one's home; the Fourth Amendment right to be secure in one's home against unreasonable searches and seizures; the Fifth Amendment right against self-incrimination; and the Ninth Amendment assertion that the enumeration of certain rights in the Constitution was not meant to deny others retained by the people. This case lay the groundwork for the Court's subsequent decision in *Roe v. Wade, infra*, striking down state laws prohibiting abortion.

Hill v. Colorado, No. 98-1856 (June 2000) upheld a Colorado statute prohibiting anyone from approaching within eight feet of someone outside a health care facility "for the purpose of passing a leaflet or handbill to, displaying a sign to, or engaging in oral protest, education, or counseling with such other person ... " The statute was attacked by individuals who were hindered in their efforts to provide counselling outside of health clinics that provided abortions. The statute was attacked as being a facially invalid restriction on the First Amendment guarantees of freedom of speech and the press, because although the statute was neutral on what message the speaker intended to convey, the intent was to stop anti-abortion demonstrations outside of abortion clinics. The U.S. Supreme Court recognized the state's legitimate interest in providing unimpeded access to health care facilities and emphasized the unwilling listener's right to be left alone from persuasion. It upheld the statute as an acceptable "time, place, and manner" restriction of speech under the test as discussed in *Ward v. Rock Against Racism*, 491 U.S. 781 (1989): "The principal inquiry in determining content neutrality, in speech cases generally and in time, place, or manner cases in particular, is whether the government has adopted a regulation of speech because of disagreement with the message it conveys."

Lochner v. New York, 198 U.S. 45 (1905) reversed the decisions of New York state courts, all of which had upheld a baker's criminal conviction for violation of New York labor law by requiring an employee to work more than sixty hours per week. The US Supreme Court held that the statute necessarily interfered with the right of contract between the employer and employees. The right to contract, however, was protected by the Fourteenth Amendment, which prohibited a state from depriving any person of life, liberty, or property without due process of law. Admitting that the state had so-called "police powers," the Court stressed that they related generally to the safety, health, morals, and general welfare of the public. It then concluded that bakers were just as capable as anyone else in society to buy and sell labor without the need of state protection. Furthermore, there was no reason to believe that the baking of wholesome bread depended on a sixty-hour work week or that there was anything unhealthy about the vocation of a baker.

Mapp v. Ohio, 367 U.S. 643 (1961) [see Unit I, Chapter 4 for a through discussion of this case] held that evidence gathered by the police in an unlawful search and seizure could not be used as evidence in a criminal trial in a state court. The Court thus extended the exclusionary rule announced in *Weeks v. United States*, 222 U.S. 383 (1914) to prosecutions in state courts.

Marbury v. Madison, 5 U.S. 137 (1803) [see Unit III, Chapter 1 for the opinion] held that Sec. 13 of the federal Judiciary Act of 1789, granting the Supreme Court the right to issue a writ of mandamus, was unconstitutional as a violation of Art. III, Sec. 2 of the U.S. Constitution.

It was the first case to declare a legislative enactment unconstitutional, thereby establishing the Court's power of judicial review over acts of the legislature.

Miranda v. Arizona, 384 U.S. 436 (1966) held that before the police could interrogate a criminal suspect they were required to inform him of his right to remain silent, his right to have the assistance of counsel, including state-appointed counsel if he was unable to afford his own attorney, and to warn him that anything he said to the police could and would be used against him in a court of law. If the police interrogated the suspect without reading him his so-called Miranda rights, the results of the interrogation could not be used as evidence in a later criminal trial. *Miranda* was recently uphold in *Dickerson v. United States*, No. 99-5525 (26 June 2000)

Mitchell v. Helms, No. 98-1648 (June 2000) held that state funds provided for lending library and media materials and computer software and hardware to public and private schools survived constitutional attack under the establishment of religion clause of the First Amendment. The original plaintiff in the case had argued that the provision of state funds to private schools that were religiously affiliated was direct state aid in support of that religion. The Supreme Court applied the test announced in *Agostini v. Felton*, 521 U.S. 203, namely whether the statute in question (1) has a secular purpose and (2) has a primary effect of advancing or inhibiting religion. To determine whether the statute's effect was to advance religion, *Agostini* examined whether: (1) it results in governmental indoctrination, (2) defines its recipients by reference to religion, or (3) creates an excessive entanglement between government and religion. The lower court in *Mitchell* had found that the statute had a secular purpose and did not create an excessive entanglement and these findings had not been challenged on appeal. The Supreme Court thus considered only whether the state aid resulted in indoctrination and defined its recipients by reference to religion answering both questions in the negative by applying a "neutrality principle" asking whether the aid is offered to a broad range of groups or persons regardless of their religion and whether the aid created a financial incentive to undertake religious indoctrination.

Plessy v. Ferguson, 163 U.S. 537 (1896) held that the equal protection clause of the Fourteenth Amendment was satisfied by a statute that provided for separate railway facilities for blacks and whites provided the facilities were equal. The case thus established the so-called "separate but equal" doctrine, which was later overruled by *Brown v. Board of Education, supra*.

Reynolds v. Sims 377 U.S. 533, 84 S.Ct. 1362, 12 L.Ed.2d 506 (1964), similar to *Baker v. Carr*, involved a challenge to a state's apportionment scheme for election of representatives to the state legislature. Here the State of Alabama based apportionment on the census of 1900 even though the state constitution required reapportionment every ten years based on population. As the population of Alabama had grown far more in some, usually urban, than in other districts, the plaintiffs in this case argued that they were being denied equal protection in violation of the 14th Amendment. The U.S. Supreme Court noted that if a state weighted the votes of some of its citizens two to ten times as high as the votes of other citizens no one would doubt that this weighting violated the Equal Protection Clause. No other result could be reached when the state gave a far larger number of citizens the same number of representatives in the state legislature as a much smaller group of citizens. Accordingly, the Court held that apportionment must be based primarily on population. This decision is often referred to as the "one-person-one-vote" holding.

Reynolds v. United States, 98 U.S. 145 (1878) upheld a Utah statute criminally prohibiting bigamy against a violation of the freedom of religion claim by a member of the Mormon congregation. This case was one of the earliest Supreme Court cases on the free exercise clause of the First Amendment. The Court upheld the statute as permissible state control over actions as opposed to beliefs. If such statutes could be struck down then anyone's religious beliefs could become the supreme law of the land.

Roe v. Wade, 410 U.S. 113 (1973) struck down state laws prohibiting abortion as denial of the right to privacy as a fundamental right protected by the Fourteenth Amendment's due process clause and the concept of personal liberty from state interference. The decision grants pregnant women in the first trimester in conjunction with their attending physician and without state interference the right to decide to have an abortion. During the second trimester, the state may impose such restrictions as are necessary to preserve the mother's health. Not until the third trimester, when the fetus is viable, does the state have the right to prohibit abortions and protect the life of the unborn child.

Schenck v. United States, 249 U.S. 47, 39 S.Ct. 247, 63 L.Ed. 470 (1919), an early free speech case, announced the clear-and-present-danger standard for determining whether speech could be restricted. The original defendants in the case had been convicted of conspiracy to violate the Espionage Act of 1917 because they had printed and circulated a document criticizing the United States' conscription of soldiers during World War I and encouraging men to oppose the draft. On appeal to the U.S. Supreme Court the convictions were upheld. The Court held that if the government had a right to prohibit obstruction of the draft, then they could prohibit speech that had the effect of influencing people to do just that. The question was "whether the words used are used in such circumstances and are of such a nature as to create a clear and present danger that they will bring about the substantive evils that Congress has a right to prevent."

Sternberg v. Carhart, No. 99-830 (June 2000) This case presented the question of whether a Nebraska statute criminally prohibiting the performance of a "partial birth abortion," violated the Constitution, as interpreted originally in *Roe v. Wade*, 410 U.S. 113 (1973). A "partial birth abortion" involves dismembering the fetus, extracting parts of its body, and finally using an incision and suction device at the base of the skull to remove its brain. This procedure is used up through the end of the sixth month of pregnancy. The Court struck down the Nebraska statute as unconstitutional because the law lacked any exception for preservation of the mother's health and imposed an undue burden on a woman's ability to choose to have an abortion.

Texas v. Johnson, 491 U.S. 397, 109 S.Ct. 2533, 105 L.Ed.2d 342 (1989) [see Unit III, Chapter 3 for the opinion] held that a Texas statute prohibiting desecration of the U.S. flag was an unconstitutional restriction on freedom of speech in violation of the First Amendment.

United States v. O'Brien 391 U.S. 367, 88 S.Ct. 1673, 20 L.Ed.2d 672 (1968) arose during the Vietnam war. The original defendant and several others had burned their draft cards on the steps of a Boston courthouse in protest against the war. The defendant was charged and convicted of the criminal offense of knowingly destroying or mutilating a military registration certificate in violation of federal law. He argued that the law infringed the First Amendment's freedom of speech clause. Although the law prohibited conduct and not speech, O'Brien argued that his conduct was intended to convey a message and was thus protected. The U.S. Supreme Court upheld the constitutionality of the law, announcing the test relevant for the regulation of expressive conduct: "a government regulation is sufficiently justified if it is within the constitutional power of the Government; if it furthers an important or substantial governmental interest; if the governmental interest is unrelated to the suppression of free expression; and if the incidental restriction on alleged First Amendment freedoms is no greater than is essential to the furtherance of that interest." This test is more lenient toward the government than the strict scrutiny test applied to laws related to the suppression of free expression, or so-called content-based regulation, as opposed to the content-neutral regulation in *O'Brien*.

United States v. Virginia 115 S.Ct. 2264 (1996) involved a constitutional challenge based on the Equal Protection Clause of the Fourteenth Amendment to Virginia Military Institute's exclusion of women from its educational program. VMI was founded in 1839 as a state-supported university dedicated to producing "citizen-soldiers," men prepared for leadership in civilian life and in military service. Its training program is particularly rigorous and physically demanding. The suit was initiated by the United States because of a complaint received from a female high school student who sought admission to the all-male VMI. The U.S. Court of Appeals agreed that VMI's policy violated the requirements of equal protection and suggested that to satisfy them VMI either admit women, establish a separate parallel program for women, or abandon state financial aid and operate as a single-sex private institution. Virginia opted for the second alternative and established Virginia Women's Institute for Leadership. The Supreme Court held that Virginia had failed to demonstrate an "exceedingly persuasive justification" for its gender-based state action by showing that the classification based on sex served "important governmental objectives" and that the means employed were "substantially related to the achievement of those objectives." This "skeptical scrutiny" test falls short of the "strict scrutiny test" but exceeds the "rational basis" test of constitutionality.

University of California Regents v. Bakke 438 U.S. 265 (1978) held that a university could not employ a quota system within the framework of an affirmative action program to admit minority applicants to medical school if the quota system denied white applicants the right to compete for those admission slots. A university could take race into account as one factor relevant to admission to its graduate school program, but it could not apply a strict quota system thereby discriminating against members of the majority race.

West Virginia State Board of Education et al. v. Barnette 319 U.S. 624 (1943) held that West Virginia's law requiring school children in public or private schools to recite the pledge of allegiance to the flag was a violation of the First Amendment's free speech clause. Although the original plaintiff was a Jehova's Witness, who also contested the statute as a violation of the First Amendment's free exercise (of religion) clause, the Court based its decision on the free speech clause with the argument that it also protected the right to remain silent.

Yick Wo v. Hopkins, 118 U.S. 356 (1886), held that the Fourteenth Amendment to the U.S. Constitution was not confined to the protection of citizens, but instead that its provisions were universal in their application, to all persons within the territorial jurisdiction, without regard to any differences of race, of color, or of nationality. The case involved a San Francisco city ordinance which required a permit to operate a laundry in a wooden building. The ordinance granted a city administrator the power to grant permits on application. Of the two hundred applications submitted by Chinese nationals all were refused, whereas all but one of the applications submitted by non-Chinese citizens were granted. The Court struck down the ordinance because it permitted the city to arbitraly grant permits and thus allowed the discrimination of which the petitioner complained.

Appendix III
Common Case Citations

1. U.S. Court Decisions

A citation to a case decided by a court in the United States generally includes 1) the volume number, 2) the abbreviation of the reporter where the case is published, 3) the page number and 4) the year of the decision and any additional information to distinguish the particular court that reached the decision. The primary source of authority on case citations in the U.S. is: *The Bluebook: A Uniform System of Citation*, which is compiled by the editors of the *Columbia Law Review*, the *Harvard Law Review*, the *University of Pennsylvania Law Review* and *The Yale Law Journal*, all scholarly journals in the field of law. The *Bluebook* is published and distributed by The Harvard Law Review Association, Gannett House, 1511 Massachusetts Avenue, Cambridge, Massachusetts 02138, U.S.A. The following provides very basic information on citation form to permit the reader to understand how to begin working with U.S. case materials.

A. Federal Court Decisions

As discussed in Unit II on U.S. Court systems, there are three basic levels of courts: the trial courts, the courts of appeals and the supreme courts.

1. Trial Courts

In the federal system, the trial courts are the U.S. District Courts. The decisions of the district courts are reported in the **Federal Supplement**, which is abbreviated "**F. Supp.**" As you know, the entire United States is divided into federal districts, each state having at least one district, some having up to four districts. To indicate the district court which reached the decision, the district is indicated in parentheses with the date of the decision. Consider the citation:

Barker v. City of Philadelphia, 134 F.Supp. 231 (E.D. Pa. 1955)

This case is reported in volume 134 of the Federal Supplement on page 231. The case was decided by the U.S. District Court for the Eastern District of Pennsylvania in 1955.

In addition to the district courts, we discussed the U.S. Court of International Trade, which is abbreviated **"Ct. Int'l Trade"** and the U.S. Court of Federal Claims, which is abbreviated **"Cl. Ct."**

2. Intermediate Appellate Courts

The intermediate appellate court in the federal system is the U.S. Court of Appeals. The United States is divided into eleven numbered circuits, each containing several districts. The courts of appeals in these circuits hear appeals from the decisions of the district courts within their circuit. U.S. Courts of Appeals decisions are reported in the **Federal Reporter**, abbreviated **F., F.2d** or **F.3d**. The "2d" and "3d" mean "second" and "third series." The volumes of the Federal Reporter are number 1-999. Rather than continue with volume 1000, the volume numbering restarts with volume 1 Federal Reporter 2d series, or 1 F.2d. Consider the citation:

United States et al. v. Carroll Towing Co., Inc., et al.
159 F.2d 169 (2d Cir. 1947)

This case is reported in volume 159 of the Federal Reporter, second series on page 169. The case was decided by the U.S. Court of Appeals for the Second Circuit. (In those days, this court was still called the U. S. Circuit Court of Appeals, Second Circuit, but that is fairly irrelevant for our purposes here because the citation form is the same). The Second Circuit includes the district courts in the states of Connecticut, New York and Vermont. This particular case was appealed from the decision of the U.S. District Court for the Eastern District of New York. It thus came to the Court of Appeals for the Second Circuit.

In addition to the eleven numbered circuits, we discussed the U.S. Court of Appeals for the District of Columbia, which is abbreviated **"D.C. Cir."** and the U.S. Court of Appeals for the Federal Circuit, which is abbreviated **"Fed. Cir."**

3. U.S. Supreme Court

The decisions of the U.S. Supreme Court are reported in three different publishers' editions, which are entitled:

United States Reports	abbreviated **"U.S."**
Supreme Court Reporter	abbreviated **"S.Ct."**
Lawyer's Edition	abbreviated **"L.Ed."** or **"L.Ed.2d"**

Accordingly, for any U.S. Supreme Court decision, you can find the same case in three different sets of volumes. Consider the following **parallel citations:**

Brown v. Board of Education,
347 U.S. 483, 74 Sup. Ct. 686, 98 L.Ed. 873 (1954)

This case can be found in volume 347 of the United States Reports on page 483; in volume 74 of the Supreme Court Reporter on page 686; and in volume 98 of the Lawyer's Edition on page 873. It was decided in 1954.

Sometimes all three citations are used when citing a Supreme Court case. Sometimes, however, you may have only one citation to work with. If it happens to be to the set of volumes you do not have access to in your library, it is still relatively easy to find the citation you need for the volumes available to you. The most simplistic way of doing this is to work with the year of the decision. If you have the cite: 347 U.S. 483 (1954), but your library only has the Supreme Court Reporter, then you need to find the volume of the Supreme Court Reporter containing decisions reached in 1954. At the front of the volume you will find a table of cases, and then you just have to look for *Brown v. Board of Education*. Although simplistic, this method is somewhat time consuming, particularly because 1954 decisions might be contained in a number of different volumes, i.e. the individual volume of the Supreme Court Reporter will not necessarily have all of the decisions reached in 1954. A more elegant and less time consuming method is to look for a table at the beginning of the volume giving you the parallel citations.

Although there are a few other publications containing federal cases and other material, generally you will be confronted with the citations explained above. Ideally, you have a *Bluebook* available to find an explanation of any citation you might have. If you do not, it is suggested that if the cite is not to one of the volumes above, you consider whether it is a cite to a state court decision.

B. State Court Decisions

Decisions reached by the individual state courts are reported both in a set of state court reports for the individual state and in regional reporters, each of which include the decisions of the courts of appeals and the supreme courts of a group of states. If you are working with legal materials in Europe, you will most likely not have the individual state reporters available. Still, it is important even when working with the regional reporters, to know the abbreviations used for the individual states:

Ala.	Alabama	Ky.	Kentucky	N.D.	North Dakota
Alaska	Alaska	La.	Louisiana	Ohio	Ohio
Ariz.	Arizona	Me.	Maine	Okla.	Oklahoma
Ark.	Arkansas	Md.	Maryland	Or.	Oregon
Cal.	California	Mass.	Massachusetts	Pa.	Pennsylvania
Colo.	Colorado	Mich.	Michigan	R.I.	Rhode Island
Conn.	Connecticut	Minn.	Minnesota	S.C.	South Carolina
Del.	Delaware	Miss.	Mississippi	S.D.	South Dakota
D.C.	Washington, D.C.	Mo.	Missouri	Tenn.	Tennessee
Fla.	Florida	Mont.	Montana	Tex.	Texas
Ga.	Georgia	Neb.	Nebraska	Utah	Utah
Haw.	Hawaii	Nev.	Nevada	Vt.	Vermont
Idaho	Idaho	N.H.	New Hampshire	Va.	Virginia
Ill.	Illinois	N.J.	New Jersey	Wash.	Washington
Ind.	Indiana	N.M.	New Mexico	W.Va.	West Virginia
Iowa	Iowa	N.Y.	New York	Wis.	Wisconsin
Kan.	Kansas	N.C.	North Carolina	Wyo.	Wyoming

Below are a list of all the regional reporters in the United States, including a list of the states whose court decisions are published in the particular reporter:

A., A.2d   Atlantic Reporter: Connecticut, Delaware, Maine, Maryland, New Hampshire, New Jersey, Pennsylvania, Rhode Island, Vermont

N.E., N.E.2d   North Eastern Reporter: Illinois, Indiana, Massachusetts, New York, Ohio

N.W., N.W.2d   North Western Reporter: Iowa, Michigan, Minnesota, Nebraska, North Dakota, South Dakota, Wisconsin

P., P.2d, P.3d   Pacific Reporter: Alaska, Arizona, California, Colorado, Hawaii, Idaho, Kansas, Montana, Nevada, New Mexico, Oklahoma, Oregon, Utah, Washington, Wyoming

So., So.2d   Southern Reporter: Alabama, Florida, Louisiana, Mississippi

S.E., S.E.2d   South Eastern Reporter: Georgia, North Carolina, South Carolina, Virginia, West Virginia

S.W., S.W.2d   South Western Reporter: Arkansas, Kentucky, Missouri, Tennessee, Texas

As a general rule, cases decided by a supreme court in one of these states will be cited, for example as follows:

> *Petterson v. Pattberg*, 248 N.Y. 86, 161 N.E. 428 (1928)

or:

> *Petterson v. Pattberg*, 161 N.E. 428 (N.Y. 1928)

In the first citation, you can tell that the case was decided by a New York state court (refer to the list of abbreviations above), because the parallel citation to New York's state reporter is given. You can also find the case in the regional reporter, namely the North Eastern Reporter (N.E.). In the second variation, without the parallel citation, you can tell the case was decided by a New York state court, because of the abbreviation given with the date in the parentheses. If the case had *not* been decided by the highest court of the state, then the abbreviation would include some form of "App.", such as (N.Y. App. Div. 1995). Consider the following citation:

> *Singer v. Marx*, 144 Cal. App. 2d 637, 301 P.2d 440 (1956)

or:

> *Singer v. Marx*, 301 P.2d 440 (Cal. Ct. App. 1956)

Here you can tell that the case was decided by a California state court (Cal.) on the intermediate appellate level (Ct. App.). You can also find the case in volume 301 of the Pacific Reporter, second series (P.2d) on page 440.

2. English Court Decisions

The highest court of appeal in the English system is the House of Lords, or more precisely the **Appellate Committee of the House of Lords**, primarily manned by professional judges called Lords of Appeal in Ordinary or the Law Lords and headed by the Lord Chancellor. The House of Lords primarily hears appeals from the **Court of Appeal**, which is composed of a **Civil Division** and a **Criminal Division**. The Civil Division of the Court of Appeal hears appeals from the **High Court of Justice**, which is composed of the **Queen's Bench Division** (or King's Bench Division), a trial court for private law disputes, the **Chancery Division**, a trial court for company law, estates, trusts, bankruptcy, equity, patents and a few other matters, and the **Family Division**, a trial court for divorce, adoption, child custody, guardianship and probate cases. It also hears appeals from the decisions of the **County Courts**, trial courts of limited jurisdiction for civil law disputes. The Criminal Division of the Court of Appeal hears appeals from the **Crown Court**, a trial court for more serious criminal cases and from the **Queen's Bench Division**, which also hears some criminal appeals from the **Magistrates Courts**, trial courts of limited jurisdiction for criminal matters.

A. House of Lords

The decisions of the House of Lords are reported in the *Law Reports*, *Appeal Cases* (**A.C.**) and cited, for example:

Chandler v. Director of Public Prosecutions, [1964] A.C. 763

The **[1964]** indicates the number of the volume and also the year of the decision, which is to be found on page 763.

Decisions of the House of Lords are also published in the *All England Law Reports* (**All ER**) and in the *Weekly Law Reports* (**W.L.R.**):

D v. National Society for the Prevention of Cruelty to Children,
[1977] 1 All ER 589, HL

Porter v. Honey, [1988] 1 W.L.R. 1420, HL

The first citation is to volume 1 of the 1977 *All England Law Reports*, page 589. This series has several volumes per year and each year the volume numbering starts again with number one. Accordingly you need the year of the decision to determine which volume 1 you are looking for. Since the *All England Law Reports* contains the decisions of a number of different courts, the **HL** following the page tells you that the case was decided by the House of Lords. The second citation is to volume 1 of the 1988 *Weekly Law Reports* page 1420, again a decision the House of Lords reached (**HL**).

B. Court of Appeal

There is no single series of the *Law Reports* for the decisions of the Court of Appeal. Instead, the Civil Division decisions are generally published in a series provided for the court from whose decision the appeal is taken, namely the Queen's Bench (**Q.B.**), or King's Bench (**K.B.**); the Chancery Division (**Ch.**) and the Family Division (**Fam.**). The decisions of the Criminal Division are reported either in the Queen's Bench series or in the *Criminal Appeal Reports* (**Cr.App.R.**). If a decision of the Court of Appeal is taken to the House of Lords, it may be published with the House of Lords decision in the *Appeal Cases* series of the *Law Reports*. Consider the following citations:

McCarey v. Associated Newspapers Ltd. [1965] 2 Q.B. 86, C.A.

Ashburn Anstalt v. Arnold, [1989] Ch. 1, C.A.

Cantliff v. Jenkins, [1978] Fam. 47, C.A.

The first case was appealed from a decision of the Queen's Bench Division and can be found in volume 2 of the 1965 *Law Reports, Queen's Bench Division*, on page 86. The second case was appealed from a decision of the Chancery Division and the third from a decision of the Family Division. The following is a citation to a decision of the Criminal Division:

Regina v. Conway (1990) 91 Cr.App.R. 143, C.A.

The *Criminal Appeal Reports*, unlike the other volumes cited above, has a continuous numbering system for its volumes extending over a number of years. Accordingly, the 1990 in parentheses rather than square brackets, indicates the year of the decision, to be found in volume 91 of the *Criminal Appeal Reports* on page 143.

The decisions of the Court of Appeal are also published in the *All England Law Reports*:

Alpha Trading Ltd. v. Dunnshaw-Patten Ltd. [1981] 1 All ER 482, C.A.

and in the *Weekly Law Reports*:

BP Exploration v. Hunt [1981] 1 W.L.R. 232, C.A.

Suggested Reading

The Bluebook: A Uniform System of Citation (17th ed.), Harvard Law Review Association: Cambridge, Mass. (2000)

Guy Holborn, *Butterworths Legal Research Guide*, Butterworths: London, et al. (1993)

M. Jacobstein, R. Mersky, *Legal Research Illustrated* (5th ed.), Foundation Press: Westbury, N.Y. (1990)

Suzanne McKie, *Legal Research*, Cavendish Publishing Ltd.: London (1993)

Answers to Language Exercises

Unit I

I. Verbs: See pp. 3-11 for the use in the original context

1. enacts
2. is divided
2. derives
4. are bound
5. held; bound; depart; overrule
6. was retracted
7. delivered
8. provides
9. adhere
10. was prosecuted
11. prosecuted; was not consummated
12. dismissed; was reversed
13. was upheld; was acquitted
14. was convicted
15. had relied; propounded

II. Terms: See pp. 3-22 for use in the original context

1. plaintiff
2. complaint
3. declaration
4. allegations
5. averments
6. contentions
7. defendant
8. court
9. appeal
10. appellant
11. appellee
12. holding
13. precedents
14. codes
15. statutes
16. House of Lords
17. Lord Chancellor
18. judiciary
19. Lords of Appeal in Ordinary (or: Law Lords)
20. facts of the case
21. legal history of the case
22. issue on appeal
23. holding
24. dicta
25. liable
26. damages
27. negligence
28. reasonable

III. See pp. 26-30 for an explanation in context:

actions ex contractu:
assumpsit
covenant
debt

actions ex delicto:
replevin
trespass
trespass on the case
trover

IV. See pp. 26-30 for an explanation in context:

a. trespass
b. debt
c. trover
d. assumpsit

e. replevin
f. trespass on the case
g. covenant

V. See pp. 38-65 for an explanation of terms in context:

1. grand jury
2. petit jury
3. indictment
4. trial jury
5. trial jury/petit jury
6. array

7. challenge to the array/motion to quash the venire/motion to quash the array
8. voir dire
9. petit jury/trial jury
10. challenge for cause
11. peremptory challenges
12. impaneled

VI. See pp. 38-65 for use in context:

1. held
2. exercised
3. petitioned; granted/denied
4. moved; dismissed
5. was tried
6. convened
7. convicted
8. sentenced

9. delivered; joined
10. brought
11. instructed; sequestered; deliberated; reached
12. testified
13. upheld; reversed
14. provides
15. establishes; shifts

VII. See pp. 38-65 for explanation in context:

1. **judgment:** decision reached by a *judge* either in a trial or on appeal

   verdict: decision reached by the *jury* in a trial

   sentence: judge's decision on the *amount of punishment* to be imposed in a criminal case

2. **felony:** most serious level of criminal offenses; punishment usually not under one year imprisonment in a high security prison

   misdemeanor: intermediate level criminal offenses; punishment usually does not exceed one year

   petty offense: least serious level of criminal offenses; punishment usually is a monetary fine

   capital crime: felony for which the death penalty can be imposed

3. **to overrule:** to declare a previous decision of either a lower court or of the court itself invalid (when the court overrules its own precedent); this term is used in relation to past precedents announced in a *different case* from the case in which they are overruled (e.g. *R. v. Shivpuri* overruled *Anderton v. Ryan*); the term is also used to mean to deny the request or objections of a lawyer during a trial

to reverse:	to declare the decision of a lower court invalid; this term is used in relation to a lower court's decision in the *same case* as the one in which the decision is reversed (e.g. in *Ballew*, the Supreme Court reversed the decision the Court of Appeals reached in *Ballew*)
to remand:	to send a case back to a lower court for some specified treatment of the case different from the treatment the lower court previously gave it
4. citation:	indication of the place where one can find a case that has been published
quotation:	actual repetition of words of someone else, either printed or previously spoken
5. deliberation:	used to refer to jury's consideration of a case in attempting to reach a verdict
sequestration:	used to refer to the isolation of the jury during deliberation

VIII. Answers in text on p. 80, lines 8-19

1. of	5. by	9. by
2. in	6 In	10. at
3. in	7. through	
4. into	8. with	

IX. See text on pp. 79-83 for an explanation in context:

1. beyond a reasonable doubt:	standard of the burden of proof in a criminal case
by a preponderance of the evidence:	standard of the burden of proof in civil cases
2. alternative dispute resolution:	method *other than going to court* of dealing with a conflict between two parties
adjudication:	method of dealing with a conflict between two parties *by going to court*

X. See pp. 86-133 for an explanation in context:

1. A lawyer is anyone who has completed the study of law. An attorney is a lawyer who is actually practicing law. A litigator is an attorney who is specialized in presenting cases in court.
2. These are all British terms. A solicitor is a lawyer who specializes in the office type of legal work. A barrister is a lawyer who specializes in presenting cases in court, particularly in the higher courts in England. A barrister who has not been appointed Queen's Counsel is called a junior. QC, also called a silk, is a barrister who has been appointed by the Queen on the recommendation of the Lord Chancellor because he or she is particularly outstanding in the practice of law.
3. An in-house lawyer is a lawyer who works on the legal staff of a company rather than in a law firm. A Wall Street lawyer is an attorney who works in one of the larger law firms in the U.S., traditionally located on Wall Street in New York and which usually caters to corporate clients. A judge's clerk is a young law school graduate who works for a judge for one to two years. A public defender is a lawyer who works for the state defending persons accused of crimes who cannot afford a lawyer.

4. A consulting fee is the fee a lawyer charges for the advice he gives the client on the client's first visit to his office. A retainer is a fee the client pays a lawyer to hire the lawyer to represent her. An hourly fee is a fee computed on the basis of the amount of time the lawyer actually spends working for the client. A flat fee is a fixed amount the lawyer charges for performing certain services, such as spending one day in court. A contingency fee is a fee that the client pays only if the lawyer wins the case for the client. A brief fee is a fee charged by a barrister for preparing a case to go to court and for the first day spent in court. A refresher is a fee paid to a barrister for each day in court following the first day.

5. An interrogatory is a written list of questions addressed to the opposing party in a law suit which have to be answered under oath. A deposition is an oral questioning session of either a witness or a party to a law suit in the presence of the lawyers representing both parties to the law suit and a court reporter. A request for admissions is a document asking the other party to agree to the truth of certain statements or not. All three of these terms designate tools of discovery.

6. These are all terms defining the purpose of criminal punishment. Deterrence is the prevention of future crimes through showing society and the offender that they will be punished if they do commit them. Rehabilitation as a purpose of punishment focuses on influencing or training the offender to accept social norms and correspond to them in the future. Retribution is oriented toward paying the offender back for the wrong he has done to society.

7. The record includes all of the documents relevant in a case, one of which is the trial transcript, which is a verbatim report of everything said in court during a trial.

8. All of these motions ask the judge to decide the case independent from the jury based only on the law as applied to the facts most favorable to the non-moving party. The defendant files the motion for a non-suit at the close of the plaintiff's case in chief. Either party may file a motion for a directed verdict at the end of the trial but before the jury is instructed and given the case to decide. The motion for judgment notwithstanding the verdict may be filed by a party who is dissatisfied with the jury's verdict after it has been rendered.

9. Prejudicial error is some mistake that was made during the law suit that could have affected the outcome, whereas harmless error is a mistake that could not have affected the outcome. Prejudicial error provides the basis for the motion for a new trial.

10. In a general verdict the jury merely states which party won the law suit and if it was the plaintiff, then also the amount of damages the plaintiff is to receive from the defendant. In a special verdict the jury states what facts it believed to be true.

XI. See pp. 89-97 for an explanation in context:

1. legislature, executive, judiciary
2. legislator, president (of the US) / governor (of an individual state), judge /justice
3. legislative, executive, judicial
4. The term **government** in US English means the entire state, including all three branches, whereas **Regierung** in German refers to the executive branch only.

XII. See pp. 102-133 for an explanation in context:

1. plaintiff	8. default judgment	15. defenses
2. complaint	9. service of process	16. counterclaims
3. jurisdiction	10. motion to dismiss	17. reply
4. defendant	11. demurrer	18. rejoinder
5. cause of action	12. answer	19. pleadings
6. prayer for relief	13. admissions	20. motion for judgment
7. summons	14. denials	on the pleadings

XIII. See pp. 137-155 for explanation in context:

1. prosecuted
2. evidence
3. search
4. seizure
5. trial
6. evidence
7. exclusionary rule
8. holding
9. retroactively

10. conviction
11. collateral review
12. appeal
13. custody
14. arrest warrant
15. search warrant
16. warrants
17. probable cause

XIV. See pp. 137-155 for an explanation in context:

1. direct attack: challenge of lower court's judgment during the normal appellate process

direct review: court's consideration of an appeal

collateral attack: challenge of a judgment that has already become final and can no longer be appealed

collateral review: court's consideration of a collateral attack

petition for a writ of habeas corpus: means of collateral attack in a criminal case

2. statute of limitations: deadline before which one must bring a law suit to avoid losing the right to sue; period of time between the injury, or discovery of the injury, and the deadline for filing a law suit; operates to bar plaintiff from bringing suit

statute of repose: time within which an injury must occur for the party injured to be able to bring suit; period of time between, for example, purchase of a product and injury caused by that product, after which time a suit may not be brought even though the product may then be the cause of injury; operates to bar plaintiff from bringing suit

res judicata: case that has already reached a final judgment on the merits of the case; operates to bar plaintiff from bringing the suit

Unit II

I. See pp. 167-185 for an explanation of terms in context:

1. plaintiff
2. defendant
3. trial court
4. appellate court
5. issue of fact
6. issue of law
7. a court's jurisdiction
8. appellant
9. appellee
10. trial de novo (U.K.: appeal)
11. direct appeal
12. administrative court
13. labor court
14. juvenile court
15. probate court
16. domestic relations court/ probate court
17. administrative agency

II. See pp. 167-185 for an explanation of terms in context:

1. limited jurisdiction
2. general jurisdiction
3. jurisdiction
4. concurrent jurisdiction
5. jurisdiction
6. exclusive jurisdiction
7. trial de novo

III. See pp. 167-185 for an explanation of terms in context:

trial courts:	Municipal Court, Superior Court, County Court, U.S. District Court, Justice Court, Court of Common Pleas, and in New York Supreme Court
intermediate appellate courts:	U.S. Court of Appeals
highest appellate court:	Supreme Court

IV. See pp. 185-204 for an explanation of terms in context:

1. admiralty/maritime
2. exclusive jurisdiction
3. original jurisdiction
4. federal question jurisdiction
5. diversity jurisdiction
6. forum shopping
7. removed
8. personal jurisdiction
9. served process
10. in rem jurisdiction
11. quasi in rem jurisdiction
12. long-arm statute
13. forum state

Unit III

I. See pp. 227-243:

1. on
2. under
3. on behalf of
4. in
5. for
6. of
7. of
8. Pursuant to
9. under
10. on
11. with respect to
12. In
13. to
14. to
15. during
16. On
17. except for
18. In
19. of
20. through
21. of
22. in
23. to
24. of/within/in
25. on
26. under
27. according to

II. See pp. 167-243 for an explanation of terms in context:

1. majority opinion
2. concurring opinion
3. dissenting opinion
4. consolidated opinion
5. docketed
6. amicus curiae brief
7. others similarly situated
8. instant case
9. expressly reserved
10. to enjoin; provisions; injunction
11. findings below
12. repealed
13. ratified
14. infra; supra
15. writ of certiorari
16. ex parte

III. Compare German text to Texas Penal Code § 42.09 p. 248 to help with the translation:

§ 90a. Desecration of the State and its Symbols. (1) A person who publicly, in a meeting of people, or through the distribution of printed materials (§ 11(3)) commits one of the following offenses shall be punished with up to three years' imprisonment or a monetary fine:

1. casting aspersion on or maliciously degrading the Federal Republic of Germany or one of its states or its constitutional order, or

2. desecrating the colors, the flag, the official seal, or the national anthem of the Federal Republic of Germany or one of its states.

(2) A person who removes, destroys, damages, physically mistreats, defaces, or defiles a publicly furled flag or an officially and publicly mounted or posted symbol of sovereignty of the Federal Republic of Germany or of one of its states is to be punished in the same manner. The attempt is also subject to punishment.

(3) If by committing the offense the offender purposely supported efforts directed against the continued existence of the Federal Republic of Germany or against its constitutional principles, then the punishment shall be up to five years' imprisonment or a monetary fine.

German Penal Code (1999)

Answers to Questions on the Text

Unit I

Chapter 1

Exercises p. 12

1. The main argument against announcing a rule in a case and applying it only to future cases is that a court would assume the function of a legislature. A court is supposed to resolve disputes by applying the law as it exists to the cases brought to it and not to create new law for the future. This topic will be discussed in depth in Chapter 4 of this Unit, but the question is intended to encourage discussion of the general retroactivity problem.
2. One could argue that applying a new precedent making conduct criminal that was formerly not criminal violates guarantees like "nulla poena sine lege." Important to realize in regard to *Shivpuri*, however, is that it was impossible for Shivpuri to rely on *Anderton v. Ryan*, because Shivpuri did not know he was mistaken about the nature of the substance he was transporting. *Anderton v. Ryan* only applies to cases of mistake about the nature of the goods involved and no one can rely on being mistaken.
3. The arguments are in lines 12-16; 16-19; 19-23; 23-26.

Exercises pp. 20-22

1. The original plaintiff was the dock owner. The ship owner lost at the trial court level, which you can tell from line 21, because the jury determined that the ship owner had to pay the dock owner $500 for the damage. Since the ship owner lost at trial, it was the ship owner who appealed and thus was the appellant in the decision printed in the book. The facts of the case are stated in the opinion in lines 4-20. The legal history of the case, as far as it can be understood from this excerpt, is that the dock owner sued the ship owner for the damage caused to his dock. The trial court found in favor of the dock owner and awarded him $500. The ship owner then appealed. The issue on appeal is whether a person acting under necessity should have to pay for the damage he causes, especially when his conduct is completely reasonable under the circumstances, i.e. not negligent. The holding is that he does.
2. People will be held responsible for intentional torts, and in some cases, like product liability, they will be responsible independent of any showing that they were at fault (**strict liability/verschuldensunabhängige Haftung**).
3. This case does not raise a question of negligence because the ship owner acted intentionally, which is sufficient as a basis for tort liability.
4. The court's consideration of any case that is different from this case is dicta, e.g. lines 40-45; 49-52. The ratio decidendi of this and the *Ploof v. Putnam* case is stated in § 904 BGB, namely that a person has a right to cause damage to someone else's property to avoid

imminent danger to his own property if the damage caused is (significantly) less than the damage avoided. (*Ploof*) Still, the actor has to pay for the damage. (*Vincent*)

5. The first sentence of the last paragraph of *Vincent* refers to the situation of necessity as described in § 228 BGB. *Vincent* cannot be a precedent for a § 228 case and lines 49-51 indeed say that *Vincent* is not a § 228 case.

Exercises p. 35

1. The main source of law in a common law system is judicial precedent; in a civil law system it is codes.
2. The doctrine of *stare decisis* states that precedents bind judges to decide future cases in the same way they have decided similar cases in the past.
3. facts of the case; legal history of the case; issue raised on appeal; holding; ratio decidendi
4. The holding is the resolution of the actual dispute before the court; dicta is anything else included in the opinion, such as hypotheticals, legislative history, etc.
5. The ratio decidendi is the principle of law needed to resolve the case.
6. a) plaintiff and defendant; b) appellant and appellee
7. assumpsit is contractual; trespass, case, replevin and ejectment are delictual
8. A remedy is anything a court can award a successful plaintiff because of an injury the defendant caused, such as money damages, specific performance, an injunction. Different words for "remedy" are: relief, recovery, redress.
9. A writ is a written order, but the word is used primarily when referring to a court order. The writ system became very rigid and led to injustice in certain types of cases, which is why equity developed.

Chapter 2

Exercises p. 47-48

1. See Chapter 2 (A) (1) and (2) for a description of the difference between the grand and petit juries.
2. a) see lines 5-10 of the opinion; b) see lines 5-10; c) the issue raised on appeal is whether a jury of 6 violates an individual's rights under the Sixth Amendment; d) the holding is that it does not
3. For the arguments see lines 11-26 regarding the jury as providing commonsense judgment and protecting the accused from the prosecutor and judge; lines 27-35 on whether the larger size of the jury benefits the defendant more than the prosecutor; lines 36-43 on the cross-section of the community requirement for the jury; lines 44-51 on the number 12 being an historical accident.
4. As the size of the jury decreases the chance that a member of a minority group will be on any particular jury decreases. If Hispanics account for 10% of the community then you need at least a ten-member jury to ensure that on average one Hispanic will sit on any particular jury. With a 6-person jury, you would expect to have about one Hispanic on every other jury, but with a 12-person jury you would expect to have one Hispanic on every jury.
5.a. too broad in the sense that it would cover even the case of a 1-person jury, which clearly would not satisfy the Sixth Amendment guarantee
5.b. too narrow because it applies only to the 6-person, but not the 7-person jury, which clearly would satisfy the Sixth Amendment guarantee

5.c. too narrow because it excludes juries of 13 or more, again clearly satisfactory under the Sixth Amendment

5.d. best formulation

5.e. too broad because the case says nothing about 5-person juries

Exercises p. 51

1. The discussion is in lines 67-79
2. The U.S. Supreme Court denied certiorari as you can tell from the citations following "cert. denied." The Georgia Court of Appeals felt bound by *Sanders* because that case was decided by the Georgia Supreme Court, whose decisions bind all Georgia courts. This point will be clearer after you read Unit II. It was the Georgia Supreme Court which held that a 5-person jury was constitutional. The Georgia Court of Appeals is bound by its own decisions, by the decisions of the Georgia Supreme Court and by the decisions of the United States Supreme Court.
3. The advantages in a unanimous verdict are similar to the advantages in having more people on a jury rather than less. See the arguments in *Williams* and *Ballew*. One major disadvantage in requiring a unanimous verdict is that if only one of twelve persons does not agree, then a new trial will have to be held with a new jury. That is expensive, time consuming and a burden on everyone's nerves.

Exercises p. 62

1.a. facts of the case (lines 5-18); legal history (lines 20-24)

1.b. The legal issue is whether a prosecutor can exercise peremptory challenges to exclude members of the defendant's race from jury participation.

2. The venire is the larger group of qualified jurors brought into the court room for the voir dire selection of individuals who will actually serve on the jury. The impaneled jury is the jury that will actually sit at trial.
3. As you will see from reading the case, the Court based its decision on the equal protection clause.

Exercises pp. 64-65

1. See lines 45-57.
2. *Batson* as it stands applies only to a prosecutor's exercising peremptory challenges in a criminal case on the basis of race, and not gender, age, religion, national origin.
3. A person could have an interest in a cross-section of the community to be sure that people like himself are not excluded from the jury. It would be more difficult to argue that people not like himself should also be included. Therefore the Sixth or Seventh Amendment arguments would not be as easy to make as the equal protection argument, especially regarding the prospective *juror's* right to equal protection and thus his right not to be excluded on the basis of his race or other characteristics. Many U.S. Americans would argue that peremptory challenges should be abolished altogether and others would argue that *Batson* and these later cases have almost abolished them anyway.

Exercises pp. 70-71

1. See the text, pp. 39-43 for the difference between the two juries.
2. This question merely requires you to formulate legal provisions in terms that a person untrained in the law can understand.
3. Generally a judicial opinion will first include the facts of the case, with some indication of how the case was decided by the lower court or courts. Sometimes the decision(s) of the lower court(s) will not be stated until the very end of the opinion where the court whose decision is reported rules to uphold or reverse them. The main body of the decision contains the court's arguments and the factors it considered in reaching the decision.
4. This question has no "correct" answer but instead is suggested as a class project requiring students to do independent legal research, report their findings and argue cases in class as in a moot court competition (appellate argumentation).

Chapter 3

Exercises p. 81

1. For arguments in favor of the interrogative system, see John Langbein, The German Advantage in Civil Procedure, 52 *University of Chicago Law Review* 823 (1986). Some of them include efficiency, legal security, reliance on professionally trained judges, etc.
2. This text relates to a private law dispute. You can tell that in part from lines 8-11. We would not usually consider a prosecutor in a criminal case as being propelled by the prospect of victory, or at least one should not see the prosecutor in this way, because the prosecutor is responsible for representing the interests of society including those of the criminal defendant. You can also tell that a private law dispute is meant from lines 35-43. Although the parties to a private law dispute will admit the truth of what can really be proved, a criminal defendant will not necessarily admit anything.
3. The answers to these questions will depend on the legal system the reader is discussing.

Exercises pp. 83-84

1. The text is based on a criminal trial as you can see immediately in line 3, where the author refers to the prosecutor, and also in lines 19-25. He is writing about a jury trial.
2. Answer depends on the legal system discussed.
3. Arguments in favor of the adversary system are that it is more democratic (lines 1-2); that it poses fewer risks of error (lines 28-29); that it minimizes bias (lines 30-32); that it permits a more vigorous defense (lines 32-35); and that it divides power over the outcome of the trial four ways thus avoiding corruption (lines 47-50). Of course any argument in favor of the adversary system is at least indirectly a critique of the accusatorial system. But the author gets pretty direct in the last two arguments.
4. Some metaphorical constructions are: "sporting approach to the truth" (line 1), "to joust in open court" (line 4), "two pitted advocates" (line 11). For the translation of this text into German see: George P. Fletcher, *Notwehr als Verbrechen*. Der U-Bahn-Fall Goetz (translated by Cornelius Nestler-Tremel) Suhrkamp (1993).
5. The trial is supposed to enable the factfinder to determine what really happened in the sense of scientific truth. Of course, as the author of the second text points out, that is not possible with 100% accuracy. Even if you adopt the attitude of the first author in lines 35-43 of the text, you still might argue that the parties feel better about having a trial and

making the effort to discover the truth than simply tossing a coin. See the last article recommended in the Suggested Reading for an interesting discussion of procedural justice and its appeal to people of many nations as a means of resolving disputes.

Exercises p. 113

1. Since it was the respondent's action that was dismissed, the respondent was originally the plaintiff in the case and the petitioner the defendant. The trial court then dismissed the complaint, so it would be the plaintiff who was the appellant on the intermediate appellate court level and the defendant was the appellee. The intermediate appellate court reversed the judgment of the trial court and therefore the plaintiff's action was reinstated. The original defendant, or appellee, then petitioned to the U.S. Supreme Court to have the decision of the intermediate appellate court reversed.

2. The facts of the case here refer not to the facts providing the basis for the antitrust action, which are not even reported here. The facts are the facts relevant for the U.S. Supreme Court's decision in the case you read, namely that the plaintiff refused to cooperate in responding to written interrogatories. The legal history of the case is that the trial court dismissed the plaintiff's action under Rule 37; the court of appeals reversed the trial court's order, and the U.S. Supreme Court granted certiorari to review the case. The issue raised on appeal is whether the trial court abused its discretion in dismissing the action. The holding is that it did not under the facts stated. The ratio decidendi is that Rule 37 provides for this extreme sanction to provide the trial court with a deterrent against parties' unwillingness to cooperate in discovery and that the trial court is in the best position to determine whether the facts justify the measure in the particular case.

3. Discovery gives the parties to a law suit extensive rights that can easily be abused. The parties can go on fishing expeditions just to expose the other party to criticism that has little to do with the real issues in the case. Discovery records, such as deposition transcripts, are available to the public. Admittedly not many people spend their afternoons in a courthouse reading discovery records, but the fact that everyone has access to them is somewhat disconcerting and an invasion of privacy. Parties have even been know to settle a case out of court to avoid having to comply with discovery requests, merely because they do not want to be exposed to the other party or to the public. Although the judge has control of the parties' conduct and of protected information, such as trade secrets, a judge is not an expert in every area that might be involved in a law suit she is hearing. As a consequence a judge's decision may not always be altogether satisfying for the parties to the law suit.

Exercises p. 133

1. These motions all ask the judge to assume the facts most favorable to the non-moving party. Still the moving party claims he should win the law suit as a matter of law. The motions thus permit the parties to have the court review the law and its correct application at various times from the beginning to the end of the trial process.

2. The main difference is the time at which they can be made. The demurrer is filed in response to the plaintiff's complaint. The motion for judgment on the pleadings is filed after all of the pleadings have been filed. The motion for non-suit is made at the close of the plaintiff's case in chief. The motion for directed verdict is made at the close of the evidentiary phase of the trial. The motion for a judgment notwithstanding the verdict is made after the verdict has been returned.

3. These questions and suggestions are intended to encourage readers to take advantage of the opportunity to observe a trial both at home and abroad. The answers to the questions will

vary depending on where the trial takes place. Generally, in Continental European nations, parties do not have the right to cross-examine witnesses. Usually it is the judge who conducts the proceedings, albeit in light of the parties' requests.

Chapter 4

Exercises p. 143

There are no "correct" answers to these questions. Rather they are intended to encourage the right kind of arguments. The *Teague v. Lane* case following the exercises resolves this question.

Exercises pp. 146-147

1. a) facts of the case (lines 7-17); b) legal history (lines 7-9 and 18-23); c) issue raised on collateral review (lines 26-27)
2. For cases on direct review (lines 59-61); for cases on collateral review (lines 70-73, 79-83)
3. The exclusionary rule does not improve the fact-finding process, but may indeed hinder it. The purpose of the exclusionary rule is to deter the police from conducting illegal searches and seizures. Applying *Mapp* retroactively will not accomplish that goal any better than simply applying it in the future. Furthermore there is not much reason to suspect that Linkletter was not guilty just because the evidence against him was seized illegally. Not having a lawyer to represent you, on the other hand, puts you at a considerable disadvantage within an adversary system, because the mechanism of two "equal" opponents battling for the truth will not function well in a completely unequal setting. Accordingly, we might worry more about whether Gideon was really guilty or whether he was just poorly represented. That would cause us to doubt the outcome of his trial.
4. Assuming that the fact-finding process depended on the race of the jury members would be the same as saying that people can never judge fairly and objectively. There is no reason to assume that a white juror will always decide against a black defendant or vice versa, even though no doubt some people do discriminate against members of races other than their own. Certainly, the Supreme Court would not want to adopt the position that a black juror will always favor a black defendant or a white juror a white defendant, because that indeed would mean that members of the defendant's own race should be excluded and that members of other races, because of their negative response, should be excluded as well. Including members of the defendant's own race might at least hinder members of a different race from expressing their discriminatory attitudes during jury deliberation. The Supreme Court's reliance on the equal protection clause with regard to the prospective juror's right to serve on a jury permits the Court to avoid this problem and also permitted it to reach the decision it did in *Powers v. Ohio*.

Exercises p. 155

1. facts of the case (lines 10-19); legal history (lines 20-34); issue on appeal (lines 6-8); holding (lines 8-9); ratio (137-140)
2. A new precedent may be applied fully retroactively (line 43), purely prospectively (line 53), or in the case in which it is pronounced and in all cases based on facts which occurred after it was pronounced (lines 65-67). *Beam* rejects the third alternative in favor of the first and does not relate to the second. Anything the Court states relating to the second alternative is thus dicta and not part of the holding or the ratio. There is language in the opinion that

indicates the Court's dissatisfaction with *Chevron Oil*, for example in line 58, the Court points out that it has resorted to pure prospectivity only infrequently and in lines 62-65 it states that this method has the drawback that it permits courts to act like legislatures. In *Harper v. Virginia Dept. of Taxation*, 113 S.Ct. 2510 (1993) the Court clearly weakened its holding in *Chevron*. The new rule in *Chevron* did not apply to the parties to that suit (lines 80-85) but rather purely prospectively.

3. This problem should arise primarily regarding new statutes and their application to facts that occurred or arose before the new statute was adopted and regarding any case decisions that are considered to be binding precedents, such as the decisions of the Bundesverfassungsgericht or the European Court of Justice.

Unit II

Chapter 1

Exercises p. 176

1. Answers depend on the legal system discussed. The German court system is generally a three-tiered system with a trial initiating in the local court (Amtsgericht), a court of limited jurisdiction, or the regional court (Landgericht), a court of general jurisdiction. A party dissatisfied with the decision of the local court can have a trial de novo (U.S.) in the regional court [can appeal to (U.K.)] but cannot appeal any further to a higher court; a party dissatisfied with the decision of the regional court can have a trial de novo in the higher regional court (Oberlandesgericht). Finally, a party dissatisfied with the higher regional court's decision can appeal [**appeal by way of case stated** (U.K.) meaning only on questions of law and not fact] (Revision) to the Federal High Court of Justice (Bundesgerichtshof). German courts are differentiated according to the types of cases they hear, such as administrative law courts (Verwaltungsgerichte), labor courts (Arbeitsgerichte), social security courts (Sozialgerichte), or are divided into senates, such as criminal or civil law senates, depending on the type of case involved. Appeal to the higher courts is a matter of right as long as certain requirements have been fulfilled, but the court has the discretion to hear a case even if the requirements have not been fulfilled if the case raises an important question of law.

2. Most German students do not know the names of more than one or two justices on the Federal Constitutional Court (Bundesverfassungsgericht) and usually know none of the justices on the Federal High Court of Justice. The point of this exercise is that judges play a more significant role in a common law system and thus are more commonly known by name than in a civil law system. The German system has a number of higher courts, rather than just one supreme court for all types of cases. Judges on the Federal Constitutional Court are appointed for a term of years and not for life. Otherwise, German judges are civil servants and have life appointments as judges, albeit not as judges on a particular court. It is difficult to imagine a legal system in which judicial appointments are not in some way politically influenced.

3. Germany has federal and state courts in the sense that the individual states (Länder) are responsible for establishing certain courts (Amtsgericht, Landgericht, Oberlandesgericht, etc.), whereby the highest courts (Bundesgerichtshof, Bundesarbeitsgericht, Bundesverwaltungsgericht, Bundessozialgericht) are established by the federal government. Still these courts form one court system, and not seventeen different court systems. For constitutional law cases, each state has its own constitutional court with jurisdiction over cases brought under the individual state constitutions. See Art. 92 et seq. of the Basic Law (Grundgesetz).

Chapter 2

Exercises pp. 200-201

1. a) facts of case (lines 13-41); b) legal history (lines 19-20; 42-56); c) issue on appeal (lines 6-11); d) holding (lines 154-156); e) ratio (lines 66-68; 74-76; 120-122; 126-130; 148-150)
2. The decisions of courts in the member states of the EU will be given full faith and credit in other member states under the European Convention on Jurisdiction and Enforcement of Judgments in Civil and Commercial Matters. If nations have not ratified treaties giving each other's judicial decisions full faith and credit, they may not be enforced outside the state in which they were reached. That of course is not true of the judicial decisions reached by courts within one single nation, such as Germany.
3. Most German-English/English-German legal dictionaries translate the terms as indicated here, but the point is to encourage discussion of the differences between the two systems because there is no perfect match for these terms.

Unit III

Chapter 1

Exercises p. 224

1. Answer is in the text of the opinion.
2. Marshall emphasizes the written nature of the U.S. Constitution, e.g. in line 116, which permits him to depart from the English tradition. Freedom of religion in Germany is drawn from the Weimarer Verfassung, for example (see Art. 140 of the Basic Law). The Basic Law does grant the Bundesverfassungsgericht the right of judicial review (see Art. 93 and Art. 100 of the Basic Law).

Exercises p. 233

1. Presumably the plaintiffs thought they would receive more objective treatment from a federal rather than a state court.
2. The defendants could have had the action **removed** to the federal court.
3. perpetually; there is no indication that any court ever granted a temporary injunction in this case.
4. Relief was denied on the basis of the separate but equal doctrine of *Plessy v. Ferguson*, which will be discussed later in the case.

Exercises pp. 234-235

1. At least two because the court is called the District Court for the Eastern District of South Carolina, meaning there is at least one more district, namely the Western District.
2. Factual difference: schools for blacks and whites were basically equal in Kansas but not in S. Carolina; factual similarity: in both states the schools were segregated
3. The District Court presumably did not grant the plaintiffs a temporary injunction, because it even "denied the plaintiffs admission to the white schools during the equalization program" (lines 36-37).

4.   See lines 27-43.

Exercises p. 239

1.   Constitutional guarantees on basic rights can be interpreted differently over time as so-
     ciety and societal values change. Accordingly, legislative intent seems less interesting in an
     equal protection case than it might be regarding a tax statute adopted last year.
2.   The lower state courts were bound by *Plessy v. Ferguson* to the extent they had to require
     facilities for blacks that were at minimum equal to those provided for whites. They were
     not bound in the sense that they could not have struck down segregation statutes, as indeed
     the Delaware court did, but they were not required to do so. The lower federal courts were
     bound by *Plessy* in both senses, because the federal courts could not interpret the constitu-
     tional guarantee broader than the U.S. Supreme Court had done. State courts can give a
     broader interpretation based on their own state constitutions, but cannot go lower than
     the minimum established by the U.S. Constitution as interpreted by the U.S.Supreme
     Court. Lawyers for the black cause used *Plessy* to gain at least equal facilities for African-
     Americans. Although the facilities remained segregated, they were improved.

Exercises p. 240

1.   Arguments will be given in the rest of the case, but students should attempt to argue the
     case themselves before reading further.
2.   A court usually states in the opinion that it is reserving decision on the particular question,
     or they indicate that they are not attempting to decide that issue now but may do so in
     some future case that presents it more directly.

Exercises p. 243

1.   If a child is not permitted by statute to go to a particular school then the child's liberty is
     being restricted without any trial or fair process in which a good reason is established for
     the restriction.
2.   The plaintiffs in *Bolling v. Sharpe* could not rely on the equal protection clause of the
     Fourteenth Amendment because the Fourteenth Amendment applies only to the states and
     Washington D.C. is not a state. They relied on the Fifth Amendment, which does not
     contain an equal protection clause but does contain the due process clause. The cases in
     Unit I involved the opposite problem. The Bill of Rights applies to citizens' rights against
     the federal government and not against the individual state governments. To use the Bill of
     Rights to one's benefit against state action, one has to argue that the Fourteenth Amend-
     ment's guarantee of due process extends the rights contained in the Bill of Rights to protect
     individuals from state action. Review discussion following *Williams v. Florida* in Chapter
     2 of Unit I.
3.   facts of the cases (lines 13-74); legal history (lines 14-26; 28-43; 45-56; 58-74); issue on
     appeal (lines 134-137); holding (lines 159-166); ratio (lines 151-159).

Exercises p. 254

1. Facts of the case in lines 6-16; legal history of the case in lines 18-30; issues raised on appeal
in lines 43-54; holding in lines 30, 221-222; ratio decidendi in lines 72-73, 115-119, 129-132,
158-160, 202-203, 217-221.

2. A law is unconstitutional on its face if for every conceivable application of the law it would be struck down. Although in *Texas v. Johnson* the Supreme Court has held only that the Texas statute was unconstitutional as applied to Johnson, the ratio decidendi of the case leaves little doubt that all similar statutes regardless of how applied would also be found unconstitutional. Consider the aftermath of *Texas v. Johnson*:

> "The decision in Johnson elicited considerable public criticism. Soon after the decision, and after outraged floor speeches, the House and Senate passed, by overwhelming votes, resolutions disagreeing with the ruling and pledging to seek means to restore penalties for "such reprehensible conduct." In short order, the battle lines were drawn between those in Congress who wanted the Constitution amended to permit restraints on flag desecration and those who supported new legislation rather than a constitutional amendment. President Bush strongly supported the amendment approach, and many of those who agreed with him believed that any new federal law would meet the same fate in the Court as did the Texas law in Johnson. But others (including many liberal Democrats) believed that a carefully drawn statute might be upheld, and that this would forestall the pressure for a constitutional amendment. Several constitutional scholars, including Laurence Tribe, Rex Lee and Geoffrey Stone, testified before Congress that a flag-burning statute might be drafted so as to pass constitutional muster ... The statutory strategy prevailed, and the Flag Protection Act of 1989 was adopted by overwhelming majorities in each House. The bill became law without the President's signature. The new law was immediately and publicly violated in order to challenge its constitutionality. The result was the 1990 Eichman case, ... [which stuck down the statute as unconstitutional under the First Amendment].
>
> The decision in Eichman spurred a renewed campaign for a constitutional amendment, but the proposed amendment that reached the floor of both Houses in 1990 fell 34 votes short of the required two-thirds majority in the House and nine votes short in the Senate. A 1995 version of the proposed amendment fared better, passing by a vote of 312-120 in the House but falling three votes short in the Senate, which voted for the amendment 63-46 ..."

G. Gunther / K. Sullivan, *Constitutional Law*, 13th ed., The Foundation Press, Inc.: New York (1997) pp.1228-1230.

3. It is fairly obvious that § 90a. of the German Penal Code would be unconstitutional under the holding in *Texas v. Johnson*, particularly because § 90a.(1) 1., 2. are directly aimed at expression rather than conduct. Arguably, subsection (2) is aimed at conduct that destroys public property, but since the subsection does not relate to public property in general but rather to public property that symbolizes the state and its principles, it too would suffer from the defects noted in *Johnson*.

4. In *Johnson* the Supreme Court applied the strict scrutiny test and not the *O'Brien* test or the rational basis test. To determine whether the strict scrutiny test applies in cases involving speech through expressive conduct one has to first determine whether the state's interest in passing the statute in question is related to the suppression of free expression. If it is not, then the *O'Brien* test applies (lines 49-54). If it is, then one must ask whether the state's interest, although related to the suppression of free expression, still justifies conviction under the statute (lines 134-135) using the strict scrutiny test (lines 144-146).

Bibliography

Cases

Anderton v. Ryan [1985] A.C. 560; [1985] 2 W.L.R. 968; [1985] 2 All E.R. 355 10

Apodaca v. Oregon, 406 U.S. 404 (1972) 51

Ballew v. Georgia 435 U.S. 223, 98 S.Ct. 1029, 55 L.Ed.2d 234 (1978) 48

Batson v. Kentucky 476 U.S. 79, 106 S.Ct. 1712, 90 L.Ed.2d 69 (1986). 62, 174

Bolling v. Sharpe, 347 U.S. 497, 74 Sup.Ct. 693, 98 L.Ed. 884 (1954) 243

Brown v. Board of Education, 347 U.S. 483, 74 Sup. Ct. 686, 98 L.Ed. 873 (1954) . . . 227

Burgett v. Texas, 389 U.S. 109 (1967) 143

Edmonson v. Leesville Concrete Co., Inc., 111 S.Ct. 2077 (1991). 65

Gebhart v. Belton, 344 U.S. 891 (1952) [granting cert.] 236

Georgia v. McCollum, 112 S.Ct. 2348 (1992). 65

Gideon v. Wainwright, 372 U.S. 335 (1963) 138

Goldfarb v. Virginia State Bar, 421 U.S. 773 (1975) 90, 97

James B. Beam Distilling Co. v. Georgia 111 S.Ct. 2439 (1991) 149

J.E.B. v. Alabama ex rel. T.B., 114 S.Ct. 1419 (1994) 65

Johnson v. Louisiana, 406 U.S. 356 (1972) 51

Kitchens v. Smith, 401 U.S. 847, 91 S.Ct. 1089 (1971) 143

Linkletter v. Walker, 381 U.S. 618, 85 S.Ct. 1731, 14 L.Ed.2d 601 (1965) 137

London Tramways v. London City Council [1898] A.C. 375 8

Loper v. Beto, 405 U.S. 473, 92 S.Ct. 1014, 31 L.Ed.2d 374 (1972). 143

Mapp v. Ohio, 367 U.S. 643, 81 S.Ct. 1684, 6 L.Ed.2d 1081 (1961) 137

Marbury v. Madison 5 U.S. (1 Cranch) 137, 2 L.Ed. 60 (1803) 218

National Hockey League v. Metropolitan Hockey Club, Inc., 427 U.S. 639 (1976) . . . 109

Plessy v. Ferguson, 163 U.S. 537 (1896) 237

Ploof v. Putnam 8 Vt. 471, 71 A. 188 (1908) 16, 103

Powers v. Ohio, 111 S.Ct. 1364 (1991). 65

Practice Statement (Judicial Precedent) [1966] 3 All E.R. 77. 8

Regina v. Smith (Roger) [1975] A.C. 476 9

Regina v. Shivpuri [1987] A.C. 1 11

Roe v. Wade 410 U.S. 113, 93 S.Ct. 705, 35 L.Ed.2d 147 (1973)   146

Sanders v. State, 234 Ga. 586, 216 S.E.2d 838 (1975).   51

Schenck v. United States 249 U.S. 47, 39 S.Ct. 247, 63 L.Ed. 470 (1919)   247

Teague v. Lane 489 U.S. 288, 109 S.Ct. 1061, 103 L.Ed.2d 334 (1989)   144

Texas v. Johnson, 491 U.S. 397, 109 S.Ct. 2533, 105 L.Ed. 2d 342 (1989).   247

United States v. O'Brian 391 U.S. 367 (1968)   250

Vincent v. Lake Erie Transportation Co. 109 Minn. 456, 124 N.W. 221 (1910)   19

Williams v. Florida 399 U.S. 78, 90 S.Ct. 1893, 26 L.Ed.2d 446 (1970)   42

World-Wide Volkswagen Corp. v. Woodson, 444 U.S. 286, 100 S.Ct. 559, 62
    L.Ed.2d 490 (1980)   194

Legislative Materials

Criminal Attempts Act 1981 § 1   9

Judiciary Act of 1789, Sec. 13 . . . .   218, 221

Model Penal Code, § 212.3 False Imprisonment   74

Model Penal Code, § 221.1 Burglary.   73

Model Penal Code, § 222.1 Robbery.   55

Model Penal Code, § 223.6 Receiving Stolen Property   73

Oklahoma's long-arm statute.   196

§ 904 BGB.   22

§§ 666, 675 BGB.   28

§§ 325, 326 BGB.   29

§ 607 BGB.   29

§§ 985, 987 et seq. BGB   29

§§ 916 et seq. ZPO   29

§ 823 BGB.   29

§ 992 BGB.   29

§ 242 BGB.   34

§ 90a StGB.   261

Sherman Antitrust Act   90

Treaty establishing the European Economic Community, Art. 2   153

Treaty establishing the European Economic Community, Art. 3   154

U.S. Code, Title 28, Part IV, Chapter 81 § 1251   173

U.S. Code, Title 28, Part IV, Chapter 81 § 1253   232

U.S. Code, Title 28, Part IV, Chapter 81 § 1257   174

U.S. Code, Title 28, Part IV, Chapter 85 § 1330   186

U.S. Code, Title 28, Part IV, Chapter 85 § 1331 186
U.S. Code, Title 28, Part IV, Chapter 85 § 1332 187
U.S. Code, Title 28, Part IV, Chapter 85 § 1333 187
U.S. Code, Title 28, Part IV, Chapter 85 § 1345 187
U.S. Code, Title 28, Part IV, Chapter 89 § 1441 188
U.S. Code, Title 28, Part IV, Chapter 155 § 2281 231
U.S. Code, Title 28, Part IV, Chapter 155 § 2284 231
U.S. Constitution, Art. I Sec. 8. 153
U.S. Constitution, Art. I Sec. 9. .... 141, 153, 225
U.S. Constitution, Art. I Sec. 10. 225
U.S. Constitution, Art. III Sec. 1 .... 171, 217
U.S. Constitution, Art. III Sec. 2 217
U.S. Constitution, Art. III Sec. 3 .... 217, 225
U.S. Constitution, Art. IV Sec. 1 199
U.S. Constitution, Amendment I 247
U.S. Constitution, Amendment IV 138
U.S. Constitution, Amendment V 39
U.S. Constitution, Amendment VI 41, 183
U.S. Constitution, Amendment VII 41
U.S. Constitution, Amendment XI. 217
U.S. Constitution, Amendment XIII. 227
U.S. Constitution, Amendment XIV 45, 227
U.S. Constitution, Amendment XV 227

Executive Materials

Attorney General's Guidelines on Exercise by the Crown of its Right of Stand-by
    (1989) 88 Cr App R 123 67

Secondary Literature

George P. Fletcher, A Crime of Self-Defense. Bernhard Goetz and the Law on Trial ... 82
G. Hazard, Jr./C. Tait/W. Fletcher, Pleading and Procedure: Cases and Materials,
    7th ed 80, 106, 180, 190
Jeffrey Abramson, We, the Jury 68
Smith and Bailey on the Modern English Legal System 31
G. Gunther/K. Sullivan, Constitutional Law, 13th ed 310

Encyclopedia and Dictionaries

Corpus Juris Secundum, vol. 15A "Common Law"   4

Black's Law Dictionary "aggravated battery"   149

Black's Law Dictionary "appearance"   195

Black's Law Dictionary "conversion"   30

Black's Law Dictionary "excise tax"   153

Black's Law Dictionary "injunction"   229

Black's Law Dictionary "res judicata"   154

Black's Law Dictionary "rule nisi"   220

Black's Law Dictionary "sheriff"   191

Black's Law Dictionary "unlawful assembly"   75

Black's Law Dictionary "venue"   201

Black's Law Dictionary "writ of mandamus"   221

Merriam Webster's Dictionary of Law "full faith and credit"   200

Terminology

Number after term indicates Unit and Chapter in which term originally appeared and was explained, e.g. (I.1) = Unit I, Chapter 1.

The terminology appearing in this book is defined *in the context* in which it appears in the texts. Some terms have more than one usage and the meaning depends on the context. You may therefore not treat this Glossary as an exhaustive dictionary. If you have a German legal term within a text you would like to translate into English, you should first look in a German-English dictionary of legal terms for the possible English equivalents. The quality of legal dictionaries varies considerably. You will find a recommendation of the better ones at the end of Chapter 1, Unit I. Once you have the English equivalents, you should check them in an English-English legal dictionary to find out their exact meaning within an Anglo-American legal system. In addition, it is helpful to cross-check the English terms by looking them up in the English-German part of the same legal dictionary you used to find the English equivalents originally. Most likely you will find several German terms indicated for one of the English terms. That should help you understand the possible contexts within which the terms may be used, particularly when translated into another language and another legal system. If you have an English term within a text you would like to translate into German, you probably will not need to do this last cross-check, because you are a native speaker of the German language and have training in German law. You will therefore know which German term to use if you understand the English term sufficiently. Suggestions for German translations of the following terms as they appeared in context are included, if at all feasible. Many terms simply cannot be translated because the two legal systems are different in a fundamental way. Sometimes approximations of terms are indicated with "ca." and sometimes a comparison is suggested or simply an explanation in German given.

abridgement of speech (III.3)	prohibition against free speech (**Beeinträchtigung der Redefreiheit**)
abuse of discretion (I.3)	unfair or unjust exercise of a decision maker's power over a situation; misuse of leeway to decide how to deal with a situation (**Ermessensmißbrauch**)
account (I.1)	common law form of action to force the defendant to give an explanation, or **account**, of how he has used the plaintiff's money which has been entrusted to his management or care (ca. **Klage auf Auskunft und Rechenschaftslegung**)

accusatorial system (I.3)	system of trial in criminal cases in which the judge is the primary gatherer of evidence at trial and works from a file the prosecutor collected on the defendant's guilt
the accused (I.2)	person who has been charged with a criminal offense (**Beschuldigter, Angeschuldigter**)
to acquit (I.1)	to find not guilty of a criminal charge (**freisprechen**)
acquittal (I.1)	a not-guilty judgment (**Freispruch**)
Act (I.1)	an enactment, a law that is in force (**Gesetz**)
act of God (I.1)	natural cause of some event; used to refer to natural catastrophes, as opposed to human actions, which cause damage (**höhere Gewalt**)
actionable (I.4)	of or relating to an injury for which a law suit may be maintained in the sense that the law supports the particular claim (ca. **einklagbar, gerichtlich verfolgbar**)
actions ex contractu (I.1)	law suit based on breach of an obligation voluntarily assumed in a contract (**Ansprüche aus Vertrag als Klagegrund**)
actions ex delicto (I.1)	law suit based on breach of obligation imposed by law and independent of any contractual relationship (**Ansprüche aus Delikt als Klagegrund**)
adjudication (I.3)	resolution of legal dispute in a court of law (ca. **richterliche Behandlung und/oder Entscheidung eines Falles in einem streitigen Verfahren**)
administration (III.3)	management of the executive branch of the government; collection of all persons working in the executive branch of government (**Verwaltung**)
administrative agency (I.3; II.1)	part of the executive branch of the government which is responsible for the enforcement of the law (**Verwaltungsbehörde**)
administrative court (II.1)	court with jurisdiction over cases arising under public law, executive orders or regulations; most common law systems do not have separate courts for administrative matters (**Verwaltungsgericht**)
admiralty jurisdiction (II.2; II.3)	power to hear cases that arose on the high seas, great lakes, or other navigable bodies of water; see also **maritime jurisdiction** (ca. **Seegerichtsbarkeit**)
admission (I.3)	agreement to the truth of a factual claim; usually contained in the defendant's answer and relating to the plaintiff's complaint (**Zugeständnis**)
adversary system (I.3)	system of trial in which the parties, as opponents, present evidence most favorable to their own view of the case in an attempt to convince either judge or jury of their right to prevail (U.K. **adversarial system**) (im Zivilrecht: **kontradiktorisches Verfahren**)

advocacy and communi- (U.K.) one of three heads offered as part of the Professional
cation skills (I.3)   Skills Course; teaches students to formulate arguments, nego-
                               tiate, get across their ideas to others (**Argumentations- und
                               Kommunikationsfähigkeiten**)

advocate (I.3)   a person who supports or defends s.o. or s.th.; often used for
                               lawyers within the adversary system (**Advokat**); **to advocate:** to
                               argue for s.th., to support or defend s.th. (**sich einsetzen für**)

affidavit (III.1)   sworn statement of facts (ca. **eidesstattliche Erklärung**)

to affirm (I.2)   to uphold, as an appellate court, the decision reached by a lower
                               court (**die Entscheidung aufrechterhalten**)

affirmation (I.2)   substitute for the oath, omitting the name of God (**Eid ohne
                               religiöse Beteuerung**)

agent to receive process   person appointed to accept process for another person; mostly
(II.2)   agents for companies doing business in various states (**Zustel-
                               lungsbevollmächtigter**); see also **process agent**

aggravated battery (I.4)   unlawful infliction of severe physical injury under circumstances
                               which make the act more serious (**aggravating circumstances**)
                               than a simple battery, such as through the use of a deadly wea-
                               pon (vergleichbar mit: **gefährliche Körperverletzung**)

allegation (I.1)   claim; used primarily in a legal context (**Behauptung**); **to allege**
                               (**behaupten**)

to allege (I.3)   to claim, to contend, to maintain that certain facts are true (**be-
                               haupten**)

to allow an appeal (I.1;   (U.K.) to decide an appeal in favour of the appellant (**der Revi-
II.2)   sion stattgeben**)

alternate juror (I.2)   juror in addition to the required number to constitute the petit
                               jury who attends the entire trial but actually participates in de-
                               liberation only if one of the regular jurors suddenly has to be
                               excused (ca. **Ersatzgeschworener**)

alternative dispute resolu- any non-judicial method of resolving disputes, such as **arbitration** (I.3)   **tion** (**außergerichtliche Streitbeilegung**)

American Bar Association   (*abbr* **ABA**) umbrella organization for all bar associations in the
(I.3)   U.S. (**amerikanische Anwaltskammer**)

amicus curiae (III.2)   friend of the court (pl. **amici curiae**); term used to refer to indi-
                               viduals, organizations, public officials, etc. who are not parties
                               to a law suit but who may have information of value to the court
                               when considering an appeal; **amici curiae** are invited by the
                               court to submit briefs, referred to as **amicus briefs** and to par-
                               ticipate in oral argumentation

amount in controversy   the amount for which the plaintiff sues the defendant (**Streit-
(I.2)   wert**); also called **value in controversy**

annotated (III.3)	commented on by including relevant cases, legislative history, etc. (**kommentiert, mit Anmerkungen**), e.g. **Texas Penal Code Annotated** (*abbr* **Ann.**) (**Kommentar zum Strafgesetzbuch von Texas**)
answer (I.1; I.3)	defendant's formal substantive response to the plaintiff's complaint (**Klageerwiderung**)
antitrust action (I.3)	law suit charging violation of the **antitrust laws** (**Klage in einer Kartellsache**)
antitrust law (I.3)	law prohibiting the formation of a cartel or anticompetitive practices (**Kartellgesetz**)
to appeal (I.1)	(U.S.) to turn to a higher court with the argument that a legal error occurred during the trial (**in die Revision gehen**); **on appeal**: during the appeal (**in der Revision**); (U.K.) appeals may be taken on points of law and fact, hence **to appeal** on points of law (**in die Revision gehen**); **to appeal** on points of fact (**in die Berufung gehen**); also **to appeal by way of case stated**: to appeal only on points of law from decisions of the Magistrates' Courts or the Crown Court in criminal cases to the Queen's Bench Division
appellant (I.1)	person bringing the appeal (**Revisionskläger** [Zivilrecht]; **Revisionsführer** [Strafrecht]);
appellate (I.1)	of or relating to an appeal, as the **appellate** court, meaning the **court of appeal(s)** (**Revisions-**)
appellate brief (I.3)	written document containing a short statement of the legal arguments supporting one party's position on appeal (**Revisionsantrag**)
appellate court (II.1)	intermediate court; considers only issues of law on appeal, namely errors that it is claimed the trial court made in the law; convenes with a panel of judges (usually three) and no jury; also called the **court of appeals** (U.S. **Revisionsgericht** [and *not* **Berufungsgericht!**]; U.K. **Berufungs-** oder **Revisionsgericht**)
appellate jurisdiction (II.1)	power of a court to hear cases after they have been decided by a lower court; power of review of lower court decisions for errors of law (**Zuständigkeit als Revisionsgericht**)
appellee (I.1)	the person against whom the appeal has been brought (**Revisionsbeklagter** [Zivilrecht]; **Revisionsgegner** [Strafrecht]); (U.K.) **respondent**
to apply for silk (I.3)	(U.K.) to file a request with the Lord Chancellor to be reviewed and recommended to the reigning monarch for appointment as QC or KC (**die Bestellung durch die Königin / den König beantragen**)
arbitration (I.3)	non-judicial method of resolving dispute between two parties whereby one or more **arbitrators** hear the parties' version of the

	problem and seek a solution based more on permitting the parties to save face and continue in their relationship rather than on determining their individual rights and providing the basis for discontinuation of the relationship (**Schiedsgerichtsbarkeit**)
armed robbery (I.4)	robbery committed with the use of a weapon (**Raub mit Waffen**)
array (I.2)	prospective jurors summoned to court for selection for jury duty, also called the **venire**, or: (U.K.) **panel** (ca. **Gesamtheit der möglichen Geschworenen**)
arrest warrant (I.2)	formal document issued by judge permitting police to take s.o. into custody (**Haftbefehl**)
assailant (I.1)	s.o. who assaults another person (ca. **Angreifer**)
to assault (I.1)	to attack or threaten s.o. (ca. **angreifen**); an assault is a criminal offense and a tort; tort of intentionally causing the victim to fear that he will be harmfully or offensively touched physically on the instant occasion (**Bedrohung**)
to assert jurisdiction (II.2)	to take control over a case and over the parties to the case as a court of law (**die eigene Zuständigkeit annehmen**)
to assess fees (I.3)	(U.K.) to establish as a court the appropriate fees for a solicitor's work involving litigation (**Anwaltsgebühren festsetzen**)
assets (II.1)	total of one's property rights and claims against others (**Vermögen**); contrast to **liabilities**
assistant solicitor (I.3)	(U.K.) beginning solicitor within a law firm who is not yet partner of the firm (**Solicitor bei Beginn seiner Tätigkeit**)
associate justices (II.1)	all judges on a court of appeals other than the head judge (**beisitzende Richter**)
associate solicitor (I.3)	(U.K.) more experienced solicitor than an assistant within a law firm before becoming partner
assumpsit (I.1)	common law form of action for damages to compensate for the defendant's failure to perform as promised under a simple contract; (ca. **Klage auf Schadensersatz wegen Nichterfüllung**) whereby the promise may be implied by law (**general assumpsit**) or expressly made by the defendant (**special assumpsit**)
attempt (I.1)	trying to do s.th. that is criminally prohibited but being unsuccessful in actually bringing about the prohibited harm (**Versuch**)
attorney (I.3)	lawyer who is actually practicing law (as opposed to e.g. a professor or judge (**Rechtsanwalt**)
Attorney General (III.2)	the lawyer who represents a state or nation, as the **Attorney General of the United States,** who is also the head of the Justice Department, and the **Attorneys General** of the individual states in the U.S. (ca. **Justizminister und Generalstaatsanwalt**)
avenue of appeal (I.4)	possibility to go to a higher court with a claim that a legal error has occurred in a lower court (**Rechtsweg**)

averment (I.1)   claim; used primarily in legal context to refer to a claim contained in the plaintiff's complaint or the defendant's answer to the complaint (**Behauptung**); **to aver** (**behaupten**)

Bachelor of Arts / Bachelor of Science (I.3)   (*abbr* **B.A.** or **B.S.**) first university-level academic degree (**Baccalaureus Artium, Baccalaureus Scientiarum**)

Bachelor of Laws (I.3)   (*abbr* **LL.B.**) academic degree awarded on the successful completion of a three-year course of legal studies at an English university (**Baccalaureus Legum**)

banking (I.3)   department of a law firm which focuses on negotiating financial agreements and preparing the necessary documents for financing (**Abteilung für Bankwesen**)

bar (I.3)   group or class of practicing lawyers within a particular jurisdiction, e.g. the California bar, the American bar (**die Anwaltschaft**)

to bar (I.4)   to hinder, to prohibit (**ausschließen**); **to be barred**: to be prohibited (**ausgeschlossen sein**)

bar association (I.3)   professional organization of lawyers, responsible for monitoring attorney's conduct (**Rechtsanwaltskammer**)

bar examination (I.3)   state licensing examination for lawyers who intend to practice law within the jurisdiction (**juristisches Staatsexamen**)

bar review course (I.3)   privately offered cram course to help students study for and pass the **bar examination** (**Repetitorium**)

Bar Vocational Course (I.3)   (U.K.) (*abbr* **BVC**) one-year graduate course of legal education to prepare student to become a **barrister** (**juristisches Aufbaustudium**)

barrister (I.3)   (U.K.) lawyer specialised in litigation rather than in the office type of legal work as the **solicitor**

Batson Challenge (I.2)   challenge to the other party's peremptory challenge with the argument that the other party has exercised the peremptory challenge on the basis of the prospective juror's race and thus should not be permitted (**Einspruch gegen einen Antrag auf Ablehnung eines Geschworenen mit der Begründung, der Antrag sei nur wegen der Rasse gestellt, der der Geschworene angehört**)

battery (I.4)   crime of unlawful infliction of severe physical injury (**Körperverletzung**)

the bench (I.2)   term used to refer to a judge or to judges in general (ca. **Gesamtheit der Richter**)

between party assessment (I.3)   (U.K.) court's assessment of the winner of a law suit's costs to be paid by the losing party (**Festsetzung der Anwaltskosten der im Prozeß obsiegenden Partei**)

beyond a reasonable doubt (I.3) standard of proof in a criminal case (U.K. **beyond all reasonable doubt**) meaning that the factfinder must be so convinced of the defendant's guilt that no rational, reasonable doubt regarding that guilt remains (ca. **ohne vernünftigen Zweifel**)

bond (I.1)
instrument of security for a debt; document indicating existence of a debt and agreement to repay which is secured by a mortgage (**Schuldschein verbunden mit der Bewirkung einer Sicherheitsleistung**)

breach of the peace (I.2)
criminal offense of disturbing the public order (ca. **Störung der öffentlichen Ruhe und Ordnung**)

brief (III.2)
document containing legal argumentation of a case submitted to an appellate court when an appeal is filed or a petition for a writ of certiorari is made (**Revisionsbegründung**)

brief fee (I.3)
(U.K.) barrister's fee for preparation of a case for litigation and for the first day in court (**Prozeßvorbereitungs- und Prozeßführungskosten für den ersten Tag vor Gericht**)

to bring s.o. to trial (I.2)
to file charges against s.o. in a court of law; usually used in the criminal law context (**anklagen**); also **to charge s.o. with an offense**

burden of persuasion (I.3)
another term for **burden of proof** (**Beweislast**); see also **onus of proof**

burden of proof (I.2)
obligation to offer enough evidence to prove the facts relevant to the legal claim (**Beweislast**); **the burden of proof shifts** to the other party when the person making the claim has established a prima facie case (**Umkehr der Beweislast**)

Bush administration (III.3)
management of the executive branch of the government under the leadership of President George W. Bush (**die Bush-Regierung**)

business administration (I.3)
graduate course of study that prepares students for later work in business management, marketing, personnel, etc. (**Betriebswirtschaftslehre**)

business law and practice (I.3)
(U.K.) LPC course covering the law of company organisation, organisation of a firm, commercial relations (**Wirtschaftsrecht und Wirtschaftspraxis**)

canon law (I.1)
church law (**kanonisches Recht**)

capital case (I.2)
a criminal trial involving a crime which can be punished by death (ca. **Kapitalfall**)

capital crime (I.2)
a crime the commission of which is threatened with the death penalty (**Kapitalverbrechen**)

case at bar (III.2)
the case the court is considering at the moment; also the **instant case** (**der vorliegende Fall**)

case in chief (I.3)
main part of a party's presentation of evidence (as opposed to the presentation of evidence on **rebuttal** (**Hauptvorbringen**))

cases on collateral review (I.4)
law suits in which a party attacks a court judgment outside the normal appellate process (**wiederaufgenommene Verfahren**)

cases pending on direct review (I.4)
law suits in which the parties are still involved in appealing the decisions of lower courts (**anhängige Verfahren**); cases that are not yet final or **res judicata** (**rechtskräftig**)

cause of action (I.1; I.3)
set of facts that permit a person to file a law suit against s.o. else (**Klagegrund**)

challenge for cause (I.2)
formal request by a party to a law suit that the judge dismiss a juror for certain specified reasons or causes relating to the juror's ability to be fair at the particular trial (ca. **Antrag auf Ablehnung eines Geschworenen wegen Befangenheit**)

challenge to the array (I.2)
formal request to dismiss the entire array or venire because of the jury commissioner's incorrect method of selection; also called: **motion to quash the venire, motion to quash the panel, motion to quash the array** (ca. **Antrag auf Ablehnung der Gesamtheit der Geschworenen**)

Chancery Division (II.2)
(U.K.) court of general jurisdiction over intellectual property cases, equity, insolvency, company law, and probate cases (**Abteilung des High Court of Justice für geistiges Eigentum, Billigkeitsentscheidungen, Insolvenzfälle, Gesellschaftsrecht und Nachlaßsachen**)

charge given by the trial court (I.1)
the trial court judge's instructions to the jury on the law (ca. **Belehrung der Geschworenen**)

charges (I.1)
formal legal claims made against s.o. (criminal law: **Anklagepunkte**; civil law: **Ansprüche**)

chattels (I.1)
movable property (**Fahrnis, bewegliche Sachen**); also referred to as **personal property, movables, personalty**; contrasted to **real property** or land and things attached to it (**Liegenschaften**)

chief justice (II.1)
the head judge of a supreme court (**Gerichtspräsident**)

child custody (I.3)
right to care, maintain, and supervise a child; on divorce the probate court will award custody rights to one of the parents (**Sorgerecht**)

circuit (II.1)
an area over which a U.S. Court of Appeals has jurisdiction to hear appeals from its district courts (**Kreis, der aus mehreren Gerichtsbezirken besteht**)

Circuit Court (II.1)
one name for state trial court of general jurisdiction (vgl. **Landgericht**)

City Hall (III.3)
the building which houses the administration of a city (**Rathaus**)

civil actions (I.1)
law suits based on theories of private law (**privatrechtliche Ansprüche als Klagegrund**)

Civil Code (I.1)
translation of the German **Bürgerliches Gesetzbuch** or the French **Code civil**

Civil Division (II.2)	the half of the Court of Appeal responsible for hearing appeals from the trial courts of general and limited jurisdiction in private and public law suits, namely from the county courts and from the High Court of Justice (**Zivilsenat des Revisionsgerichts**)
civil law system (I.1)	a system of law, such as the legal systems of continental European nations, with a strong Roman law tradition and the main source of law in written codes
civil procedure (I.3)	area of law dealing with the requirements of private litigation, e.g. how to initiate a law suit, jurisdiction of the courts, etc. (**Zivilprozeßrecht**)
claim barred by procedural requirements (I.4)	law suit may not be brought because of some defect in the manner in which the claim has been filed, rather than because of substantive legal problem (**die Klage ist unzulässig**)
claim barred by res judicata (I.4)	law suit may not be brought because a final judgment has already been reached in the same case (**die Rechtskraft steht der Klage entgegen**)
claim barred by the statute of limitations (I.4)	law suit may not be brought because the period of time allowed by statute for filing the suit has already expired (**der Anspruch ist verjährt**)
claim barred by a statute of repose (I.4)	law suit may not be brought because the period within which the legal violation had to occur expired before the injury in fact did occur (**Anspruch, der erloschen ist**)
Class A offense (III.3)	offense in highest category of seriousness with respect to punishment threatened, e.g. Class A misdemeanor, Class A felony (**Straftat der Kategorie A**)
class action (III.2)	law suit filed by one or more plaintiffs on behalf of themselves and all individuals like them in the sense that they too have suffered from the same violation of their rights
Clayton Act (I.3)	antitrust act; addition to the Sherman Act prohibiting mergers, price discrimination, exclusive dealing if effect is to reduce competition (**Gesetz zur Ergänzung des Bundeskartellgesetzes**)
clear and present danger test (III.3)	test of constitutionality of a statute restricting speech that asks whether the state has a right to prevent the occurrence of some harm and whether the speech in question is likely to incite someone to cause that harm; if so then the speech can also be prohibited (**Test, ob eine Rede eine nicht bezweifelbare und gegenwärtige Gefahr für die Begehung von Straftaten schafft**)
to clerk for a judge (I.3)	to work for a judge as a young lawyer, usually immediately upon leaving law school (**als wissenschaftlicher Mitarbeiter bei einem Obergericht arbeiten**)
client (I.3)	person who hires a lawyer to represent him (**Mandant / Mandantin**)

closing argument (I.3)   final address to the jury in an attempt to sum up the evidence that has been presented during trial and convince the jury that one's own client should prevail in the law suit (**Schlußplädoyer**)

cloud (II.2)   a claim against another person's property, such as to secure a debt, or because one holds a lease on the property or right of way across the property (**Belastung**)

code (I.1)   organized and theoretically consistent treatment of an entire body of law (**Gesetzbuch**); **to codify**: to formulate a body of law in sections of a code (**kodifizieren**)

Code of Civil Procedure (I.3)   compilation of laws relating to the permissible manner of pursuing a law suit in court (**Zivilprozeßordnung**)

collateral attack (I.4)   means of challenging a court's decision that is separate from the normal trial-appellate process, e.g. through a petition for a **writ of habeas corpus** (**Antrag auf Wiederaufnahme eines Verfahrens**)

collateral review (I.4)   court's consideration of a collateral attack (**Wiederaufnahmeverfahren**)

college (I.3)   school within a university, e.g. college of law, college of medicine; if the college offers a program of undergraduate education it is called a college of liberal arts and can exist alone as an institution, or within a university (**Fakultät**)

commentary (I.1)   expert's analysis of the law including references to cases and legal theories (**Kommentar**)

Commerce Clause (I.4)   contained in Article I Section 8 of the U.S. Constitution; permits the U.S. Congress to regulate trade between the individual states

commercial cases (II.2)   law suits between merchants, or those who are in the business of selling goods or services (**wirtschaftsrechtliche Fälle**)

to commit a crime (I.1)   to act in a way, or to bring about a result that is criminally prohibited (**eine Straftat begehen**); **commission** as contrasted with **omission** means acting, as opposed to not acting, and thereby fulfilling the definition of a criminal offense (**Handlung - Unterlassung**)

to commit the defendant for trial (II.2)   to indict a defendant for trial at the crown court (**eine Anklage erheben und den Angeklagten an den crown court überweisen**)

committal proceedings (II.2)   proceedings in the magistrates' court to determine whether a defendant should be indicted for trial in the crown court (**Verfahren zur Klärung der Frage, ob der Angeklagte an den crown court überwiesen werden soll**)

common-law crime (I.2)   criminal offense under the principles of the common law rather than under any particular statutory enactment

common law system (I.1)	a system of law such as found in England and in countries influenced by England with the main source of law in the opinions of judges
Common Professional Examination (I.3)	(U.K.) (*abbr* **CPE**) name for the conclusion of the conversion course (**Abschluß des Umschulungskurses für den Anwaltsberuf**)
company law (II.2)	law governing business associations, i.e. firms, companies (**Gesellschaftsrecht**)
compelling state interest (III.3)	state goal that is absolutely necessary to pursue, state interest that is absolutely necessary to protect, e.g. public health (**zwingendes, übergeordnetes Staatsinteresse**)
compensatory damages (I.1)	primary common law remedy for breach of contract; puts non-breaching party in position he would have been had contract been performed (**Schadensersatz wegen Nichterfüllung**); primary remedy for tort; also **money damages**
complaint (I.1; I.3)	formal document setting forth the plaintiff's claims against the defendant to a private law suit (**Klage, Klageschrift**); the law suit is initiated by the plaintiff's filing the complaint with the appropriate court
compulsory areas (I.3)	(U.K.) mandatory or required subjects for the LPC; include conveyancing, wills probate and administration, business law and practice, litigation and advocacy (**Pflichtfächer**)
concurrent jurisdiction (II.1)	the power to decide a case as one of several courts with that same power over the subject matter of the case; a plaintiff may decide to initiate the law suit in any one of these several courts (**konkurrierende Zuständigkeit**)
concurring opinion (II.1)	the opinion of one or more judges who agree on the holding but not on the reasons for that holding (**Sondervotum, das eine in der Begründung abweichende Meinung eines Richters enthält**)
consent decree (I.3)	court order to which the parties to a law suit have agreed and which they have recognized as a just determination of their rights
consolidated opinion (III.2)	a court's decision for a group of cases that have been joined together and for which the court writes only one opinion (**Entscheidung in verbundenen Verfahren**)
constitutional law (I.3)	area of law dealing with the provisions of the **constitution**, which is the fundamental law of a nation and establishes the various branches or departments of the government, their powers, and guarantees civil and human rights (**Verfassungsrecht**)
consulting fee (I.3)	initial fee a lawyer charges for the time he expends in first meeting the client and hearing the alleged facts of the case (**Beratungsgebühr**)

to consummate a crime (I.1)	to act in a way that fulfills all of the elements of the definition of a criminal offense (**eine Straftat vollenden**)
contempt of court (I.2)	criminal offense of showing disrespect for the court; hindering the court in the administration of justice; can be punished with a fine or imprisonment (**Mißachtung des Gerichts**)
contention (I.1)	claim (**Behauptung**); **to contend**: to claim (**behaupten**)
contentious work (I.3)	legal services involving litigation (**juristische Dienstleistungen, die mit der Führung eines Prozesses verbunden sind**)
non-contentious work (I.3)	legal services not involving litigation (**juristische Dienstleistungen, die nicht mit der Führung eines Prozesses verbunden sind**)
contested divorce (II.2)	dissolution of marriage when partners are not in agreement over the division of their property or the custody of their children; also called defended divorce (**streitige Scheidung**)
contingency fee (I.3)	lawyer's fee that is charged only if the lawyer wins the case for her client; usually a percentage, currently between 33.3 and 50 percent, of what the client is awarded at trial (**Erfolgshonorar**)
contract (I.1)	agreement between two private parties, or between a private party and the state (**Vertrag**); term is *not* used for international agreements, which are called **treaties, conventions, agreements** (**Verträge**)
contract law (I.1; I.3)	the law of obligations as between two or more persons who have voluntarily entered into an agreement involving rights and obligations for each of those persons (**Vertragsrecht**)
conversion (I.1)	unlawful exercise of ownership rights over another person's property (ca. **Unterschlagung**)
conversion course (I.3)	(U.K.) one-year course of legal study to teach students who have completed a university program leading to the B.A. or the B.Sc., rather than the LL.B., the basics of law so that they can continue with practical legal education (**Umschulungskurs für den Anwaltsberuf**)
conveyancing (I.3)	(U.K.) LPC course covering the law of real property transfers (**Lehre von der Eigentumsübertragung**)
to convict (I.1)	to find the defendant in a criminal trial guilty of the offense charged (**für schuldig erklären**)
copyright (II.1; II.2)	intellectual property right protecting an author's ownership of his or her own creations from unauthorized use (**Urheberrecht**)
core subjects (I.3)	six areas of law that form the basics of first-level legal education in England (**Hauptfächer**)
corporate client work (I.3)	legal services aimed at the legal problems companies usually have (**juristische Praxis für Firmen**)
corporate hierarchy (I.3)	structure of responsibility and power within a corporation (**Hierarchie innerhalb einer Firma**)

corporate litigation (I.3)	trial in which at least one party is a corporation (**Führung eines Prozesses für eine Gesellschaft; Gerichtsverhandlung im Namen einer Gesellschaft**)
corporation (I.4)	legal entity organized under law with legal personality distinct from the personalities of its shareholders (**Aktiengesellschaft**)
costs follow the event (I.3)	(U.K.) costs are borne by the loser of the law suit (**Anwaltskosten werden von der unterlegenen Partei getragen**)
count (I.1; I.2)	a separate and distinct legal claim; one crime charged in the indictment (**Anklagepunkt**) or one civil law claim made in a complaint (**Anspruch**)
to countenance a presumption (III.3)	to permit one to conclude *sth*, to support an inference (**den Schluß erlauben, daß**)
counterclaim (I.3)	legal claim filed by defendant in response to plaintiff's complaint; statement of a cause of action against the original plaintiff in a case (**Widerklage**)
County Court (II.1)	one name for state trial court of general jurisdiction (vgl. **Landgericht**); also used as a name for a state trial court of limited jurisdiction (**Gericht mit beschränkter Zuständigkeit,** e.g. **Amtsgericht**); a **county** is a governmental unit in the sense of **Kreis** or **Landkreis**
county court (II.2)	(U.K.) trial court of limited jurisdiction responsible primarily for hearing private law disputes (**erstinstanzliches Gericht mit beschränkter Zuständigkeit**)
court clerk (II.2)	(U.K.) trained lawyer who advises the magistrates on the law (**wissenschaftlicher Mitarbeiter an einem Obergericht**)
court costs (I.3)	the price of having a court involved in resolving a legal dispute; usually the losing party to a law suit is required to pay the court costs for both parties (**Gerichtskosten**)
Court of Appeal (II.2)	intermediate court of appeal in England composed of a civil division and a criminal division (**Revisionsgericht**)
court of appeal(s) (I.1)	court on a level higher than the trial court, which considers issues of law and not of fact (**Revisionsgericht**)
Court of Chancery (I.1)	original court of equity
Court of Common Pleas (II.1)	one name for state trial court of general jurisdiction (vgl. **Landgericht**); original name of the court that heard legal disputes arising between the King's subjects; a **plea** (**Gesuch**), like **pleadings** (**Schriftsätze**), is a formal request addressed to a court
court of competent jurisdiction (I.4)	court with the power to decide a law suit; a court that has authority to decide a case (**zuständiges Gericht**)
court of first impression (II.1)	term used to describe a trial court because it is the first court to hear a case (**erstinstanzliches Gericht**)

court of last resort (II.1)	final court in a hierarchy of courts to which a party can turn on appeal (**letztinstanzliches Gericht**)
court of record (II.1)	court that keeps a detailed protocol of exactly what happened in a case
court reporter (I.3)	a court official responsible for recording testimony verbatim and preparing the transcript of the session (**Protokollführer**)
covenant (I.1)	common law form of action for **damages** to compensate for the defendant's failure to perform as promised under a contract which is written and has been **signed, sealed and delivered** to the plaintiff (ca. **Klage aus einem nach besonderen Formvorschriften geschlossenen Vertrag**)
Criminal Division (II.2)	(U.K.) the half of the Court of Appeal responsible for hearing appeals in criminal cases from the crown court (**Strafsenat des Revisionsgerichts**)
criminal law (I.3)	area of law dealing with violations of statutes for which punishment is imposed; also called penal law (**Strafrecht**)
criminal procedure (I.3)	area of law dealing with the requirements of criminal litigation and the rights of an accused (**Strafprozeßrecht**)
cross-complaint (III.2)	complaint filed by the defendant to a law suit against either the plaintiff or against any other person who is directly involved in the controversy (**Widerklage, Drittwiderklage**, bzw. **Streitverkündung**)
cross-examination (I.3)	questioning of a witness by the lawyer opposed to the lawyer who called the witness (**Kreuzverhör**)
to cross-examine (I.3)	to ask a witness who has been questioned by the opposing party questions related to the witness' testimony for the purpose of discrediting it (**ein Kreuzverhör vornehmen**)
cross-petition (III.2)	petition filed by the respondent to an appeal to a supreme court; the petitioner is the party filing the appeal, or petitioning for the writ of certiorari, and the respondent is the party against whom the appeal is filed, who may also raise a point to be considered on appeal in a **cross-petition** (ca. **Anschlußrevision**)
cross-section of the community (I.2)	group of people who represent all demographic aspects, such as income, educational and professional or vocational levels, race, gender, political opinion, religious persuasion, ethnic background, etc. of a particular area where they live (**Bevölkerungsdurchschnitt**)
crown court (II.2)	(U.K.) criminal court of general jurisdiction (**erstinstanzliches Gericht für Strafsachen mit unbeschränkter Zuständigkeit**)
custody (I.4)	security of and control over a person (**Haft**) or a thing (**Gewahrsam**)

damage (I.1)   harm caused the victim of a tort (**Schaden**)

damages (I.1)   money that the defendant has to pay the plaintiff for causing the plaintiff's injuries (**Schadensersatz**); to be distinguished from **damage**, which is the common word for harm; used in a tort and contract law context; **to recover damages**: to be awarded damages by a court to be paid by the defendant to a private law dispute for injury caused

de facto segregation (III.2)   separation of the races in fact, rather than as required by law (ca. **tatsächliche, aber nicht rechtlich vorgeschriebene Trennung der Rassen**)

de jure segregation (III.2)   separation of the races as required by law (ca. **rechtlich vorgeschriebene Trennung der Rassen**)

debt (I.1)   common law form of action to recover a specific sum of money the defendant owes the plaintiff (ca. **Zahlungsklage**)

decedents' estates (II.1)   **decedent** is the commonly used legal term for someone who has died, e.g. within the context of the law of inheritance (**Erblasser**); and in this context "**estate**" is the total amount of property left after death (**Nachlaß**); used together they identify an area of law relating to the administration of the estate after death but before it is distributed to the decedent's heirs and to the legal rules governing that distribution, including the law of last wills and testaments (**Erbrecht**)

decision on the merits (I.4)   a judgment that resolves the substantive claims of the parties and not one based on some procedural defect, such as lack of jurisdiction (ca. **Sachurteil**)

declaration (I.1)   another name less commonly used for **complaint** (**Klageschrift**)

defamation (I.2)   intentionally making false statement to injure another person's reputation; ridiculing a person in public; can be both a crime and a tort; if published it is **libel**; if spoken it is **slander** (**üble Nachrede; Beleidigung und Verleumdung**)

default judgment (I.3)   judgment entered against the defendant for failure to answer the plaintiff's complaint, or against either party for failure to proceed with the action as required (**Versäumnisurteil**)

defendant (I.1)   in a private law dispute, the person against whom a law suit has been brought (**Beklagter**); in a criminal case, the person who has been formally charged with a crime (**Angeklagter**)

defended divorce (II.2)   dissolution of marriage when partners are not in agreement over the division of their property or the custody of their children; also called contested divorce (**streitige Scheidung**)

defense (I.1; I.3)   (U.K. **defence**) anything a defendant to criminal or civil law charges can argue to his benefit (**Verteidigungsvorbringen**)

defense counsel (I.2) lawyer representing the defendant in either a civil case (**Prozeßvertreter**) or criminal case (**Strafverteidiger**)

Delaware corporation (I.4) corporation organized under the laws of the State of Delaware, a state which has particularly beneficial laws for corporations and thus a common state of incorporation

deliberation (I.2) the jury's consideration of a case in an attempt to reach a verdict (ca. **Beratung der Geschworenen**)

to deliver an opinion (I.2) to announce, as an appellate judge, the holding one has reached for a law suit on appeal and to give reasons for that holding (**ein Urteil verkünden**)

demurrer (I.3) motion for dismissal of the complaint because it fails to state a cause of action (**Antrag auf Klageabweisung wegen Unschlüssigkeit**)

denial (I.3) claim that a factual claim is false; usually contained in the defendant's answer and relating to the plaintiff's complaint (**Bestreiten**)

to deny (I.2) to reject or disagree, as a court, with a motion a party has made (**ablehnen**); or with a remedy a party seeks

to deny relief (III.2) to refuse to give the plaintiff the remedy she has filed suit to get (ca. **das Klagebegehren ablehnen**)

Department of Revenue (I.4) name used in some states for the tax office (**Finanzamt**)

deponent (I.3) person being questioned during a deposition (**der Befragte**)

to depose (I.3) to take the sworn testimony of a witness or party to a law suit during the pretrial discovery process (**befragen**)

deposition (I.3) oral interview of a witness or party to a law suit taken under oath and recorded by a court reporter in the presence of both parties (**mündliche Befragung zur Aufklärung der Beweislage**)

to deter (I.3) to keep *s.o.* from doing *sth*; to threaten *s.o.* with negative consequences for engaging in criminal behavior (**abschrecken**)

deterrence (I.3) one purpose or effect of punishment, namely preventing the commission of crimes (**Abschreckung**)

deterrent (I.3) *n. sth*, such as the threat of punishment, that has the effect of preventing *s.o.* from doing *sth* (**Abschreckungsmittel**); *adj* of or relating to a **deterrent**, having the effect of preventing certain conduct (**abschreckend**)

detinue (I.1) common law form of action to recover specific personal property, or the value of that property, which the defendant unlawfully **detains**, or refuses to give back to the plaintiff, who is the owner of the property, and for **damages** to compensate plaintiff for loss of use of property (ca. **Vindikationsklage, Herausgabeklage**)

dictum (I.1)

(pl. **dicta**) any comment or discussion in a judicial opinion that is not necessary for resolving the dispute in the case; often includes hypotheticals used for the sake of argumentation, analogies, legislative history; sometimes referred to as **obiter dictum** or **obiter dicta,** especially if the discussion goes far astray from the basis of the decision

to die intestate (I.3)

to die without leaving a will (**sterben, ohne ein Testament zu hinterlassen**)

to die testate (I.3)

to leave a will at death (**ein Testament hinterlassen**)

Diploma in Law (I.3)

(U.K.) another name for the conclusion of the conversion course (**Abschluß des Umschulungskurses für den Anwaltsberuf**)

direct appeal (II.1)

appeal from the decision of a trial court to a supreme court without first appealing to the intermediate court of appeals (**Sprungrevision**)

direct attack (I.4)

an appeal from a judgment within the normal appellate process (ca. **Anfechtung eines Urteils in einem noch nicht abgeschlossenen Verfahren**)

direct examination (I.3)

questioning of a witness by the lawyer who called the witness to testify (**Vernehmung eines Zeugen, den der vernehmende Anwalt selbst benannt hat**)

direct review (I.4)

a court's consideration of a **direct attack** within the normal trial-appellate process, for example on appeal

discovery (II.1)

also called **pretrial discovery;** evidence gathering phase which extends from the filing of the complaint to the beginning of the trial; gives each party the right to evidence in the possession of the other party (**Beweiserhebungsverfahren, in dem jede Partei ein Recht hat, Beweise durch Zeugenvernehmungen, Vorlage von Urkunden usw. zu erheben**)

discretion (I.2; I.3)

right or power to exercise judgment in making a decision independent of any exact rules on how to proceed (**Ermessen**); **discretion** is **abused** if the person exercising it acts unfairly or arbitrarily (**Ermessensmißbrauch**)

to dismiss an action (I.3)

judge's decision refusing to hear a case; court's rejection of a law suit (**eine Klage abweisen**)

to dismiss an appeal (II.2)

(U.K.) to decide an appeal in favour of the appellee (**die Revision abweisen**)

dissenting opinion (II.1)

the opinion of one or more judges in the minority of the court of judges hearing an appeal who do not agree on the holding the majority reached in the case (**Sondervotum, das eine im Ergebnis abweichende Meinung eines Richters enthält**)

distributor (II.2)   intermediate seller, sells to other wholesalers or to retailers, but not to the consumer (**Zwischen- oder Großhändler**); also **wholesaler**

district (II.1)   an area of a state over which a U.S. District Court has jurisdiction; each state comprises at least one and currently at most four districts (**Gerichtsbezirk**)

District Court (II.1)   one name for state trial court of general jurisdiction (vgl. **Landgericht**)

diversity jurisdiction (II.2)   power granted to the federal district courts to hear civil law disputes between citizens of different states, assuming the amount in controversy is more than $50,000 (**Zuständigkeit eines Bundesgerichts, weil die Parteien Einwohner verschiedener Bundesstaaten sind**); cases brought to the federal district courts on this basis are called **diversity cases**

divorce (I.3)   dissolution of marriage (**Scheidung**)

docket (III.2)   court's calendar of official business; calendar of dates set for hearing cases (**Terminkalender eines Gerichts**); a case is **restored to the docket** (**in den Terminkalender neu eingetragen**) when it is rescheduled for an additional hearing at a later date

to docket a case (III.2)   to register a case in the court's calendar of official business; to assign a specific date and time for a case to be heard by a court (**einen Rechtsstreit in den Terminkalender des Gerichts eintragen**)

domestic relations court (II.1)   court with jurisdiction over family law issues (**Familiengericht**)

double jeopardy (I.2)   to be endangered twice; refers to prohibition against trying s.o. twice for the same crime (**ne bis in idem**)

due process of law (I.2)   expression used in the U.S. Constitution to mean fairness in legal procedures (**Rechtsstaatlichkeit**); the due process guarantee is contained in the Fifth and Fourteenth Amendments and as a part of the Fourteenth Amendment is referred to as the **due process clause**

either-way offence (II.2)   criminal offence for which the defendant can decide whether to have the trial in the magistrates' court or in the crown court, also called hybrid offence (**Straftat, die entweder durch summarisches Verfahren oder durch Eröffnung einer Hauptverhandlung vor dem crown court zu beurteilen ist**)

ejectment (I.1)   common law form of action to recover possession of real property from the defendant who is in unlawful possession of it and for **damages** for loss of use of that land (ca. **Räumungsklage**)

elective (I.3)	non-required course at a university or within a course of studies (**Wahlfach**)
to enact (I.1)	to formally adopt a law and put it into force (**verabschieden**)
encumbrance (II.2)	a claim against another person's property, such as to secure a debt, or because one holds a lease on the property or right of way across the property (**Belastung**)
to enjoin (III.2)	to prohibit s.o. from doing s.th. (**eine einstweilige Verfügung erlassen**); the remedy is an **injunction** (**einstweilige Verfügung**)
equal protection of the laws (I.2)	expression used in the Fourteenth Amendment to the U.S. Constitution to mean that every U.S. citizen has equal rights; to distinguish this guarantee from other guarantees in the Fourteenth Amendment, it is referred to as being contained in the **equal protection clause** (**Gleichheitsgrundsatz**)
equity (I.1; II.3)	body of principles that developed to compensate for the rigidity of the common law; permitted the King's Chancellor to do justice in cases that could not be resolved justly under common law principles alone (**Billigkeit; Billigkeitsrecht; Recht nach Prinzipien von Treu und Glauben**)
to establish guilt (I.2)	to prove guilt (**die Schuld beweisen**)
estates and trusts (I.1)	another name for the law of inheritance (**Erbrecht**)
ethics and client responsibilities (I.3)	(U.K.) one of three heads offered as part of the Professional Skills Course; teaches students professional rules of conduct and their obligations toward clients (**Standesrecht**)
evidence (I.1)	proof offered at trial (**Beweismaterial**)
evidence (I.3)	title of required course in U.S. law schools; teaches students the law relating to the admission of evidence at trial (**Recht der Beweisführung**)
the evidentiary case (I.2)	the sum total of proof for or against s.o. who is a party to a law suit
evidentiary value (I.3)	value of *sth* as proof of what happened or of what the facts are (**Wert als Beweismittel**)
ex parte (III.2)	in the absence of a party to a law suit
ex post facto law (III.1)	a law passed after the fact, meaning after an act has been committed or an event occurred, which changes the legal evaluation of the circumstances retroactively; Art. I, Section 9 of the Constitution prohibits the federal government, and Art. I, Section 10 prohibits the individual state governments from passing any **ex post facto law** (**Gesetz mit Rückwirkung**)
excise tax (I.4)	any one of a number of taxes imposed on sales, property transfers, the manufacture of goods, etc.
exclusionary rule (I.4)	rule of evidence prohibiting the admission at trial of proof of the commission of a crime when the evidence has been gathered in

	an unreasonable search and seizure in violation of constitutional guarantees (**Beweisverwertungsverbot wegen unzulässiger Durchsuchung und Beschlagnahme**)
exclusive jurisdiction (II.1)	power of a court alone to hear a case exclusive of all other courts (**ausschließliche Zuständigkeit**)
executive branch (I.3)	branch of the government that is responsible for enforcing laws (**Exekutive**)
to exercise a challenge (I.2)	to make use of a right to object to a prospective juror or to the entire array of prospective jurors by requesting the judge to dismiss that person or the entire array (**einen Antrag auf Ablehnung eines oder aller Geschworenen stellen**)
to exercise jurisdiction (II.2)	to take control over a case and over the parties to the case as a court of law (**die eigene Zuständigkeit annehmen**)
exhibit (I.3)	physical object introduced as evidence at trial (**Beweisstück**)
expert witness (I.2; I.3)	a person who has expertise on an issue raised in a law suit, such as a medical doctor, who can provide this knowledge to the court (**Gutachter**); witness who is qualified to give an opinion in a court (**Sachverständiger**)
F.R.D. (I.3)	*abbr* **Federal Rules Decisions**, published collection of federal court decisions on the interpretation of the Federal Rules of Civil Procedure (**Sammlung bundesgerichtlicher Entscheidungen zur Regelung von Verfahren**)
factfinder (I.2; I.3)	the person or body responsible for determining the facts of a case from the evidence presented at trial; it is the jury if a jury is used, otherwise the judge acts as the factfinder (**Richter oder Geschworenenbank, die für die Feststellung des Sachverhalts zuständig ist; Tatsachenrichter**)
facts of a case (I.1)	truths that directly relate to the issue raised in a law suit (ca. **Sachverhalt**)
false imprisonment (I.2)	crime of intentionally interfering with another person's freedom of movement (**Freiheitsberaubung**)
Family Division (II.2)	(U.K.) court of general jurisdiction over family law cases, particularly contested divorce cases (**Abteilung des High Court of Justice für Familienrechtssachen**)
family law (I.1)	the law of marriage, divorce, responsibilities to children (**Familienrecht**)
fast-track case (I.3)	(U.K.) case that is expected to be litigated within one day (**Schnellverfahren**)
federal question jurisdiction (II.2)	power granted to the federal district courts to decide cases raising legal questions under the Constitution, laws or treaties of the United States (**Zuständigkeit eines Bundesgerichts, weil sich eine**

Rechtsfrage mit Bezug auf das Bundesrecht stellt); cases raising such issues are referred to as **federal question cases**

Federal Rules of Civil Procedure (I.3)

rules governing the pretrial, trial, and post-trial process for the federal courts (*abbr* Fed.R.Civ.P.) (**Zivilprozeßordnung für die Bundesgerichte**)

federal system (I.2)

the legal system of the United States as opposed to the legal systems of the individual states (**System des Bundesrechts**)

felony (I.2)

a serious crime for which the prison term threatened normally exceeds one year (ca. **Verbrechen**)

financial and business skills (I.3)

(U.K.) one of three heads offered as part of the Professional Skills Course; covers commercial skills and financing arrangements (**Finanz- und Wirtschaftswesen**)

findings below (III.2)

refers to determinations made by a lower court before the case reached a higher court on appeal (**die Feststellungen der Vorinstanz**)

flag desecration (III.3)

physical destruction or maltreatment of a state flag (**Verunglimpfung der Flagge**)

flat fee (I.3)

lawyer's fee that is set, rather than calculated for hours of work, for a particular job, e.g. a day of representing the client in court (**festes Honorar**)

foreperson (I.2)

member of the jury selected to speak for the entire body (**Obmann**); also **foreman, forewoman**

form of action (I.1)

case specification at common law including factual, procedural and remedial elements and contained in a writ issued by the King's Chancellor, which a plaintiff had to purchase in order to file a private law suit; includes the actions of **account, assumpsit, covenant, debt, detinue, ejectment, replevin, trespass, trespass on the case** and **trover**, which today are merely referred to as **civil actions**

forum (II.2)

court (**Gericht**)

forum shopping (II.2)

looking around and choosing among several courts with **concurrent jurisdiction** to find the court most suitable for filing one's own cause of action

forum state (II.2)

state in which a court is located

The Framers (I.2)

the writers of the U.S. Constitution; also called the **Founding Fathers**

fraud (I.2)

tort and crime of knowingly false representation designed to induce reliance and cause the victim of the fraud to part with his property or rights (**Betrug**)

freedom of speech clause (III.3)

clause in the First Amendment guaranteeing that the state shall not enact laws that restrict a person's right to say what he wants (**Klausel in der Verfassung, die die Redefreiheit schützt**)

friendly witness (I.3)   a person who is expected to testify favorably toward the party who questions him (**Zeuge der eigenen Partei**)

full faith and credit (II.2)   clause in Article IV of the U.S. Constitution requiring each state in the United States to recognize and enforce all public acts, records, and judicial proceedings issued or conducted in one of the other states

fundamental right (III.3)   basic right, which enjoys the highest level of constitutional protection, e.g. freedom of speech (**schrankenlos gewährleistetes Grundrecht**)

general appearance (II.2)   coming to a court for the purpose of litigating a case, usually used to refer to a defendant who comes to court to defend against the substantive claims contained in the plaintiff's complaint and who thereby submits himself to the court's jurisdiction (ca. **vorbehaltlose Einlassung**); contrast to: **special appearance** (ca. **beschränkte Einlassung zum Zweck der Rüge formeller Mängel**)

general deterrence (I.3)   deterrence of society in general from committing crimes by punishing those who have committed them (**Generalprävention**)

general jurisdiction (II.1)   power of a court to hear any type of case as a trial court, regardless of the subject matter or amount in controversy (**unbeschränkte Zuständigkeit**); contrast to: **limited jurisdiction** (**beschränkte Zuständigkeit**)

general part (I.1)   the introductory book or part of a code in a civil law system containing basic sections that apply to the rest of the code provisions (**Allgemeiner Teil**); contrast to: **specific part**

general verdict (I.3)   jury's final decision in a case in favor of one of the parties to the law suit (**Wahrspruch, Spruch der Geschworenen**)

government (I.3)   the executive and legislative branches of the state, the state in general (**Staat**)

grade point average (I.3)   (*abbr* **GPA**) average grade attained during an educational program; computed by multiplying the value attached to the grade (A = 4.0, B = 3.0, C = 2.0, D = 1.0, F = 0) by the number of **credits** given for the course (1 hour of class per week for one semester is one credit) and dividing by the total number of credits received during the program (**Notendurchschnitt**)

graduate education (I.3)   program of study following completion of a bachelor's program, e.g. law or medicine (**Universitätsausbildung nach einem ersten Universitätsabschluß**)

grand jury (I.2)   body of traditionally 23 persons from the community which is responsible for determining whether an individual should be charged with a serious crime; contrast to: **petit jury**

grievance (I.1)   complaint, suffering, distress (**Beschwer**)

habeas corpus (I.4)   Latin: you may have the body

habeas corpus challenge   legal attack against constitutionality of a person's confinement
(I.4)   in prison (ca. **Antrag auf richterliches Gehör wegen der Verfas-
                                       sungswidrigkeit einer Inhaftierung**)

to hang out a shingle (I.3)   to begin working independently as a one-man law firm (**sich
                                       selbständig machen**)

heads (I.3)   (U.K.) main areas of study or emphasis during the Professional
                                       Skills Course (**Hauptfächer**)

heir (I.3)   *s.o.* who has a right to property left after another person's death
                                       (**Erbe**)

High Court of Justice   court of general jurisdiction that hears private and public law
(II.2)   cases; divided into three divisions, namely the Queen's (or
                                       King's) Bench Division, the Family Division, and the Chancery
                                       Division (**erstinstanzliches Gericht mit unbeschränkter Zustän-
                                       digkeit**)

high school (I.3)   secondary school of learning; usually includes grades 9-12 or
                                       10-12; on graduation the student receives the high school di-
                                       ploma (**Gymnasium, Oberschule**)

to hold (I.1)   (held, held) to make a determination which resolves a legal dis-
                                       pute (**für Recht erkennen**)

to hold s.o. liable (I.1)   to determine as a court that s.o. is responsible and must pay for
                                       damage caused (ca. **jemanden haftbar machen**)

holding (I.1)   the decision of a court that resolves the actual dispute before it
                                       (**Urteilstenor**); the part of the opinion that becomes a binding
                                       precedent, or principle of law, for the future; contrasted to **dicta**
                                       or **obiter dicta**, which are the additional comments, hypotheses,
                                       speculations, analogies, arguments of a court in the court's opin-
                                       ion and which are not binding precedents

hostile witness (I.3)   a person who has been called to testify by the opposing party; a
                                       person who is expected to testify unfavorably toward the party
                                       who questions him; also called **unfriendly witness** (**Zeuge der
                                       Gegenpartei**)

hourly fee (I.3)   fee a lawyer charges depending on how many "hours" she
                                       spends working on a legal problem for a client; usually recorded
                                       in terms of minutes and not full hours (**Stundenhonorar**)

House of Lords (I.1)   highest appellate court in England; term more commonly used
                                       to designate the upper house of the British Parliament

hung jury (I.2)   jury that cannot agree on a verdict; if the jury is hung, the judge
                                       will have to declare a **mistrial** and the trial has to be repeated

	with a new jury (**blockierte oder nicht entscheidungsfähige Geschworenenbank**)
hybrid offence (II.2)	criminal offence for which the defendant can decide whether to have the trial in the magistrates' court or in the crown court, also called either-way offence (**Straftat, die entweder durch summarisches Verfahren oder durch Eröffnung einer Hauptverhandlung vor dem crown court zu beurteilen ist**)
to impanel the jury (I.2)	to officially record the names of the individuals selected to serve on a petit jury (ca. **die Geschworenenliste zusammenstellen**)
to impeach a verdict (I.3)	to give a reason to believe that a verdict has not been reached properly (**Gründe dafür angeben, daß an einem Wahrspruch zu zweifeln ist**)
implicated on the record (III.3)	involved in a case as can be seen from reading the record (**ergibt sich aus den Gerichtsakten**)
impossible attempt (I.1)	the attempt to do s.th. that is criminally prohibited in a situation in which the criminally prohibited harm cannot possibly occur (**untauglicher Versuch**)
in banc (II.1)	as a whole court, describes method of hearing cases whereby all judges on the court convene together rather than in panels or groups of judges
incarceration (I.2)	imprisonment (**Haft**)
to incite (III.3)	to encourage *s.o.* to do *sth* (**anstiften**)
to incite a riot (III.3)	to encourage people to revolt or become very unruly (**zum Landfriedensbruch anstiften**)
incorporated (II.2)	to be organized under law as a corporation (**als Aktiengesellschaft eingetragen**)
to indict (I.2)	to charge an individual with a serious crime (**anklagen**); pronounced with a silent "c" as "in-dite"
indictable offence (II.2)	(U.K.) criminal offence over which the crown court has exclusive jurisdiction; more serious criminal offence (**Straftat, die nur vor dem crown court angeklagt werden kann**)
indictment (I.2)	formal document containing criminal charges against a defendant (**Anklageschrift**); pronounced "in-dite-ment"
infra (III.2)	see below; contrasted to **supra**, meaning: see above
infringement (II.1)	violation, usually of s.o.'s rights (**Verletzung, Rechtsverletzung**)
to inherit property (I.3)	to acquire ownership rights in real or personal property as a result of *s.o.'s* death (**erben**)
inheritance law (I.1)	the law governing property disposition on death, also called estates and trusts (**Erbrecht**)

in-house lawyer (I.3)   lawyer who works within a company on the company's legal staff (**Syndikus**)

injunction (I.1)   equitable remedy ordering a defendant not to do s.th. (ca. **gerichtliche Verfügung**); see also: **interlocutory injunction, permanent injunction, perpetual injunction, preliminary injunction, temporary injunction, temporary restraining order**

Inns of Court (I.3)   (U.K.) professional association of barristers responsible for providing barristers with sets of chambers, offering courses of legal education, and controlling admission to the Bar; include Gray's Inn, Lincoln's Inn, the Inner Temple, and the Middle Temple (**Vereinigungen der Barristers**)

inquisitorial system (I.3)   system of trial commonly used during the Middle Ages in which one person was both prosecutor and judge (**Inquisitionsprozeß**)

in rem jurisdiction (II.2)   court's power over property in dispute (**Gerichtshoheit über eine Sache**)

insolvency (II.2)   condition of having more debts than assets; results in dissolution of property and distribution to creditors (**Insolvenz**)

instant case (III.2)   the case the court is considering at the moment; also: **the case at bar** (**der vorliegende Fall**)

to instruct a barrister (I.3) (U.K.) to pass a case file on to a barrister to permit the barrister to prepare the case for litigation (**einem Barrister einen Fall anvertrauen**)

to instruct the jury on the law (I.2; I.3)   to explain, as a judge, the applicable law to the jury at the end of a trial in terms that lay persons can understand and apply to the facts as they determine them (ca. **die Geschworenen belehren**); jury instructions: the explanations of the law the judge gives at the end of the trial

intellectual property (II.2)   ownership rights over ideas, as opposed to physical objects; includes copyrights and patents (**geistiges Eigentum**)

intent (I.1)   a state of mind required by the law for holding a person responsible for the commission of a crime; indicates that the actor was aware of what he was doing and did it purposely (**Vorsatz**)

interlocutory injunction (III.2)   interim measure a court can take to prohibit a party to a law suit from engaging in some type of conduct until the court can reach a final judgment (**einstweilige Verfügung**)

Internal Revenue Service (I.4)   federal tax authority (**Finanzamt**); commonly referred to as the **IRS**

interrogative system (I.3)   system of trial common in civil law cases in continental European nations in which the judge is the primary gatherer of evidence at trial

interrogatory (I.3)   written list of questions addressed to a party to a law suit that have to be answered in writing under oath; one tool of discovery (**Fragenkatalog zur Aufklärung der Beweislage**)

involuntary servitude (III.2)   slavery, prohibited by the Thirteenth Amendment (**Sklaverei**)

issue in controversy (I.3)   legal question raised in a law suit, topic of dispute between the parties (**Streitfrage**)

issue of fact (II.1)   question about what actually happened in a case (**Tatfrage**)

issue of law (II.1)   question about what law to apply in a case or how to interpret that law (**Rechtsfrage**)

issue raised on appeal (I.1)   legal problem confronting an appellate court when deciding a case (ca. **Rechtsfrage in einem Revisionsverfahren**)

JD (I.3)   (*abbr* = **juris doctor**) degree awarded after completion of law school (**Doktor der Rechte, erster juristischer Grad**)

judgment (I.1)   judge's decision in a case (**Urteil**); (U.K.) judgement

judgment by default (I.3)   judgment against one of the parties for failure to proceed as required with the law suit (**Versäumnisurteil**)

judgment enforcement (II.2)   forcing a defendant to do what he is ordered to do in a final judicial decision (**Vollstreckung**); also **judgment execution**

judgment execution (II.2)   forcing a defendant to do what he is ordered to do in a final judicial decision (**Vollstreckung**); also **judgment enforcement**

judgment notwithstanding the verdict (I.3)   (*abbr* **j.n.o.v.**) judge's decision contrary to the conclusion reached by the jury in a trial; the test for granting a motion for a j.n.o.v. is to assume the evidence most favorable to the non-moving party is true and still decide as a matter of law that the moving party should prevail in the law suit; permits judge to control jury verdicts (**Urteil im Gegensatz zu dem Wahrspruch der Geschworenen**)

judgment on the merits (I.4)   judgment that resolves substantive claims of the parties and not one based on some procedural defect, such as lack of jurisdiction (ca. **Sachurteil**)

judgment on the verdict (I.3)   judge's decision based on the conclusion the jury reached in a trial; when the judge enters judgment on the verdict, the verdict receives legal effect (**Urteil in Übereinstimmung mit dem Wahrspruch der Geschworenen**

judicial review (III.1)   court's exercise of its power to consider the decisions of a lower court or of any branch of the government, in particular in light of their correspondence with the Constitution but also with established law (**gerichtliche Überprüfung**)

judicial sale (II.2)   method of enforcing a judgment by selling the defendant's property to satisfy the plaintiff's claims (**Zwangsversteigerung**)

judiciary (I.1)	branch of government responsible for hearing and deciding legal disputes (**rechtsprechende Gewalt**); a **judge** or **justice** (for higher courts) is the person who determines the rights of the parties to a law suit (**Richter**); **to judge:** to act as a judge in a case, to determine the rights of the parties to a law suit; **judicial:** of or relating to a judge, as in **judicial opinion** (**Urteil**)
junior (I.3)	(U.K.) barrister who is not QC; less experienced, less outstanding barrister (**junger Barrister**)
jurisdiction (I.2)	authority of a court to hear and decide a case (**Zuständigkeit**); **the court has jurisdiction** (**das Gericht ist zuständig**); the area over which a legal system is applicable, e.g. "the jurisdiction of California" means the State of California as a distinct legal system where California laws apply and are applied by California courts; see also: **appellate jurisdiction, diversity jurisdiction, exclusive jurisdiction, general jurisdiction, in rem jurisdiction, limited jurisdiction, original jurisdiction, personal jurisdiction, quasi in rem jurisdiction, subject matter jurisdiction, territorial jurisdiction**
jurors in waiting (I.2)	(U.K.) members of the jury panel (array) who have not as yet been sworn in to serve on the jury
jury box (I.2)	the rows of seats, usually two in number, around which walls are constructed and where the members of the jury sit during trial (ca. **Geschworenenbank**)
jury commissioner (I.2)	public official responsible for selecting prospective jurors for both the grand and petit juries; (U.K.) **summoning officer** (ca. **Beamter, der für die Auswahl der Geschworenen zuständig ist**)
jury instruction (I.1)	explanation by the prosecutor to the grand jury or by the judge to the petit jury on what the applicable law is (ca. **Belehrung der Geschworenen**); the judge **instructs the jury on the law**
jury nullification (I.2)	power jury has in a criminal case to ignore the law and acquit the defendant
a jury of one's peers (I.2)	expression used to emphasize the lay, or non-professional, nature of a jury composed of individuals who are like the parties to a law suit; a group of fair-minded individuals who are representative of the community in general
jury vetting (I.2)	(U.K.) investigation into prospective jurors' personal backgrounds for the purpose of enabling a lawyer to better select them for jury service; limited to the Attorney-General, who passes the information on to the prosecutor and defense counsel; also limited in scope to juror's criminal conviction record and a few other matters
justice (II.1)	judge, usually used for judges on a supreme court (**Richter**)

Justice Court (II.1)   one name for a state trial court of limited jurisdiction (**Gericht mit beschränkter Zuständigkeit, z.B. Amtsgericht**)

justice of the peace (III.1)   lower level court judge; judge on court of limited jurisdiction (**Friedensrichter**); usually empowered to perform marriages (**Standesbeamter**)

justification (I.1; I.3)   a good reason recognized by law for committing what otherwise would be a civil or criminal wrong; a justification negates the wrongfulness normally associated with conduct defined as a crime or tort and gives the actor a right to commit it (**Rechtfertigungsgrund**); examples include **self-defense** (**Notwehr**) and **necessity as a justification** (**rechtfertigender Notstand**)

justificatory defense (I.3)   defendant's claim that he had a good and legally recognized reason for what he did; defeats a plaintiff's claim in a private law suit and a criminal charge (**Rechtfertigung als Verteidigungsvorbringen**)

juvenile court (II.1)   court of limited jurisdiction with power to hear only cases involving **minors** (those under eighteen years of age) and usually relating to juvenile delinquency problems (**Jugendgericht**)

to keep term (I.3)   (U.K.) to attend twelve educational qualifying sessions at the barrister-student's Inn (**regelmäßig juristische Vorträge besuchen**)

knowingly and willfully (I.3)   with the intent to act under full awareness of the circumstances (**wissentlich und willentlich**)

labor court (II.1)   court with jurisdiction over disputes arising between employer and employee within the employment relationship (**Arbeitsgericht**)

land law (I.3)   law of real estate transfers from one person to another during life or after death (**Sachenrecht**)

landmark decision (I.2)   judicial opinion that significantly changes further development of the law (**bahnbrechendes Urteil**)

Law Commission (I.1)   committee of judges, lawyers and professors appointed to review the law, make proposals for reform and prepare draft codifications in an attempt to simplify the law and make it more consistent

law firm (I.3)   partnership of lawyers practicing together within one business organization (**Rechtsanwaltskanzlei**)

Law Lords (I.1)   judges of the House of Lords; also **Lords of Appeal in Ordinary**

law of obligations (I.1)   area of the law which includes contracts and torts (**Schuldrecht**)

law office (I.3)   office of a number of solicitors working within one business structure (**Rechtsanwaltskanzlei**)

Law School Admission Test (I.3)	(*abbr* **LSAT**) standardized test given to college graduates nationwide to determine their ability to study law; one of the more important scores on which admission to a law school is based (**Zulassungsprüfung für ein rechtswissenschaftliches Studium**)
lay assessor (I.2)	layperson who participates in the trials of most civil law systems (**Schöffe**)
lay witness (I.3)	witness who testifies as to what she saw or heard, but who is not qualified to give an opinion upon which a jury can base a decision (**Zeuge**)
layperson (I.2)	person who is not an expert (**Laie**)
to lead a witness (I.3)	to put words into a witness's mouth; to ask a question in a way that suggests or already states the answer (**suggestive Fragen stellen**)
leading question (I.3)	a question that is formulated to suggest or state the answer to that question (**Suggestivfrage**)
least intrusive means (III.3)	method employed to pursue state interest that is drawn as narrowly as possible to attain its goal (**mildestes Mittel**)
leave to amend (I.3)	permission granted by the court to a party to revise a pleading, usually the complaint after the court has sustained the defendant's demurrer (**Zulassung der Ergänzung oder Berichtigung eines Schriftsatzes**)
leave to appeal (II.2)	permission to file an appeal in a case granted by the court whose decision is being appealed or by the court to which the appeal is taken (**Zulassung der Revision**)
legal guardian (III.2)	someone who is responsible for the legal affairs of a person who does not have the capacity, because of age or any other reason, to govern his own legal affairs (**gesetzlicher Vertreter**)
legal history (of a case) (I.1)	disposition lower courts, such as the trial court and any intermediate appellate court, reached in a case (ca. **die Entscheidung(en) der Vorinstanz(en)**)
legal personality (I.4)	entity's ability to act with legal effect such that the entity is then subject to duties and can be attributed with violations of those duties; feature of a legal or juridical person (**Rechtspersönlichkeit**)
Legal Practice Course (I.3)	(U.K.) (*abbr* **LPC**) one-year course of graduate legal education to prepare for the profession of solicitor (**juristisches Aufbaustudium**)
legal representative (I.2)	a person who acts for s.o. else in legal matters, usually a lawyer (**juristischer Vertreter**); **to be represented by a lawyer** means to have a person trained in law act for you in legal matters
legislative (I.1)	of or relating to the legislature, as in **legislative enactment**

legislative history (III.2)   events, attitudes, cultural context surrounding adoption of a law (**Gesetzgebungsgeschichte**)

legislative intent (I.1)   purpose or reason legislature had for adopting a law (ca. **Wille des Gesetzgebers**)

legislator (I.1)   person who is a member of the legislature (**Abgeordneter**)

legislature (I.1)   one of three branches of government common to democratic republics; branch of government responsible for making law (**Legislative**)

legitimate state interest (III.3)   some goal or purpose that states generally have a right to pursue (**berechtigtes Staatsinteresse**)

lenity rule (I.3)   rule requiring a judge to resolve any statutory ambiguity in favor of the defendant (**in dubio mitius, Gebot restriktiver Gesetzesauslegung zugunsten des Angeklagten**)

lesser evils justification (I.3)   defense to a criminal charge based on the defendant's claim to have saved a higher-valued interest by sacrificing the lower-valued interest protected by the criminal norm he is charged with violating, also called justification of necessity, necessity as a justification (**rechtfertigender Notstand**)

liabilities (II.1)   total of one's obligations, debts, claims others have against oneself (**Verbindlichkeiten**); contrast to **assets**

liability (I.1)   responsibility in the legal sense; meaning person responsible has to pay for damage he has caused (**Haftung**); conclusion of a private law dispute determining that defendant has to pay for plaintiff's injuries; also used in a criminal context but only if specifically referenced, as **criminal liability**

libel (I.2)   tort of character **defamation** through writing, pictures, symbols, etc. that are published and serve to damage s.o.'s reputation; contrast to: **slander**

lien (II.2)   claim against another person's property, such as to secure a debt, or because one holds a lease on the property or right of way across the property (**Pfandrecht**)

limited jurisdiction (II.1)   power of a court to hear a case as a trial court which is restricted according to subject matter of case or amount in controversy (**beschränkte Zuständigkeit**)

litigant (I.1)   party to a law suit (**Partei**)

litigation (I.3)   presentation of one's case in a court of law for resolution of a dispute (**Prozeßführung**)

litigation and advocacy (I.3)   (U.K.) LPC course covering the skill of presenting and arguing cases in court (**Prozeßführung und Vertretung**)

litigator (I.3)   lawyer specialized in representing clients in court

long-arm statute (II.2)	law granting a court personal jurisdiction over individuals who are not physically within the court's geographical area of jurisdiction
Lord Chancellor (L.C.) (I.1; I.3)	head of the British judiciary and speaker of the House of Lords
Lord Chief Justice (II.2)	judge who presides over the Criminal Division of the Court of Appeal
Lords of Appeal in Ordinary (I.1)	judges of the House of Lords; also **Law Lords**
magistrates' court (II.2)	(U.K.) trial court of limited jurisdiction responsible primarily for hearing criminal cases involving less serious crimes and family law cases that are uncontested (**erstinstanzliches Gericht mit beschränkter Zuständigkeit**)
major (I.3)	main field of study during undergraduate education (**Hauptfach**)
majority opinion (II.1)	written decision of the simple majority of judges who hear an appeal; majority opinion contains the holding of the case and the reasons for that holding; it is the majority opinion that is decisive for the precedent of the case (**Mehrheitsvotum**)
to make a prima facie case (I.3)	to provide reasonable evidence of each element of a cause of action such that if the other party remains silent one will win the law suit (**Beweise, die die Schlüssigkeit der Klage nachweisen**)
malicious prosecution (I.2)	tort of causing criminal charges or civil proceedings to be brought against s.o. without good reason and for the purpose of harming that person
maritime jurisdiction (II.2)	power granted to the federal district courts to hear cases that arose on the high seas, great lakes, or other navigable bodies of water (ca. **Seegerichtsbarkeit**); see also **admiralty jurisdiction**
Master of the Rolls (II.2)	(U.K.) judge who presides over the Civil Division of the Court of Appeal
member of professional chambers (I.3)	(U.K.) barrister practising law within a set of chambers (**Mitglied einer Bürogemeinschaft**)
memorandum opinion (I.3)	judicial opinion indicating what decision the court reached and what orders it issued but not including any argumentation for its conclusions (**verkürzte Entscheidung ohne Angabe von Gründen**)
mental examination (I.3)	medical examination conducted by a psychiatrist or psychologist to determine a person's mental capacities; one tool of discovery (**psychiatrische oder psychologische Untersuchung**)
mergers and acquisitions (I.3)	(*abbr* **M&A**) department of a law firm which focuses on preparing the documents and agreements necessary to bring about the

purchase of one firm by another (acquisition) or the combination of two firms into one (merger) (**Fusionen und Übernahmen**)

minimum fee schedules (I.3) lists of minimum amounts a lawyer is permitted to charge for specified legal services; usually established by the bar association responsible for the particular lawyer; considered to be illegal price fixing in the United States; see Appendix II for U.S. Supreme Court's decision in *Goldfarb v. Virginia State Bar* (**Bundesanwaltsgebührenordnung oder Anwaltsgebührenordnungen der Einzelstaaten**)

misdemeanor (I.2) a less serious crime for which a prison term of not more than one year is threatened (ca. **Vergehen**)

mistrial (I.2) legally invalid trial that has no legal consequences (ca. **aus Formgründen ungültiges Verfahren**)

money damages (I.1) primary common law remedy for breach of contract; puts non-breaching party in position he would have been had contract been performed (**Schadensersatz wegen Nichterfüllung**); primary remedy for tort; also **compensatory damages**

mortgage (II.2) type of **lien** against property; security for creditor's claim for repayment of a debt; secured by giving creditor a right to sell property to satisfy debt if debtor defaults (**Hypothek**)

motion (I.2) formal request addressed to judge in a law suit (**Antrag**); one **files** or **makes** a motion (**einen Antrag stellen**)

motion for a directed verdict (I.3) plaintiff's or defendant's formal request addressed to the court to decide the case as a matter of law rather than give it to the jury to decide; motion asks judge to believe the evidence most favorable to the non-moving party but to still decide as a matter of law that the moving party should prevail in the law suit (**Antrag auf Klageabweisung wegen Unschlüssigkeit**)

motion for a new trial trial (I.2; I.3) post-trial motion asking the judge to void the trial and order a new trial to take place; motion is based on claim that legal error was committed which could have affected the outcome of the trial (**Antrag auf Wiederaufnahme des Verfahrens**)

motion for a non-suit (I.3) defendant's formal request addressed to the court to dismiss the plaintiff's law suit for failure to make a prima facie case; made following plaintiff's case in chief (**Antrag auf Klageabweisung wegen Unschlüssigkeit**)

motion for judgment on the pleadings (I.3) formal request addressed to the court asking it to reach a judgment for the party making the motion, or the moving party, on the assumption that the facts most favorable to the other party, or the non-moving party, are true; this motion, unlike the motion for summary judgment, is not made because the parties agree on the facts, but because one party is of the opinion that the law does not permit the other party to prevail in the law suit

	even if the one assumes that the facts he claims are true (**Antrag auf ein Urteil, das allein auf den Schriftsätzen beruht und auf Rechtsfragen beschränkt ist**)
motion for reconsideration (II.2)	formal request that a court rethink a ruling it has made and possibly change that ruling
motion for summary judgment (I.3)	formal request addressed to the court asking it to reach a judgment in the case without a trial because the parties are not in disagreement on the facts of the case (**Antrag auf ein Urteil im summarischen Verfahren**)
motion to dismiss (I.3)	formal request addressed to the court asking it to refuse to hear the plaintiff's case because of some procedural defect, such as the court's lack of jurisdiction over the defendant's person or over the subject matter of the law suit; under federal law the motion to dismiss includes the demurrer (**Antrag auf Klageabweisung wegen Unzulässigkeit**)
motion to quash the array (I.2) **motion to quash the panel** **motion to quash the venire**	formal request to dismiss the entire array or venire because of the jury commissioner's incorrect method of selection; also called **challenge to the array** (ca. **Antrag auf Ablehnung der Gesamtheit der Geschworenen**)
movables (I.1)	movable property (**Fahrnis, bewegliche Sachen**); also referred to as **personal property, chattels, personalty**; contrasted to **real property** or land and things attached to it (**Liegenschaften**)
moving party (I.3)	party making a motion (**Antragsteller**)
Municipal Court (II.1)	one name for a state trial court of limited jurisdiction (**Gericht mit beschränkter Zuständigkeit, e.g. Amtsgericht**); as an adjective **municipal** is primarily used to mean city or town (**Stadt**)
naturalized (I.2)	made a citizen of a nation, having received citizenship rights on application rather than on birth (**eingebürgert**)
necessity (I.1; I.3)	a justification or excuse based on a situation of emergency that can only be avoided by harming s.o. else's legally protected interest to protect one's own interest; distinguished between **necessity as a justification (rechtfertigender Notstand)** and **necessity as an excuse (entschuldigender Notstand)**
negligence (I.1)	failure to take adequate measures to avoid harming others; failure to act like a reasonable person would to avoid harming others; failure to see a risk of harm that a reasonable person would see (**Fahrlässigkeit**)
non-moving party (I.3)	party against whom a motion has been made (**Antragsgegner**)
non-profit organization (I.3)	charitable foundation, organization that survives on donations and does not work for profit (**gemeinnütziger Verein**)

notarization (I.1)   method of formalizing a document by having a **notary** witness the signing of the document and place stamp on it (ca. **Beurkundung durch einen Notar, notarielle Beglaubigung**)

to nullify the law (I.3)   to ignore the law and decide a case as a jury; permissible in criminal cases if jury acquits defendant regardless of the law

oath (I.2)   solemn promise invoking the name of God that one will do s.th., such as tell the truth or fulfill one's duties, to the best of one's abilities (**Eid**)

objection (I.2)   formal claim to judge that some error has been, or is in the process of being, committed during a judicial hearing (**Einspruch**)

offense (I.1)   (U.K. **offence**) crime (**Straftat**)

omission (I.1)   failure to act to avoid occurrence of criminally prohibited harm when one has duty to so act (**Unterlassung**)

onus of proof (I.2)   obligation to provide enough evidence to prove a legal claim (**Beweislast**)

opening statement (I.3)   lawyer's description of the trial to come to give the jury a framework within which to understand the evidence that will be presented (**einleitender Vortrag vor dem Gericht**)

optional areas (I.3)   non-required courses, electives (**Wahlfächer**)

oral argument (III.3)   oral presentation of arguments on appeal (**Plädoyer, mündlicher Vortrag**)

order to compel compliance (I.3)   judicial order addressed to a party who is not cooperating in the discovery process requiring his cooperation (**Anordnung, ein Begehren zu erfüllen**)

original jurisdiction (II.1)   the power to hear a case as a trial court (**Zuständigkeit als Tatsacheninstanz; Zuständigkeit in erster Instanz**)

original matter (I.3)   case, or issues raised in a case, on the trial, as opposed to appellate, court level (**erstinstanzliche Sache**)

others similarly situated (III.2)   class of individuals who are all like the plaintiff to a law suit in a legally significant way; used for **class actions**

to overrule (I.1; I.2; I.3)   to declare a previous decision of either a lower court or of the court itself invalid (when the court overrules its own precedent) (**außer Kraft setzen**); this term is used in relation to a past precedent announced in a *different case* from the case in which it is overruled (e.g. *Shivpuri* overruled *Ryan*); term is also used to mean: to deny the request or objections of a lawyer during a trial (**einen Antrag oder Einspruch ablehnen**); opposite of: **to sustain**

panel (I.2)	(U.K.) prospective jurors summoned to court for selection for jury duty; (U.S.) **array, venire** (ca. **Gesamtheit der Geschworenen**)
parole (I.2)	release of prisoner before prison term has been completely served accompanied by the imposition of certain requirements (**bedingte Entlassung**)
party complainant (III.2)	party filing a complaint, plaintiff (**Kläger**)
party defendant (III.2)	party against whom a complaint has been filed, defendant (**Beklagter**)
patent (II.1; II.2)	intellectual property right protecting an individual's inventions from unauthorized use (**Patent**)
pendente lite (III.2)	pending the law suit, awaiting the final outcome of the litigation
pending action (I.3)	law suit that has been initiated but not yet decided (**anhängiges Verfahren**)
to be pending (I.3; I.4)	to be within the judicial process waiting for a judgment (**anhängig sein**)
per curiam opinion (I.3; II.1)	opinion of the court; usually short opinion published without extensive argumentation in support of the holding; unsigned opinion representing the opinion of the court in general rather than that of a particular judge or group of judges (**Rechtsauffassung eines Kollegialgerichts**)
peremptory challenge (I.2)	privilege each party has to eliminate prospective jurors from service without giving any reason for the exclusion; limited in number (ca. **Antrag auf Ablehnung eines Geschworenen ohne Angabe von Gründen**)
permanent injunction (III.2)	injunction granted until the final disposition of a law suit
permanent relief (III.2)	final remedy granted for unlimited amount of time
perpetual injunction (III.2)	injunction granted as the final disposition of a law suit (**Leistungsurteil auf Unterlassung**)
personal jurisdiction (II.1)	authority of a court to reach decisions binding on the defendant in the case (**Gerichtshoheit über eine Person**)
personal property (I.1)	movable property (**Fahrnis, bewegliche Sachen**); also referred to as **chattels, movables, personalty**; contrasted to **real property** or land and things attached to it (**Liegenschaften**)
personal service (II.2)	delivery of process to the defendant by handing it over to him, or in some other way placing it within his reach
personalty (I.1)	movable property (**Fahrnis, bewegliche Sachen**); also referred to as **chattels, movables, personal property**; contrasted to **real property** or land and things attached to it (**Liegenschaften**)

in pertinent part (I.3)   to the extent relevant; generally used when quoting only part of a text (**soweit hier relevant**)

petit jury (I.2)   jury used to determine the facts and apply the law as the judge instructs in order to reach the outcome of a trial (**die Geschworenen**); traditionally a body of 12 persons chosen randomly from a cross-section of the community; also called the **trial jury**, as opposed to the **grand jury**; note that "jury" is singular in U.S. and plural in British English (U.S. "the jury is"; U.K. "the jury are")

petition (I.1)   formal request (**Antrag**)

to petition (I.2)   to formally request that a court do s.th. (**einen Antrag stellen**)

petition for a writ of habeas corpus (I.4)   a form of **collateral attack** that can be filed after the person's conviction has become final and all **avenues of appeal have been exhausted** (**Antrag auf richterliche Haftprüfung**)

petitioner (I.2; I.3)   name given to the person who files for a writ of certiorari (**Revisionskläger** [Zivilrecht]; **Revisionsführer** [Strafrecht])

petty offense (I.2)   a minor criminal violation, usually punished with a fine (ca. **Ordnungswidrigkeit**)

physical examination (I.3)   medical examination conducted by a physician to determine a person's physical capacities or the extent of any injuries; one tool of discovery (**medizinische Untersuchung**)

physical exhibits (I.2)   objects that can be considered in a court of law as evidence (**Gegenstand des Augenscheins**)

plaintiff (I.1)   in a private law dispute, person who sues, who initiates the law suit (**Kläger**); also called the **complainant**, because it is the plaintiff who files a complaint to initiate a law suit

pleadings (I.3; II.1)   documents filed in the initiation of a law suit which define the parties' factual claims; they include the plaintiff's complaint, the defendant's answer, the plaintiff's reply, and the defendant's rejoinder (**Schriftsätze**)

post-trial motion (I.3)   formal request by either party to the law suit addressed to the judge following completion of the trial, e.g. motion for a new trial, motion for a judgment notwithstanding the verdict (**Antrag nach der Hauptverhandlung**)

post-War Amendments (III.2)   Thirteenth, Fourteenth and Fifteenth Amendments to the U.S. Constitution, which were ratified following the Civil War

prayer for relief (I.3)   formal request addressed to the court asking it to declare the plaintiff's right to receive a specified remedy, e.g. money damages (**Klagebegehren**)

precedent (I.1)   principle of law announced by court when reaching decision that binds that court and all lower courts when reaching decisions in future similar cases, thus **binding precedent**

preliminary injunction (III.2)

interlocutory injunction granted after party to be restrained has had opportunity to be heard (**einstweilige Verfügung**)

preliminary pleading (II.1)

documents filed with court in preparation and initiation of law suit; includes: **complaint** (**Klageschrift**), **answer** (**Klageerwiderung**), **reply** (**Replik**)

preponderance of the evidence (I.3)

standard of proof in civil law dispute (U.K. **on a balance of probabilities**) meaning factfinder must be somewhat more convinced of plaintiff's case than of defendant's in order to decide in favor of plaintiff (ca. **überwiegendes Ergebnis der Beweisaufnahme**)

to present one's case (I.3)

to call witnesses and present evidence of each element of the cause of action or defense one has against the other party (**den Beweis antreten**)

to preside at trial (II.1)

to act as authority over a trial; to direct or control proceedings as a judge (**den Vorsitz führen**); (U.K. **to pursue a claim**)

to press a claim (I.4)

to sue s.o. for s.th. (**klagen**)

pretrial conference (I.3)

judge's conference with the parties to a pending law suit held before the trial begins in an effort to reach a pretrial settlement (**Besprechung vor der Eröffnung der Hauptverhandlung**)

pretrial discovery (I.3)

process of gathering evidence before the trial begins (**Sammeln von Beweismaterial vor der Eröffnung der Hauptverhandlung**)

pretrial motion (I.2)

motion made before trial begins (ca. **Antrag, der während eines Vorverfahrens gestellt wird**)

pretrial settlement (I.3)

voluntary agreement between the parties that ends their dispute before the trial has begun (**außergerichtlicher Vergleich vor der Eröffnung der Hauptverhandlung**)

prima facie case (I.2)

enough evidence to establish legal claim; enough evidence that if other party remains silent he or she will lose to the person making the **prima facie showing**

prior restraints (III.3)

controls imposed on free speech that take effect before the word is spoken or written as opposed to statutes imposing punishment for expression after the fact (**Genehmigungsvorbehalt**)

private client work (I.3)

legal services aimed at the legal problems individuals usually have (**juristische Praxis für Privatpersonen**)

private process server (II.2)

private party who is hired to serve process on defendant

probable cause (I.4)

reasonable grounds for a belief; used often in connection with standard for deciding whether to issue an arrest warrant or a search warrant (ca. **dringender Tatverdacht**)

to probate a will (I.3)

to have the validity of a will determined, pay off any remaining debts, collect the assets, and distribute them to the testator's heirs (**einen Nachlaß verwalten**)

probate court (II.1)   special court, or special type of court procedure, for inheritance, and in some states also for family law problems such as adoption of minor children (**Nachlaß- und Familiengericht**)

probate jurisdiction (II.1)   the authority as a court to hear cases involving inheritance, and perhaps also family law problems (**Zuständigkeit als Nachlaß- und Familiengericht**)

probation (I.2)   release of a person from the requirement to serve a prison term under the imposition of certain requirements, such as attending regular meetings with a **probation officer** (**Bewährungshelfer**), keeping a certain job, curfew, etc. (ca. **Bewährung**)

procedural justice (I.3)   justice defined in terms of outcome of established or defined process (**Gerechtigkeit durch Verfahren**)

procedure (I.1)   manner of conducting a case from start to finish in a court of law (**Verfahren**); as a body of law it contains rules on how to initiate a law suit and conduct it to its close (**Prozeßrecht**)

process (I.3; II.2)   copy of plaintiff's complaint and a **summons** ordering defendant to answer complaint and appear in court to defend against charges in complaint; must be served on defendant to give notice of law suit (ca. **Klage und Ladung**)

process agent (II.2)   person appointed to accept process for another person; mostly agents for companies doing business in various states (**Zustellungsbevollmächtigter**); see also **agent to receive process**

process server (II.2)   person who delivers the summons and copy of the plaintiff's complaint to the defendant (ca. **Zusteller von Klage und Ladung**)

products liability (II.2)   (U.K.: **product liability**) strict liability of a producer, seller, distributor, retailer of a product for any harm caused by that product if the harm resulted from a product defect, from the failure to warn of potential risks involved in using the product, or from the misrepresentation of the purpose for which the product can be used (**Produzentenhaftung**)

professional judgeship (I.3)   judge's position within a legal system that appoints lawyers as judges immediately after they have finished law school (**Berufsrichterschaft**)

Professional Skills Course (I.3)   (U.K.) twelve-day, sixty-hour program of vocational education offered to trainee solicitors at some time during their two-year training contract

prohibition against cruel and unusual punishment (I.4)   prohibition contained in the Eighth Amendment to the U.S. Constitution prohibiting inhumane, unreasonable forms of punishment (**Verbot unmenschlicher oder erniedrigender Strafe**)

property law (I.1)   law of ownership, possession and other rights relating to movable and immovable objects (**Sachenrecht**)

to proscribe (I.4; III.3)	to prohibit (**verbieten**); opposite of **to prescribe:** to require (**gebieten**)
to prosecute (I.1)	to formally charge s.o. with a crime (**anklagen**)
prosecutor (I.1; I.3)	public official responsible for developing and bringing criminal cases to court (**Staatsanwalt**)
prosecutor's office (I.3)	office of the government responsible for bringing individuals accused of having committed a crime to court to answer for the charges (**Staatsanwaltschaft**)
prospective juror (I.2)	person jury commissioner has selected to come to court for potential jury duty; it is from this group that the actual jurors on a grand or petit jury will be selected (ca. **möglicher Geschworener**)
protective order (I.3)	court order stopping one party to a law suit from discovering information from the other which the latter is not under a legal obligation to release (**Anordnung einer Schutzmaßnahme**)
to provide in full (III.3)	to state in its full and complete text (as opposed to **to provide in pertinent part**)
provision (I.1)	what the law **provides** (**vorsieht**), laws and parts of laws (**gesetzliche Bestimmungen**)
provisional practising certificate (I.3)	(U.K.) authorisation to practice law awarded to a student barrister after completing six months of pupilage (**vorläufige Zulassung als Barrister**)
public defender (I.3)	public official hired to work within a state office by defending indigent persons who have been accused of having committed a crime (**vom Staat gestellter Verteidiger**)
public defender's office (I.3)	office of the government responsible for defending individuals accused of having committed a crime who cannot afford to pay for a private attorney (**Behörde für die öffentliche Verteidigung von Angeklagten**)
pupilage (I.3)	(U.K.) one year of practical legal training with a barrister; required to be admitted to the Bar (**Lehrlingszeit bei einem Barrister**)
pursuant to (III.2)	according to, under (the authority of) (**gemäß**)
to qualify a witness as an expert (I.3)	to show the court that a witness is a specialist and can thus express an opinion within her field of expertise (**die Fähigkeit eines Zeugen belegen, als Sachverständige(r) auszusagen**)
quasi in rem jurisdiction (II.2)	court's power over the person of the defendant by virtue of the fact that he owns property within the court's geographical area of jurisdiction (**fingierte in rem-Zuständigkeit, Gerichtshoheit über eine Person, die von der Belegenheit einer Sache abgeleitet wird**)

Queen's Bench Division (II.2)	(U.K.) (*abbr* **QBD**) one of three divisions of the High Court of Justice; court of general jurisdiction over private law disputes, admiralty, and commercial cases (**Abteilung des High Court of Justice für Zivilsachen**)
Queen's Counsel (I.3)	(U.K.) (*abbr* **QC**) outstanding barrister who is appointed by the Queen (or King, in which case the barrister is called King's Counsel, *abbr* **KC**) on the recommendation of the Lord Chancellor (**von der Königin / dem König bestellter Barrister**)
random selection (I.2)	choice made in manner intended to ensure that every member of group from which one is selecting has an equal probability of being chosen (**Auswahl nach dem Zufallsprinzip**)
ratification (III.2)	approval of an amendment to constitution (**Verabschiedung einer Verfassungsänderung**)
ratio decidendi (I.1)	(pl. **rationes decidendi**) principle of law necessary to arrive at holding in case
rational basis test (III.3)	test of constitutionality of a law requiring that the state be pursuing a legitimate state interest and employing a reasonable means of attaining its goal; applied in cases involving non-fundamental rights, e.g. economic rights, or distinctions not considered suspect (**allgemeiner Maßstab für die Legitimation eines Grundrechtseingriffs, Verhältnismäßigkeitsprüfung im weiteren Sinne**)
to reach a verdict (I.2)	to come to a resolution of a trial as a jury (ca. **zu einem Urteilsspruch [der Geschworenenbank] kommen**)
real estate (I.1)	land and everything attached to the land (**Liegenschaften, unbewegliche Sachen**); also: **real property; realty**
real property (I.1)	land and everything attached to the land (**Liegenschaften, unbewegliche Sachen**); also: **real estate, realty**
realty (I.1)	land and everything attached to the land (**Liegenschaften, unbewegliche Sachen**); also: **real estate; real property**
reasonable means (III.3)	one of several possible ways of pursuing an interest that is likely to be successful (**geeignetes Mittel**)
reasonable person standard (I.1)	standard used in all areas of the common law as a test for whether conduct was that of a normal person in the situation under consideration; one way of expressing the standard of care applicable to torts of negligence; measures defendant against the average person in the community (vgl.: **die im Verkehr erforderliche Sorgfalt**)
rebuttal (I.3)	plaintiff's presentation of evidence following defendant's case in chief that is aimed at discrediting the defendant's case (**Antwort auf das Vorbringen des Beklagten**)

receipt of stolen goods (I.2)	crime of accepting stolen movable property to keep or sell (**Hehlerei und Begünstigung**)
record (I.1; I.3)	all of the documents relevant to a law suit assembled by the court (ca. **Gerichtsakten, Protokoll**)
recovery (I.1)	judge's award to successful plaintiff to be paid by defendant in order to make up for injury defendant caused plaintiff; also **redress, relief, remedy** (ca. **Klagebegehren**)
recross-examination (I.3)	lawyer's questioning of the opposing party's witness following redirect examination (**nochmaliges Kreuzverhör**)
redirect examination (I.3)	lawyer's questioning of his own witness following the other party's cross-examination (**wiederholte Vernehmung eines Zeugen, den der vernehmende Anwalt selbst benannt hat**)
redress (I.1)	judge's award to successful plaintiff to be paid by defendant in order to make up for injury defendant caused plaintiff; also **recovery, relief, remedy** (ca. **Klagebegehren**)
refresher (I.3)	(U.K.) barrister's fee for an additional day in court after the first day (**zusätzliche Prozeßführungskosten**)
refund action (I.4)	law suit for return of taxes paid based on the claim that the taxes were not due (**Klage auf Rückzahlung einer Steuer**)
to rehabilitate witness (I.3)	to build a witness' credibility back up in the mind of the factfinder following cross-examination (**die Glaubwürdigkeit eines Zeugen wiederherstellen**)
rehabilitation (I.3)	one purpose or effect of punishment, namely training the individual to accept and correspond to social norms in the future (**Resozialisierung**)
to reinstate an action (I.3)	to restore a law suit that has been dismissed; to revive a dismissed law suit (**Aufhebung eines die Klage abweisenden Urteils**)
rejoinder (I.3)	defendant's response to plaintiff's reply (**Duplik**)
relief (I.1)	judge's award to successful plaintiff to be paid by defendant in order to make up for injury defendant caused plaintiff; also **recovery, redress, remedy** (ca. **Klagebegehren**)
to remand (I.2)	to send back case, as an appellate court, to lower court for some specified treatment of case (**zurückverweisen**), such as: **to remand for further proceedings not inconsistent with this opinion**, meaning lower court has to deal with case as directed in decision of higher appellate court
remedies (I.3)	title of required course in U.S. law schools; teaches students the law determining what a plaintiff may be awarded by a court to compensate for injury caused by a defendant and the implications of suing for that remedy (**Recht der zulässigen Rechtsbehelfe**)

remedy (I.1; I.3)   what plaintiff to law suit is suing to obtain from defendant to compensate plaintiff for injury defendant is claimed to have caused him; what court can order defendant to do to compensate for causing injury to plaintiff (**Klagebegehren**); also **relief, recovery, redress,** examples being money damages or specific performance

removal (II.2)   taking a civil action filed in a state court out of that court and putting it into a federal district court; can be done at the defendant's option (ca. **Verweisung an ein anderes Gericht**)

to render a verdict (I.2)   to announce a verdict as a jury (ca. **das Urteil [der Geschworenenbank] verkünden**); U.K. **to return a verdict**

to repeal a law (III.2)   to cancel effectiveness of a law; to put a law out of force (**ein Gesetz aufheben**)

replevin (I.1)   common law form of action to recover personal property from defendant who unlawfully detains it, whereby the plaintiff may secure possession of that property on the posting of a **bond** or **security** at any time before judgment

reply (I.3; II.1)   plaintiff's response to the defendant's counterclaim, also called **replication** (**Replik**)

reporter (II.1)   collection of complete decisions of a court or courts (see Appendix III for a list of reporters in the U.S. and England) (**Entscheidungssammlung**)

Republican National Convention (III.3)   meeting of members of the Republican (or other) Party for the purpose of nominating a candidate for president (**Parteitag der Republikaner**)

request for admission (I.3)   written question asking the opposing party to a law suit whether he agrees that an certain statement is true with the effect that if he does that fact does not have to be proved at trial; one tool of discovery (**Aufforderung, etwas zuzugestehen**)

request for the production of documents (I.3)   request that the other party to the law suit or a witness turn over written records for inspection prior to trial; one tool of discovery (**Aufforderung, Urkunden vorzulegen**)

res judicata (I.4)   case that has already been finally judged (**rechtskräftig entschiedene Sache**); used to mean that law suits which have already reached a final judgment may not be filed again

to reserve decision (III.2)   to not make a decision at the moment but to postpone it to a later time (**sich die Entscheidung vorbehalten**)

resocialization (I.3)   one purpose or effect of punishment, namely training the individual to accept and correspond to social norms in the future (**Resozialisierung**)

respondent (II.1)   party against whom appeal to supreme court has been taken by **petitioner** via a **writ of certiorari** (**Revisionsbeklagter [Zivil-**

recht]; **Revisionsgegner** [Strafrecht]); (U.K.) person against whom an appeal has been taken

to rest one's case (I.3)

to conclude presenting evidence in support of one's case (**sein Vorbringen abschliessen**)

to restore a case to the docket (III.2)

to reschedule a case for another hearing in the future; to re-enter case in court's calendar of official business (ca. **einen Rechtsstreit in den Terminkalender des Gerichts erneut eintragen**)

retailer (II.2)

seller to the final consumer (**Einzelhändler**)

to retain a lawyer (I.3)

to hire a lawyer to represent you (**einem Rechtsanwalt ein Mandat erteilen**)

retainer (I.3)

fee paid to retain, or hire, a lawyer as one's own representative; this fee closes the contract between the individual and the lawyer and prohibits the lawyer from representing anyone from the opposing side of the dispute (**Honorar bei der Erteilung eines Mandats**)

retribution (I.3)

one purpose or effect of punishment, namely paying the criminal offender back for the wrong he has done to the victim and to society according to the biblical "eye for an eye" theory (**Vergeltung**)

retroactive application of a new precedent (I.4)

application of a legal rule newly announced in a case to facts or law suits that arose before that rule was announced (**rückwirkende Anwendung einer neuen Rechtsregel**)

to reverse (I.2)

to change, as an appellate court, the decision of a lower court in the same case (**aufheben**)

to ride circuit (I.1)

to travel as a judge from one area to another and back again to hear cases

right to stand by (I.2)

(U.K.) for right of prosecutor in Great Britain to exclude a juror from the jury without giving any reason; similar to (U.S.) **peremptory challenge**, but reserved only to prosecutor

robbery (I.2)

unlawful taking of property from owner or from person in lawful possession of property through use of force or threat of force (**Raub, räuberische Erpressung**)

Roll of Solicitors (I.3)

(U.K.) list of solicitors admitted to practice law

rule nisi (III.1)

order to give a good reason why a court ruling should not become final and enforced (ca. **Ladung mit Aufforderung, etwaige Einwendungen vorzubringen**)

the rule of law (I.4)

principle that cases should be decided in accordance with established principles of law and not by arbitrary determination (**Rechtsstaatsprinzip**); to be contrasted with **a rule of law**, which means any legal rule (**Rechtsregel**)

rule to show cause (III.1)	order to give a good reason why a court ruling should not become final and enforced (ca. **Ladung mit Aufforderung, etwaige Einwendungen vorzubringen**)
rules of evidence (I.2; I.3)	formal legal rules specifying what can and cannot be used as proof at a trial (**Beweiserhebungs- und Beweisverwertungsregeln**)
to run concurrently (I.2)	to begin to expire on the same day (ca. **gleichzeitig ablaufen**); used with prison sentences to mean that if a person has been sentenced to more than one prison term, the terms start to run together, such that the first day in prison counts as serving one day of two or more prison terms simultaneously (ca. **gleichzeitig zu verbüßende Gefängnisstrafen**)
to run consecutively (I.2)	to expire one after the other (ca. **nacheinander ablaufen**); used with prison sentences to mean that if a person has been sentenced to more than one prison term, the first term runs first and after that term has been served, the second term starts to run (ca. **nacheinander zu verbüßende Gefängnisstrafen**)
run-away jury (I.3)	jury that strongly exaggerates the serious of the defendant's wrong or of the plaintiff's injury by awarding excessive damages (**außer Rand und Band geratene Geschworenenbank**)
sanction (I.3)	punishment, measure to discourage or punish conduct (**Sanktion**)
scale fees (I.3)	(U.K.) fixed solicitor's fees based on the value of property conveyed (**in einer Gebührenordnung festgelegte Anwaltsgebühren**)
search and seizure (I.4)	looking through s.o.'s belongings and taking into custody those things that may prove criminal activity (**Durchsuchung und Beschlagnahme von Beweismaterial**)
search warrant (I.2)	formal document issued by judge permitting police to search s.o.'s home (**Durchsuchungsbefehl**)
second-degree burglary (I.2)	burglary is crime of unlawfully entering building with intent to commit crime in the building (ca. **Einbruch zum Zweck der Begehung eines Verbrechens**); **second degree** indicates that burglary was committed under circumstances in aggravation of the offense, which would otherwise be a **third-degree offense**
section (I.1)	one provision of a code or collection of statutes (§)
self-defense (I.1)	criminal law justification; permits person wrongfully attacked to use what otherwise would be unlawful force to ward off the attack (ca. **Notwehr**)
to sentence (I.2)	to impose, as a judge, some form of punishment on person found guilty of a crime (ca. **das Strafmaß festsetzen**); the **sentence** is the formal order of punishment; should not be confused with the

	judgment, which is the judge's formal conclusion in a law suit in favor of, or against, one of the parties to that suit; in a criminal case with a jury, if the jury **renders a verdict** of guilty, the judge will **enter judgment on the verdict**, meaning that the judge will give the jury's verdict the force of law, and then the judge will determine the punishment and **sentence** the defendant to, for example, five years in prison
separate but equal doctrine (III.2)	principle for interpreting the equal protection clause of the Fourteenth Amendment whereby "equality of treatment is accorded when the races are provided substantially equal facilities, even though these facilities be separate"; doctrine rejected in *Brown v. Board of Education*
sequestration (I.2)	isolation of jury from any contact with outside world; usually done when jury goes into deliberation; judge can sequester jury at beginning of trial if case is widely publicized and jury could be influenced by media or other individuals' comments (ca. **Klausur der Geschworenen**)
service of process (I.3; II.2)	delivery of **summons** and copy of plaintiff's **complaint** to defendant for purpose of notifying defendant that an action has been filed against him (**Klagezustellung**)
set of chambers (I.3)	(U.K.) group of individual offices within which a barrister practices law (**Bürogemeinschaft**)
settlement negotiations (I.3)	discussions between the parties aimed at reaching a resolution of their dispute without going to or completing trial (**Verhandlungen zur Herbeiführung eines Vergleichs**)
shareholder (I.4)	person or legal entity holding shares of a company (**Aktionär**)
sheriff (II.2)	chief executive and administrative officer of a county; may be required to **serve process** within the county over which he is responsible
Sherman Antitrust Act (I.3)	antitrust act; federal statute prohibiting anticompetitive behavior (**Bundeskartellgesetz**)
to show cause (III.1)	to give a good reason for s.th. (**Behauptungen substantiieren**)
silks (I.3)	(U.K.) another name for barristers who are QCs / KCs (**von der Königin / dem König bestellte Barristers**)
slander (I.2)	tort of character defamation through oral expression
small claims court (I.3)	simplified lower level trial court procedure for considering civil law disputes regarding a very small amount in controversy, such as $500
solicitor (I.3)	(U.K.) lawyer specialised in the office type of legal work rather than in litigation as the **barrister**

solicitor and own client assessment (I.3)	(U.K.) court's determination whether the client has to pay his solicitor the full amount of the fees the solicitor has charged the client (**Kontrolle der Anwaltsgebühren durch das Gericht**)
source of law (I.1)	origin of legal principles applied by judges to solve cases (**Rechtsquelle**)
special appearance (II.2)	coming to court for the limited purpose of objecting to the court's jurisdiction; not an appearance to defend against substantive claims, but rather to argue that the court has no jurisdiction over one's person (ca. **beschränkte Einlassung zum Zweck der Rüge formeller Mängel**); contrast to: **general appearance** (ca. **vorbehaltlose Einlassung**)
special verdict (I.3)	jury's indication of what facts it believes are true following a trial (**Tatsacheninterlokut**)
specific deterrence (I.3)	deterrence of an individual from committing crimes, *e.g.* by imprisoning him so that he is not a threat to society (**Spezialprävention**)
specific part(s) (I.1)	one or more books or parts of a code dealing with a particular area of the law (**Besonderer Teil**)
specific performance (I.1)	remedy for breach of contract whereby the defendant is forced to do exactly what he promised to do under the contract (**Vertragserfüllung**)
speech (I.1)	(U.K.) opinion of a judge of the House of Lords in a case
to stand trial (I.2)	to face formal criminal charges at trial on issue of guilt (ca. **sich vor Gericht in einem Strafverfahren verantworten**)
standard of proof (I.3)	test of when burden of proof has been satisfied; defined measurement of how convinced factfinder at trial has to be before deciding in favor of party bearing the burden (**Beweismaßstab**)
standard of review (I.3)	norm to be followed by an appellate court in determining whether lower court erred in reaching its decision (**Revisionsmaßstab**)
stare decisis, doctrine of (I.1)	principle that courts are bound by their former decisions when deciding later similar cases
statute (I.1)	a single written law that has been adopted by the legislature; sometimes used to designate a single section of a code (**Gesetz**); **statutory**: of or relating to written enacted law
statute of limitations (I.3; I.4)	(U.K. **limitation period**) period within which a law suit may be initiated after a violation of rights has occurred (**Verjährungsfrist**)
statute of repose (I.4)	period within which damage must occur in order to be the basis for a law suit (**Frist, nach deren Ablauf ein Anspruch erloschen ist**)

to stay the proceedings proceedings (I.3)	to postpone the trial process; to bring the law suit to a temporary standstill (**das Verfahren aussetzen**)
strict scrutiny test (III.3)	test of constitutionality of a law requiring that the state be pursuing a compelling state interest and employing the least intrusive means of attaining its goal; applied in cases involving fundamental rights, e.g. freedom of speech, or where the law distinguishes on the basis of a suspect classification, e.g. race, gender, age (**strenge Prüfung der Verfassungsmäßigkeit eines Gesetzes bei schrankenlos gewährleisteten Grundrechten und bei der Verwendung von diskriminierenden Unterscheidungsmerkmalen**)
to strike out the pleadings (I.3)	to exclude all or part of the factual claims included in the plaintiff's complaint or the defendant's answer (**Teile der Klage abweisen**)
subject matter jurisdiction (II.1)	authority of a court to decide a particular type of case according to the legal issues it raises and the amount in controversy (**sachliche Zuständigkeit**)
substantive justice (I.3)	justice defined in terms of higher truths and principles (**materiale Gerechtigkeit**)
to sue in tort (I.1)	to sue s.o. for a tort
summary trial (II.2)	shortened version of a trial; common in the magistrates' courts; also called trial summarily (**erstinstanzlicher Prozeß im summarischen Verfahren**)
summary-only offence (II.2)	(U.K.) criminal offence over which the magistrates' courts have exclusive jurisdiction (**in einem summarischen Verfahren zu beurteilende Straftat**)
summing up (I.2)	(U.K.) judge's instructions on law and summary of evidence presented during trial, including judge's comments on this evidence; given at end of trial and before the jury deliberates on verdict (ca. **Belehrung der Geschworenen**)
summoning officer (I.2)	(U.K.) public officer responsible for calling in individuals from society to be prospective jurors; (U.S.) **jury commissioner** (ca. **Beamter, der für die Auswahl der Geschworenen zuständig ist**)
summons (I.2; I.3; II.2)	formal court order to a person to appear before that court, for example to testify as a witness, to serve as a juror, etc.; attached to a complaint ordering the defendant to answer the complaint and appear in court to defend himself against the plaintiff's claims (**Ladung**)
Superior Court (II.1)	one name for state trial court of general jurisdiction (vgl. **Landgericht**)
supra (I.2)	commonly used in legal texts to mean "see above"; contrasted to "**infra**" meaning "see below"

supreme court (II.1)   highest court in a court system; considers only issues of law on appeal; decision to hear a case is within the discretion of the court; convenes in banc; usually has seven to nine judges (**oberstes Revisionsgericht**)

surrebuttal (I.3)   defendant's presentation of evidence following plaintiff's **rebuttal** that is aimed at discrediting the rebuttal (**Replik auf die Antwort des Klägers**)

Surrogate's Court (II.1)   one name for a **probate** or **domestic relations court**

suspect classification (III.3)   statutory distinction drawn on the basis of a characteristic that is immutable, has no relation to an individual's abilities or rights, and has been used as the basis of discrimination in the past (**diskriminierendes Unterscheidungsmerkmal**)

to suspend a sentence (I.2)   to cancel criminal defendant's obligation to actually serve time in prison; not to be confused with **probation** (**Bewährung**), which requires the defendant to fulfill certain conditions, such as attending regular meetings with a **probation officer** (**Bewährungshelfer**), keeping a certain job, curfew, etc.; also not to be confused with **parole** (**bedingte Entlassung**), which releases defendant before prison term has been completely served but also imposes certain requirements on him

to sustain (I.1; I.3)   to uphold, to grant or support the validity of a formal request made by a lawyer during a trial (**einem Antrag oder Einspruch stattgeben**); the opposite of **to overrule** (**ablehnen**)

tax (I.3)   department of a law firm which focuses on fiscal problems, e.g. personal and corporate income tax, and devises methods of saving taxes for its clients (**Steuerabteilung**)

temporary injunction (III.2)   interlocutory injunction granted after party to be restrained has had opportunity to be heard; also **preliminary injunction**

temporary restraining order (III.2)   interlocutory injunction granted without hearing party to be restrained

tenancy (I.3)   (U.K.) right to use an office within a set of chambers as a barrister (**Bürobenutzungsrecht**)

term (III.1)   period during which a court hears cases; the U.S. Supreme Court's term begins on the first Monday in October (ca. **Sitzungsperiode**)

territorial jurisdiction (II.2)   term that includes: **personal jurisdiction**, which is a court's power over the person of the defendant (**Gerichtshoheit über eine Person**); **in rem jurisdiction**, which is a court's power over property in dispute (**Gerichtshoheit über eine Sache**); and **quasi in rem jurisdiction**, which is a court's power over the person of the defendant by virtue of the fact that he owns property within the court's geographical area of jurisdiction (**fingierte in rem-Zu-**

ständigkeit, Gerichtshoheit über eine Person, die von der Belegenheit einer Sache abgeleitet wird)

testament (II.1) document containing instructions on how to dispose of a person's property after death; **testament** originally limited to the distribution of personal property and **will** to the distribution of real property, but today terms are synonymous (**Testament**)

testator / testatrix (I.3) person who leaves a last will and testament; person who dies testate, as opposed to *s.o.* who dies without leaving a will who is said to die intestate (**Testator / -in**)

to testify (I.2) to tell what one knows relating to a law suit in a court of law (**aussagen**)

testimony (I.3) what a witness says under oath in response to either lawyer's questions (**Zeugenausage**)

title (II.2) ownership right to property (**Eigentumsrecht** [and *not* **Titel**(!), meaning in German the right one acquires through a final judicial judgment in a case])

tools of discovery (I.3) methods of gathering evidence before trial available to both parties as a matter of right; they include the interrogatory, deposition, request for admissions, request for the production of documents, and physical and mental examinations (**Mittel der Entdeckung von Beweismaterial**)

tort an injury inflicted intentionally or accidentally upon s.o. for which that person can sue for compensation, pain and suffering, etc. ([zivilrechtliches] **Delikt**)

tort law (I.1; I.3) the area of the law dealing with rights against a person who has committed a tort (**Deliktsrecht**), also referred to simply as **torts**

toxic torts case (I.3) law suit involving the emission into the atmosphere, the depositing into the water, or the burial into the ground of extremely poisonous substances (**Rechtsfall, der ein Umweltdelikt betrifft**)

trainee solicitor (I.3) (U.K.) apprentice solicitor, student working within a training establishment learning the practical skills needed to be a solicitor (**auszubildene(r) Jurist(in)**)

training contract (I.3) (U.K.) two-year contract entered into by the trainee solicitor and the training establishment providing for the practical legal education of the trainee (**Ausbildungsvertrag**)

training establishment (I.3) (U.K.) law office or organisation that gives students who have finished the LPC practical legal instruction to prepare them to become a solicitor (**Ausbildungskanzlei**)

training principal (I.3) (U.K.) solicitor within a training establishment to whom a trainee is assigned for one-on-one practical legal training (**Ausbildungsleiter**)

transcript (I.1; I.3)	written record of everything said during a court proceeding, such as the grand jury hearings (also called **minutes**) or the trial (usually called the **trial transcript**) (**Wortprotokoll**)
treason (III.1)	"Treason against the United States, shall consist only in levying war against them, or in adhering to their enemies, giving them aid and comfort. No person shall be convicted of treason unless on the testimony of two witnesses to the same overt act, or on confession in open court..." Art. III, Section 3 U.S. Constitution (ca. **Landesverrat, Hochverrat**)
treaty (I.1)	international agreement (**Vertrag**); *not* used for agreement between two private parties
trespass (action of) (I.1)	common law form of action to recover damages to compensate for injury caused by the defendant's unlawful interference with the plaintiff's person, property or rights
trespass (I.1)	a tort at common law involving direct injury to s.o. committed either intentionally or negligently for which the injured party could sue for compensation
trespass on the case (I.1)	form of action to recover damages to compensate for injury resulting from the defendant's wrongful act which was not an act of direct or immediate force (**trespass**) but instead which caused the harm indirectly or as a secondary consequence; generally referred to simply as "**case**" (ca. **Schadensersatzklage wegen widerrechtlicher Verletzung von Rechtsgütern bei mittelbarem Schaden**)
trial (I.1)	the first proceeding in which a legal dispute is resolved (**Hauptverhandlung**)
trial court (II.1)	first court to hear a case, considers both issues of fact and issues of law, convenes with one judge and possibly a jury (**Tatsacheninstanz**)
trial de novo (II.1)	a second trial held by court of general jurisdiction of a case already decided by trial court of limited jurisdiction (**Verfahren in der Berufungsinstanz**); (U.K.) also called **appeal** on points of fact
trial summarily (II.2)	shortened version of a trial; common in the (U.K.) magistrates' courts; also called summary trial (**erstinstanzlicher Prozeß im summarischen Verfahren**)
to be tried by a jury (I.2)	to have a petit jury as the factfinding body at a trial; also called **trial by jury** (ca. **Geschworenenprozeß**)
trover (I.1)	common law form of action to recover damages to compensate for the value of personal property which the defendant has wrongfully **converted** to his own use, such as by finding the plaintiff's property and keeping it for himself (ca. **Schadenser-**

	satzklage wegen rechtswidriger Aneignung, z.B. wegen Fundunterschlagung)
trust (I.3)	cartel (**Kartell**)
trusts and equity (I.3)	course offered within program of legal studies covering the trust, which is a method of passing property on to later generations or of establishing a foundation, and the field of equity (**Stiftungs- und Billigkeitsrecht**)
to try a case (I.1)	to act as a judge in a trial court in resolving a legal dispute (ca. **über einen Fall gerichtlich verhandeln**)
U.S. Court of Appeals (I.3)	intermediate appellate court in the federal court system (**Bundesrevisionsgericht**)
U.S. Court of Federal Claims (II.1)	trial court in the federal court system with jurisdiction over some claims because of their subject matter, such as claims against the United States
U.S. Court of International Trade (II.1)	trial court in the federal system with jurisdiction over claims relating to tariffs and trade, imports, embargoes and other quantitative restrictions on imports
U.S. District Court (I.3; II.1)	trial court in the federal court system (**Bundesbezirksgericht**)
U.S. Supreme Court (I.1; II.1)	highest court in the federal court system (combination of all the **oberste Bundesgerichte** and the **Bundesverfassungsgericht**)
unanimous verdict (I.2)	a verdict in which all members of the jury agree; usually a requirement for jury trials in the U.S. (ca. **einstimmiges Geschworenenurteil**)
unconstitutional as applied to *s.o.* (III.3)	in violation of the constitution in the particular case, but not in other cases
unconstitutional on its face (III.3)	in violation of the constitution regardless of how applied (**verfassungswidrig bei jeder denkbaren Anwendung**)
undergraduate education (I.3)	university-level education following high school and preceding the first university degree; contrasted to graduate education (**Ausbildung, die zu einem ersten Universitätsabschluß führt**)
unfriendly witness (I.3)	a person who has been called to testify by the opposing party; a person who is expected to testify unfavorably toward the party who questions him; also called hostile witness (**Zeuge der Gegenpartei**)
United States Code (II.1)	multi-volume collection of the laws of the United States; abbreviated **U.S.C.**; also comes in an annotated edition: **United States Code Annotated** (**U.S.C.A.**) which includes comments on the legal history of the section, case decisions relating to the various legal provisions, etc.

university (I.3)   union of two or more colleges within one educational institution (**Universität**)

unlawful assembly (I.2)   crime of meeting or gathering together and disturbing the public peace with the intention of committing some unlawful act

to uphold (I.1)   to maintain the validity of, for example, a decision reached by a lower court (**aufrechterhalten**)

to vacate (III.2)   to declare void or empty of effect, as in: **to vacate the lower court's judgment** (**das Urteil der Vorinstanz aufheben**)

value in controversy (I.2)   the amount for which the plaintiff sues the defendant (**Streitwert**); also **amount in controversy**

venire (I.2)   prospective jurors summoned to court for selection for jury duty; also **array**; (U.K.) **panel** (ca. **Gesamtheit der möglichen Geschworenen**)

venireperson (I.2)   prospective juror; person on the **array** or **venire**; also **venireman**, **venirewoman**

venue (II.2)   location of a court with subject matter and personal jurisdiction; relates to where the court is and not to the power of the court to hear the case (**örtliche Zuständigkeit**)

verdict (I.2)   result of trial as jury determined; in a criminal case the verdict will be "guilty" or "not guilty;" in a private law dispute either "for the plaintiff in the amount of..." or "for the defendant;" (ca. **Spruch der Geschworenen**); also referred to as a **general verdict** in contrast to a **special verdict,** which is merely a list of facts the jury believes are true to which the judge will apply the law in reaching the final judgment in a case; a **special verdict** is required when, for example, the judge feels the law is too complicated for the jury to apply correctly (ca. **Tatsacheninterlokut**)

voir dire (I.2)   examination of prospective jurors for the purpose of determining who will actually serve on petit jury; conducted by judge, but permits lawyers to question prospective jurors and exercise challenges to have them removed

to waive a right (I.2)   to give up a right, to not insist on exercising a right (**auf ein Recht verzichten**)

waiver of service (II.2)   substitute for personal service of process; plaintiff mails process to defendant requesting that defendant give up his right to (**waives**) personal service (ca. **Verzicht auf Zustellung von Klage und Ladung**)

Wall Street firm (I.3) law firm located in the financial district of New York, originally on Wall Street; today a general term for any large law firm that pursues business with corporate clients (**Wall-Street Kanzlei**)

warrant (I.2) formal document issued by a judge permitting a law enforcement officer, for example to arrest s.o., in which case it is referred to as an **arrest warrant** (**Haftbefehl**); or to search that person's home, in which case it is called a **search warrant** (**Durchsuchungsbefehl**)

wholesaler (II.2) intermediate seller, sells to other wholesalers or to retailers, but not to the ultimate consumer (**Zwischen- oder Großhändler**); also **distributor**

will (I.3; II.1) document containing instructions on how to dispose of a person's property after death; **will** originally limited to the distribution of real property and **testament** to the distribution of personal property but today terms are synonymous (**Testament**)

wills probate and administration (I.3) (U.K.) LPC course covering the law of executing a will, probate court procedure, and administration of an estate (**Testamentsvollstreckung und Nachlaßverwaltung**)

witness (I.2) a person who has personal knowledge of facts relevant to a law suit called into court to tell the court those facts (**Zeuge**)

witness stand (I.3) seat in which witness sits while testifying in court (**Zeugenbank**)

writ (I.1) written order issued by a court or some other official responsible for judicial matters (ca. **gerichtliche Anweisung**)

writ of certiorari (I.2) formal order issued by supreme court and addressed to lower court ordering lower court to certify record in a case and send it to supreme court for further judicial review (ca. **Zulassung der Revision**); if the supreme court agrees to hear a case it will: **grant the writ, grant certiorari, grant cert.**; if it decides not to hear the case it will: **deny the writ, deny certiorari, deny cert.**

writ of habeas corpus (I.4) also called the Great Writ; court order that s.o. be released from prison because confinement involves potential violation of a constitutionally guaranteed right; does not revolve around question of guilt (**richterliche Haftprüfung**)

writ of mandamus (III.1) court order directed to a lower court or to a public officer ordering him to perform some act which he is legally obligated to perform as part of his official duties (ca. **gerichtliche Anweisung, eine Amtshandlung vorzunehmen**)

writ of prohibition (II.2) order issued by a higher court to stop a lower court judge from asserting jurisdiction over a case because the lower court judge would be exceeding the power granted to him (ca. **gerichtliche Feststellung, daß ein unteres Gericht die Grenzen seiner Zuständigkeit überschritten hat**)